Defending Possession Proceedings

THIRD EDITION

Jan Luba, BARRISTER

Nic Madge, SOLICITOR

Derek McConnell, SOLICITOR

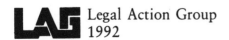 Legal Action Group
1992

Third edition published in Great Britain 1993
by LAG Education and Service Trust Limited
242 Pentonville Road, London N1 9UN

Reprinted 1994

First edition 1987
Second edition 1989

British Library Cataloguing in Publication Data
A CIP catalogue record for this book is available from the
British Library.

ISBN 0 0905099 35 4

Phototypeset by Kerrypress Ltd, Luton, Beds
Printed in Great Britain by BPC-Wheatons Ltd, Exeter

Preface

The three years since the publication of the second edition of *Defending Possession Proceedings* have again seen a marked increase in the numbers of residential occupiers threatened with possession claims by landlords and mortgage lenders. In 1987 164,650 possession actions were started in England and Wales resulting in 98,970 possession orders being granted. The figures for 1991 were 305,783 and 237,918 respectively.[1] In 1992 the political outcry over mortgage repossessions in particular turned the problem into one of national priority. In what was seen by some as pre-election posturing the Conservative administration announced the first 'mortgage rescue schemes' to assist the thousands of borrowers in arrears. It remains to be seen to what extent the initiative will be of benefit.

In January 1989 the new private sector residential security regime introduced by the Housing Act 1988 came into effect. In one way this Act has simplified the task of those advising private sector residential tenants. The widespread use of the assured shorthold tenancy has removed most tenants' ability to contest their landlord's claim to recover possession. However, the poor drafting of the 1988 Act has also highlighted a number of points which require consideration in the higher courts.

In turn the inadequacies of the current law protecting residential mortgage borrowers continue to be exposed daily in county courts. In view of this it is all the more surprising that the Law Commission's proposals to reform the law, published in November 1991, did not receive wider recognition.[2] It can only be hoped that it will not be long before their draft Land Mortgages Bill is considered by Parliament.

As in previous editions, an effort has been made to present the law and practice in a way accessible to those called upon to advise residential occupiers. While there has not been extensive statutory revision of the law regulating the three principal tenures, there has, as always, been

1 *Judicial Statistics 1987* Cm 428 and *1991* Cm 1990, HMSO.
2 *Transfer of Land—Land Mortgages* 1991 HC 5, HMSO.

significant case law development and we hope this has been accurately recorded in this third edition.

Many of the issues dealt with in this book are the subject of discussion at the bi-monthly meetings of the Housing Law Practitioners Association.[3] In addition the material can be updated by reference to Nic Madge and Jan Luba's 'Recent Developments in Housing Law', a quarterly series in *Legal Action* (published by LAG), and by the annual review 'Owner-Occupiers : Recent Developments' by Derek McConnell which also appears in *Legal Action* in April each year. The authors would like to express gratitude to their colleague Russell Campbell from the National Housing Law Service for his assistance in the preparation of this third edition. The authors welcome information on recent cases for inclusion in 'Recent Developments'.

The law in England and Wales is stated as at 1 May 1992 but it has been possible to take account of case law up to 1 November 1992.

Jan Luba, Nic Madge, Derek McConnell

3 Contact Professional Briefings, 120 Wilton Road, London SW1V 1JZ, tel. 071–233 8322.

Contents

Table of Cases

Table of Statutes

Table of Statutory Instruments

Part I

Public Sector Occupiers

Introduction

Since 1980 most occupiers of public sector accommodation have enjoyed security of tenure as *secure* tenants or licensees. Their code of protection, today set out in Housing Act (HA) 1985 Pt IV, prevents landlords from recovering possession except by establishing before a county court judge that grounds set out in the Act can be proved. In most cases, occupiers are further protected by a discretion the court exercises as to whether the particular circumstances justify the making of the order.

On paper therefore, public sector occupiers have considerable protection against loss of their homes. However, that protection and with it the considerable 'charter of rights' associated with secure occupancy status, is being steadily eroded.

The first responsibility for this erosion lies with the county courts which, until very recently, have failed to grasp the importance of possession actions commenced against secure occupiers. About 100,000 actions are started each year. Research has repeatedly shown that public sector possession cases receive insufficiently thorough attention in many county courts. In some parts of the country the rapidity with which possession orders are issued indicates scant regard for security of tenure and an emphasis on speedy disposal. Possession orders are made in the majority of cases and thousands of occupiers are actually evicted each year as a result.

Most of these cases are in reality 'debt collecting actions' – the main thrust of the proceedings being to threaten repossession on the ground of rent arrears unless the occupier resumes regular and full payment of rent due and owing. This happens, notwithstanding the readily available remedy of a direct action for the rent due and the Government's repeated exhortations to public landlords to see possession proceedings only as the last resort in recovering arrears. Landlords presumably regard possession proceedings as a 'bigger stick' to wield against defaulting tenants. This practice, which might appear to verge on an abuse of the process of the court, has now received critical scrutiny from the Lord Chancellor's Civil

3

Justice Review and, it is hoped, will either die out or be prevented by effective amendment to the court rules. A changed approach should lead to a reduction in the overall number of possession proceedings and a sharper focus on the statutory criteria limiting the circumstances in which possession orders can be granted.

The second aspect of the erosion of secure occupiers' rights emerges from the policy objectives of the HA 1988. In broad terms these are to move housing associations out of the 'public sector' provision of housing and into the private market sector. This will be achieved gradually by preventing new occupiers of housing association accommodation from acquiring secure status. For decades to come therefore, within the housing stock of any housing association, there will be both tenants continuing to enjoy secure status and newer occupiers with more limited rights akin to those available in the 'new' private rented sector. In order to respond to this change, this part of this book has been restructured to deal separately with housing associations and housing action trusts (see below).

The majority of this part is concerned with advising in the routine case – a rent arrears possession action brought against a secure occupier. It is, of course, possible for secure occupiers to 'lose' their secure status as a result of circumstances other than repossession and indeed some residents never acquire security at all. The situation of such occupiers is considered in this part also.

The first chapter provides a short summary of security in the public sector. Chapter 2 deals with the situations in which security is threatened or lost. The third chapter deals with the grounds for possession proceedings against secure occupiers and chapter 4 deals with preparation of defences. Chapter 5 covers a miscellany of other situations affecting public sector occupiers. Chapters 6 and 7 deal with the occupiers of housing association and housing action trust properties respectively. Reference should also be made to Part III which deals with possession procedure.

Throughout Part I, statutory references are to the HA 1985 unless otherwise stated.

CHAPTER 1

The Secure Occupier

As with security of tenure in the private rented sector (see Part II below), the rights to security of those in the public sector operate as a supplement to the ordinary common law rules of landlord and tenant law. Under those rules, the occupier would be let into possession by the landlord. The landlord at common law thereafter needed only to bring the arrangement to an end in accordance with its terms and the occupier's right to possession then ceased. Security of tenure in the public sector, first introduced by the Housing Act (HA) 1980, now derives from HA 1985 Pt IV and operates by way of prohibiting a landlord from bringing the tenancy to an end. As we shall see, in an ordinary case, the landlord can end the tenancy only by application to a court.

Secure tenancies

The greatest security of tenure available in the public sector is given to those who are 'secure tenants'. Most council and other public sector tenants are secure tenants. However, it is always important to check that all the hallmarks of a secure tenancy as set out below are present in each case.

A secure tenancy exists at any time when all of the following conditions are satisfied:

- the property is a 'dwelling-house'
- the landlord is a prescribed public body
- the tenant is an individual
- the tenant occupies the property as his or her only or principal home
- the property was let as a 'separate dwelling'
- the tenancy is not in an exempt category.

Each of these requirements is discussed in turn below.

The property is a 'dwelling-house'

Security of tenure covers both houses and parts of houses (s112(1)) and extends to any land let together with the dwelling-house other than agricultural land exceeding two acres (s112(2)). The word 'house' is not further defined in Pt IV. It is suggested that the phrase 'part of a house' is sufficiently broad to include flats, rooms, apartments and bed-sitting rooms and possibly accommodation in some hostels. However, a single room without cooking facilities and situated in a hostel is not a 'dwelling-house' for the purposes of the security of tenure provisions.[1]

The landlord is a prescribed public body

The landlord must be one of the 'prescribed public bodies' within the list set out in s80(1) and (2) as amended. If there are joint landlords they must all be 'prescribed public bodies'.[2]

> 80(1)   The landlord condition is that the interest of the landlord belongs to one of the following authorities or bodies:
> a local authority
> a new town corporation
> [a housing action trust]
> an urban development corporation
> the Development Board for Rural Wales
> *the Housing Corporation*
> *a housing trust which is a charity* or
> *a housing association* or housing co-operative to which this section applies.
> (2)   *This section applies to–*
>   *(a)   a registered housing association other than a co-operative housing association, and*
>   *(b)   an unregistered association which is a co-operative housing association.*
> (4)   This section applies to a housing co-operative within the meaning of section 27B (agreements under certain superseded provisions) where the dwelling-house is comprised in a housing co-operative agreement within the meaning of that section.

The words in square brackets were added by HA 1988 s83(2). The words in italics are repealed by HA 1988 s140 and Sch 18 but are retained for transitional purposes (Sch 18 para 4). The changes reflect the policy

---

1   *Central London YMCA Housing Association Ltd v Goodman* (1992) 24 HLR 109, CA.
2   *R v Plymouth City Council and Cornwall County Council ex parte Freeman* (1987) 19 HLR 328.

intention (see p4) that new letting by housing associations and trusts should not come within the secure tenancy regime.

For the position of housing association, housing co-operative and housing trust occupiers see chapter 6. For the position of housing action trust occupiers see chapter 7.

Management co-operatives carrying out housing management functions for public bodies (under s27B) are themselves capable of granting secure tenancies and licences in respect of the property they manage (s80(4) and HA 1988 s35(4)(b)).

If the interest of the landlord is transferred after the grant of the tenancy to a non-prescribed body, for example by the sale of council property into the private sector, any sitting tenants will lose secure status although they may become 'protected' or 'assured' tenants under provisions regulating private sector tenancies (see Part II below and HA 1988 s38). For the circumstances in which a public sector landlord may seek to recover possession prior to sale, see p13.

The tenant is an individual

The tenant must be an individual person (s81) or a group of individuals holding as joint tenants. Therefore a tenancy cannot be secure if the tenant is a company, a charity, a short-life housing association, a co-op or a public authority. The sub-tenants of such bodies may themselves be secure or protected tenants (see below p57).

The 'only or principal home' rule

The tenant must occupy the property as his or her only *or* principal home: s81. A secure tenant may, therefore, have more than one home but have a 'secure' tenancy only in relation to the principal one: see p20. Where there are joint tenants, at least one of them must occupy as his or her only or principal home (s81).

Temporary absences caused by holidays, stays in hospital, working abroad etc do not affect security, but a permanent or very long-term absence may lead to loss of security (see below p17).

If the absent tenant is married and the home has been the matrimonial home, his or her spouse may preserve the security of the tenancy by continuing in occupation during the other's absence (Matrimonial Homes Act 1983 s1(6)).[3] There is no equivalent provision for cohabitees or other

---

3   As amended by the Housing (Consequential Provisions) Act 1985 Sch 2 para 56(2). See also p19 below.

family members. But, if the absence of the tenant is only temporary, see p17.

The 'let as a separate dwelling' requirement

This has three components: the letting must have been 'as' a separate dwelling; the premises let must be a 'dwelling' (in a 'dwelling-house' – see above p6); and the dwelling must have been let as a 'separate' dwelling (s79(1)).

The first of these requirements deals with the nature of the tenancy. Was it a letting of premises 'as' a separate dwelling? In *Webb v London Borough of Barnet*[4] the council let a house, yard, workshop and associated buildings for use as a motor repair business. The tenant so used it until retirement and continued in occupation of the house once the business had closed. It was held that the tenancy was not secure. The original letting had been for commercial user not for use as a separate dwelling.

It should be noted that the security of tenure provisions only cover 'a' separate dwelling, ie, one unit of accommodation. It may be possible for two adjoining units let to the tenant to be combined to form a single dwelling for these purposes.[5]

The second reuirement deals with the subject of the letting. It must be a 'dwelling'. This is something more than simply a physical unit of four walls, a floor and a ceiling (as that test would be satisfied by a garage or store), but it can be difficult to identify with precision. In *Central London YMCA Housing Association Ltd v Goodman*[6] the premises comprised a furnished twin-bedded room in a tower block with private bathroom and lavatory en suite. The agreement prohibited the use of any heating or cooking apparatus in the room. The Court held that the room was not a dwelling. It declined to adopt any test as to what would constitute a dwelling, simply stating that '[t]he court has to look at all the circumstances of the particular case'.

Thirdly, property must have been let to the tenant as a 'separate' dwelling (s79(1)). Usually this condition is satisfied because the tenant and family are the only occupiers of the property concerned. If, however, facilities are shared with other tenants this does not affect security unless the sharing is of living accommodation (kitchen, lounge, dining room or

4   (1988) 21 HLR 288, CA.
5   *Jenkins v Renfrew District Council* (1989) SLT (Lands Tr.) 41, but cf. *Kavanagh v Lyroudias* [1985] 1 All ER 560.
6   (1992) 24 HLR 109, CA.

bedroom[7]). Security is not affected if such living accommodation is shared by other members of the tenant's household or by lodgers.

Applying these principles, a letting of a room or rooms not having a cooking facility within the room(s) will not be secure as the letting fails the tests of 'as', 'separate' and 'dwelling' just described.[8]

The tenancy is not in an excluded category

The HA 1985 sets out several categories of tenant excluded from full security of tenure:

a) tenants in one of the classes exempted from protection by Sch 1 (s79(2)(a)). Detailed consideration of each of the classes is beyond the scope of this work, but the categories may be summarised as:

      long leases;

      premises occupied in connection with employment;[9]

      land acquired for development;[10]

      accommodation for homeless persons (see p59);

      temporary accommodation for persons taking up employment;[11]

      'private sector leasing' (see p61);

      temporary accommodation during works;

      agricultural holdings;

      licensed premises;

      student lettings;

      1954 Act tenancies; and

      almshouses;

b) tenancies ceasing to be secure after the death of the secure tenant (s79(2)(b)); see below p15;

---

7 See *Kensington and Chelsea RBC v Haydon* (1984) 17 HLR 114 on the effect of sharing with a 'resident caretaker', and generally *Thomson v Glasgow CC* (1986) SLT 6, noted at December 1986 *Legal Action* 165, Lands Tr.

8 *Central London YMCA Housing Association Ltd v Saunders* (1990) 23 HLR 212, CA.

9 *South Glamorgan DC v Griffiths* [1992] EGCS 10, CA; *Hughes v Greenwich LBC* [1992] EGCS 76, CA; *Campbell v City of Edinburgh DC* (1987) SLT 51; noted at June 1987 *Legal Action* 19, CS and *DeFontenay v Strathclyde Regional Council* [1990] SLT (Ex Div) 605, noted at December 1990 *Legal Action* 14, CS.

10 *Attley v Cherwell District Council* [1989] 21 HLR 613, CA, *Harrison v Hyde Housing Association Ltd* [1990] 23 HLR 57, CA, *London & Quadrant Housing Trust v Robertson* (1991) unreported, but noted at September 1991 *Legal Action* 15, cc and *Lillieshall Road Housing Co-op v Brennan* (1992) 24 HLR 193, CA.

11 *Campbell v Western Isles Island Council* (1989) SLT 602, CS noted at December 1989 *Legal Action* 13.

c) tenancies ceasing to be secure following assignment or full subletting (see further pp20–21).

Tenants who were served with notices to quit which expired before 3 October 1980 (the commencement date of the new provisions for security of tenure) are also excluded from protection unless they have subsequently been granted an express or implied licence (see below) to remain in possession or a new tenancy.[12]

Secure 'licensees'

Although it is not a common occurrence, a landlord authority may grant a licence rather than a tenancy to the occupier of council or other public sector property (eg, because the occupier is under 18 years of age and thus incapable at law of holding a tenancy). Whether or not the occupier pays 'rent' or a 'licence fee' or any other charge, such licence will be secure if all the hallmarks outlined in relation to a secure tenancy apply (s79(3)). This extension of security to public sector licensees renders substantially less significant the distinction, still important in the private sector, between those with licences and those with tenancies (see below p81). It should be stressed that the licence agreement must have conferred the exclusive right to a occupy a 'separate dwelling'. Thus, a resident in a hostel with specialist support facilities under an agreement permitting the owners unrestricted access to the room and containing power to require the occupier to share (and/or require the occupier to move to another room), will not have a licence to occupy as a separate dwelling and will not therefore have security of tenure.[13] Similarly, a licence which is simply a subsidiary agreement associated with a secure tenancy of a dwelling (such as permission temporarily to use additional rooms during building work) does not itself amount to a licence to occupy premises as a 'separate dwelling'.[14]

Occupiers who initially enter the property as trespassers and are then given licence to remain as a temporary expedient do not benefit from security of tenure (s79(4)).[15] Thus most 'licensed squatters' are outside the main protection of security (for their situation see p62 below). It should be noted that if the licence is granted to the squatter other than as a temporary expedient, for example, in recognition of the *full* rehousing obligation of a housing authority under the HA 1985 Pt III (homeless

---

12   *Hammersmith and Fulham LB v Harrison* [1981] 2 All ER 588, CA.
13   *Westminister City Council v Clarke* (1992) 24 HLR 360, HL.
14   *Tyler v Royal Borough of Kensington & Chelsea* (1990) 23 HLR 380, CA.
15   See *R v Southwark LBC ex parte Bannerman* (1989) 22 HLR 459, QBD.

persons) the licensee immediately benefits from security. Alternatively, the squatter could acquire security from being granted a tenancy of the property.

[If a check through this chapter has revealed that the occupier is not a secure tenant or licensee, go directly to p61 below.]

CHAPTER 2

Security Threatened

This chapter considers the circumstances in which the landlord *or* occupier can place the security of tenure in jeopardy. The initial focus is, of course, on the typical case of landlord-initiated action. Throughout this chapter the term 'secure tenancy' is used to refer to both secure tenancies and secure licences unless the contrary is expressed.

Landlord initiated

Landlord threatens possession proceedings

A secure tenancy cannot legally be brought to an end by a landlord other than by obtaining a court order for possession: s82(1). The landlord must therefore initiate court proceedings to recover possession unless the occupiers themselves have brought to an end the security of tenure, in one of the ways described below (pp14–21). Usually, the landlord gives the tenant some informal notice by letter or by visit of an officer, that possession proceedings may be contemplated unless the tenant remedies a specific default, for example, pays any outstanding rent, ceases to commit nuisances etc. The first formal step the landlord must take if intending to press ahead to recover possession is service of a notice (usually known as Notice of Seeking Possession–NSP). In order to be effective the notice must meet the requirements of s83(2):

> (2) The notice shall—
>   (*a*)   be in the form prescribed by regulations made by the Secretary of State,
>   (*b*)   specify the ground on which the court will be asked to make an order for the possession of the dwelling-house or for the termination of the tenancy, and
>   (*c*)   give particulars of that ground.

Where the tenancy is a periodic tenancy the notice ceases to be effective 12 months from the specified date (s83(3)(b)). The 'specified date' is to be no earlier than the date on which the tenancy could, under common law or in contract, have been brought to an end by notice to quit served on the tenant that day. The 'specified date' must be shown on the notice (s83(3)(a)).

If the landlord wishes to proceed to recover possession on the basis of the notice, possession proceedings must be begun within 12 months of the specified date (s83(4)).

Any failure to comply with any of these strict procedural requirements gives rise to a complete defence to any proceedings brought on the basis of that notice (see below chapter 4).

Landlord proposes to sell the property

A secure tenancy remains secure only for so long as the landlord condition remains satisfied, ie the landlord is a 'prescribed public body' (s80(1)). Once the freehold or head lease is transferred to a body other than one of those prescribed in s80(1) (see above) security of tenure under HA 1985 collapses. In place, the sitting tenants will usually obtain protection against the new owners under the Rent Acts (see Part II below) or as assured tenants under HA 1988 Pt I (HA 1988 s38).

A proposal by the landlord to sell thus threatens the 'secure' status of the tenants. Once the proposal becomes a positive decision to sell to a particular buyer, the secure tenants must be consulted through the procedures established by s105.[1] Details of these procedures can be inspected at the landlord's principal office, usually the town hall, or a copy purchased (s105(5)). As from 11 March 1988, the procedures for disposal to non-public sector landlords are governed by the consultation requirements of s106A and Sch 3A (added by Housing and Planning Act 1986 s6) which make more detailed provision than s105 arrangements (see DoE Circular 6/88). Where the landlord is a housing action trust the s105/106A procedure is replaced by arrangements specified in HA 1988 s84.

The landlord may not wish to sell with 'sitting' tenants and may attempt to secure vacant possession, in which case the procedures as to notice (above) and grounds for possession (below) must be satisfied. The Housing and Planning Act 1986 introduced a new ground 10A to HA 1985 Sch 2 to allow landlords a limited opportunity to recover possession in such circumstances (see p37).

---

1   *Short v LB Tower Hamlets* (1985) 18 HLR 171, CA.

If a public sector landlord is compelled to transfer tenanted stock to the private sector as a result of the 'tenants' choice' procedure for change of landlord contained in HA 1988 Pt IV, those tenants who wish to transfer will lose secure status. Any tenant wishing to remain secure can give the appropriate notice (HA 1988 s103(2)) and continue as a secure tenant of the public sector landlord. The new purchaser will grant leases of the property occupied by continuing secure tenants to the public sector organisation which will remain their immediate landlord: HA 1988 s100.

Tenant initiated

Tenant gives notice to quit or surrenders the tenancy

Nothing in the HA 1985 restricts the ability of tenants to determine their own tenancies. In the case of periodic tenancies this can be achieved by serving on the landlord proper notice to quit. This brings to an end both security of tenure and the tenancy itself. To be effective any such notice must be in writing and meet contractual[2] and statutory requirements[3] (see p86).

Apart from those cases in which the tenant is genuinely giving notice in order to quit the premises, notice to quit is often deployed as a device in disputes following a breakdown of the domestic relationship. A sole tenant is free to end his/her tenancy by notice to quit irrespective of the concerns or interests of family members. There may, however, be an exception if the property has been the matrimonial home, a spouse remains in occupation and the simple purpose of the notice to quit was to render that spouse homeless. The courts have been reluctant to uphold notices which are used as devices to overcome spouses's rights of occupation in this way. If the notice to quit is not valid or is set aside in subsequent matrimonial proceedings, the secure tenancy continues. The position is different if there is a joint tenancy. While the joint tenancy subsists neither party is usually able permanently to exclude the other from the home. If, however, one party gives notice to quit to the landlord the whole tenancy lapses leaving the landlord free to re-grant a sole tenancy (pursuant to prior arrangement) to one of the former joint tenants. This device has obtained the judicial seal of approval.[4] However,

---

2   *Community Housing Association v Hoy* (1988) CC. Noted at December 1988 *Legal Action* 18.
3   *Wandsworth LBC v Brown* (1986) CC. Noted at September 1987 *Legal Action* 13.
4   *Hammersmith & Fulham LBC v Monk* (1992) 24 HLR 203, HL, approving *Greenwich LBC v McGrady* (1982) 6 HLR 36, CA.

the ramifications of deploying this device and in particular the breach of any rules in equity which apply, are beyond the scope of this work.[5]

Secure tenants may also end their tenancy by surrender by deed (see p94 for surrender by operation of law, ie, without a deed) or, in the case of a fixed-term tenancy, by giving notice as permitted by any break-clause. It is not possible for one joint tenant, acting alone, to surrender the tenancy or (subject to the express terms of the tenancy) give a 'break-clause' notice.

Tenant dies

If the tenant dies, neither the tenancy agreement itself nor security of tenure automatically lapses. If there is a person in occupation entitled to succeed the tenant and the tenant was not himself a 'successor' (defined in s88) the secure tenancy automatically vests in the successor.

In summary, those entitled to succeed are (a) the spouse of the tenant or (b) another member of the tenant's family. In both cases the successor must have been occupying the dwelling as his or her only or principal home[6] at the time of the tenant's death. In the case of family members other than spouses, the potential successor must have lived with the tenant throughout the 12-month period ending with the tenant's death (s87). The full 12 months need not have been spent in the property succession to which is claimed.[7] The situation where there is more than one successor is dealt with by s89(2). The phrase 'member of the family' is defined by s113 and extends to the cohabitee of the deceased:[8]

> **113.**—(1) A person is a member of another's family within the meaning of this Part if—
>
> > (*a*) he is the spouse of that person, or he and that person live together as husband and wife, or
> >
> > (*b*) he is that person's parent, grandparent, child, grandchild, brother, sister, uncle, aunt, nephew or niece.
>
> (2) For the purpose of subsection (1)(*b*)—
>
> > (*a*) a relationship by marriage shall be treated as a relationship by blood,

---

5 See Jan Luba 'Joint secure tenants: clarification or confusion?' February 1983 *LAG Bulletin* 26 and Matthews 'Terminating secure periodic joint tenancies' (1983) 80 LS Gaz 603.

6 *Peabody Donation Fund Governors v Grant* (1982) 6 HLR 41; (1982) 264 EG 925, CA.

7 *Waltham Forest LBC v Thomas* (1992) 24 HLR 622, HL.

8 For these purposes, cohabitees of the same sex as the deceased are excluded: *Harrogate BC v Simpson* (1984) 17 HLR 205. See also *Application No 11716/85 v UK* (1986) 83 LS Gaz 2320, European Commission of Human Rights.

(b)   a relationship of the half-blood shall be treated as a relationship of the whole blood,

(c)   the stepchild of a person shall be treated as his child, and

(d)   an illegitimate child shall be treated as the legitimate child of his mother and reputed father.

Where there is no person entitled to succeed, security is lost and the tenancy itself vests in the estate. Thereafter it will be disposed of as a non-secure tenancy in the administration of the estate – usually being surrendered to the landlord.[9] However, special provision is made to deal with the situation which arises if a divorce court has earlier pronounced on what is to happen to the tenancy in the event of the tenant's death. For example, in divorce proceedings the court may order transfer of the tenancy from husband to wife on terms that if the wife dies, the tenancy is to revert to the husband (s89(3) and Matrimonial Causes Act 1973 s24).

Following the death of a tenant, disputes not infrequently arise between the landlord authority and occupiers who assert that they are entitled to succeed to the tenancy. In such cases the landlord may seek to determine the tenancy by notice to quit in the usual way and start ordinary possession proceedings. It would obviously not be appropriate for the landlord to serve a NSP while asserting that the occupier has not become the secure tenant. The occupier then defends on the basis that s/he is a secure tenant having properly 'succeeded' the deceased tenant. The burden of proof is on the occupier to establish the right to succeed.[10] If the landlord admits that a succession has taken place but claims that the successor is under-occupying, see p42.

If the landlord authority is asserting that the occupier is a trespasser (often bureaucratically described as an 'unauthorised occupier') it cannot simply rush into CCR Ord 24 or RSC Ord 113 proceedings (see below p235). The occupier who is able to show, in such proceedings, that the deceased tenant's tenancy has not been properly determined (eg, by service of notice on the executor/administrator or President of the Family Division[11]) will have a complete defence to the action.[12] Once the landlord authority has served effective notice to quit on the person responsible for the deceased tenant's estate it may, if there is no occupier, recover possession directly.

9   See M Lee 'The periodic tenancy and death of a tenant' (1983) 80 LS Gaz 883.
10   *Peabody Donation Fund Governors*, n6.
11   As to service of such notice, see *Practice Direction* [1985] 1 All ER 832.
12   *Wirral BC v Smith and Cooper* (1982) 4 HLR 81.

Absentee tenant

Absence from the property, however longstanding, will not bring the *tenancy* to an end. That can only be achieved in one of the ways recognised by common law, ie notice to quit, surrender, forfeiture etc (see chapter 9).

However, the *security of tenure* of the secure tenant may be placed in jeopardy by long-term absences. A secure tenancy remains secure only for so long as the tenant (or one of the joint tenants) 'occupies the dwelling-house as his only or principal home' (s81). A very prolonged absence may indicate that the tenant no longer occupies the property as a home and thus the security may lapse. There are several possible variations on the circumstances of the absentee tenant:

T has 'assigned' the tenancy and left   For discussion of this see p20 below.

T has sublet the whole property to others and is living elsewhere   Here the security of tenure is brought to an end not only by the failure to occupy but also by the specific provision in s93(2):

> If the tenant under a secure tenancy parts with the possession of the dwelling-house or sublets the whole of it (or sublets first part of it and then the remainder), the tenancy ceases to be a secure tenancy and cannot subsequently become a secure tenancy.

If prior to departure the tenant has granted a true *licence* of the whole and then left, s93(2) may be avoided but security is still threatened by failure to occupy.[13] In such circumstances the landlord authority may serve an ordinary notice to quit[14] and start possession proceedings to recover possession against the true tenant and the other occupiers. The position of any sub-tenants is considered at p57 below.

T is absent for a long period but intends to return   The issue here is whether the tenant is still occupying as his or her home the property in question. The caselaw developed under the Rent Acts (see p113 below) suggests that relevant factors in applying the occupation test would be: length of absence; the intention of the tenant; furniture and belongings; and presence of a caretaker.

A person may be absent for many years (working abroad, travelling, visiting relatives etc) but intend to return to his or her 'home'. Possibly furniture and other belongings will be left in the property and a 'caretaker'

---

13   *London Borough of Islington v LaMarque* (1992) unreported, noted at September 1991 *Legal Action* 14, CC.

14   Some local authorities react to such situations by serving a NSP as well as ordinary notice to quit.

(usually a friend or relative) let into residence to take care of the property, ensure the rent is paid etc. In such circumstances, the tenant usually retains security of tenure.

However, the phrasing of the Rent Act provisions ('. . . if and so long as he occupies the dwelling-house as a residence . . .') is sufficiently wider than '. . . occupies the dwelling-house as his only or principal home' to suggest that cases decided under that provision are only useful as pointers. More direct guidance on the interpretation of the phrase can be gleaned from cases decided under the equivalent provision in the Leasehold Reform Act 1967 (ie, 'only or main residence' in s1(2)). In that jurisdiction, intention to return is also a key factor.[15]

The Court of Appeal has now determined that the correct approach in secure tenancy cases is to consider all the surrounding circumstances. In *Crawley Borough Council v Sawyer*, a tenant was away from his home for over a year. The gas and electricity were disconnected. The tenant had moved in with his girlfriend and they intended to buy a property together. The council served notice to quit. The couple's relationship broke down and the tenant moved back to his home. The county court judge held that the council property had throughout remained his home as the tenant always intended to return. The Court of Appeal would not interfere with that finding.[16]

Disputes may arise when a landlord finds either an apparently empty property or the 'caretaker' in occupation. The landlord then serves an ordinary notice to quit on the absentee tenant (on the basis that security has lapsed) and recovers possession if there is no one in occupation or starts possession proceedings. The landlord may face not inconsiderable difficulties in serving the true tenant with notice to quit. A tenant who can show that, notwithstanding the prolonged 'temporary' absence, s/he continues to occupy the home, will retain security of tenure and may successfully defend the action or secure re-instatement.

The most common difficulties over long-term absence arise from: tenants going abroad for indeterminate periods to visit relatives or to travel; tenants serving terms of imprisonment; tenants receiving long-term hospital treatment or treatment in residential care homes. The case of the prisoner is usually relatively straightforward as s/he can be promptly located and will usually assert an intention to return even when serving a lengthy term.[17] The case of the very elderly or mentally ill tenant in a

---

15   *Poland v Earl Cadogan* [1980] 3 All ER 544, CA.
16   *Crawley BC v Sawyer* (1988) 20 HLR 98, see also *Miller v Falkirk DC* 1990 SLT (Lands Tr.) 111 noted at March 1991 *Legal Action* 13, and *Roxborough DC v Collins* (1991) 8 GWD 483.
17   See *Notting Hill Housing Trust v Etoria* April 1989 *Legal Action* 22.

caring institution is more problematic, as it will be difficult to establish that they have both the intention and prospect of returning to resume occupation (but see cases in the Rent Act context, discussed at p114. For the position of a tenant clearly having two homes, see p20.

T has 'disappeared'   It is not unusual, particularly in serious rent arrears cases, for the landlord to find that the tenant has abandoned the premises leaving them vacant or with 'unauthorised' occupiers in possession. If the authority immediately commences CCR Ord 24 or RSC Ord 113 proceedings (see p235) to recover possession without first determining the tenancy at common law, the unlawful or other occupier will have a complete defence to the action on the basis that the landlord does not have an immediate right to possession.[18] In certain limited circumstances it may be possible for the landlord to show that the tenants have, by their actions, surrendered the property, thus entitling the landlord authority to recover possession. In order for this to be established the court must be satisfied that, at very least, 'a tenant had left owing a very substantial sum of money and had been absent for a substantial time'.[19] The burden of proof is on the landlord authority.

The courts have varied in their approach as to whether abandonment is sufficient, on the facts, to amount to surrender, in the public sector. In *Preston BC v Fairclough*[20] the tenants had left another family in occupation but there was no evidence of the tenants' own date of departure or the amount of rent in arrears if any: it was held that surrender was not established. In *R v Croydon LBC ex parte Toth*,[21] the premises had been left empty for several weeks, all furniture had been removed and £488 rent was outstanding: here it was held that surrender was made out.

If the landlord authority deals with a case of 'abandonment' by serving proper notice to quit, it may recover possession of the vacant property on expiry or commence summary proceedings for possession against any occupiers.

T has left non-tenant spouse/cohabitee in possession   The spouse's presence in the property makes good the tenant's failure to occupy and is treated as occupation by him or her (Matrimonial Homes Act 1983 s1(6)[22]). This situation continues for so long as the parties are married and lasts up to decree absolute. If the landlord authority successfully takes

18 *Preston BC v Fairclough* (1982) 8 HLR 70.
19 Ibid per Griffiths LJ at 73.
20 See n18.
21 (1988) 20 HLR 576, CA.
22 As amended by Housing (Consequential Provisions) Act 1985 Sch 2 para 56(2).

possession proceedings against the tenant on one of the HA grounds (p22 below) and an order is made, the remaining spouse (or indeed a former spouse having rights of occupation) can apply to stay or suspend the order (s85(5)).

No such special protection is available to a cohabitee. S/he must simply argue that, on the specific facts, his or her occupation is indicative of the tenant's intention to return.

T has two homes, one of which is the public-sector tenancy   The tenant will lose the benefit of security in the property if it is neither his or her only nor principal home. It is a question of fact in relation to persons having two homes, which of them is the principal home.[23]

Tenant assigns

Security of tenure may obviously be threatened if the tenant seeks to transfer the whole tenancy to a third party. As seen above, *subletting* of the whole property brings to an end the security of tenure of the tenant (although not the tenancy itself): s93(2).

Similarly, s91 provides that except in prescribed cases the secure tenancy is not capable of *assignment* at all. The three prescribed cases are:

a) assignment by way of mutual exchange (in which circumstances the strict provisions of s92 and Sch 3 must be complied with);
b) assignment pursuant to a property transfer order made under the Matrimonial Causes Act 1973 s24;
c) assignment to a person who would have been qualified to succeed the tenant if the tenant had died immediately before the assignment.

If the assignment takes place in one of the prescribed circumstances, the assignee receives the full secure tenancy (notwithstanding any prohibition on assignment in the tenancy agreement itself[24]). The landlord authority can obtain possession only by serving a NSP (see above) and commencing possession proceedings on one of the grounds applicable to a secure tenant. Assignment in breach of a prohibition on assignment in the tenancy, for example, would prima facie satisfy ground 1.[25]

If the assignee in possession did not receive the property under one of

---

23   *Sutton LBC v Swann* (1986) 18 HLR 140 and *Camden LBC v Coombs* (1988) CC, noted at March 1988 *Legal Action* 17, and see Thompson 'The two-home tenant' (1986) 83 LS Gaz 2073.
24   *Peabody Donation Fund Governors v Higgins* [1983] 3 All ER 122; (1983) 10 HLR 82, CA.
25   Ibid.

the prescribed methods or the purported assignment was ineffective,[26] s/he will nevertheless have a complete defence to premature CCR Ord 24 or RSC Ord 113 proceedings. The landlord must first determine properly the tenancy of the original tenant or of the assignee in the normal way and then take proceedings (ordinary or summary) against the assignee.

Summary

In the usual case the prerequisite of taking possession proceedings against a secure tenant is the issue of a NSP in the prescribed form.

If the *tenancy* has earlier been ended by the secure tenant him or herself and the premises are vacant, the landlord may recover possession directly, ie the right to possession arises without the need for proceedings. If the former tenant remains in occupation, the landlord will require a court order before recovering possession (see 223).

If the tenancy continues, but *security* has been lost or is in question, the landlord must bring the tenancy to an end in accordance with contractual and common law principles before seeking to recover possession.

26   *LB Croydon v Bustin and Triance* (1991) 24 HLR 36, CA, *Newham LB v Bennett* [1984] CLY 1960, CC (both cases of ineffective transfer from mother to son) and *Crago v Julien* [1992] 1 All ER 744, CA (spouse to spouse).

CHAPTER 3

Grounds for Possession against Secure Occupiers

A landlord can bring to an end a secure tenancy or secure licence only by successful application to a court (s82(1)). The prerequisite of an action to recover possession is service of a NSP in the prescribed form (s83(1)).

Thereafter the landlord authority may decide to press the matter by taking proceedings for possession. The usual procedure is the issue of a summons and particulars of claim in the local county court (see Part III below). This must be done at a time when the notice is still effective (see below p49). At the hearing of the action the landlord must show that the necessary grounds and conditions are made out. Before considering these matters and the substantive merits, the court must be satisfied on a number of technical issues (eg that the notice was properly served). These are dealt with in chapter 4 (technical defences).

Note that the concept of a 'consent order' is not applicable in the case of secure tenants or licensees. Section 84(1) prevents the making of any form of possession order until the court is satisfied that a ground and condition for ordering possession are made out. The court can only be so satisfied if it hears evidence or is presented with express admissions by the defendant.[1]

Grounds and conditions

Once the court is seized of the matter it must first be satisfied that a ground for possession is made out. Section 84(1) provides that:

> 84.—(1) The court shall not make an order for the possession of a dwelling-house let under a secure tenancy except on one or more of the grounds set out in Schedule 2.

If a ground within Sch 2 cannot be established the proceedings must inevitably be dismissed. Each of the grounds is separately considered

1 *Wandsworth LBC v Fadayomi* (1987) 19 HLR 512; [1987] 3 All ER 474, CA.

below (pp23–43). Even if satisfied that a ground is made out, possession is not to be ordered unless the ground has been specified in the NSP (see chapter 2) which was served before the proceedings were commenced. The only routes available to a landlord who makes out an alternative ground are either (a) to seek leave of the court to amend the NSP to embrace the new ground (s84(3)) or (b) to abandon the proceedings and serve a fresh NSP based on the new ground.

The burden of proof is throughout on the landlord to show that the ground is made out on the balance of probabilities. Furthermore, no order for possession will be made simply because a ground for possession has been established. The landlord must also prove that relevant *conditions* are made out.

Each ground for possession carries with it a condition or set of conditions which must also be satisfied before possession is ordered. Indeed s84(2) provides:

> (2)   The court shall not make an order for possession—
>
> (a)   on the grounds set out in Part I of that Schedule (grounds 1 to 8), unless it considers it reasonable to make the order,
>
> (b)   on the grounds set out in Part II of that Schedule (grounds 9 to 11), unless it is satisfied that suitable accommodation will be available for the tenant when the order takes effect,
>
> (c)   on the grounds set out in Part III of that Schedule (grounds 12 to 16), unless it both considers it reasonable to make the order and is satisfied that suitable accommodation will be available for the tenant when the order takes effect;
>
> and Part IV of that Schedule has effect for determining whether suitable accommodation will be available for a tenant.

Each of these conditions is considered below in relation to the relevant ground. If the landlord cannot show on the balance of probabilities that the conditions are satisfied the proceedings will be dismissed even though the grounds have been proved.

Ground 1: Rent arrears

This is the most common basis on which possession is sought against secure occupiers. The first part of ground 1 of Sch 2 on which the landlord relies will be satisfied only if the landlord proves that:

> rent lawfully due from the tenant has not been paid.

In order to recover possession the landlord must also satisfy the court that the appropriate condition is met – in this case that it is reasonable to make the order (s84(2)(a)). It is important to check carefully that each element of both the ground and condition have been proved to the satisfaction of the court.

The ground

Almost every word of ground 1 requires careful interpretation.

'rent'

The rent in question is the gross rent due in respect of the relevant property. However, neither of the terms 'rent' or 'gross rent' is defined in the HA 1985. It is suggested that 'rent' for these purposes does not include service charges, amenity payments, overpaid housing benefit (HB) or any other indebtedness which is not strictly rent.[2] In the Rent Act (RA) jurisdiction, the courts have inclined to the view that 'rent' embraces the total monetary payment made to the landlord.[3] Public sector landlords have a tendency to use the rent payment system to collect a variety of charges from tenants ranging from fees for communal TV aerials to tenants' association membership subscriptions, and from rent for separate garages to heating charges. It is doubted whether all of these elements can properly be said to be part of the 'rent' unless so described or defined expressly in the tenancy agreement. In *Dudley MBC v Bailey*[4] it was hoped that the Court of Appeal would provide an authoritative definition of 'rent' in the context of a public sector tenancy. However, the council in that case conceded that general rates owed by the tenant and normally collected with the rent were not part of the rent and the case turned on other issues. The concession was in line with earlier decisions in the lower courts.[5]

It may be shown that in spite of indebtedness on paper, there are in fact no true arrears of rent, eg, because the money has earlier been properly used by the tenant to pay for repairs as a result of the landlord's default (see p227) or, more commonly, the alleged arrears have arisen from the landlord's failure to pay into the tenant's rent account the appropriate amounts of HB (see p268). In the latter case it is important to note that entitlement to housing benefit does not serve to reduce or eliminate liability for rent. It is only when such benefit is paid to the landlord that liability for rent is satisfied. From that point in time the rent will have

---

2   See Ann McAllister and Siobhan McGrath 'Grounds for possession: rent lawfully due' Parts 1–3 December 1985 *Legal Action* 169, January 1986 p9 and February 1986 p21.

3   *Sidney Trading Co v Finsbury Corp* [1952] 1 All ER 460 at 461 and *Markworth v Hellard* [1921] 2 KB 755.

4   (1990) 22 HLR 424, CA.

5   *Trafford BC v Mullings* (1989), unreported, noted at March 1990 *Legal Action* 12, CC.

been 'paid' even if there is an administrative delay in attributing it to the particular tenant's rent account. Delay in payment of benefit to the landlord by the benefit authorities will, of course, be material in considering the reasonableness condition (see p26).

Alternatively, the 'arrears' may in fact have arisen where, after satisfaction of the rent liability by payment or credit of HB, the benefit authority (which may or may not also be the landlord) has discovered an overpayment and improperly sought to recover the overpayment by adjusting the tenant's rent account. Obviously, in such a case, there are no arrears of rent as the rent has already been paid. The benefit authority must look to methods other than the 'adjustment' of rent accounts for the recovery of overpayments (*HB Guidance Manual* DSS, para 11.26).

'lawfully due'

The rent must be lawfully due from the current tenant. It is open therefore to the tenant to assert in a defence that the rent has been improperly fixed or increased. Where the landlord is a local housing authority this involves the assertion that in breach of its statutory duty the council has not fixed a reasonable rent[6] (s24). Although this is a straightforward assertion to make, it is exceptionally difficult to prove.[7] A successful defence of not 'lawfully' due may be raised if the rent increase was based on some misinterepretation by the landlord of the relevant housing finance legislation (as in *R v Ealing LBC ex parte Lewis*[8]). Similarly, the rent claimed will not be lawfully due if the landlord has failed to observe any contractual or statutory requirements as to notice of increase (s102). Such requirements will be strictly construed.[9] Further, rent cannot normally be lawfully increased on account of any improvement work by the tenant (s9X).

'from the tenant'

Only the rent due from the tenant is relevant. Any rent owed by a previous occupier, former tenant or spouse/cohabitee of the current tenant is irrelevant. Thus a defendant who took the tenancy by way of statutory succession or assignment starts with a 'clean slate' as against the present landlord and is only liable for rent accruing from the date of succession or assignment.[10] It should be noted, however, that any one of a number of joint tenants may be sued for the whole rent due.

---

6   *Wandsworth LBC v Winder* [1985] AC 461; (1984) 17 HLR 196, HL.
7   *Wandsworth LBC v Winder (No 2)* (1987) 20 HLR 400, CA.
8   (1992) 24 HLR 484, QBD.
9   *Clements & O'Boyle v Brent LBC* (1990) unreported, noted at March 1990 *Legal Action* 12.
10 *Tickner v Clifton* [1929] 1 KB 207.

'has not been paid'

If all arrears have been cleared before the issue of proceedings, the ground manifestly is not made out unless further arrears accrue before the date of the hearing.[11] This is so, even though the landlord may prove arrears as at the date of the NSP.

If arrears were outstanding at the date of issue of the proceedings but are cleared before the hearing or on the hearing date, the court may still find the ground satisfied but is unlikely also to be satisfied that it is reasonable to make the order (see below).[12]

If a landlord fails to prove any element of ground 1, proceedings founded solely on that ground must be dismissed. In the usual case, the landlord proves the ground by putting in evidence – the tenancy agreement, the current rent due, the record of payments made by the tenant and copies of demands made for payments of arrears.

The condition

Even if the court is satisfied that there has been a failure to pay rent lawfully due it cannot make a possession order of any description unless also satisfied that in all the circumstances of the case it would be reasonable to do so (s84(2)(a)).

In applying the 'reasonableness' test the court is required to have regard to all relevant factors including the length of the tenancy, the past rent record of the tenant, whether the failure to pay rent is persistent, whether there have been earlier agreements to clear arrears, the conduct of the landlord in seeking or waiving amounts due and the personal circumstances of the tenant. *Woodspring DC v Taylor*[13] provides a good example of the application of these principles. The Court of Appeal held that it was not appropriate for an order to be made against longstanding tenants with a previous good rent record presently in financial difficulties, even though arrears of over £700 (in 1982) were proved. Where the root cause of the arrears of rent is the low income of the defendant, the court will need to consider the availability of, and entitlement to, social security benefits. In *Second WRVS Housing Society v Blair*[14] the Court of Appeal set aside an order for possession made against a young, single man who owed £1,200 rent and had been tenant for only eight years. The county

11   *Bird v Hildage* [1948] 1 KB 91, CA.
12   *Dellenty v Pellow* [1951] 2 KB 858, CA.
13   (1982) 4 HLR 95, CA.
14   (1986) 19 HLR 104, CA.

court judge had not adequately considered: (a) the possibility of arranging direct payment to the landlord of current rent from the welfare benefit authorities, (b) the possibility of the social security office deducting small amounts from the tenant's welfare benefits and paying them direct to the landlord towards the arrears and (c) the tenant's medical condition.

If possession proceedings have been initiated for a very modest amount of arrears, or without much regard by the landlord to other collection methods, the attention of the court should be directed to DoE Circular 18/87, which suggests that court action should be only the last resort procedure.

Where the rent has been withheld because the amount due or outstanding is genuinely disputed, or because the tenant has a legitimate grievance over disrepair, the court would not usually find it reasonable to make an order but is more likely to adjourn the proceedings with directions (eg that a defence and counterclaim be entered in respect of the alleged repairing default). In *LB Haringey v Stewart*,[15] the tenant withheld rent on account of alleged disrepair. At trial a counterclaim for damages for disrepair was dismissed. In relation to the possession claim the tenant was unable to repay the withheld rent amounting to over £1,000 (because it had been spent rather than set aside) and made no proposals as to payment of current rent and payment of the arrears. The Court of Appeal declined to interfere with a decision that it was reasonable to order possession.

In resisting rent arrear possession claims brought by housing associations, advisers can usefully refer to the Tenants' Guarantee published by the Housing Corporation for its constructive guidance on tackling rent arrears. Although the document has statutory force only in relation to assured tenancies, the Housing Corporation expects the benefits of it to be enjoyed equally by secure tenants. In particular, the Guarantee requires the association to issue its tenants with a rent arrears policy and procedure. Failure to follow these procedures will be helpful on the 'reasonableness' of the association's claim to possession.

Surprisingly, public landlords frequently bring possession proceedings in respect of rent arrears owed by tenants on very low incomes, including those on welfare benefits. The key issues on reasonableness in such cases are:

– why did the landlord not arrange direct payment of housing benefit to themselves either voluntarily or, once eight weeks' worth of arrears had accrued, as of right[16]

15   (1991) 23 HLR 557, CA.
16   Housing Benefit (General) Regulations 1987 (SI no. 1971) regs 93–95.

- why did the landlord not arrange deduction at source of a small amount from the tenant's welfare benefit to pay off the arrears[17] instead of bringing possession proceedings?

Advisers may well find that, as the landlord will by this stage have proven that arrears are owed, the court is very inclined to make some sort of order. In such cases, if there is no evidence as to why it is reasonable for possession to be granted, any form of possession order must be resisted. The adviser could invite the court to dismiss the possession claim but enter a judgment for a money claim made by the landlord, if the amount of the arrears claimed is agreed. This gives the court and landlord the satisfaction of an order against the tenant in default, but it is agruable that no order for costs should be made against the tenant as a money claim could have been brought by ordinary action or by a rent action under CCR Ord 24 P II rather than by possession proceedings. A further alternative would be an adjournment on terms (p52).

Ground 1: Other breach of tenancy agreements

Ground 1 of Sch 2 further provides that (subject to it being reasonable in all the circumstances) an order can be made if:

an obligation of the tenancy has been broken or not performed.

The obligation must arise from the tenancy, that is, it must be an express or implied term of the tenancy agreement itself, and not of some collateral agreement (eg the separate renting of a garage). A failure to comply with the conditions attached to grant of permission to carry out improvements is however specifically brought within ground 1 (s99(4)).

Advisers should ensure that the tenancy agreement relied on by the landlords is in fact the agreement applicable to the tenant. Public sector landlords often produce to the court the 'latest version' of their tenancy agreements. The true tenancy agreement is the one originally entered into by the tenant, subject to the statutory procedure for variation (ss102–103). A variation cannot be achieved simply by sending the tenant a 'fresh' tenancy agreement.[18]

Many local authorities have recently introduced provisions into tenancy agreements which expressly prohibit acts of domestic violence or racial harassment. Even if the authority can show that the provision has been properly incorporated into the tenancy agreement,[19] it remains to be

17   Social Security (Claims and Payments) Regulations 1987 SI No 1968 Sch 9, para 5.
18   *Palmer v MB Sandwell* (1987) 20 HLR 74, CA.
19   See *Camden LBC v Hawkins* (1987) unreported, CA.

seen whether breach of such terms constitutes breach of an 'obligation' of the tenancy rather than the simple contravention of some personal undertaking given by the tenant as to future conduct.[20]

Another more common provision is the prohibition contained in the tenancy agreement against the keeping of pets or other animals on the premises let. Proceedings under ground 1 based on this particular breach provide a good illustration of the distinction between the ground for possession and the reasonableness requirement. The tenant may well admit clear and continuing breach of the agreement by keeping an 'animal companion' but an order may be refused because in particular circumstances it would not be reasonable to order possession notwithstanding that the tenant intends to continue keeping the pet at the premises.[21]

In other cases where the ground is proved, the condition of reasonableness will be affected by considerations such as: whether the breach is continuing, persistent or repeated; the seriousness of the breach; its implications for the landlord; and the personal circumstances of the tenant. Advisers should also draw the attention of the court to the landlord's readily available alternative of injunction proceedings against the tenant in respect of the alleged breach, rendering possession unnecessary.[22]

Advisers should argue against the apparently attractive option of an order suspended on terms that there be no further breach, as such an order will usually attract an award of costs against the tenant. A suspended order can be resisted on the basis generally that it would not be reasonable in the circumstances or specifically that the same objective can be met by adjourning the proceedings on terms (see below p52) giving the landlord liberty to restore in the event of further breach. A suspended order would be an acceptable result in a 'breach of term' case only if made upon terms that it was not to be enforced without leave of the court and with no order for costs. Without such an express restriction the landlord can obtain a warrant without further hearing.

Ground 2: Nuisance and annoyance

The first part of ground 2 of Sch 2 is satisfied where:

> the tenant or any person residing in the dwelling-house has been guilty of conduct which is a nuisance or annoyance to neighbours.

---

20   *RMR Housing Society v Combs* [1951] 1 KB 486, CA.
21   *Bell London and Provincial Properties Ltd v Reuben* [1947] KB 157, CA.
22   *Sutton Housing Trust v Lawrence* (1987) 19 HLR 520.

Note that the ground imputes the tenant with responsibility for the actions of others living in the property – not just family members. However, a casual visitor, guilty of causing annoyance, is probably not 'residing in the dwelling-house' for the purpose of this ground. (It is unclear therefore whether the ground is available where the nuisance is caused by departing party guests.) 'Neighbours' is clearly a broader concept than 'immediately adjoining occupiers' and therefore embraces other residents sufficiently nearby to be affected by the nuisance or annoyance emanating from the property (see caselaw developed on this point in the private sector p130 below). Similarly, the words 'or annoyance' broaden the concept of nuisance. Both words are given their normal rather than their technical legal meanings. The necessary 'conduct' to be proved may possibly be constituted by one single act but is more likely to be shown through a number of examples of similar behaviour.

Proceedings under ground 2 have succeeded[23] where allegations proved were of racially motivated harassment of other residents in a purpose-built block of flats by the children of the tenant.[24]

However, there is no implied term in a tenancy agreement which requires the landlord to take action under ground 2 in the case of neighbour nuisance. The affected neighbour accordingly cannot compel the authority to act under this ground.[25]

Note that the 'reasonableness condition' must always be satisfied before an order can be made. It is not, however, uncommon to see cases in which a judgment proceeds from a finding that ground 2 is made out, directly to a suspended possession order, thus missing the vital issue as to whether it be reasonable for *any* order to be made. In considering 'reasonableness' the court should be invited to consider inter alia: the seriousness and frequency of the nuisance; whether it is continuing, persistent or recently abated; the effects on the neighbours; warnings issued by the landlord; and the relevant personal circumstances of the tenant.

Witnesses called by landlords frequently fail to distinguish between their own evidence of acts of nuisance and the repetition of details told to them by others. Unless acts are specifically admitted, the neighbours affected by the nuisance will usually be required to attend the hearing to give evidence directly.

---

23 *Newham LBC v McDonnell* (1985) unreported, Bow County Court.
24 See the later cases noted in D Forbes *Action on Racial Harassment* (Legal Action Group 1988) in appendix five.
25 *O'Leary v Islington LBC* (1983) 9 HLR 81, CA.

Ground 2: Criminal activity

A landlord may also rely on ground 2 where the tenant or a person residing in the dwelling-house

> has been convicted of using the dwelling-house or allowing it to be used for immoral or illegal purposes.

This part of ground 2 is also subject to the condition that it must be shown to be reasonable in all the circumstances for possession to be awarded before an order is made (s84(2)(a)).

There has been little or no experience of use of this ground in the public sector since its first introduction in 1980. Reference may usefully be made therefore to the developed caselaw on the almost identically expressed wording found in RA 1977 for private tenants (p131).

Ground 3: Deterioration

Schedule 2 ground 3 provides a remedy for the landlord where

> The condition of the dwelling-house or any of the common parts has deteriorated owing to acts of waste by, or the neglect or default of, the tenant or a person residing in the dwelling-house and, in the case of an act of waste by, or the neglect or default of, a person lodging with the tenant or a sub-tenant of his, the tenant has not taken such steps as he ought reasonably to have taken for the removal of the lodger or sub-tenant.

The ground is subject to the condition that an order for possession may be made only if it would be reasonable to do so (s84(2)(a)).

Useful guidance on the construction of this provision is to be derived from cases on RA 1977 Sch 15 Case 3 (see p132). However, unlike that case, the present ground 3 embraces deterioration in the condition of 'common parts'. This is defined (s116) as meaning

> any part of a building comprising the dwelling-house and any other premises which the tenant is entitled, under the terms of the tenancy, to use in common with the occupiers of other dwelling-houses let by the landlord

and the ground may therefore cover the situation in which the tenant or other person residing in the dwelling-house has been responsible for damaging the lifts, stairways, rubbish chutes, communal lighting etc in the block of which the dwelling-house forms part. The acts or omissions must be proved on the balance of probabilities to have been the responsibility of the tenant or co-resident.

Ground 4: Deterioration of furniture

Ground 4 of Sch 2 provides:

> The condition of furniture provided by the landlord for use under the tenancy, or for use in the common parts, has deteriorated owing to ill-treatment by the tenant or a person residing in the dwelling-house and, in the case of ill-treatment by a person lodging with the tenant or a sub-tenant of his, the tenant has not taken such steps as he ought reasonably to have taken for the removal of the lodger or sub-tenant.

Although they have power to provide furniture for residents (s10) local authorities rarely do so. Most council and other public sector properties are let unfurnished. However, the ground extends to furniture provided by the landlord authority in the common parts of the property. (Given the extended definition of 'common parts' in s116, this would embrace vandalism by the tenant in such places as the communal laundry or children's playing area.)

Ground 4 is subject to the condition that even if the terms of the ground are established an order may be granted only if it is reasonable in all the circumstances (s84(2)(a)).

Ground 5: Tenancy by deception

Schedule 2 ground 5 will be satisfied if

> The tenant is the person, or one of the persons, to whom the tenancy was granted and the landlord was induced to grant the tenancy by a false statement made knowingly or recklessly by the tenant.

The ground extends not only to representations known to be false at the time of making, but also to 'reckless' statements. However, only statements attributable to the *tenant* (or one of the joint tenants) are relevant, so that if a spouse or partner induces the landlord to let the accommodation in the sole name of the other spouse or partner, the ground cannot be relied upon.

In order to substantiate a ground 5 case the landlord must prove not only a false statement but also that the statement *induced* the grant of the tenancy.

However, it is important to remember that the landlord must also show that it is reasonable for possession to be ordered (s84(2)(a)). In defending such a case, the court should be reminded that the landlord already has a specific remedy if induced to grant the tenancy by the deception of a *homeless* applicant – prosecution under s74. The loss of the home would be 'excessive punishment' in all but the most exceptional cases. It should be noted too that the tenant may also be liable to prosecution for 'obtaining by deception', contrary to the Theft Act 1968.

In *Ruschcliffe BC v Watson*[26] the tenant recorded on her application form that she had been a lodger in her former home. The landlord subsequently discovered that she had held a housing association tenancy. The entry on the form was unquestionably 'false' for the purposes of ground 5. The county court judge was satisfied that all the other elements of the ground were similarly proven and ordered possession. An appeal on the basis, *inter alia*, that it was not reasonable to render the tenant homeless by repossession, was dismissed.

Ground 6: An illegal premium

The HA 1985 permits assignment by way of exchange between secure occupiers (s92) but payment of a premium renders both parties liable to possession proceedings based on ground 6. This applies where

> The tenancy was assigned to the tenant, or to a predecessor in title of his who is a member of his family and is residing in the dwelling-house, by an assignment made by virtue of section 92 (assignments by way of exchange) and a premium was paid either in connection with that assignment or the assignment which the tenant or predecessor himself made by virtue of that section.
>
> In this paragraph 'premium' means any fine or other like sum and any other pecuniary consideration in addition to rent.

In order to recover possession the landlord must, in addition to proving the ground, show that it would be reasonable for an order of possession to be made (s84(2)(a)).

It should be noted that the ground is met whichever party to the assignment pays a premium and also extends to the current tenant where the assignment was carried out by a predecessor in title. In the latter case the predecessor must be a member of the tenant's family still living in the tenant's home. Thus if a NSP is served relying on this latter aspect of the ground, the claim can be defeated if the family member responsible moves permanently out of residence prior to the issue of proceedings.

Ground 7: Non-housing accommodation

Ground 7 of Sch 2 makes very specific provision for those residing in non-housing accommodation (eg, in a social service or educational facility) who are guilty of inappropriate conduct:

> The dwelling-house forms part of, or is within the curtilage of, a building which, or so much of it as is held by the landlord, is held mainly for purposes other than housing purposes and consists mainly of accommodation other than housing accommodation, and—
>
> (a) the dwelling-house was let to the tenant or a predecessor in title of his in consequence of the tenant or predecessor being in the employment of the landlord, or of—
>
> a local authority,
> a new town corporation,
> an urban development corporation,
> the Development Board for Rural Wales, or
> the governors of an aided school,
>
> and
>
> (b) the tenant or a person residing in the dwelling-house has been guilty of conduct such that having regard to the purpose for which the building is used, it would not be right for him to continue in occupation of the dwelling-house.

The examples that legislators presumably had in mind were of 'misbehaviour' by staff or their successors accommodated within the buildings or grounds of schools, colleges and residential homes. Note that the misconduct must be related to the purpose for which the main building is used. Note also that the dwelling must be within the 'curtilage' of some non-housing building. It is not sufficient simply to show that the dwelling is within the same grounds as that building.[27] Whether the dwelling is within the 'curtilage' of another building is largely an issue of fact. Advisers will find helpful guidance in the caselaw relating to applications for exercise of the right to buy, which turn on whether the property sought to be purchased is within the curtilage of another building (HA 1985 Sch 5 ground 5).[27A] If the accommodation has been provided to an employee, required to occupy it for the better performance of his or her duties, the tenancy may not be secure at all (Sch 1 para 2 – see p9 above).

Possession may be ordered under ground 7 only if in all the circumstances it is reasonable for an order to be made (s84(2)(a)).

---

27   *Dyer v Dorset CC* (1988) 20 HLR 490, CA.
27A See *Barwick v Kent County Council* (1992) 24 HLR 341, CA.

Ground 8: Temporary accommodation

Not infrequently landlords temporarily rehouse secure tenants while works of repair or improvement are in progress at their homes. If the secure tenant is offered and accepts an alternative secure tenancy or licence while work is in progress, ground 8 of Sch 2 deals with the situation if that tenant or his or her successor refuses to return 'home'.

> The dwelling-house was made available for occupation by the tenant (or a predecessor in title of his) while works were carried out on the dwelling-house which he previously occupied as his only or principal home and—
>
> (a)   the tenant (or predecessor) was a secure tenant of the other dwelling-house at the time when he ceased to occupy it as his home,
>
> (b)   the tenant (or predecessor) accepted the tenancy of the dwelling-house of which possession is sought on the understanding that he would give up occupation when, on completion of the works, the other dwelling-house was again available for occupation by him under a secure tenancy, and
>
> (c)   the works have been completed and the other dwelling-house is so available.

Note that ground 8 is not concerned with requiring the tenant to move out for works to be done – that is covered by ground 10 (see below); rather it concerns the tenant refusing to return to the former home. It must be shown both that the tenant had agreed to move back and that the works have been completed.

The ground is subject to the condition that the grant of an order must be reasonable in all the circumstances (s84(2)(a)). Relevant factors will include: the circumstances under which the tenant was initially required to move; the terms of any understanding reached at that time with the landlord; the length of time the tenant has been in the present property etc. The court may be particularly reluctant to disturb the tenant if works at the former home were scheduled to take a few months and were completed years later.

Ground 9: Overcrowding

A ground for possession is made out where the dwelling-house

> is overcrowded within the meaning of Part X in such circumstances as to render the occupier guilty of an offence

(Sch 2 ground 9).

Overcrowding is generally prohibited by Pt X (as to what may constitute overcrowding see p156 below) but not all overcrowding renders the occupier likely to be guilty of an offence. In particular, overcrowding caused by visiting family members or natural growth in family size is excepted and a council may licence overcrowding (s330) to prevent the occupier being liable to conviction. However, a council which places secure tenants in overcrowded property may itself be liable to conviction.[28]

If reliance is placed on this ground, the landlord must show that suitable alternative accommodation will be available to the tenant if an order is made (s84(2)(b)). In addition, Sch 2 Pt IV para 3 makes special provision as to what is suitable alternative accommodation for those against whom possession is sought on overcrowding grounds:

> 3.   Where possession of a dwelling-house is sought on ground 9 (over-crowding such as to render occupier guilty of offence), other accommodation may be reasonably suitable to the needs of the tenant and his family notwith-standing that the permitted number of persons for that accommodation, as defined in section 326(3) (overcrowding: the space standard), is less than the number of persons living in the dwelling-house of which possession is sought.

Of course, the accommodation must also be suitable in the other respects referred to in Sch 2 Pt IV (see below p43).

Ground 10: Landlord's works

Possession proceedings may be brought on ground 10 of Sch 2 where:

> The landlord intends, within a reasonable time of obtaining possession of the dwelling-house—
> (a)   to demolish or reconstruct the building or part of the building comprising the dwelling-house, or
> (b)   to carry out work on that building or on land let together with, and thus treated as part of, the dwelling-house,
> and cannot reasonably do so without obtaining possession of the dwelling-house.

The landlord must intend to carry out substantial work but in order to satisfy this ground must also show that the work cannot be carried out without obtaining possession of the dwelling-house. The landlord needs to establish that legal possession of the property and termination of the tenancy is necessary, not simply access or temporary occupation of the premises by the landlord's contractors. Arguably, it must be proved that either the tenant has refused to co-operate with the landlord's proposals

---

28   See DPP v Carrick DC (1985) 31 Housing Aid 5.

for temporary displacement to other accommodation or that the landlord does not have and cannot secure any accommodation to provide a temporary dwelling for the tenant while works are in progress. It is also suggested that the ground cannot be made out if the tenant demonstrates a willingness to move out of the premises (eg, to stay with relatives) while work is in progress. On the other hand there will be cases in which the proposed works are so extensive as to amount to reconstruction, in which circumstances the recovery of possession seems sensible and the ground will be satisfied.

The Court of Appeal has held that in order to establish ground 10, the landlord must be in a position to (a) specifically identify the proposed works and (b) show why it is necessary to recover possession in order for the works to be carried out.[29]

Even if the ground is made out, possession cannot be ordered unless suitable alternative accommodation is available to the tenant and his or her family[30] (s84(2)(b)). If the tenant is forced to give up possession s/he will usually seek permanent suitable accommodation rather than negotiate an 'understanding' for return to the original accommodation once work is completed as such an understanding opens the way to later proceedings under ground 8.

As to financial compensation payable where the occupier is displaced by works of renovation or major repair, see Luba *Repairs: Tenants' Rights* chapter 8 (LAG) and any specific provision in the tenancy agreement.[31]

A tenant attached to his or her home in its present condition might frustrate the landlord's intentions for demolition or reconstruction by exercising the statutory right to buy. If the application to buy has reached the stage at which the tenant would be enabled to compel completion by injunction, the tenant will be entitled to complete the purchase rather than face eviction under ground 10.[32]

Ground 10A: Landlord seeking to sell with vacant possession

The Housing and Planning Act 1986 s5 inserted[33] ground 10A into HA 1985 Sch 2, which assists landlords who want to achieve vacant possession and sell property for redevelopment. Ground 10A provides that

29 *Wansbeck DC v Marley* (1987) 20 HLR 247, CA.
30 See n1.
31 *Borg v Southwark LBC* (1987) unreported, CA.
32 *Dance v Welwyn Hatfield DC* [1990] 22 HLR 339.
33 Housing and Planning Act 1986 Commencement (No 5) Order 1987 SI No 754. Effective date 13 May 1987; see DoE Circ 14/87.

a court may order possession if suitable alternative accommodation is available (see p43) and:

> The dwelling-house is in an area which is the subject of a redevelopment scheme approved by the Secretary of State or the Housing Corporation in accordance with Part V of this Schedule and the landlord intends within a reasonable time of obtaining possession to dispose of the dwelling-house in accordance with the scheme.
>
> *or*
>
> Part of the dwelling-house is in such an area and the landlord intends within a reasonable time of obtaining possession to dispose of that part in accordance with the scheme and for that purpose reasonably requires possession of the dwelling-house.

In order for the ground to become available, the dwelling must be in a 'redevelopment area'. Part V to HA 1985 Sch 2 sets out the terms under which the Secretary of State may designate such an area. The procedure requires an element of prior consultation with tenants (Pt V para 2) and allows the Secretary of State to require information from relevant landlords (para 3(2)), take into account a variety of factors (para 3(1)) and grant conditional or outright approval (para 5(1)). If the scheme is approved conditionally, the landlord may rely on a NSP served on ground 10A even though the conditions are not satisfied at the date of service, so long as they are fulfilled at the date of the hearing (para 5(3)). Where the landlord is a registered housing association, the Pt V functions fall upon the Housing Corporation rather than the Secretary of State (para 7). The Secretary of State has set out his approach to Pt V applications in DoE Circular 14/87.

In order to obtain possession on ground 10A, the landlord need *not* satisfy the court that an order is reasonably required. The only relevant condition is that suitable alternative accommodation is available.

Tenants displaced as a result of ground 10A proceedings may be entitled to home loss payments (Land Compensation Act 1973 s29 as amended by the Housing and Planning Act 1986 s5(3)).

Ground 11: Charitable landlords

A ground for possession arises where

> the landlord is a charity and the tenant's continued occupation of the dwelling-house would conflict with the objects of the charity.

(Sch 2 ground 11).

The condition which the landlord must also satisfy is that suitable alternative accommodation is available to the tenant (s84(2)(b)): see p43. But the landlord need not show that it is reasonable to require the tenant to move.

If the conflict with the objects of the charity is caused by the tenant's breach oi the tenancy agreement, the tenant runs the risk that the landlord may in the alternative rely on ground 1 and secure possession without being required to provide alternative accommodation (see p28 above).

Ground 12: Tied accommodation

Ground 12 may be relied upon where

> The dwelling-house forms part of, or is within the curtilage of, a building which, or so much of it as is held by the landlord, is held mainly for purposes other than housing purposes and consists mainly of accommodation other than housing accommodation, or is situated in a cemetery, and—
> (a)   the dwelling-house was let to the tenant or a predecessor in title of his in consequence of the tenant or predecessor being in the employment of the landlord or of—
> a local authority,
> a new town corporation,
> an urban development corporation,
> the Development Board for Rural Wales, or
> the governors of an aided school,
> and that employment has ceased, and
> (b)   the landlord reasonably requires the dwelling-house for occupation as a residence for some person either engaged in the employment of the landlord, or of such a body, or with whom a contract for such employment has been entered into conditional on housing being provided.

Clearly the ground is not restricted to the situation in which the same public body is both landlord and employer. It expressly incorporates situations where the landlord is a prescribed public body (see above p6) and the tenant is an employee of another or different authority.

It is not sufficient simply that the tenant or the person from whom the tenant derived title is an ex-employee of the landlord: the original letting must have been 'in consequence' of that employment. See the discussion on the similar RA provision (below) and 'Premises occupied by employees' (p211). As to the meaning of 'within the curtilage of' see p34 above.

Note that the landlord must already be employing the person for whom the property is required or have a contract for the employment of that person. The property must also be 'reasonably required' by the landlord (cf RA Case 8 below).

Additionally, the landlord must satisfy the dual conditions that (a) there will be suitable alternative accommodation (see p43) for the tenant and any family and (b) it is reasonable to order possession in all the circumstances of the case (s84(2)(c)).

In considering whether it would be reasonable to order possession, the court will have regard to, inter alia, the ex-employee's age and length of service, other accommodation possibilities for the new employee and the nature of the accommodation of which possession is sought.

Ground 13: Accommodation for the disabled

Special provision is made for the recovery of premises adapted for the disabled. Ground 13 applies where

> The dwelling-house has features which are substantially different from those of ordinary dwelling-houses and which are designed to make it suitable for occupation by a physically disabled person who requires accommodation of a kind provided by the dwelling-house and—
>
> (a)   there is no longer such a person residing in the dwelling-house, and
> (b)   the landlord requires it for occupation (whether alone or with members of his family) by such a person.

Note that the special features must be 'substantially' different from those of an ordinary dwelling and they must have been 'designed' (in the technical sense) for the special needs of the physically disabled. A simple additional ground-floor lavatory would not fulfil those requirements.[34] It should be noted that the ground is not available where the premises are adapted for use by a mentally disabled tenant (recovery of possession in such cases would be sought under grounds 14 or 15).

Also, the landlord must show that possession is required (not necessarily reasonably) for a disabled person requiring the particular special features. If the ground is made out, the landlord must prove, in addition, that (a) suitable alternative accommodation is available (see p43) and (b) it would be reasonable for a possession order to be made (s84(2)(c)).

Ground 14: Special accommodation provided by housing associations etc

Schedule 2 ground 14 applies where

34   *Freeman v Wansbeck DC* (1983) 10 HLR 54; [1984] 2 All ER 746, CA.

The landlord is a housing association or housing trust which lets dwelling-houses only for occupation (whether alone or with others) by persons whose circumstances (other than merely financial circumstances) make it especially difficult for them to satisfy their need for housing, and—

    (*a*)   either there is no longer such a person residing in the dwelling-house or the tenant has received from a local housing authority an offer of accommodation in premises which are to be let as a separate dwelling under a secure tenancy, and

    (*b*)   the landlord requires the dwelling-house for occupation (whether alone or with members of his family) by such a person.

Note that the limbs of paragraph (a) are expressed in the alternative. The second limb makes special provision for those reluctant to move on from 'half-way' or 'bridging' accommodation into permanent public-sector tenancies. The second limb of paragraph (a) cannot be satisfied by the association or trust making available a secure or an assured tenancy with the same or another association or trust – only a local authority secure tenancy satisfies the provision. However, whichever limb is relied upon, the landlord must also show that a person with the appropriate special housing need would take the defendant's place.

In order to succeed in reliance upon this ground the landlord must show that both the 'suitable alternative accommodation' (see p43) and 'reasonableness' conditions are satisfied (s84(2)(c)).

As to the position of housing association and housing trust tenants generally see chapter 6.

Ground 15: Special needs accommodation

Provision is made by ground 15 for recovery of possession of one of a group of dwellings let to those with special needs. It applies where

The dwelling-house is one of a group of dwelling-houses which it is the practice of the landlord to let for occupation by persons with special needs and—

    (*a*)   a social service or special facility is provided in close proximity to the group of dwelling-houses in order to assist persons with those special needs,

    (*b*)   there is no longer a person with those special needs residing in the dwelling-house, and

    (*c*)   the landlord requires the dwelling-house for occupation (whether alone or with members of his family) by a person who has those special needs.

The special needs dwellings must be in a 'group' within the ordinary meaning of that term. It is suggested that this requirement would not be met where the relevant dwellings said by the landlord to comprise the 'group' were spread throughout the area of the landlord's ordinary housing stock.[35]

Limbs (a), (b) and (c) must all be satisfied, and in order to succeed in recovering possession the landlord must also show that 'suitable alternative accommodation is available' (see p43) and that the making of an order would be reasonable in all the circumstances (s84(2)(c)).

Ground 16: Underoccupation

No ground for possession is available to the landlord simply on the basis that the original tenant no longer requires such extensive accommodation. However, if the present tenant is a successor (defined by s88) other than the tenant's spouse, ground 16 makes limited provision for recovery of the property by the landlord where

> The accommodation afforded by the dwelling-house is more extensive than is reasonably required by the tenant and—
> (a)   the tenancy vested in the tenant by virtue of section 89 (succession to periodic tenancy), the tenant being qualified to succeed by virtue of section 87(b) (members of family other than spouse), and
> (b)   notice of the proceedings for possession was served under section 83 more than six months but less than twelve months after the date of the previous tenant's death.
> The matters to be taken into account by the court in determining whether it is reasonable to make an order on this ground include—
> (a)   the age of the tenant,
> (b)   the period during which the tenant has occupied the dwelling-house as his only or principal home, and
> (c)   any financial or other support given by the tenant to the previous tenant.

Note therefore that ground 16 does not provide for recovery of possession from a widow or widower of the deceased tenant who is underoccupying. Nor does it apply to the underoccupying successor to a fixed-term tenancy (s90). It can also be avoided if the late tenant had sufficient foresight to assign the tenancy to the successor in advance of his or her death (s91(3)(c)). In the latter case the new assignee tenant cannot be ousted under ground 16 although ground 1 may be applicable if the assignment was made in breach of a prohibition against assignment.[36]

---

35   *Martin v Motherwell DC* [1991] SLT (Lands Tr) 4, noted at September 1991 *Legal Action* 15.
36   *Peabody Donation Fund Governors v Higgins* [1983] 3 All ER 122; (1983) 10 HLR 82, CA.

Ground 16 sets a specific timetable for action by the landlord. The NSP must be served no earlier than six months from the date of death of the former tenant and no later than 12 months after the death. Note the time runs from the actual date of death, not the date on which the landlord learned of the death (contrast with HA 1988 Sch 2 ground 7, p191 below).

The landlord must not only satisfy each limb of ground 16 but also show that (a) suitable alternative accommodation is available (see below) and (b) it would be reasonable for an order to be made (s84(2)(c)). As to (a), because the present tenant is a successor s/he will take the fresh secure tenancy also as a successor unless the landlord can be persuaded to agree otherwise (s88(4)). Such an agreement may provide sufficient 'edge' to achieve a compromise at the door of the court in a ground 16 case where the defence is not strong and the successor is attracted by the possibility of alternative accommodation which is not only suitable but which will also provide the opportunity for a further succession within the family.

As to (b), the reasonableness test, note that the second paragraph of ground 16 makes specific provision for identified factors to be taken into account by the court. In addition, it has been held that if the successor tenant has exercised the right to buy, the court, in considering reasonableness, should take into account the reasons why the landlord wishes to recover possession and the fact that the tenant may have established a right to purchase.[37]

Suitable alternative accommodation

In any proceedings based on grounds 9 to 16 the landlord must show that suitable alternative accommodation is available to the tenant and family (s84(2)(b) and (c)). Where the landlord is not the local housing authority the obligation is satisfied by production of a certificate issued by the housing authority to the effect that it will provide suitable accommodation before a specified date (Sch 2 Pt IV para 4). Where the landlord is the housing authority or there is no certificate, the landlord must prove that suitable accommodation is available within the terms of Sch 2 Pt IV paras 1 and 2.

> 1. For the purposes of section 84(2)(*b*) and (*c*) (case in which court is not to make an order for possession unless satisfied that suitable accommodation will be available) accommodation is suitable if it consists of premises—
>   (*a*)   which are to be let as a separate dwelling under a secure tenancy, or
>   (*b*)   which are to be let as a separate dwelling under a protected

37   *Enfield LBC v McKeon* [1986] 2 All ER 730; (1986) 18 HLR 330, CA.

tenancy, not being a tenancy under which the landlord might recover possession under one of the Cases in Part II of Schedule 15 to RA 1977 (cases where court must order possession), *or*

(c)   *which are to be let as a separate dwelling under an assured tenancy which is neither an assured shorthold tenancy, within the meaning of the Housing Act 1988 nor a tenancy under which the landlord might recover possession under any of the Grounds 1 to 5 in Schedule 2 to that Act.*

and, in the opinion of the court, the accommodation is reasonably suitable to the needs of the tenant and his family.

2.   In determining whether the accommodation is reasonably suitable to the needs of the tenant and his family, regard shall be had to—

(a)   the nature of the accommodation which it is the practice of the landlord to allocate to persons with similar needs;

(b)   the distance of the accommodation available from the place of work or education of the tenant and of any members of his family;

(c)   its distance from the home of any member of the tenant's family if proximity to it is essential to that member's or the tenant's well-being;

(d)   the needs (as regards extent of accommodation) and means of the tenant and his family;

(e)   the terms on which the accommodation is available and the terms of the secure tenancy;

(f)   if furniture was provided by the landlord for use under the secure tenancy, whether furniture is to be provided for use in the other accommodation, and if so the nature of the furniture to be provided.

The words in italics were added by HA 1988 Sch 17 para 65. As to the quality of security offered by an assured tenancy see p177.

In applying these provisions, note that:

–   'family' is defined broadly (s113);

–   if family members have different or conflicting views as to the suitability of the accommodation offered, the court should grant leave for them to be joined as parties to the proceedings in addition to the tenant[38];

–   the list of factors set out in para 2 is not exhaustive[39];

–   the factors are not identical to those set out for RA tenants. Although caselaw developed in that jurisdiction may provide useful aids to construction (see p119), the RA authorities must be approached with some caution[40];

---

38   See n1.
39   *Enfield LBC v French* (1984) 17 HLR 211, CA.
40   Ibid at 216–217.

- it may be helpful to invite the judge to view the accommodation offered;
- paragraph 2(a) has no parallel in the RAs. It allows the court to consider the landlord's usual allocation policy for families of the same size etc as that of the tenant. Thus it will be open to the landlord to suggest in the case of a single person that their usual policy is to provide a small flat or bed-sitter. The defence for a tenant faced with such an assertion relies upon showing that it is an unreasonable rule or that an exception should be made;
- if the alternative accommodatiom will be provided by a different landlord, the court should be invited to direct that the tenancy of the accommodation be a secure rather than an assured tenancy: HA 1988 s35(4)(e).

Appeals

Advisers should be aware that although a general right of appeal lies from the county court to the Court of Appeal, that Court is singularly reluctant to disturb findings at first instance on issues of reasonableness and suitability of alternative accommodation. Every effort should be put into ensuring a successful outcome at the first hearing of a possession action.

CHAPTER 4

Preparing the Defence

General preparation

The preparation of the defence should take place at the first possible opportunity. In the usual case the adviser will have taken full instructions from the client (see checklist, appendix A). In addition to the client's statement and background material relating to the particular possession proceedings the adviser will wish to gather a file containing:

a) copy of the tenancy agreement (a copy may be obtained from the landlord authority: s104(1));
b) copy of the NSP (see p12);
c) rent book/rent payment book;
d) a welfare benefit assessment;
e) a housing benefit assessment;
f) report on condition of the property.

Items d) and e) can be prepared under separate green forms for each item. Item f) can be prepared by an expert surveyor or environmental health officer pursuant to a separate action for any disrepair or a possible counterclaim in the present proceedings, and can be paid for through green form or civil legal aid, as appropriate.

Full civil legal aid should be applied for immediately if the tenant may meet the financial criteria, as the litigation concerns an issue of vital importance – the tenant's continued occupation of his or her home. If the adviser is instructed only days or weeks prior to the hearing, emergency legal aid should be obtained (see chapter 23). If a defence is to be submitted this should be in the appropriate form and properly served on the landlord authority (see p226 Possession Procedure and precedent A5 for an example), but the adviser instructed at the last moment will simply have to pass a copy to the landlord at court or apply for an extension of time in which to file a defence. In the latter case it would be sensible to have an outline or early draft of the defence available at court.

The following pages set out the so-called technical defences and a review of the substantive defences which can be successfully deployed to resist possession proceedings.

Technical defences

Although these defences are described as 'technical' they are as effective as the substantive defences in preventing the landlord from obtaining an order for possession against a secure occupier.

Defective notice

As seen above (p12) the proper notice must be served upon the tenant as a prerequisite to the commencement of possession proceedings. If the notice is deficient, the proceedings must fail. A copy of the notice in the current prescribed form is reproduced on pp343–4. (The different prescribed form for fixed-term secure tenancies is not reproduced.) Every NSP should be carefully inspected with a view to discovering any possible deficiency.

Form

The notice must be in the form prescribed in regulations made by the Secretary of State: s83(2)(a). Those regulations are made by statutory instrument. The earliest prescribed form was contained in the Secure Tenancies (Notices) Regulations 1980 SI No 1339.[1] Those regulations were saved for the purposes of the 1985 Act by the Housing (Consequential Provisions) Act 1985 s2(2). A new form is prescribed by the Secure Tenancies (Notices) Regulations 1987 SI No 755 which came into force on 13 May 1987.

If the notice is not made in the form as prescribed at the date of service it is bad on its face and ineffective. Possession proceedings based on such a notice cannot succeed. However, since minor technical deficiencies would otherwise invalidate notices, the 1987 regulations provide that a NSP not in the prescribed form will be valid if 'in a form substantially to the same effect' (reg 2(1)). This use of delegated legislation to save otherwise faulty notices has been held to be within the relevant powers of the Secretary of State: *Dudley MBC v Bailey*.[2] As that case was fought entirely on the point as to the *vires* of the saving power (rather than on the faults in the notice actually served), there is little judicial guidance as to the degree of error necessary to remove a form from the category of 'substantially to the

---

1   As amended by SI 1984 No 1224 and upheld in *Wansbeck DC v Charlton* (1981) 42 P & CR 162, CA.
2   (1990) 22 HLR 424.

same effect' as that prescribed. Arguably, a notice would differ in substance if the Notes for Guidance contained in the body of the prescribed form were omitted from the notice actually served or set out on the reverse or on a separate sheet without an indication to 'See overleaf' or 'See attached'. Similarly, the words 'names of secure tenants' in para 1 are crucial, as the later guidance notes distinguish secure tenants from other tenants and licensees. It should also be noted that the words 'Notice of Seeking Possession' and the statutory reference at the head of p343 are themselves an important part of the preseribed form.

Ground

The notice must 'specify the ground on which the court will be asked to make an order for possession': s83(2)(b). It must therefore correspond with the ground that is (a) pleaded in the particulars of claim and (b) relied upon in court. As to (a), landlords not infrequently fail to set out in particulars of claim the ground on which possession is being sought, contrary to the relevant court rules (see chapter 22, Procedure in Possession Proceedings). If a different ground for possession is made out at trial, the proceedings must be dismissed unless the court gives leave for an alternative ground to be pleaded by alteration or addition (s84(3)).

Particulars

The notice must, on its face, give 'particulars' of the ground for possession (s83(2)(c)). These particulars must give the tenant sufficient details of the circumstances the landlord relies on in asserting that a ground for possession is made out.[3] Clearly the simple statement 'arrears of rent' is an insufficient particular.[4] Similarly 'various acts of nuisance' or 'instances of dilapidation' would be inadequate.[5]

If insufficient particulars are given, the court cannot entertain the proceedings, which must, therefore, be struck out.[6] The court cannot give the landlord leave to amend the NSP for the purpose of improving the particulars.

If inaccurate particulars are given, the court may (according to the degree of inaccuracy) permit the matter to proceed. Thus if the notice gives particulars that the 'arrears of rent are £X' and it is shown at hearing that the landlord has innocently and in error included in £X items which are not arrears of rent (eg, water rates), the action can proceed but the

---

3   *Torridge DC v Jones* (1985) 18 HLR 107; (1985) 276 EG 1253, CA.
4   Ibid.
5   *South Buckinghamshire DC v Francis* (1985) 11 CL 152.
6   *Torridge DC*, n3.

judge will take into account the nature and extent of the error in determining whether possession should be given.[7]

The specified date

The specified date must be no earlier than the date on which the tenancy or licence could have been brought to an end by notice to quit or notice to determine given by the landlord on the same date that the NSP was served (s83(3)). Accordingly, the adviser should check carefully the minimum period of notice the landlord would have been required to give under contract, statute or common law. In the ordinary case of a weekly periodic tenancy the specified date must be no earlier than four weeks after the next rent day.[8] If the 'specified date' is too early the notice will be bad on its face and the proceedings will inevitably be dismissed.

Proceedings issued before the specified date will also be struck down, as no summons should be issued until after the specified date has passed (s83(4)).

Has the notice lapsed?

The notice is valid for only 12 months from the specified date (s83(3)(b)). Upon its first anniversary the notice lapses. No proceedings can be brought in respect of a notice that has lapsed (s83(4)). Thus an action for possession started more than 12 months after the specified date is defective.[9] It must be noted that the 12 months runs not from the date of service but from the specified date. This means that effectively the landlord has 13 months from service to begin proceedings (contrast the position for Notices Seeking Possession of Assured Tenancies, p183). For these purposes the proceedings 'begin' on the date the relevant county court issues the summons.

Service

The HA 1985 requires that the notice has been served by the landlord 'on the tenant' (s83(1)). Nothing in Pt IV or s617 (service of notices) assists on the form that service of the notice must take.[10] It is for the landlord to prove that the notice was served on the tenant. As to the rules developed by the courts in relation to forms of service of notice to quit on private tenants see p91. Obviously, the tenant deliberately avoiding service will not attract the court to a technical defence based on deficient service. However, the burden of proof remains on the landlord to show that the

7   *Dudley MBC v Bailey* n2 *supra.*
8   Protection from Eviction Act 1977 s5 as amended.
9   *Edinburgh DC v Davis* (1987) SLT 33 noted at June 1987 *Legal Action* 19.
10   See January 1982 *Housing* 27.

notice was properly served. Local authority landlords may be assisted in establishing service by the Local Government Act 1972 s233, which permits service by post or hand delivery to the 'proper address' – usually the last known address.

The adviser might also usefully refer to the terms and conditions of tenancy. These not infrequently require that notices relating to the tenancy be served by some particular means (eg, recorded delivery post).

The right court and the right judge?

The county court has jurisdiction to determine possession proceedings brought against a secure tenant irrespective of the amount of any money sum also claimed 'in connection with a secure tenancy': s110(1). If proceedings are started in the High Court, the landlord will not be entitled to recover any costs (s110(3)) but the action may otherwise proceed.

Prima facie, actions of such importance to the individual as possession proceedings ought to be tried initially by a county court circuit judge. However, the Lord Chancellor has the power to direct that district judges shall have jurisdiction to hear these cases (s111(2)(a)) and he has exercised that power in his *Housing Act 1980 (Registrars' Jurisdiction) Direction 1985* (1985) NLJ 1085. Although the defendant has a right to object, in practice the defendant generally agrees to the district judge having jurisdiction since, if unsuccessful in his or her defence, there will be a right of appeal to the circuit judge.

Defective pleadings

The usual rules as to pleading in civil litigation apply in possession proceedings against secure occupiers in the county court (see Procedure in Possession Proceedings, chapter 22). Common technical deficiencies in landlords' pleadings in the public sector include:

a) failure to join all joint tenants;
b) failure to plead own title;
c) failure to plead the NSP;
d) insufficient particulars pleaded (particularly of 'reasonableness')[11];
e) failure to restrict pleading to the ground in the NSP.

However, as the landlord will generally easily acquire leave to amend the pleadings, reliance on pleadings defects will rarely amount to a long-term defence.

11   CCR Ord 6 r3, and see *Midlothian DC v Brown* 1990 SCLR 765 and *Renfrew DC v Inglis* 1991 SLT (Sh Ct) 83.

Action improperly brought

If the possession proceedings have been improperly brought, for example they are motivated by bad faith, abuse of power or dishonesty by a public-sector landlord, the tenant may be able to secure an order of prohibition restraining pursuit of the action, by an application for judicial review in the High Court. It would be usual for the county court proceedings to be adjourned in such circumstances (s85(1)) to await the outcome of the High Court action.[11A] Alternatively, the county court may either be asked to strike out the action as an abuse of process or the occupier could perhaps set up the unlawful action of the landlord by way of defence.[12]

Set-off

Tenants have a complete defence to an action for possession based on a failure to pay monies due to the landlord, if they can properly set-off (eg, by a successful counterclaim) an amount equal to or greater than the amount claimed by the landlord. Such circumstances usually arise from disrepair (see p227) or a failure to pay HB (see p268). However, reliance should not solely be placed on the set-off by way of defence as there is never a guarantee that the counterclaim will succeed.[13]

Substantive Defences

Ground not made out

The first substantive line of defence for the secure tenant, assuming that the technical defences mentioned above have proved inappropriate, is to argue that the ground asserted by the landlord is not made out on the balance of probabilities. The usual issues dealt with in possession proceedings and common methods of defending are set out in the discussion of the appropriate grounds (see above).

Condition not made out

The second line of defence, assuming that the landlord has proved (or the tenant admits) that a ground has been made out, is to show that a necessary condition is not satisfied. The conditions are discussed above together with the ground to which they relate.

11A *Avon CC v Buscott* (1988) 20 HLR 385, CA.
12   *Wandsworth LBC v Winder* [1984] AC 461; (1984) 17 HLR 196, HL.
13   *LB Haringey v Stewart* (1992) 23 HLR 557, CA.

Possession orders and eviction

Possession order inappropriate

It need not inevitably follow that, because both a ground and a condition are made out, a possession order (immediate or suspended) should be made. Indeed, there are cases in which, despite its being shown that the landlord has acted reasonably in bringing possession proceedings, it is nevertheless worthwhile to give the tenant another 'chance'. The mechanism readily available to the court is the adjournment of the proceedings (s85(1)), in all cases except those brought under grounds 9–11 inclusive.

The specific power to adjourn (additional to any other discretion in the court) arises in all cases where the ground relied upon is 1 to 8 or 12 to 16. In any of these cases the court may adjourn the proceedings for such period or periods as it thinks fit (s85(1)). This has the substantial benefit to the claimant that the costs of the action are not usually awarded if the matter is adjourned generally.

The safeguard for the landlord is that the court is free to make the adjournment conditional (s85(3)). For example, the adjournment may be conditional upon the tenant paying the current rent plus £x towards the arrears. The check on excessive conditions is s85(3)(a) which provides that conditions are not to be imposed if they would cause exceptional hardship to the tenant or would otherwise be unreasonable. A form of order or adjournment on terms meeting these points has recently been published.[14]

If the court cannot be persuaded to deal with the matter by way of adjournment, the adviser must take steps to avoid the making of an absolute order for possession.

Resisting an absolute possession order

There are, of course, cases in which the tenant is unable to resist the conclusion that (the landlord having established both the grounds and conditions) a possession order must be made. If a possession order is made, the tenancy ends on the date on which the tenant is to give up possession in pursuance of the order: s82(2).

When considering the circumstances in which an absolute possession order may be avoided it must be stressed that it is no 'victory' for the tenant to achieve a suspended or otherwise non-immediate possession order. First, costs will usually be awarded against the tenant on the making of the order whether suspended or otherwise. Although a legally

14   See Platt and Madge 'Suspended Possession Orders' (1991) 141 NLJ 853, and p381 below.

aided tenant has some protection against an award of costs (see chapter 25 below), these may cause considerable hardship to other occupiers. Second, there is the possibility at any time of the landlord simply applying ex parte for a warrant for possession in respect of any further default (thus illustrating the importance of securing an order subject to the condition that it is not to be enforced without leave of the court). Third, the suspension may be on terms which – although they must not be unreasonable or cause exceptional hardship (s85(3)) – may nevertheless cause *some* hardship. Fourth, if the terms of a suspended order are broken (for whatever reason) the order becomes effective to determine the tenant's secure tenancy.[15] Thus, although simply missing a single payment will not of itself usually cause the landlord to seek execution of the suspended order, it would appear to lose the tenant all benefits associated with 'secure' status, eg, the right to buy, the right to assign etc.[16]

If a suspended possession order is to be made, the court should be discouraged from using the present standard form N28. Other alternative models are available which better protect the interests of occupiers.[17] Any such order should, however, be expressed so as to ensure that it cannot be implemented once the outstanding sum or arrears expressed in it has been paid.[18]

Preventing an eviction

Where an order for possession has been made, occupiers retain secure status until the date on which they are to give up possession in pursuance of the order: s82(2). On that date both security and the tenancy end.

In the case of an absolute order for possession the date on which the tenant is to give up possession will be clearly shown in the order itself or identified by a reference to 'x days from today's date' (very commonly 28 days from the date of hearing). In the case of a suspended order the date that both security and the tenancy end is the date on which the terms of the order are breached.[19] If the terms are not breached but are complied with, the tenancy and security with it continue indefinitely.

Whether the order is expressed to be absolute or suspended, the court can further suspend or stay the order or postpone the date for possession on any grounds that it 'thinks fit': s85(2). This can be done at any time

---

15   *Thompson v Elmbridge BC* (1987) 19 HLR 526, CA.
16   See J Driscoll 'Rent arrears, suspended possession orders and the rights of secure tenants' (1988) 51 MLR 371.
17   See pp377–81.
18   *Blaenau Gwent BC v Snell* (1989) unreported, noted at March 1990 *Legal Action* 13.
19   See n15.

before the moment of execution of the order by the bailiffs, even a matter of hours or minutes beforehand. The procedure for making an application for a stay or postponement is described on p255. Note that this procedure is not available where the possession order has been obtained under grounds 9, 10, 10A or 11, but that in all other cases it is available even if the original date for possession has passed or a suspended order has been breached. (The subsequent status of an occupier who lost his or her tenancy and security as a result of breach of a suspended order but who has successfully applied for a stay or further suspension is unclear.[20])

Reinstating the tenant after eviction

Even if the order has been executed by the bailiff taking possession (whether or not the occupier was forced immediately, physically to leave) it is still not too late to set aside the possession order. This can only be done, however, by application to the court under CCR Ord 37. If the application succeeds, the original order is set aside as well as the warrant for possession issued under it and the occupier can re-enter the premises.[21] Grounds for such an application might include non-receipt of the summons for possession[22] (Ord 37 rr2–3) or compliance with a money judgment to which the possession proceedings were linked.[23]

'Duty advocate' plan

This section illustrates how an adviser might respond to the public sector possession case which occurs with greatest frequency (rent arrears), where instructions are received at the last moment.

The proper preparation of a defence in a rent arrears case requires careful study and consideration. In particular, all the documents must be examined, statements taken and negotiations pursued.

If instructed at 'the door of the court' the adviser should avoid the temptation of negotiating a 'suspended order' for current rent and a modest level of weekly payment off the arrears (for reasons, see p52). After all, closer examination may establish that there are in fact no arrears at all.

---

20   See n16.
21   *Governors of the Peabody Donation Fund v Hay* (1986) 19 HLR 145.
22   *Tower Hamlets LBC v Abadie* (1990) 22 HLR 264, CA, *Islington LBC v Hassan* (1991) unreported but noted at September 1991 *Legal Action* 15, *Islington LBC v Bakari* (1991), noted at March 1992 *Legal Action* 11, *Lancaster CC v Cohen* (1991), noted at March 1992 *Legal Action* 11, and *Tower Hamlets LBC v McCarron* noted at September 1988 *Legal Action* 13.
23   See n21.

If instructions are received literally at the last moment, the adviser should make an initial application for the case to be put back in the list and then take some brief particulars from the client. Although the court list may contain dozens of cases it does not always follow that there will be the opportunity to have a lengthy discussion – cases can be processed very quickly in some courts.

The adviser should try to take a preliminary statement from the tenant covering the duration of the tenancy, the personal circumstances of the tenant, the circumstances surrounding the 'arrears', details of income and details of HB received (see checklist, appendix A).

If the tenant has any documents with him or her the adviser should inspect:

- the NSP (see p47);
- the summons and the particulars of claim (see p50);
- the rent book/payment book; and
- any correspondence.

If there is time, a green form should be completed at this stage so that upon return to court the adviser can seek dispensation for the green form to cover representation.[24]

If it emerges (as it usually does) that the arrears are disputed and/or the tenant is in hardship and/or there is disrepair etc, the immediate objective will be the securing of an adjournment to another date. Before returning to make such an application in court the adviser should be briefed as to:

- the likely eventual defence;
- the tenant's circumstances;
- the possibility of an agreement to pay current rent;
- the possibility of an agreement to pay something off the arrears;
- the reason why advice was not sought earlier;
- the minimum directions necessary to achieve the next stage in the action (eg, time within which a defence can be served).

The adviser then returns to court with the tenant and indicates to the landlord's representative that a request for an adjournment will be made. The adviser then argues that:

- s/he has just been instructed;
- those instructions reveal that the client has both an arguable defence (eg, that the arrears are disputed or it would not be reasonable to order

24   Legal Advice and Assistance (Scope) Regulations 1989 SI No 550 reg 8.

possession) and/or that the tenant has a potential counterclaim and defence by way of set-off based on disrepair or failure to pay HB etc;
- an adjournment is sought;
- the tenant will submit to a condition that current rent be paid throughout the period of the adjournment (s85(3));
- further conditions would be unreasonable or would cause excessive hardship (s85(3)(a));
- directions be given for a defence to be filed within (say) 21 days and such other steps as may be appropriate, eg discovery, experts' reports etc;
- costs be reserved to the trial judge.

In most cases the above procedure ought to achieve an adjournment. If not, the adviser has to do his or her best to defend successfully on the day and appeal any adverse order made. In an appropriate case, an appeal may be entered against the refusal to adjourn, in addition to an appeal against the order made.[25]

Once the adjournment is secured, the adviser should make the necessary arrangements for full legal aid to be obtained and for all technical and substantive defences and counterclaims to be considered. If the matter is to be conducted by a solicitor, advisers should bear in mind the possible delays in obtaining a full legal aid certificate and the time limit allowed for service of a defence.

25   See *Janstan Investments Ltd v Corregar* (1973) 21 November (unreported), CA and *Spitaliotis v Morgan* (1985) 277 EG 750, CA.

CHAPTER 5

Special Cases

Sub-tenants of Secure Occupiers

The first important point to be established is that the occupier is indeed the *sub-tenant* of the secure tenant. It is often the case that the occupier was let into possession as a lodger. This will usually be what the secure tenant argues as s/he requires no permission from the head landlord to allow lodgers onto the premises (s93(1)(a)).

Lodgers

The occupier will be a lodger in the tenant's home if the tenant provides services or attendances (eg, changes of bed-linen, cleaning, removing refuse) which require unrestricted access to the occupier's room. Traditionally, the lodger will also receive cooked or otherwise prepared meals. The lodger will be a licensee of the tenant and liable to exclusion by the tenant at the end of any period of lodging without the need for a formal notice in any prescribed form. This results from the exclusion of the lodger from the Protection from Eviction Act 1977 as a result of sharing use of the premises with his or her licensor, the true tenant (PEA 1977 s3A(2)(a)).

A lodger is not a sub-tenant, and secure tenants are free to take in lodgers as they wish (s93(1)(a)).

Other licensees

The tenant may also have allowed others in as licensees, eg, visiting family members. Some tenants invite relatives or friends to move into their homes on a short-term informal basis during the tenant's temporary absence. Other take in 'sharers', who may then remain in the home during the tenant's absence. None of these occupiers has a sub-tenancy, either because they do not have exclusive possession (a prerequisite of tenancy) or because there has been no intention to create a legal relationship.

Sub-tenants of part

Secure tenants are free to sub-let parts of their homes with the written consent of their landlords (s93(1)(b)). Many do not seek or obtain such consent (s94), and as between the landlord and the tenant such sub-lettings are unlawful, although any sub-letting is enforceable as between tenant and sub-tenant. However, such a sub-letting will not acquire any security of tenure or protection under the PEA 1977 as the 'landlord' (the secure occupier) will be resident and sharing accommodation with the tenant (PEA 1977 s3A(2)(a)).

Sub-tenants of the whole

It is not uncommon for secure tenants to move out of their homes and put others in occupation on long- or short-term arrangements. Even if the secure tenant intends to return and resume occupation at a later date, security of tenure is lost by the sub-letting of the whole and cannot be regained (s93(2)). In such circumstances, therefore, little is to be achieved by the tenant displacing the sub-tenant and attempting to regain occupation.[1] As between the secure tenant and the sub-tenant, the letting will be enforceable; and if made after 15 January 1989, may be an assured tenancy.

The sub-tenant and the public landlord

The position of a sub-tenant may be placed in jeopardy by action taken against the tenant by the landlord. If the landlord achieves a possession order against the secure tenant, the landlord may be able to proceed directly against the *sub*-tenants under the procedures for summary possession in RSC Ord 113 or CCR Ord 24[2] (see chapter 24 below), or indeed rely on the primary possession order to recover vacant possession of the whole property.[3]

The sub-tenant could perhaps obtain some additional time by showing that the interest of the true tenant had not been properly

1   *Merton LBC v Salama* (1989), unreported CAT 169, noted at June 1989 *Legal Action* 25; *Jennings v Epping Forest DC* [1992] NPC 93, CA; and *Muir Group HA v Thornley* [1992] EGCS 112, CA.
2   *Moore Properties v McKeon* [1976] 1 WLR 1278.
3   *R v Wandsworth County Court ex parte Wandsworth LBC* [1975] 1 WLR 1314 and *Thompson v Elmbridge BC* (1987) 19 HLR 526, CA.

determined by the landlord. This will especially be relevant wh true tenant has died or simply 'disappeared' (see above pp16 a respectively).

Sub-tenants of a secure tenant will not be secure themselves because their immediate landlord is not a public sector body (see p6). However, if the true tenant surrenders the premises to the landlord or gives notice to quit, the landlord accepting such surrender or receiving such notice is bound to recognise the title of the sub-tenant.[4] The sub-tenant might in this way be elevated to the position of secure tenant of the landlord, providing s/he fulfils the conditions listed on p5. The most difficult of the conditions for the sub-tenant of part to establish will be that s/he occupies a dwelling which 'was let as a separate dwelling'.[5]

Homeless persons

Placement in council-owned property

There are four main situations in which a public landlord might be providing temporary accommodation for homeless persons in its *own* housing stock:

a) while enquiries are being conducted to establish the circumstances of the homelessness of an applicant in apparent priority need (s63(1));

b) while an applicant having been declared intentionally homeless, is given an opportunity to secure his or her own accommodation (s65(3)(a))[6];

c) pending the outcome of a referral made to another housing authority (ss67–68);

d) when the local housing authority has accepted the obligation permanently to house the applicant (s65(2)), but is awaiting a suitable unit of property for letting on a secure tenancy.

In cases a) to c), the occupier, whether a tenant or licensee, cannot achieve 'secure status' before the local authority concludes its enquiries and issues notification under s64 or s68(3). (If no notification is given, the occupier is not able to assert that, on the facts, it should be treated as having been given).[7] Even then, a one-year period must pass in that

---

4 *Parker v Jones* [1910] 2 KB 32 (surrender) and *Mellor v Watkins* (1874) LR 9 QB 400 (notice).

5 W Birtles 'Sub-tenants: Problems for local authorities when properties are surrendered' 18 September 1987 *Local Government Chronicle* p12.

6 *Family Housing Association v Miah* (1982) 5 HLR 94.

7 *Swansea City Council v Hearn* (1991) 23 HLR 284.

accommodation before the occupier's tenancy of it can become secure (Sch 1 para 4).

It is, therefore, open to the landlord to determine the tenancy or licence in the normal way before the tenancy becomes secure and recover possession.[8] If the tenancy or licence is not properly determined it will continue, and possession cannot be ordered.[9] Usually, however, *unless the landlord specifically gives notice to the contrary*, the tenancy remains non-secure for 12 months.

In category b) cases, the family may wish to dispute the finding of intentionality and decline to take to the streets when the period of temporary accommodation is ended by notice to quit etc. In such circumstances, the landlord authority may seek to recover possession in the county court. The homeless applicant will need to have those proceedings adjourned while an action is in progress by way of judicial review in the High Court to test the legality of the finding of intentionality.[10]

In case d), the person immediately becomes secure as tenant or licensee of the property occupied. This applies even though the landlord may have intended only to provide temporary accommodation in that dwelling until alternative property became available. The homeless person made a 'better offer' is of course free to take it and surrender the current secure tenancy.

If, however, the homeless person in case d) is in the *same* property as that occupied during case a) above (ie, while enquiries were made), the normal one-year waiting period from service of s64 notice applies for accrual of security of tenure.

It has been suggested in one division of the Court of Appeal that the rights granted to homeless applicants to occupy accommodation in the temporary situations described above, do not amount to the status of either licence or tenancy.[11] Subsequently, another division of the Court has held that view to be inconsistent with House of Lords authority and directed it not be followed.[12]

As a further way of avoiding security of tenure for homeless applicants, many of those accepted for permanent rehousing are placed in short-life council accommodation awaiting redevelopment, and are thus excepted from secure status (see p9). Alternatively, temporary housing is provided in non-council accommodation (see below).

8   *Restormel BC v Buscombe* (1982) 14 HLR 89, CA.
9   *Eastleigh BC v Walsh* (1985) 17 HLR 392.
10 See, for example, *R v LB Croydon ex parte Toth* (1986) 18 HLR 493, QBD.
11 *Restormel BC v Boscombe* n6 at 100–101 and *Ogwr BC v Dykes* [1989] 1 WLR 295, CA.
12 *FHA v Jones* (1989) 22 HLR 45.

Placement in non-council-owned accommodation

Many homeless households are placed temporarily in the private rented sector in short-term tenancies or bed-and-breakfast accommodation. Their rights and security can be ascertained from Part II (Private Sector Tenants).

Those placed in housing association accommodation will have the same security (or lack thereof) as those placed in council-owned property if the initial placement was made before 15 January 1989. For consideration of whether those placed subsequently can be assured tenants, see p66.

In recent years, the phenomenon of 'short-term leasing' has developed to meet the temporary accommodation needs of homeless households. A local authority may take a lease or licence[13] of vacant privately owned property for use as temporary accommodation for the homeless. The council then installs as their tenants the homeless household. Schedule 1 para 6 exempts the tenancy from secure status, irrespective of the period for which it continues or the reasons why the homeless household is being accommodated. For their protection, see Non-Secure Tenants (below).

Non-secure tenants

There remains a substantial number of public sector tenants who have never acquired security (eg, because they are excepted by Sch 1) or who have lost it in one of the ways described above in chapter 2. They remain contractual tenants liable to pay rent and the other obligations of both parties continue to bind them and be enforceable by either landlord or tenant. The landlord seeking to recover possession must therefore determine the contractual tenancy and bring proceedings for possession.

There are broadly two lines of defence open to the non-secure tenant:
a) *Defective notice to quit.* The tenant can successfully resist possession proceedings (if only temporarily) by showing that the contractual tenancy has not been properly determined. The circumstances in which this can be established are set out in Part II p86.
b) *Administrative law grounds.* The non-secure tenant may be able to defend on the grounds that the proceedings are improperly brought by the landlord, that is, that a public body is acting in abuse of its powers. Examples would include authorities motivated by bad faith or dishonesty,

13   *LB Tower Hamlets v Miah* (1992) 24 HLR 197, CA.

or otherwise acting unreasonably.[14] The onus is on the tenant to make out the allegation of abuse of power or breach of duty.[15]

Non-secure licensees

Those who hold licences from local authorities which do not achieve secure status (see above p10 for the exceptions to security) are not entitled to the benefits of the HA 1985. Possession proceedings brought against them may be defended on only one of two grounds:
a)   *Insufficient notice.*   A licence can be determined only by the giving of contractual or reasonable notice.[16] 'What is a reasonable time depends on all the circumstances of the case and where the licence has been to occupy premises for residential purposes the reasonable time has reference to enabling the licensee to have an opportunity of taking his effects away from the property.'[17] The licensee given insufficient notice may have a short-term defence that longer notice should have been given. Any proceedings to recover possession under Ord 113 or 24 (see chapter 24 below) can be started only *after* reasonable notice has expired.[18]

From 15 January 1989, any notice given to determine a non-secure licence (whether the licence was granted before or after that date) must: (a) be in writing, (b) contain the prescribed information and (c) be given not less than four weeks before it takes effect (HA 1988 s32(2)). The only licences not covered by the statutory rules are those granted to squatters as a temporary expedient (Protection from Eviction Act 1977 s3A(6)) or to licensees of hostels provided by public sector landlords (s3A(8)).
b)   *Administrative law grounds.*   The non-secure public sector licensee is as able as the non-secure public-sector tenant to argue that the proceedings are improperly brought by the landlord authority (see above).[19]

---

14   *Bristol DC v Clark* [1975] 3 All ER 976; *Bristol CC v Rawlins* (1977) 34 P & CR 12; and *Sevenoaks DC v Emmott* (1979) 39 P & CR 404.
15   *Cannock Chase DC v Kelly* [1978] 1 All ER 152.
16   *Minister of Health v Bellotti* [1944] KB 298.
17   *GLC v Jenkins* [1975] 1 All ER 354 per Diplock LJ at 357c.
18   Ibid.
19   *Cleethorpes BC v Clarkson* (1977) noted at July 1978 *LAG Bulletin* 166 and at (1978) 128 NLJ 860; *R v Wear Valley DC ex parte Binks* [1985] 2 All ER 699; and *Kensington and Chelsea RBC v Haydon* (1984) 17 HLR 114, CA.

CHAPTER 6

Housing Associations

Those who occupy housing association property may do so as tenants or licensees and may fall within either the public sector regime for security of tenure or the private sector regime. This chapter explains the protection available according to the type of arrangement under which the occupier is in residence.

Tenants of housing associations

Under the provisions of HA 1985 s80, tenants of all housing associations (whether registered or unregistered) were within the 'secure tenancy' regime described in chapter 2. The intention behind the HA 1988 however, is to produce a situation in which all *new* housing association lettings are on an assured tenancy basis. Assured tenants have a more limited form of security of tenure than they would have had as secure public sector tenants and are placed in the same category of protection as most new tenants of private sector landlords (see pp177–198).

Subject to the limited exceptions described below, all housing association tenancies granted on or after 15 January 1989 are assured rather than secure tenancies (HA 1988 s35(4)). They may be normal assured tenancies or assured shorthold tenancies, although the Housing Corporation in its statutory role of guiding the activities of housing associations (HA 1988 s49) has indicated that shorthold arrangements should be used 'only in exceptional circumstances . . . where shorthold is the only practicable way of meeting the housing association's housing objectives'.[1]

The key to determining whether the tenant of the housing association is assured or secure is usually the date of grant of the tenancy. On or after

1 *Housing Corporation Guidance on the Management by Registered Housing Associations of Housing Accommodation Let on Assured Tenancies Under The Housing Act 1988* Part C.

15 January 1989 will be prima facie assured, on or before 14 January 1989 will be prima facie secure. However, housing association tenancies granted on or after 15 January 1989 will be secure rather than assured if:

- the tenant was previously a secure occupier (whether as sole or joint tenant or as secure licensee) with the same housing association (HA 1988 s35(4)). Therefore a secure tenant can transfer to other property within the same housing association's stock without loss of secure status; or
- the tenancy was granted following the re-acquisition of defective property (which a former secure tenant had bought) under the procedure set out in Pt XVI (formerly the Housing Defects Act 1984) pursuant to s554(2A) (HA 1988 s35(4)(f)). This embraces not only the original tenant who bought the defective house from the association but also certain members of his or her family (see HA 1988 Sch 17 para 61); or
- the tenancy was granted pursuant to a contract to let made before 15 January 1989 (HA 1988 s35(4)(c)); or
- the tenancy is offered as 'suitable alternative accommodation' to a former secure occupier against whom a possession order has been made in proceedings taken under s84(2)(b) or (c) and the court has directed that the new tenancy or licence should be secure (HA 1988 s35(4)(e)). This exception will be relevant to the former tenant of a public sector body rehoused by a housing association in accommodation arranged by the former landlord (see p44); or
- the tenant was a private sector protected or statutory tenant and the housing association has taken over from the private landlord (HA 1988 s34(5)).

Further modifications apply where the association is temporarily housing homeless families or is a housing co-operative. These are discussed separately below.

Defending housing association tenants

The first step is to determine (in accordance with the section above) whether the tenant holds an assured or a secure tenancy. Wherever possible it should be argued that the tenancy is secure as this confers a greater degree of security of tenure (as well as the right to buy etc).

Assured tenants

The principles for defending possession proceedings brought against assured tenants are set out in detail at pp177–198. If proceedings are brought under any of the discretionary grounds (see p184) the attention of the court could usefully be drawn to the management guidance issued by the Housing Corporation to housing associations. This includes the requirement that associations should have policies and procedures that tenants should be informed about and which cover various matters.[2] These include the circumstances in which requiring tenants to move to alternative accommodation might be necessary and the circumstances in which the association may take legal action in pursuing arrears of rent and other charges (which should be only after full investigation and consideration of the tenant's circumstances). Note also that associations should offer tenants information, advice and assistance in applying for HB, so that they receive their proper entitlement.

Demonstrating a failure to comply with this guidance may be useful in persuading the court that it is not reasonable in all the circumstances to grant an order for possession.

Secure tenants

The approach to defending secure tenants of housing associations and other public sector landlords is discussed at pp46–58.

Housing association licensees

Many housing associations make property available to occupiers on licence rather than by way of tenancy. The first step for the adviser assisting such an occupier is to determine whether what has been granted is truly a licence or is in law a tenancy (see p81). If, despite its description, the licence is a tenancy, see p63 above.

If the arrangement is a true licence then the security of tenure it attracts is determined by the date on which it was granted. A licence granted by a housing association on or before 14 January 1989 may be a secure licence attracting considerable security of tenure (see p10 for a discussion of the conditions for such a licence being secure). If the licence was granted on or before 14 January 1989 but does not fulfil the conditions for being a secure licence, see p62 which deals with non-secure licensees.

If the licence was granted on or after 15 January 1989 it cannot be

---

2   Ibid Part G.

secure unless it falls into one of the excepted categories set out on p64 above. The occupier consequently will have only the most limited protection. See p205 for the conditions governing the recovery of possession from licensees.

Housing associations and the homeless

In discharging their statutory duties toward the homeless, local authorities are urged to seek the help and co-operation of housing associations[3] and registered housing associations are obliged by statute to provide reasonable help on request: s72(a). As a result, in many areas of the country housing associations provide temporary accommodation for homeless people where:

- investigations by the local authority under HA 1985 Pt III are under way; or
- the person became homeless intentionally and is entitled only to temporary accommodation; or
- the person is awaiting acceptance by a different housing authority to which s/he has been referred under the local connection provisions.

In any of these situations the occupier does not immediately gain secure status as against the housing association (see further p59).

If the accommodation is first provided on or after 15 January 1989 and is provided by way of tenancy, that tenancy will not immediately be assured. Such a tenancy will be assured only if either:

a) the tenant is so notified by the association (HA 1988 s1(6)); or
b) 12 months have expired since service on the tenant of the local authority's decision on the homelessness application (HA 1988 s1(7)).

In order to avoid the possible accrual of secure or assured status, many associations grant licences, rather than tenancies, of temporary accommodation to homeless people. If the licence was granted before 15 January 1989 it will become secure unless determined within 12 months of the local authority homelessness decision (see p59). If granted on or after 15 January 1989 it will be neither secure nor assured and attract only the limited protection indicated on p62.

Whether what has been granted to the homeless person pursuant to a temporary obligation is a licence or a tenancy is to be determined according to the usual legal principles (see p81).[4] The Court of Appeal has

3   *Code of Guidance* DoE, 3rd edn, para 12.7.
4   *Eastleigh BC v Walsh* (1985) 17 HLR 392; [1985] 2 All ER 112, HL.

recently[5] resiled from the view that the usual principles can be modified in these cases.[6] Whether the arrangement is in law a tenancy or a licence can have important implications, eg as to the correct method by which it may be ended.

If the housing association grants a tenancy of 'temporary accommodation' to a person whom the local authority has accepted for permanent rehousing but for whom the council does not yet have appropriate accommodation, that tenancy may immediately be either secure or assured depending upon the date it is granted (see p63 above). The tenant will thus have considerable protection from eviction by the association, although a possession order might be granted if suitable alternative accommodation is made available (see p43 for secure tenants, p192 for assured). The association could not avoid this result by granting a licence to such a person prior to 15 January 1989 as they were secure licensees (see p10). However, since 15 January 1989 it has been possible to grant licences in such cases which attract neither secure nor assured status.

Housing co-operatives and housing trusts

A tenancy or licence granted before 15 January 1989 will be secure and covered by the provisions described in Part I of this book if granted by:

- a housing trust which is a charity; or
- an unregistered housing association which is a co-operative housing association; or
- a registered housing association other than a co-operative housing association (s80(1) and (2)); or
- a management co-operative exercising the functions of a public sector landlord (s80(4)).

Accordingly, occupiers of property held by housing trusts which are not charities or by registered housing co-operatives are not within the secure status regime. If a registered housing co-operative de-registers however, the tenants must be notified that they have become secure (s80(3)).

Each of the variations in landlord type is closely defined by the HA 1985 and the technical definitions may be found as follows:
'charity' s622
'co-operative housing association' s5(2)
'housing association' s5(1)

---

5   FHA v Jones (1990) 22 HLR 94, expressly not following Ogwr BC v Dykes [1989] 1 WLR 295.
6   Ogwr BC v Dykes [1989] 1 WLR 295.

'housing trust' s6
'registered' s5(4).

For tenancies granted on or after 15 January 1989, those granted by housing trusts, co-operatives and associations will normally attract assured or assured shorthold status and thus be governed by the regime described in Part II of this book. However, a 'fully mutual housing association' cannot grant an assured tenancy (HA 1988 Sch 1 para 12(1)(h)) and after 15 January 1989 it cannot grant a secure tenancy. New tenants of fully mutual housing associations are therefore outside both schemes of security (see p209 for their protection against eviction). The term 'fully mutual' is defined by s5(2).

The tenants and licensees of management co-operatives administering council property under arrangements made within s27B will continue as secure tenants whatever the date of grant.

CHAPTER 7

Housing Action Trusts

Housing action trusts (HATs) are intended to revitalise, improve and regenerate areas of run-down local authority housing. The statutory basis of their operation is to be found in HA 1988 Pt III. Each individual HAT is established by statutory instrument (HA 1988 s62) for an area of land itself identified by a separate statutory order (HA 1988 s60). That area will largely (but not necessarily exclusively) comprise tenanted local authority housing. The Secretary of State will, by further order, give the HAT the housing management powers held by the local authority in relation to that property (HA 1988 s65) and may transfer ownership of the council property itself to the HAT (HA 1988 s74). The HAT will thus become the 'new landlord' for existing council tenants and will be free to grant new tenancies or otherwise dispose of any empty property transferred to it from the local authority.

Effect on existing tenants

Tenants and licensees who have secure status as described in the earlier chapters of this Part will retain that status following transfer of the freehold of their homes to a HAT. This is achieved by the addition of HATs to the list of prescribed public landlords: s80 as amended by HA 1988 s83(2) (see p6). In order to obtain possession the HAT would therefore have to serve a NSP in the normal way (p12) and take proceedings based on fulfilment of the grounds and conditions for possession. The wording of the various grounds has been amended to make provision for HATs (HA 1988 s83(6)).

    It is expected that rent arrears will be the most common ground on which possession proceedings will be based and there are two aspects of defending such cases which are particularly relevant to HATs.

Challenging the rent

The HAT can establish a ground for possession for rent arrears only if rent is 'lawfully due' from the tenant (ground 1 Sch 2). A HAT can lawfully make only a 'reasonable charge' for housing accommodation (HA 1988 s85(1)). It may accordingly be possible to raise a defence by showing that the charge levied is not reasonable.[1] This might be on the basis that the property let is de facto in the midst of a 'building and redevelopment site' and therefore of reduced value. Alternatively, it might be that the rent has been substantially raised in advance of the improvement of the buildings and local environment contrary to assurances[2] that rents would not be increased until improvement work had been carried out.

Old arrears

If the tenant was in arrear with rent at the date the property was taken over by the HAT, the liability for the arrears does not necessarily transfer to the HAT (HA 1988 s74(4)). The tenant might thus be able to start with a 'clean slate' with the HAT. As long as no further arrears accrue, the tenant will be free from the risk of possession proceedings brought by either the HAT or the former council landlord (although obviously the former landlord can sue for the old rent arrears as a civil debt). If there are further arrears and the HAT takes possession proceedings it will be important to make it clear to the court that the former arrears are not part of the HAT's claim.

To find out whether liability for the arrears has been transferred it will be necessary to consult the terms of the transfer order made by the Secretary of State under HA 1988 s74. This will be relatively easy as the order will be published as a statutory instrument.

Access for renovation

In the course of its works to improve the property acquired, the HAT may need possession of dwellings for the purpose of renovation. For this purpose reliance will be placed on grounds 10 or 10A of HA 1985 Sch 2 (see pp36–37) in obtaining possession although suitable alternative accommodation must be provided. Obviously, the more acceptable alternative would be for the HAT to offer temporary alternative

---

1   *Wandsworth LBC v Winder* [1985] AC 461, HL and *Wandsworth LBC v Winder (No2)* (1987) 20 HLR 400, CA.
2   *HATs: A consultation document* (DoE, October 1987) paras 20–21.

accommodation while the works are undertaken and for the tenant thereafter to resume occupation.

New tenants of housing action trusts

Tenancies granted by HATs are outside the lettings regime of the Rent Act 1977 (RA 1977 s14(h) as amended by HA 1988 s62(7)) and HATs are incapable of granting the new assured tenancies introduced by HA 1988 (Sch 1 para 12(1)(i)). Accordingly, unless they fall into one of the exceptional categories described on p9, all tenancies or licences granted by HATs will be secure (ss4(f) and 80(1) as amended). This is true even if the tenancy is first granted after the HA 1988 came into force (HA 1988 s35(4)(a)).

As the HAT is one of the categories of organisation that local authorities can require to assist them in the discharge of their duties towards the homeless (s72 as amended by HA 1988 s70), it is expected that the exceptions from security applicable to the temporarily housed homeless (p59) will be particularly relevant. In defending possession proceedings against the new tenants of HATs the reader is referred to the early chapters of this Part.

Advisers may find it possible to develop new lines of defence by paying close attention to the terms of the order establishing the trust (HA 1988 s62), the limited objects and powers of the trust (HA 1988 s63) and the rules as to constitution (HA 1988 Sch 7). For example, it might be possible to establish in a given case that a decision to take possession proceedings or serve a NSP was taken in excess of the powers of the trust and was thus ultra vires and a nullity.

Winding-up of the trust

It is not intended that HATs retain control of areas of housing beyond the completion of their task of renovation and improvement. With the consent of the Secretary of State the HAT will dispose of the tenanted (and any empty) property to new landlords. The consultation requirements of s105 do not apply (HA 1988 s84(8)) and the tenants have no veto over the sale or transfer of their homes. Instead the HAT invites the local housing authority to consider whether it wishes to acquire any of the properties and the HAT then informs the tenants of its plans for disposal and their right to make representations (HA 1988 s84).[3]

Unless the properties are transferred to another public body (eg, back

3   *HATs: The struggle begins* (Shelter/LHU pamphlet October 1988).

to the local housing authority) the tenants lose their secure status and are likely to be assured tenants of the new landlord (HA 1988 s38), notwithstanding that the tenancy may originally have been granted long before HA 1988 was brought into force.

Part II

Private Sector Tenants

Introduction

The HA 1988 introduced fundamental changes to private sector security of tenure. Its effect is that there are now two separate regimes governing security of tenure, and accordingly possession proceedings, depending upon the date when a particular tenancy was created.

Section A – Tenancies created before 15 January 1989

Apart from amendments concerning succession after the death of a tenant, the security of tenure of those tenants whose tenancies were created before 15 January 1989 has not been affected. Such occupiers may have:

- a protected or statutory tenancy with full RA security of tenure and rent regulation (see p79); or
- a restricted contract without full RA protection, but with the possibility of delaying eviction for a limited time – see p166. The most common categories of tenants or licensees with restricted contracts are those deprived of full RA protection by resident landlords or the provision of substantial services or board; or
- a tenancy which is unprotected because it comes within one of the categories excluded from protection by RA 1977 ss4 to 16A (see p80). See also 'Rent Act Evasion' on p81; or
- a licence which enjoys no statutory protection.

These tenancies are discussed in chapters 8 to 13.

Section B – Tenancies created on or after 15 January 1989

A tenancy created on or after 15 January 1989 may be:

- an assured tenancy with security of tenure but minimal rent control (see p177). Unless a tenancy created on or after 15 January 1989 falls within one of the exceptions in HA 1988 Sch 1 or is an assured shorthold tenancy, it is likely to be an assured tenancy; or

- an assured shorthold tenancy with no long-term security of tenure and minimal rent control (see p199). An assured shorthold tenancy must be for a fixed term of not less than six months and must be preceded by a notice informing the tenant that the tenancy will be an assured shorthold tenancy; or
- a RA protected tenancy, but only if three limited exceptions apply (see p175). A tenancy created on or after 15 January 1989 can only be a RA protected tenancy if it is entered into in pursuance of a contract created before the HA came into force, if it is granted to an existing protected tenant by the same landlord or if the property is let following the making of an order for possession based on suitable alternative accommodation (see p119); or
- a tenancy which is unprotected because it falls within one of the exceptions in HA 1988 Sch 1 (see p178). The rights of an unprotected tenant whose tenancy was created on or after 15 January 1989 are very similar to those of an unprotected tenant whose tenancy was created before 15 January 1989 (see p209).

These tenancies are discussed in chapters 14 and 15.

Although the number of Rent Act tenancies is gradually declining, they are still significant in terms of the litigation that they generate. In view of the security of tenure which they have, Rent Act tenants tend to live in premises for longer and to have far more reason to defend possession proceedings. In contrast, most new tenancies in the private rented sector are assured shorthold tenancies without security of tenure. Most assured shorthold tenants realise this, and so far fewer seek advice when asked to leave. This difference is reflected by the fact that by May 1992, there had still been no Court of Appeal case relating to the provisions in the Housing Act 1988 dealing with security of tenure or possession proceedings – despite the poor drafting of some sections. In contrast, Rent Act cases were still coming before the Court of Appeal in significant numbers.

Tenancies Created Before 15 January 1989

CHAPTER 8

The Rent Acts

Introduction

The law relating to private tenants' security of tenure (or lack of it) and possession proceedings is an amalgam of the common law and protection superimposed on the common law[1] by the Rent Acts. Prior to the passing of the first Rent Act, a landlord bringing possession proceedings had to prove only that s/he owned or had an interest in the premises in question and that s/he was entitled to possession. Normally this involved proving that any occupant had never had permission to be on the premises, or, alternatively, that any such permission had been terminated in accordance with the provisions of the licence or tenancy. Apart from when landlords sought to forfeit tenancies for breach of covenant, there was no question of a landlord having to prove any ground or reasons for seeking possession or that it was reasonable for the court to make an order.

Although landlords' and tenants' rights were very greatly modified by the RAs, the old common-law rules remain highly relevant to residential occupiers who wish to defend possession proceedings. If an occupier is outside full RA or HA protection (see below) the only defence which s/he may have to possession proceedings is likely to be that the landlord has failed to terminate his or her tenancy or licence in the proper way. Even if a tenant has full RA protection, a landlord must prove that any occupant's contractual tenancy has been determined properly before relying on the RA grounds for possession.[2] A landlord's failure to determine a contractual tenancy, for example by serving an invalid notice to quit (see below), provides a complete defence even though there may be unanswerable RA grounds for possession. For this reason, the common law rules relating to determination of tenancies are dealt with in detail (see below).

1   Common-law rules have themselves been considerably modified, eg the restrictions on forfeiture in Law of Property Act 1925 s146 and County Courts Act 1984 s138. See pp98 and 102 below.
2   Rent Act (RA) 1977 Sch 15. See p118 below. The position is different for assured and assured shorthold tenants. See chapters 14 and 15.

The effect of most of the RAs since 1915 was to provide tenants who enjoyed full RA status with two forms of rights, namely control over recoverable rents and security of tenure. The RA 1977 s1 defines a protected tenancy as:

> Subject to this Part of this Act, a tenancy under which a dwelling-house (which may be a house or part of a house) is let as a separate dwelling is a protected tenancy for the purposes of this Act.
>
> Any reference in this Act to a protected tenant shall be construed accordingly.

The opening words of s1 refer to the various exceptions to full RA protection which are listed in the 1977 Act Pt I. Although it is outside the scope of this book to deal in detail with RA security of tenure, the exceptions are as follows:

dwelling-houses with rateable values above certain limits (if granted before 1 April 1990) or where the rent is more than £25,000 pa (if granted after 1 April 1990) (s4)[3];

tenancies where no rent is payable or the rent is less than two-thirds of the rateable value (if granted before 1 April 1990) or less than £1,000 pa in Greater London or £250 elsewhere (if granted after 1 April 1990) (s5)[4];

some dwelling-houses let with other land (s6);

tenancies where the tenant is obliged to pay for board or substantial attendances (s7);

lettings by certain educational establishments to students (s8);

holiday lettings (s9);

agricultural holdings (s10);

licensed premises (s11);

some resident landlords (s12);

landlord's interests belonging to the Crown, but not to the Crown Estates Commissioners (s13);

landlord's interests belonging to local authority etc (s14);

landlord's interests belonging to housing association or housing co-operative (ss15–16); and

assured tenancies (s16A) (see below).

Full RA protection gives residential tenants the right to continue as 'statutory tenants'[5] even after their contractual tenancy has terminated, provided that they continue to occupy the premises 'as a residence'. However, this status of 'virtual irremovability' is qualified – landlords are

3   As amended by the References to Rating (Housing) Regulations 1990 SI No. 434
4   As amended by the References to Rating (Housing) Regulations 1990 SI No. 434
5   See RA 1977 s2.

given various 'grounds for possession'[6] which, if proved, may enable the county court to make a possession order.

There are two categories of grounds for possession: 'discretionary grounds'[7] and 'mandatory grounds'.[8] If a landlord proves that a tenant's contractual tenancy has been terminated and that one of the *mandatory* grounds for possession exists, s/he is automatically entitled to an order for possession. However where a contractual tenancy has been terminated and one of the *discretionary* grounds for possession exists, the landlord must in addition satisfy the court that it is reasonable to make an order for possession (see below).

The RA also provides for an intermediate category of tenants and licensees who have the benefit of 'restricted contracts'.[9] They are tenants and licensees who do not have full RA security, usually because their landlord comes within the 'resident landlord exception'[10] or because their landlord provides board or substantial attendances.[11] Tenants or licensees with restricted contracts enjoy only minimal rights to delay the operation of a possession order (see below).

Throughout this section of this book dealing with tenancies created before 15 January 1989, all references are to the RA 1977 unless otherwise stated.

Rent Act evasion

Many landlords attempted to evade statutory protection by devices designed to deprive residential occupants of full RA security.[12] The rest of this chapter examines the principal forms of RA evasion. Some of these forms of evasion are also used to deprive occupants of security of tenure under HA 1988.

Licences

Only tenants can enjoy full RA protection.[13] Although a licensee may have a restricted contract, there is no question of a licensee having full RA

---

6   Ibid Sch 15.
7   Cases 1 to 10 and the availability of suitable alternative accommodation.
8   Cases 11 to 20.
9   RA 1977 s19.
10 Ibid s12.
11 Ibid s7. See eg *Otter v Norman* [1988] 2 All ER 897, HL.
12 It is not possible to deal with this in detail. See eg, *Megarry on the Rent Acts*, chapters 4 to 8, Farrand and Arden *Rent Acts (Amended and Annotated)* (Sweet & Maxwell 2nd edn 1981) pp6–15.
13 RA 1977 s1.

security. In the late 1970s and early 1980s, licence agreements became the most popular form of RA evasion. The most common arrangement was for landlords to arrange for 'sharers' in premises to sign separate forms of agreement, each purporting to give 'non-exclusive occupation' of the premises.[14] However, since *Street v Mountford* and *AG Securities v Vaughan*,[15] many who signed such agreements have become recognised as fully protected tenants. The principal requirements for a tenancy are the right to exclusive possession of premises for a term[16] in return for payment of rent.[17] Although the purpose of 'non-exclusive occupation agreements' is to attempt to deprive occupants of exclusive possession, it seems from *Street* and *AG Securities* that the court should look at the 'substance and reality' of each transaction and that, notwithstanding a written agreement, if there is a right to exclusive possession, the court should find that there is a tenancy. Lord Templeman in *Street* emphasised that when premises are in single occupation the principal class of occupants who are licensees and not tenants are lodgers whose landlords exercise a substantial degree of control over the premises occupied.[18]

Holiday lets

Section 9 provides that 'a tenancy is not a protected tenancy if the purpose of the tenancy is to confer on the tenant the right to occupy the

14   *Somma v Hazelhurst* [1978] 1 WLR 1014; *Aldrington Garages Ltd v Fielder* (1978) 247 EG 557; *Sturolson & Co v Weniz* (1984) 17 HLR 140; cf *Demuren v Seal Estates Ltd* (1978) 7 HLR 83.

15   *Street v Mountford* [1985] 2 WLR 877. N Madge 'The licence/tenancy distinction after *Street*' June 1985 *Legal Action* 77; *AG Securities v Vaughan* [1988] 3 All ER 1058 and see February 1989 *Legal Action* 21.

16   *Street v Mountford* n15. The term may be fixed or periodic.

17   Although there are cases where courts have held that there have been tenancies even though no rent was payable (eg, *Ashburn Anstalt v Arnold* [1988] 2 WLR 706, [1988] 2 All ER 147, 55 P&CR 137, CA, *Morris v Carey* [1989] EGCS 53, CA and see Law of Property Act 1925 s205(1) (xxvii)), even if a court were to decide that an occupier of residential premises who had no obligation to pay rent was a tenant, the tenancy could not be a protected or an assured tenancy (see Rent Act 1977 s5 and Housing Act 1988 Sch 1, para 3). Cf *Bostock v Bryant* (1990) 22 HLR 449, [1990] 2 EGLR 101, CA.

18   Cases in which the distinction between tenancies and licences situations has been considered since *Street* and *AG Securities* include *Nicolau v Pitt* (1989) 21 HLR 487, [1989] 1 EGLR 84, CA, *Stribling v Wickham* (1989) 21 HLR 381, (1989) 27 EG 81, CA, *Mikeover Ltd v Brady* (1989) 21 HLR 513, (1989) 59 P&CR 218, CA, *Aslan v Murphy* [1990] 1 WLR 766, [1990] 3 All ER 130, (1989) 21 HLR 532, CA, *Nunn v Dalrymple* (1989) 21 HLR 569, 59 P&CR 231, CA, *Ward v Warmke* (1990) 22 HLR 496, CA, and *Norris v Checksfield* (1991) 23 HLR 425, CA.

dwelling-house for a holiday'.[19] So, if there is a genuine 'holiday letting' the tenant does not enjoy security of tenure or the right to rent control. It is up to a tenant to prove that an agreement which purports to create a holiday let does not reflect the substance and reality of the situation or alternatively that the reference to a 'holiday' is a false label.[20] A tenant can succeed, and so establish full RA security, or a post-January 1989 assured tenancy if, for example, s/he can show that the length of the tenancy is inconsistent with a holiday, or that at the commencement of the tenancy the landlord knew that s/he was not on holiday. Common ways of proving this are to show that the landlord obtained a work reference or knew the prospective tenant's previous address.[21]

Company lets

Even if the tenant is a company, it enjoys RA protection while the contractual tenancy subsists.[22] However, because a company cannot 'reside', if there is a genuine letting to a company there is no question of a statutory tenancy arising after a contractual tenancy has been determined.[23] It may, however, be possible for a tenant to prove either that, although the written tenancy agreement purported to create 'a company let' this did not reflect the substance or reality of the transaction, or that the company was a mere nominee for an individual or individuals who were in fact the true tenants.[24]

Board

Some landlords sought to evade the RA by pretending that they provided board and that they were accordingly outside the RA due to the effect of s7. It seems clear that provision of a box of groceries weekly does not

19   HA 1988 Sch 1 para 9.
20   *Buchmann v May* [1978] 2 All ER 993.
21   *R v Rent Officer for Camden ex parte Ebiri* [1981] 1 All ER 950; *R v Rent Officer for Camden ex parte Plant* (1980) 257 EG 713.
22   Cf HA 1988 s1(1)(b) and (c). *Carter v SU Carburetter Co Ltd* [1942] 2 All ER 228; *Ronson Nominees Ltd v R C Mitchell* (1980) 8 August (unreported), SC, but noted at Institute of Rent Officers' *Selected Case Law Guide* 237.
23   RA 1977 s2; *Hiller v United Dairies (London) Ltd* [1934] 1 KB 57; *Hilton v Plustitle Ltd and Rose* [1988] 3 All ER 1051; (1988) 21 HLR 72 and February 1989 *Legal Action* 23; *Kaye v Massbetter Ltd and Kanter* [1991] 39 EG 129, (1992) 24 HLR 28, CA.
24   *Firstcross Ltd v East West Ltd* (1980) 255 EG 355; *Evans v Engelson* (1979) 253 EG 577; *Cove v Flick* [1954] 2 QB 326 at 328 and *Dando v Hitchcock* [1954] 2 QB 317 at 322.

suffice[25], and that to constitute 'board' food must both be prepared and served and be available at the rented premises.[26] A proper continental breakfast is sufficient.[27]

Representing tenants

If a tenant wishes to be legally represented at the hearing, it is vitally important that emergency legal aid forms are submitted to the Legal Aid Board as quickly as possible. Emergency legal aid may be refused if there has been delay (see chapter 23).

A landlord must always terminate a tenant's contractual tenancy (eg, by serving a valid notice to quit) *before* issuing proceedings. Unless a tenant is already a statutory tenant, failure by a landlord to terminate the contractual tenancy provides a complete defence, even if the tenant is outside the protection of the RA or however overwhelming the RA grounds for possession may be. This is not, however, the case if the contractual tenancy has been terminated at some time in the past and the tenant is already a statutory tenant (see chapter 10).

If statutory tenants cease to 'occupy premises as a residence' they lose their RA protection, and a landlord then only has to prove that the contractual tenancy has, at some stage, been terminated. However, statutory tenants may keep RA protection even though they are temporarily absent or live in two different homes (see chapter 10).

After proving that any contractual tenancy has been terminated, a landlord of a RA protected tenant must prove to the court that one of the grounds for possession is satisfied and, in many cases, also that it is reasonable for the court to make an order for possession (see chapter 11).

There are some RA grounds which are mandatory – ie if the landlord proves the ground for possession, the court *must* make a possession order and cannot consider whether or not it is reasonable to do so.

Even after a possession order has been made, the court may still have power to vary, stay, suspend or set aside the order (see chapter 27).

---

25   *Gavin v Lindsay* (1985) SCOLAG 153; also noted at March 1986 *Legal Action* 31.
26   Ibid and *Wilkes v Goodwin* [1923] 2 KB 86.
27   *Otter v Norman* n11.

CHAPTER 9

Termination of Contractual Tenancies

Before a landlord can succeed in obtaining a possession order against an unprotected tenant or any kind of RA protected tenant, the original contractual tenancy must be terminated (see chapter 8, above). If a landlord fails to prove that this has happened, the tenant has a complete defence to possession proceedings,[1] even if the landlord has grounds[2] for possession.

If a landlord does not issue possession proceedings after the termination of a contractual tenancy, or if such proceedings are unsuccessful, where the tenant has full RA protection (ie, is a protected tenant) and occupies the premises as his or her residence, the effect of the termination is to convert the tenancy into a statutory tenancy.[3] The most common ways in which a contractual tenancy can be terminated are expiry of a fixed-term tenancy, service of a notice to quit by a landlord or tenant, service of a notice of increase of rent, surrender and forfeiture. These various methods are considered in more detail in the following sections.

Expiry of fixed-term tenancies

If a tenancy is initially granted for a fixed period ('a fixed term') such as six months or one year, the contractual tenancy normally ends at the expiry of that period by effluxion of time. If the tenancy is a protected tenancy,[4] any tenant who still occupies the premises as his or her residence automatically becomes a statutory tenant. If a fixed-term tenancy has expired, a landlord usually need not serve a notice to quit before bringing possession proceedings because the contractual tenancy has already been terminated.[5] Occasionally, however, the terms of the original contractual

1 *Wallis v Semark* [1951] 2 TLR 222.
2 See below and RA 1977 Sch 15 cases 1 to 20.
3 Ibid s2(1)(a).
4 Ibid s1 and p80 above.
5 Ibid s3(4) and *Morrison v Jacobs* [1945] KB 577.

tenancy may be such that it continues even after the expiry of the initial fixed-term period. For example, if the tenancy agreement states that the tenancy is for a term 'of one year, and thereafter from month to month until determined by notice to quit' the landlord will have to terminate the contractual tenancy after the expiry of the initial year before bringing possession proceedings.

Once a fixed-term tenancy has come to an end by effluxion of time, the courts generally lean against implying a new contractual tenancy, unless there has been an express agreement for a new tenancy. The fact that a tenant continues to pay rent does not by itself imply a new contractual tenancy.[6] Occasionally, however, a landlord and a tenant may make an express agreement which will be construed either as commencing a new contractual tenancy or as a variation of the original tenancy, which means that a contractual tenancy continues to exist.[7] In such a case a landlord has to serve a notice to quit before starting possession proceedings.

Notice to quit by landord or tenant

The most common way of terminating a contractual periodic[8] tenancy is by either the landlord or the tenant serving a notice to quit. Unlike surrender (see below), when both parties agree to the tenancy coming to an end, a notice to quit operates to terminate the contractual tenancy whether or not the other party agrees. If the tenancy has not been terminated in any other way, failure to serve a valid notice to quit is a complete defence to possession proceedings.[9] A notice to quit should be strictly construed by the court. If invalid, it cannot be amended.[10] It is for a landlord seeking possession to prove that a valid notice to quit has been served.[11]

Notices to quit have no application during a fixed-term tenancy unless the tenancy agreement expressly provides that it may be terminated by a notice to quit. The normal method for a landlord to terminate a

---

6   Ibid; cf *Hartell v Blackler* [1920] 2 KB 161. See too *Longrigg, Burrough and Trounson v Smith* (1979) 251 EG 847, *Cardiothoracic Institute v Shrewdcrest Ltd* [1986] 3 All ER 633 and *City of Westminster v Basson* (1991) 23 HLR 225, [1991] 1 EGLR 277.

7   *Bungalows (Maidenhead) Ltd v Mason* [1954] 1 WLR 769.

8   Ie, a tenancy which was not originally granted for a fixed period of time. Note that completely different rules apply for assured and assured shorthold tenants. See chapters 14 and 15.

9   See eg *Plaschkes v Jones* (1982) 9 HLR 110 and *Franklyn v Tingey* (1975) BLT No 441A, (1976) 120 NLJ 767.

10 *Precious v Reedie* [1924] 2 KB 149.

11 *Lemon v Lardeur* [1946] KB 613.

fixed-term tenancy is by forfeiture (see below). There is no need for a notice to quit where the tenancy has already become a statutory tenancy.[12]

A notice to quit must comply both with the statutory requirements of the Protection from Eviction Act 1977 s5 and with common-law requirements.

Protection from Eviction Act 1977 s5

5.—(1) No notice by a landlord or a tenant to quit any premises let (whether before or after the commencement of this Act) as a dwelling shall be valid unless—

    (*a*)   it is in writing and contains such information as may be prescribed, and

    (*b*)   it is given not less than 4 weeks before the date on which it is to take effect.

    (1A) Subject to subsection (1B) below, no notice by a licensor or a licensee to determine a periodic licence to occupy premises as a dwelling (whether the licence was granted before or after the passing of this Act) shall be valid unless—

    (*a*)   it is in writing and contains such information as may be prescribed, and

    (*b*)   it is given not less than 4 weeks before the date on which it is to take effect.

    (1B) Nothing in subsection (1) or subsection (1A) above applies to—

    (*a*)   premises let on an excluded tenancy which is entered into on or after the date on which the Housing Act 1988 came into force unless it is entered into pursuant to a contract made before that date; or

    (*b*)   premises occupied under an excluded licence.

    (2) In this section 'prescribed' means prescribed by regulations made by the Secretary of State by statutory instrument, and a statutory instrument containing any such regulations shall be subject to annulment in pursuance of a resolution of either House of Parliament.

    (3) Regulations under this section may make different provision in relation to different descriptions of lettings and different circumstances.

Subsections (1A) and (1B) were inserted by HA 1988 s32. Section 5 now applies to:

- all tenancies granted before 15 January 1989;
- all licences whenever created, apart from excluded licences;
- all tenancies granted on or after 15 January 1989, apart from excluded tenancies.

12   RA 1977 s3(4) and *Morrison v Jacobs* n5.

Tenancies and licences are excluded if:
- the occupier shares with the landlord or licensor accommodation which is part of the owner's 'only or principal home'. However a tenancy or licence is not 'excluded' if the accommodation shared consists only of storage areas or means of access, such as corridors or staircases;
- the occupier lives in the same building as the landlord or licensor and shares accommodation with a member of the landlord's or licensor's family. The definition of 'member of the family' which appears in HA 1985 s113 applies. This includes spouses, parents, children, grandparents, grandchildren, siblings, uncles and aunts;
- the tenancy or licence is granted as a temporary expedient to a person who entered the premises or any other premises as a trespasser;
- the tenancy or licence merely confers the right to occupy for a holiday;
- the tenancy or licence is not granted for money or money's worth;
- a licensee occupies a hostel provided by a local authority, development corporation, housing action trust, the Housing Corporation, a housing trust etc.[13]

Section 5 applies to notices served by both landlords and tenants. However the Notices to Quit (Prescribed Information) Regulations 1988[14] which specify what information must be included apply only to landlords. Tenants' notices to quit must accordingly give four weeks' notice and be in writing, but need not follow any particular form.

The requirement for a minimum of four weeks' notice does not mean 28 'clear' days.[15] In calculating the four weeks, one should include the day on which the notice to quit is served, but not the last day referred to in the notice to quit. A notice served on a Friday complies with the Protection from Eviction Act 1977 s5 if it expires on a Friday four weeks later.[16]

The 'prescribed information' to be included in notices served by landlords is contained in the Notices to Quit (Prescribed Information) Regulations 1988:

1   If the tenant or licensee does not leave the dwelling, the landlord or licensor must get an order for possession from the court before the tenant or licensee can lawfully be evicted. The landlord or licensor cannot apply for such an order before the notice to quit or notice to determine has run out.

2   A tenant or licensee who does not know if he has any right to remain in possession after a notice to quit or notice to determine runs out can obtain

13   HA 1988 s31.
14   SI No 2201.
15   *Schmabel v Allard* [1967] 1 QB 627.
16   Ibid.

advice from a solicitor. Help with all or part of the cost of legal advice and assistance may be available under the Legal Aid Scheme. He should also be able to obtain information from a Citizens' Advice Bureau, a Housing Aid Centre or a Rent Officer.

It has been held that an old, standard-form notice to quit which complied with the former regulations (the Notices to Quit (Prescribed Information) (Protected Tenancies and Part VI Contracts) Regulations 1975) but which was served after the introduction of the Notices to Quit (Prescribed Information) Regulations 1980, was effective in terminating a tenancy, even though it did not follow the precise wording of the current regulations. Similarly, a notice to quit served on a tenant in 1989 which complied with the 1980 Regulations but not the 1988 Regulations was also held to be valid. The position might well be different if, for some reason, condusion or uncertainty was caused by using the old form rather than the current form.[17]

Common law

A notice to quit must comply with the common-law rules (see below) relating to validity. The first such requirement is that the notice must comply with any express provisions relating to service or validity which are contained in the tenancy agreement. Any such express provision overrides the rules, which are implied where there is no express provision. However, no express provision in the tenancy agreement can override the Protection from Eviction Act 1977 s5. An express provision may, for example, state that a notice to quit should give more notice than usual[18] or less notice than usual.[19] Similarly an express provision may provide that a notice to quit may be validly served in the middle of a rental period.[20]

Clarity and timing

The main common-law requirement is that a notice to quit should state with certainty when the notice expires. Landlords have a duty 'to give notices in terms which are sufficiently clear and unambiguous in that the right date is either stated or can be ascertained by the tenant by reference to his tenancy agreement with the terms of which he must be taken to be familiar . . .'.[21] The time between the date on which notice is served and

---

17   *Beckerman v Durling* (1981) 6 HLR 87, CA, and *Swansea CC v Hearn* (1991) 23 HLR 284, CA; cf *Shah v Emmanuel* December 1988 *Legal Action* 17, CC.
18   *Doe d Peacock v Raffan* (1806) 6 Esp 4.
19   *Wembley Corporation v Sherren* [1938] 4 All ER 255.
20   Ibid.
21   *Addis v Burrows* [1948] 1 All ER 177 per Evershed LJ at 182.

the date on which it purports to take effect should be at least as much as the rental period of the tenancy.[22] If the tenancy is a monthly tenancy, the notice to quit should give at least one month's notice. If the tenancy is a quarterly tenancy, the notice should give at least three months' notice.[23] However, in addition to giving the correct length of time, it is vital that the notice expires on the correct day. A notice to quit a weekly tenancy may expire either on the same day as the date on which the tenancy commenced or on the date on which the rent is paid[24] or on the day before.[25] For example, if the tenancy began on the first day of the month or rent is payable on the first day of the month, the notice may validly expire on the first or last day of the month.[26] Any notice to quit expiring on any other day is completely invalid and the tenant will have a complete defence to possession proceedings.[27] The normal rule is that a contractual tenancy ends at midnight on the date on which the notice to quit expires.[28] Possession proceedings cannot be issued until the notice to quit has expired.

It is usual for landlords to serve notices to quit which as well as giving a specific date also include the phrase 'or at the end of the period of your tenancy which will end next after the expiration of four weeks from the service upon you of this notice'. Such a saving clause is valid[29] provided that proceedings are not issued before the date on which the tenancy could have been validly determined.

Although the overriding consideration is that a notice to quit must be clear and unambiguous, it may well be that minor misdescriptions are not fatal. The question which a court should ask is: 'Is the notice quite clear to a reasonable tenant reading it? Is it plain that he cannot be misled by it?'.[30] For example a notice referring to 'The Waterman's Arms' which should have referred to 'The Bricklayer's Arms' has been held to be valid.[31]

22   Doe d Peacock v Raffan n18. See too Manorlike Ltd v Le Vitas [1986] 1 All ER 573, CA for the meaning of 'within three months'.
23   Lemon v Lardeur n11. A yearly tenancy can be determined by six months' notice.
24   Crane v Morris [1965] 1 WLR 1104 and Harley v Calder (1989) 21 HLR 214; [1989] 1 EGLR 88, CA. As to a yearly tenancy see Sidebotham v Holland [1895] 1 QB 378.
25   Newman v Slade [1926] 2 KB 328 and Harley v Calder (1989) 21 HLR 214; [1989] 1 EGLR 88, CA.
26   Precious v Reedie n10; and Queen's Club Gardens Estates v Bignell [1924] 1 KB 117. NB the definition of 'month' in Law of Property Act (LPA) 1925 s61(a).
27   Precious v Reedie n10; Queen's Club n26.
28   Bathavon RDC v Carlile [1958] 1 All ER 801.
29   Addis v Burrows n21; Bathavon RDC v Carlile n28 and Queen's Club n26.
30   Carradine Properties Ltd v Aslam [1976] 1 All ER 573 per Goulding J at 576.
31   Doe d Armstrong v Wilkinson (1840) 1 A&E 743 and other cases cited in Woodfall Law of Landlord and Tenant (Sweet & Maxwell 28th edn 1978) at 1–2013. Cf Jankovitch v Petrovitch (1977) August 1978 LAG Bulletin 189, CA.

Similarly, a notice served in 1974 stating that the tenant should give up possession in 1973 rather than 1975 has been held to be valid because it was clear to the tenant that there was a clerical error and the landlord intended the notice to refer to 1975.[32]

There are no common-law requirements relating to signature of notices to quit. It is necessary only that a tenant should be able to ascertain who has sent the notice to quit.

Service

A notice to quit may be served either by a landlord or tenant or by an authorised agent. In some circumstances a notice to quit may be given in the name of the agent[33] but it is more usual for notice served by an agent to state that it is served 'for and on behalf of' the landlord. One joint owner may validly serve notice to quit on behalf of other joint owners even if they are not named in the notice.[34] Similarly, one joint tenant may serve a notice to quit on the landlord and so determine the contractual tenancy even if the other joint tenant does not agree.[35] A notice to quit served by a landlord on only one out of several joint tenants is sufficient to determine the joint contractual tenancy.[36] It is not possible for a landlord to purport to terminate one joint tenant's interest in the premises without determining the interest of the other joint tenants.[37] A notice to quit must include all of the premises let under the particular tenancy agreement. A notice to quit which purports to terminate a tenant's interest in only part of the property covered by the tenancy is completely ineffective.[38]

The notice to quit must be served on or before the date in the notice from which time starts to run, otherwise it is invalid and totally ineffective. It need not be served personally by handing it to the tenant.[39] However, the common law rules as to what is valid service are far from clear. There are few recent cases and many of the cases cited in Woodfall appear to conflict. It has been held sufficient to leave a notice to quit with a tenant's wife or servant even though it did not actually come to the

32   *Carradine v Aslam* n30.
33   See Woodfall op cit n31 1-1995 and *Lemon v Lardeur* n11.
34   *Doe d Aslin v Summersett* (1830) 1 B & Ad 135 and *Annen v Rattee* (1984) 17 HLR 323, CA. Cf *Jacobs v Chaudhuri* [1968] 2 All ER 124 and *Featherstone v Staples* [1986] 2 All ER 461, CA; *Leckhampton Dairies Ltd v Artus Whitfield* (1986) 130 SJ 225.
35   *Greenwich LBC v McGrady* (1982) 6 HLR 36.
36   *Doe d Bradford v Watkins* (1806) 7 East 551 and *LB Hammersmith and Fulham v Monk* (1992) 39 EG 135, (1992) 24 HLR 206.
37   *Greenwich LBC v McGrady* n35.
38   *Woodward v Dudley* [1954] Ch 283.
39   See Woodfall op cit n31 1-2001.

tenant's attention before the time started running. On the other hand, service on a tenant's wife when she was not on the premises rented has been held to be bad service.[40] However, if the tenancy was created by a written agreement it is likely that the Law of Property Act 1925 s196 will apply. Section 196(4) states that a notice will 'be sufficiently served, if it is sent by recorded delivery addressed to the lessee at his or her abode or business, office or counting house' if that letter is not returned through the Post Office undelivered. Service is deemed to be made at the time at which the recorded delivery letter would arrive in the ordinary course of the post. Where s196 applies, a notice may be validly served even though it was not received by the addressee.[41] Where a tenant rents a bed-sitting room, there is no need for the notice to be delivered to or fixed to the door of that room. It is sufficient for it to be delivered through the letter box in the main door on the ground floor of the building.[42] The notice should be addressed to the tenant of the premises, and not to the sub-tenant, although it will operate to determine the sub-tenancy as well as the head tenancy.[43] If a tenant has died, the notice must be served either on the person who becomes legally entitled to the tenancy or, if the tenant died without making a will, on the President of the Family Division[44] or administrator of the estate (see p213 below).

Statutory tenants and notices to quit

Although there is no need for a landlord to serve a notice to quit on a statutory tenant before starting possession proceedings (see above), a tenant will remain liable for rent until a statutory tenancy has been validly determined[45] even if s/he has moved out of the premises. This liability can be ended only by a possession order, voluntary agreement of landlord and tenant or a notice to quit served by the tenant.

RA 1977 s3(3) provides:

> Subject to Section 5 of the Protection from Eviction Act 1977 (under which at least 4 weeks' notice to quit is required), a statutory tenant of a dwelling-house shall be entitled to give up possession of the dwelling-house if, and only

---

40   Ibid at 1-2001-1-2003.
41   *Re 88 Berkeley Road, London NW9, Rickwood v Turnsek* [1971] Ch 648. See too *Cannon Brewery Company Ltd v Signal Press Ltd* (1928) 139 LT 384.
42   *Trustees of Henry Smith's Charity v Kyriacou* [1989] 2 EGLR 110, CA.
43   *Mellor v Watkins* (1874) LR 9 QB 400 per Blackburn J. Cf the effect of RA 1977 s137 at p206 below.
44   Administration of Estates Act 1925 s9; *Practice Direction* [1985] 1 All ER 832 and *Wirral BC v Smith and Cooper* (1982) 43 P & CR 312.
45   *Trustees of Smith's (Henry) Charity v Willson* [1983] 1 All ER 73.

if, he gives such notice as would have been required under the provisions of the original contract of tenancy, or, if no notice would have been so required, on giving not less than 3 months' notice.

A tenant cannot unilaterally determine a statutory tenancy without serving a notice to quit and the normal strict requirements relating to notices apply.[46] Advisers should therefore counsel tenants against simply departing without giving notice or reaching agreement with the landlord.

Acceptance of rent after service of a notice to quit

Payment of rent after a notice to quit has been served does not normally operate to create a new contractual tenancy.[47] In order to establish that a new contractual tenancy has been created a tenant has to establish that this was the intention of both landlord and tenant. Payment and acceptance of rent may, however, operate as a waiver on the landlord's part of any breach of any clause in the tenancy agreement (see below).

Notice of increase of rent

In some circumstances a notice of increase of rent may terminate a periodical RA protected contractual tenancy in exactly the same way as a notice to quit.

RA 1977 s49(4) provides:

> Where a notice of increase is served during a contractual period and the protected tenancy could, by a notice to quit served by the landlord at the same time, be brought to an end before the date specified in the notice of increase, the notice of increase shall operate to convert the protected tenancy into a statutory tenancy as from that date.

If a landlord wishes to increase a tenant's rent to take into account an increased rent registered by a rent officer[48] or, in certain circumstances, to pass on an increase in rates,[49] s/he must serve a notice of increase in the prescribed form.[50] In addition, those increases can normally take effect

---

46 *King's College Cambridge v Kershman* (1948) 64 TLR 547; *Boyer v Warbey* [1953] 1 QB 234 and RA 1977 s5(1).

47 *Clarke v Grant* [1950] 1 KB 104 and *City of Westminster v Basson* (1991) 23 HLR 225, [1991] 1 EGLR 277. An invalid agreement for an irrecoverable rent increase does not vary an existing tenancy agreement or amount to a new contractual tenancy – *Sopwith v Stutchbury* (1983) 17 HLR 50.

48 See RA 1977 s72 and Pt III.

49 Ibid s46.

50 Ibid s49(2).

only if the tenancy is already a statutory tenancy or if the landlord can convert the contractual tenancy into a statutory tenancy. Rather than requiring the landlord to serve both a notice to quit and a notice of increase, a notice of increase which gives at least as much notice as would be necessary in a notice to quit, fulfils both functions.

If the notice of increase is invalid (eg fails to comply with statutory requirements), purports to operate retrospectively or does not give sufficient notice, it is ineffective in converting a contractual tenancy into a statutory tenancy. If tenants pay increases in rent after the service of invalid notices of increase, they are not estopped from maintaining that there is still a contractual tenancy.[51]

Surrender

Surrender by express agreement

A surrender is a voluntary agreement of both landlord and tenant that the tenancy should come to an end before the expiry of its fixed term without the service of a notice to quit. An express surrender must state an immediate intention that the tenancy should come to an end. It cannot operate to take effect in the future. Surrenders by express agreement must be made by deed,[52] although in some circumstances an oral agreement may be effective as a surrender by operation of law (see below).

If there are joint tenants all tenants must agree to the surrender.[53] A husband has no implied authority to surrender a tenancy on behalf of his wife.[54]

Surrender by operation of law

Even if there is no express surrender by deed, the law may consider that a landlord and tenant have behaved in an unequivocal way which is inconsistent with the continuance of the contractual tenancy. In such circumstances, if their behaviour makes it inequitable for one of the parties to claim that the tenancy still exists, the law will imply a surrender. In *Foster v Robinson* Sir Raymond Evershed MR stated:

> It has been laid down that in order to constitute a surrender by operation of law there must be, first, an act or purported surrender invalid per se by reason

---

51 *Wallis v Semark* n1.
52 LPA 1925 s52.
53 *Leek and Moorlands Building Society v Clark* [1952] 2 QB 788.
54 *Re Viola's Indenture of Lease, Humphrey v Stenbury* [1909] 1 Ch 244.

of non-compliance with statutory or other formalities, and secondly, some change of circumstances supervening on, or arising from, the purported surrender, which, by reason of the doctrine of estoppel or part performance, makes it inequitable and fraudulent for any of the parties to rely upon the invalidity of the purported surrender.[55]

There are three main examples of situations where there may be an effective surrender by operation of law:

First, there is surrender by an agreement that the tenant should abandon the tenancy and that the landlord should resume possession of the premises.[56] It seems that it is necessary for the tenant to hand back the premises to the landlord. In *Hoggett v Hoggett and Wallis*[57] the tenant tried to surrender premises to the landlord while his wife was still living in the premises. This was not a valid surrender. Similarly, the mere departure by a tenant from the premises while rent is owing is not an implied surrender unless there is agreement.[58] The position may be different if substantial rent arrears are outstanding.[59]

Secondly, there is surrender by delivery of the key. Delivery of the key to the premises by the tenant to the landlord and its acceptance by the landlord may be a surrender by operation of law. However, it depends on the circumstances. In *Furnivall v Grove*[60] there was a surrender where a tenant handed back the key and a few days later the landlord demolished the building. On the other hand, in *Boynton-Wood v Trueman*[61] a tenant handed the key of a cottage to his landlord so that repairs could be carried out. The court held that there was no surrender because there was 'no unequivocal act on the part of the tenant . . . which would indicate that he was surrendering his tenancy.'

Thirdly, there is surrender by agreement for a new lease. The creation of a new lease between landlord and tenant or between the landlord and some third party with the agreement of the tenant determines the original

---

55   [1950] 2 All ER 342 at 346, quoting from Foa *General Law of Landlord and Tenant* (Hamish Hamilton 7th edn 1947) pp617–618. See too *Dibbs v Campbell* (1988) 20 HLR 374.
56   *Phene v Popplewell* (1862) 12 CBNS 334.
57   (1979) 39 P & CR 121.
58   *Preston BC v Fairclough* (1982) 8 HLR 70.
59   Ibid and *R v LB Croydon ex parte Toth* (1986) 18 HLR 493.
60   (1860) 8 CB(NS) 496. See too *Phene v Popplewell* (n56) where the tenant delivered the key to the landlord who then painted out the tenant's name above the premises and instructed an auctioneer to put up a 'To let' sign.
61   (1961) 177 EG 191.

contractual tenancy.[62] This is the case even if the new lease is for a shorter period than the old lease[63] or if there is an agreement that instead of a tenancy the tenant should enjoy a rent-free licence for the rest of his or her life.[64] If the new lease is for some reason invalid, there is no surrender of the earlier lease unless the surrender has been effected by deed.[65] The new agreement must be more than a variation of the terms of the existing tenancy[66], although an agreed increase in rent may, depending on the circumstances, take effect either as an implied surrender and regrant of a new lease, or as a variation of the terms of the existing lease.[67] A request by the tenant that the landlord should relet the premises to someone else does not operate as a surrender if his wife is still in occupation of the premises.[68]

If a tenancy is surrendered and the tenant moves out with an intention to cease residing at the premises, that is the end of the tenancy. In these circumstances a surrender by operation of law takes effect irrespective of the parties' intentions.[69] No statutory tenancy can arise and there is no need for the landlord to bring possession proceedings. If, however, a landlord and a contractual protected tenant agree to the surrender of a tenancy, but the tenant continues to occupy the premises as a residence, the only effect of the surrender is to convert the contractual tenancy into a

---

62   For example *Climping Park Ltd v Barritt* (1989) *Independent* 15 May, CA. In these circumstances a tenant is estopped from denying the validity of the new lease and so cannot deny the implied surrender of the old lease, for a landlord cannot validly grant a new lease without first procuring a surrender of the old lease – *Jenkin R Lewis & Son Ltd v Kerman* [1970] 1 All ER 833, but cf *Rhyl UDC v Rhyl Amusements Ltd* [1959] 1 All ER 257 and *Ashton v Sobelman* [1987] 1 WLR 177 (agreement between freeholder and sub-tenant alone not sufficient).

63   *Phene v Popplewell* n56.

64   *Foster v Robinson* n55 – provided that it is a genuine transaction.

65   *Rhyl UDC v Rhyl Amusements* n62 and the cases reviewed therein by Harman J at 267.

66   *Smirk v Lyndale Developments* [1975] 1 All ER 690, although an agreement that a tenant will rent additional land or an extra part of premises and that the total should be held as one parcel with an increased rent does operate as an implied surrender and regrant – *Jenkin Lewis v Kerman* n62. Similarly the variation of the term (ie, length) of a lease so that it subsists for a longer period also operates as an implied surrender and regrant – *Re Savile Settled Estates, Savile v Savile* [1931] 2 Ch 210.

67   Cf *Jenkin Lewis v Kerman* n61 and *Gable Construction Co Ltd v Inland Revenue Commissioners* [1968] 2 All ER 968.

68   *Hoggett v Hoggett* n57. See too *Fredco Estates v Bryant* [1961] 1 All ER 34 where the landlord said that the tenant could use three extra rooms with no increase in rent. Held there was no surrender.

69   *Jenkin Lewis v Kerman* n62.

statutory tenancy.[70] The landlord still has to prove a RA ground for possession, and, if appropriate, that it is reasonable for the court to make an order for possession (see below). This is the case even if the landlord, the tenant and a prospective purchaser all agree that the purchaser will acquire the property with vacant possession and that the tenant will not make any claim to occupy the premises against the purchaser.[71]

A surrender of a tenancy does not terminate any sub-tenancy which the tenant has previously created. The sub-tenant becomes a direct tenant of the landlord[72] even if the head tenancy contained a covenant against subletting without the landlord's consent.[73]

Forfeiture

Nature of forfeiture

Forfeiture is the procedure which allows a landlord to bring to an end a contractual fixed-term tenancy or lease before the fixed period of time for which the lease was originally granted expires. Forfeiture of a fixed-term tenancy has the same effect as a notice to quit on a periodic tenancy (see p86). If the tenancy is outside statutory protection, forfeiture means that the landlord is entitled to repossess the premises. If the tenancy has full RA protection, forfeiture merely converts the contractual protected tenancy into a statutory tenancy. Forfeiture can take place only if there is an express provision in the lease allowing the landlord to 're-enter' or forfeit. In practice all leases contain such clauses. At common law there was no need for a landlord to bring court proceedings to forfeit a lease: an unequivocal act on the part of the landlord sufficed.[74] Most commonly this consisted of the landlord entering the premises and taking possession. However, the Protection from Eviction Act 1977 s2 provides:

> Where any premises are let as a dwelling by a lease which is subject to a right of re-entry or forfeiture it shall not be lawful to enforce that right otherwise than by proceedings in the court while any person is lawfully residing in the premises or part of them.

The service of court proceedings is an unequivocal act which amounts to

---

70 RA 1977 s2(1)(a) and *R v Bloomsbury and Marylebone County Court ex parte Blackburne* (1985) 275 EG 1273, CA.
71 *Appleton v Aspin and Plane* (1987) 20 HLR 182, CA.
72 *Mellor v Watkins* n43.
73 *Parker v Jones* [1910] 2 KB 32.
74 An agreement with an existing sub-tenant that the sub-tenant will change the locks is not sufficient to forfeit the headlease – *Ashton v Sobelman* n62.

forfeiture.[75] In view of the various forms of relief available to lessees (see below), the lease is not actually terminated until a court order is made, but the effect of an order is that forfeiture takes effect from the date when proceedings were served.[76] If proceedings include a claim for an injunction to restrain the lessee from future breaches of covenant, however, the issue and service of proceedings is not an unequivocal act and so does not give rise to forfeiture.[77] A landlord claiming forfeiture in the county court must use Form N6 and specify the daily rate of rent accruing.[78]

When issuing proceedings, a landlord must notify any person who may be entitled to relief from forfeiture (see below).[79]

Even before issuing proceedings for forfeiture, a landlord may have to comply with various requirements. If the landlord is claiming forfeiture due to rent arrears, the general rule is that there must be a formal written demand before proceedings are issued. In practice, however, this rule is usually excluded by a provision in the lease which gives the landlord a right to re-enter if there are arrears 'whether the rent has been lawfully demanded or not'. In addition, the County Courts Act 1984 s139(1) provides that if six months' rent is owing at the commencement of the action and if there are insufficient goods on the premises to cover the arrears, proceedings may be issued without a formal demand for rent even if there were no corresponding provision in the lease. If forfeiture proceedings are issued for breach of any other covenant in the lease, a notice must be served pursuant to the Law of Property Act 1925 s146 before the issue of proceedings. Section 146 provides:

> *Restrictions on and relief against forfeiture of leases and underleases*
> **146.**—(1)   A right of re-entry or forfeiture under any proviso or stipulation in a lease for a breach of any covenant or condition in the lease shall not be enforceable, by action or otherwise, unless and until the lessor serves on the lessee a notice—
> (a)   specifying the particular breach complained of; and
> (b)   if the breach is capable of remedy, requiring the lessee to remedy the breach; and
> (c)   in any case, requiring the lessee to make compensation in money for the breach;
> and the lessee fails, within a reasonable time thereafter, to remedy the breach, if it is capable of remedy, and to make reasonable compensation in money, to the satisfaction of the lessor, for the breach.

75   *Grimwood v Moss* (1872) LR 7 CP 360; *Canas Property Co Ltd v KL Television Services Ltd* [1970] 2 WLR 1133.
76   *Borzak v Ahmed* [1965] 2 QB 320.
77   *Moore v Ullcoats Mining Co* [1908] 1 Ch 575.
78   CCR Ord 6 r3(e) and *Canas Property Co Ltd v KL Television Services* n75.
79   County Court (Amendment No 2) Rules 1986 SI No 1189 amending CCR Ord 6 r3.

(2)   Where a lessor is proceeding, by action or otherwise, to enforce such a right of re-entry or forfeiture, the lessee may, in the lessor's action, if any, or in any action brought by himself, apply to the court for relief; and the court may grant or refuse relief, as the court, having regard to the proceedings and conduct of the parties and the foregoing provisions of this section, and to all the other circumstances, thinks fit; and in case of relief may grant it on such terms, if any, as to costs, expenses, damages, compensation, penalty, or otherwise, including the granting of an injunction to restrain any like breach in the future, as the court, in the circumstances of each case, thinks fit.

(3)   A lessor shall be entitled to recover as a debt due to him from a lessee, and in addition to damages (if any) all reasonable costs and expenses properly incurred by the lessor in the employment of a solicitor and a surveyor or valuer, or otherwise, in reference to any breach giving rise to a right of re-entry or forfeiture which, at the request of the lessee, is waived by the lessor, or from which the lessee is relieved, under the provisions of this Act.

(4)   Where a lessor is proceeding by action or otherwise to enforce a right of re-entry and forfeiture under any covenant, proviso, or stipulation in a lease, or for non-payment of rent, the court may, on application by any person claiming as under-lessee any estate or interest in the property comprised in the lease or any part thereof either in the lessor's action (if any) or in any action brought by such person for that purpose, make an order vesting, for the whole term of the lease or any less term, the property comprised in the lease or any part thereof in any person entitled as under-lessee to any estate or interest in such property upon such conditions as to execution of any deed or other document, payment of rent, costs, expenses, damages, compensation, giving security, or otherwise, as the court in the circumstances of each case may think fit, but in no case shall any such under-lessee be entitled to require a lease to be granted to him for any longer term than he had under his original sub-lease.

(5)   For the purposes of this section—
   (a)   'Lease' includes an original or derivative under-lease; also an agreement for a lease where the lessee has become entitled to have his lease granted; also a grant at a fee farm rent, or securing a rent by condition;
   (b)   'Lessee' includes an original or derivative under-lessee, and the persons deriving title under a lessee; also a grantee under any such grant as aforesaid and the persons deriving title under him;
   (c)   'Lessor' includes an original or derivative under-lessor, and the persons deriving title under a lessor; also a person making such grant as aforesaid and the persons deriving title under him;
   (d)   'Under-lease' includes an agreement for an under-lease where the under-lessee has become entitled to have his under-lease granted;
   (e)   'Under-lessee' includes any person deriving title under an under-lessee.

(6)   This section applies although the proviso or stipulation under which

the right of re-entry or forfeiture accrues is inserted in the lease in pursuance of the directions of any Act of Parliament.

(7)   For the purposes of this section a lease limited to continue as long only as the lessee abstains from committing a breach of covenant shall be and take effect as a lease to continue for any longer term for which it could subsist, but determinable by a proviso for re-entry on such a breach.

(8)   This section does not extend—

(i)   To a covenant or condition against assigning, underletting, parting with the possession, or disposing of the land leased where the breach occurred before the commencement of this Act; or

(ii)   In the case of a mining lease, to a covenant or condition for allowing the lessor to have access to or inspect books, accounts, records, weighing machines or other things or to enter or inspect the mine or the workings thereof.

(9)   This section does not apply to a condition for forfeiture on the bankruptcy of the lessee or on taking in execution of the lessee's interest if contained in a lease of—

(a)   Agricultural or pastoral land;

(b)   Mines or minerals;

(c)   A house used or intended to be used as a public-house or beer-shop;

(d)   A house let as a dwelling-house, with the use of any furniture, books, works of art or other chattels not being in the nature of fixtures;

(e)   Any property with respect to which the personal qualifications of the tenant are of importance for the preservation of the value or character of the property, or on the ground of neighbourhood to the lessor, or to any person holding under him.

(10)   Where a condition of forfeiture on the bankruptcy of the lessee or on taking in execution of the lessee's interest is contained in any lease, other than a lease of any of the classes mentioned in the last subsection, then—

(a)   if the lessee's interest is sold, within one year from the bankruptcy or taking in execution, this section applies to the forfeiture condition aforesaid;

(b)   if the lessee's interest is not sold before the expiration of that year, this section only applies to the forfeiture condition aforesaid during the first year from the date of the bankruptcy or taking in execution.

(11)   This section does not, save as otherwise mentioned, affect the law relating to re-entry or forfeiture or relief in case of non-payment of rent.

(12)   This section has effect notwithstanding any stipulation to the contrary.

Section 146 in effect gives tenants two opportunities to resist forfeiture, first an opportunity to remedy any breach which is capable of remedy and second to apply for relief from forfeiture.[80] It applies to breaches of all covenants except for non-payment of rent. It does not apply to furnished tenancies.[81] A landlord cannot avoid the provisions by dressing up a forfeiture as a surrender of the lease.[82] Here it should be noted that there are special provisions relating to service of notices where a landlord alleges that a lessee has been in breach of the lessee's repairing covenant.[83]

If the notice given under s146(1) (above) does not state whether or not the breach is capable of remedy or, if it is remediable, does not require the lessee to remedy it within a reasonable time, the notice is invalid.[84] Breaches of 'positive covenants' (eg, to keep premises in repair) are normally capable of remedy if the lessee can comply with them within a reasonable time.[85] This applies even if the lessee is in breach of a continuing positive covenant. However, it is often more difficult to remedy a breach of a negative covenant. For example, a breach of a covenant not to assign, sublet or part with possession is incapable of remedy because the assignment or subletting has already taken place and cannot be undone.[86] Breaches of covenant against immoral user (prostitution) cannot usually be remedied due to the stigma which attaches to the premises and the possible effect on property values,[87] although this is not an automatic rule[88] particularly if the tenant does not know about the breach. A breach involving a criminal conviction cannot be remedied.[89]

Waiver of breach

If landlords waive particular breaches of covenant, they cannot rely on those breaches to bring proceedings for forfeiture. Landlords may waive a breach expressly or by implication. Waiver takes place where the landlord does an unequivocal act which recognises the continued existence of the lease after having knowledge of the ground for forfeiture. There are certain actions which amount to waiver of forfeiture irrespective of the

80 *Expert Clothing Service and Sales v Hillgate House Ltd* [1985] 2 All ER 998, per Slade LJ.
81 S146(7).
82 *Plymouth Corp v Harvey* [1971] 1 WLR 549.
83 Leasehold Property (Repairs) Act 1938.
84 *Expert Clothing v Hillgate* n80.
85 *Rugby School (Governors) v Tannahill* [1935] 1 KB 87; *Expert Clothing v Hillgate* n80.
86 *Scala House and District Property Co v Forbes* [1974] QB 575.
87 *Rugby School v Tannahill* n85; *British Petroleum Pension Trust v Behrendt* (1985) 276 EG 199 and *Egerton v Jones* [1939] 2 KB 702.
88 *Glass v Kencakes Ltd* [1966] 1 QB 611.
89 *Hoffmann v Fineberg* [1949] Ch 245 (gaming club, no licence); *Ali v Booth* (1966) 110 SJ 708; (1966) 199 EG 641, CA (food hygiene offences); *Dunraven Securities Ltd v Holloway* (1982) 264 EG 709 (Obscene Publications Act offences).

landlord's intention,[90] for example, a demand for or receipt of rent which accrues after the cause of forfeiture[91] even if the demand is made 'without prejudice'.[92] The knowledge or actions of agents[93] or employees such as porters[94] are deemed to be equivalent to direct knowledge of the landlord. Suspicion that there is a breach without actual knowledge of the facts is not enough to constitute waiver.[95]

No demand for rent after proceedings have been issued can amount to waiver because the landlord has already acted unequivocally in issuing those proceedings. Similarly, there is no waiver of a breach even if the landlord knows about it, if s/he merely stands by without interfering while the lessee carries on the breach.

A continuing breach of covenant continually gives rise to new causes of forfeiture and so waiver cannot affect future breaches.[96] Waiver operates to prevent a landlord from relying on a particular breach only, not on subsequent future breaches. Subletting is a 'one off' breach which only occurs at the time when premises are initially sublet. However sharing premises may be a continuing breach which persists even after waiver.[97]

Relief from forfeiture

Even if the landlord establishes that a tenant has breached a covenant, the tenant may still be entitled to apply for relief from forfeiture. If the court grants relief, the tenant's contractual tenancy continues as if the landlord had not sought to forfeit. Relief from forfeiture may be expressed to be conditional, for example, on the tenant not committing future breaches of covenant. There are several forms of relief which operate in different ways. The county court and High Court powers to grant relief from forfeiture differ.

Arrears of rent – county court

Procedure in the county court is governed by the County Courts Act 1984 s138. The 1984 Act has been amended by the Administration of Justice Act 1985 s55. Section 138, as amended, provides:

90   *Central Estates (Belgravia) v Woolgar (No.2)* [1972] 3 All ER 610.
91   *Blackstone Ltd v Burnetts* [1973] 1 WLR 1487.
92   *Segal Securities v Thoseby* [1963] 1 All ER 500.
93   *Central Estates v Woolgar* n90.
94   *Metropolitan Properties Co Ltd v Cordery* (1979) 251 EG 567.
95   *Chrisdell Ltd v Johnson and Tickner* (1987) 19 HLR 406, CA.
96   *Segal Securities v Thoseby* n92.
97   *Metropolitan Properties Co Ltd v Crawford and Wetherill* March 1987 *Legal Action* 20, CC.

Forfeiture for non-payment of rent

Provisions as to forfeiture for non-payment of rent

138.—(1)   This section has effect where a lessor is proceeding by action in a county court (being an action in which the county court has jurisdiction) to enforce against a lessee a right of re-entry or forfeiture in respect of any land for non-payment of rent.

(2)   If the lessee pays into court or to the lessor not less than 5 clear days before the return day all the rent in arrear and the costs of the action, the action shall cease, and the lessee shall hold the land according to the lease without any new lease.

(3)   If—

(a)   the action does not cease under subsection (2); and

(b)   the court at the trial is satisfied that the lessor is entitled to enforce the right of re-entry or forfeiture,

the court shall order possession of the land to be given to the lessor at the expiration of such period, not being less than 4 weeks from the date of the order, as the court thinks fit, unless within that period the lessee pays into court or to the lessor all the rent in arrear and costs of the action.

(4)   The court may extend the period specified under subsection (3) at any time before possession of the land is recovered in pursuance of the order under that subsection.

(5)   If—

(a)   within the period specified in the order; or

(b)   within that period as extended under subsection (4),

the lessee pays into court or to the lessor—

(i)   all the rent in arrear; and

(ii)   the costs of the action,

he shall hold the land according to the lease without any new lease.

(6)   Subsection (2) shall not apply where the lessor is proceeding in the same action to enforce a right of re-entry or forfeiture on any other ground as well as for non-payment of rent, or to enforce any other claim as well as the right of re-entry or forfeiture and the claim for arrears of rent.

(7)   If the lessee does not—

(a)   within the period specified in the order; or

(b)   within that period as extended under subsection (4),

pay into court or to the lessor—

(i)   all the rent in arrear; and

(ii)   the costs of the action,

the order shall be enforceable in the prescribed manner and so long as the order remains unreversed the lessee shall, subject to subsections (8) and (9A), be barred from all relief.

(8)   The extension under subsection (4) of a period fixed by a court shall not be treated as relief from which the lessee is barred by subsection (7) if he fails to pay into court or to the lessor all the rent in arrear and the costs of the action within that period.

(9)   Where the court extends a period under subsection (4) at a time when—
  (a)   that period was expired; and
  (b)   a warrant has been issued for the possession of the land,
the court shall suspend the warrant for the extended period; and, if, before the expiration of the extended period, the lessee pays into court or to the lessor all the rent in arrear and all the costs of the action, the court shall cancel the warrant.

(9A)   Where the lessor recovers possession of the land at any time after the making of the order under subsection (3) (whether as a result of the enforcement of the order or otherwise) the lessee may, at any time within six months from the date on which the lessor recovers possession, apply to the court for relief; and on any such application the court may, if it thinks fit, grant to the lessee such relief, subject to such terms and conditions, as it thinks fit.

(9B)   Where the lessee is granted relief on an application under subsection (9A) he shall hold the land according to the lease without any new lease.

(9C)   An application under subsection (9A) may be made by a person with an interest under a lease of the land derived (whether immediately or otherwise) from the lessee's interest therein in like manner as if he were the lessee; and on any such application the court may make an order which (subject to such terms and conditions as the court thinks fit) vests the land in such a person, as lessee of the lessor, for the remainder of the term of the lease under which he has any such interest as aforesaid, or for any lesser term.

In this subsection any reference to the land includes a reference to a part of the land.

(10)   Nothing in this section or section 139 shall be taken to affect—
  (a)   the power of the court to make any order which it would otherwise have power to make as respects a right of re-entry or forfeiture on any ground other than non-payment of rent; or
  (b)   section 146(4) of the Law of Property Act 1925 (relief against forfeiture).

Section 138 provides three different forms of relief from forfeiture:

a)   if all the rent arrears and costs are paid into court at least five days before the hearing, the action automatically ceases and the lease continues as if no proceedings had been issued (s138(2)). The tenancy remains a contractual tenancy;
b)   at the hearing, if there is a claim based on arrears of rent, the court must automatically delay possession for at least four weeks. If during this period the lessee pays all the arrears and costs, there is again complete relief from forfeiture (s138(3)) and the tenancy continues as a contractual tenancy. The court may, of its own motion, adjourn the

hearing once for enquiry to ascertain the lessee's ability to pay rent, but it is normally wrong for there to be two such adjournments without the lessor's consent.[98] The period of suspension may be extended at any time before possession is actually recovered (s138(4));

c) the lessee may apply to the court within six months of the landlord recovering possession (eg, by sending in the bailiff or otherwise) for relief against forfeiture (s138(9)).[99] Similar applications for relief where there has been peaceable re-entry may be made under s139(2), although in view of the Protection from Eviction Act s2 (see above) this will rarely be applicable to residential premises.

Other breaches of covenants – county court

The Law of Property Act 1925 (LPA) s146(2) provides that a lessee may apply for relief from forfeiture and that the court may grant such relief, subject to whatever conditions it thinks fit. This does not apply where there are arrears of rent (LPA s146(11)). Although the most common way for lessees to apply for relief from forfeiture is to counterclaim in forfeiture proceedings which the landlord has issued, it is possible for lessees themselves to issue proceedings in which they claim relief. Indeed, that is the only way in which relief may be sought if a landlord peacably re-enters premises which are 'not let as a dwelling' and so not protected by the Protection from Eviction Act 1977 s2. Lord Templeman summarised the law in *Billson v Residential Apartments* (1992) 91 EG 91, by stating:

> A tenant may apply for . . . relief from forfeiture under section 146(2) after the issue of a section 146 notice but he is not prejudiced if he does not do so. A tenant cannot apply for relief after a landlord has forfeited a lease by issuing and serving a writ, has recovered judgment and has entered into possession pursuant to that judgment. If the judgment is set aside or successfully appealed the tenant will be able to apply for relief in the landlord's action but the court in deciding whether to grant relief will take into account any consequences of the original order and repossession and the delay of the tenant. A tenant may apply for relief after a landlord has forfeited by re-entry without first obtaining a court order for that purpose, but the court in deciding whether to grant relief will take into account all the circumstances including delay on the part of the tenant.

Under-lessees have, in all cases, including rent arrears cases, the right to apply for relief and to have leases vested in themselves instead of the lessees

---

98   *R v A Circuit Judge ex parte Wathen* (1976) 33 P & CR 423 (tenant admitted arrears of rent, but said that he had an expectancy of money under a trust at an unknown future date).

99   Reversing the effect of *Di Palma v Victoria Square Property Company Ltd* [1985] 2 All ER 676; cf *Jones v Barnett* [1984] 3 All ER 129.

(LPA s146(4)). This operates by granting a new lease which comes into effect from the date when relief is given.[100]

If there are joint lessees of premises, all must apply together for relief under LPA s146.[101] The court may grant relief in respect of part only of premises if, for example, the breaches of covenant were confined to one distinct part of the building.[102]

Equitable jurisdiction – county court
The court has a further equitable jurisdiction, wider than LPA s146(4), to grant relief to under-lessees or mortgagees.[103] This jurisdiction does not, however, extend to lessees in rent arrears cases because of the inclusion of the words 'shall be barred from all relief' in s138(7).[104]

The High Court
Proceedings for forfeiture of RA protected leases are normally brought in the county court however large the arrears of rent,[105] because costs are not recoverable in the High Court.[106] Briefly, the High Court's powers to grant relief are contained in the Common Law Procedure Act 1852 ss210–212. These provisions state that a lessee must seek relief within six months of the execution of judgment, although it appears that there is an equitable jurisdiction for the court to grant relief outside that period if there has been peaceable re-entry.[107] The LPA s146 applies equally to High Court proceedings.

Principles on which relief is granted
The circumstances in which relief is granted vary considerably and the courts are reluctant to lay down general principles.[108] It is clear, however, that courts must take into account all relevant circumstances. The harm caused to a landlord by breach of covenant (for example, the effect on the value of the property[109]) is important. For this reason relief is frequently

---

100 *Cadogan v Dimovic* [1984] 1 WLR 609.
101 *Fairclough (TM) and Sons v Berliner* [1931] 1 Ch 60.
102 *GMS Syndicate Ltd v Gary Elliott Ltd* [1982] Ch 1.
103 *Abbey National BS v Maybeech* [1984] 3 All ER 262.
104 *Di Palma v Victoria Square* n99.
105 RA 1977 s141(3) and (5).
106 S141(4).
107 *Thatcher v Pearce and Sons* [1968] 1 WLR 748.
108 *Leeward Securities Ltd v Lilyheath Properties* (1983) 271 EG 279; (1983) 17 HLR 35, CA and *Bickel v Duke of Westminster* [1977] QB 517 at 524 per Lord Denning MR.
109 *Central Estates v Woolgar* n90.

refused where an unlawful subletting or assignment leads to the creation of a statutory tenancy where there would not otherwise have been one and where it would have been reasonable for a landlord to refuse consent to the subletting or assignment.[110] Similarly, it is rare for relief to be given where the covenant broken is a covenant against immoral user since the courts take the view that a 'stigma' may attach to the property.[111] If a breach has been brought to an end, or ended some time ago, the court is more likely to grant relief.[112] If the breach complained of would not have been a breach if the landlord had consented, it is relevant to consider whether the landlord could reasonably have withheld his or her consent.[113] Similarly, the intention of the lessee at the time of committing the breach is important (for example where the lessee had no intention of breaching the lease, but the breach was brought about by a solicitor's mistake, relief was granted[114]). The landlord's conduct is also relevant, and in a case where the conduct of the landlord throughout had been to harass the lessee and in which the court held that the landlord's conduct was unreasonable, relief was given without hesitation.[115] The tenant's age and health may be relevant.

Forfeiture and RA protection

A landlord who wishes to evict a RA-protected tenant for breach of a covenant during a fixed-term tenancy has to go through two stages, although both may be dealt with at the same hearing. First, the court must consider whether the lease should be forfeited, and, if appropriate, whether relief against forfeiture should be given.[116] If the lease is forfeited, the tenancy becomes a statutory tenancy. The court has then to consider whether a RA ground for possession exists (most commonly under Case 1), and if so, whether it is reasonable to make an order for possession.[117]

If the tenancy is forfeited and the court considers it reasonable to make an order for possession, the order should be in Form N27. If, however, the lease is forfeited but the court, on RA grounds, does not make an order for possession (for example because it is not reasonable to do so), the order

---

110 *Leeward Securities v Lilyheath* n108 and *West Layton Ltd v Ford* [1979] QB 593.
111 *British Petroleum v Behrendt* n87.
112 *Scala House v Forbes* n86.
113 Ibid.
114 Ibid.
115 *Segal Securities v Thoseby* n92.
116 *Central Estates v Woolgar* n90.
117 See below and *Wolmer Securities v Corne* [1966] 2 All ER 691.

should be in Form N27(1). If the lease is forfeited, but on RA grounds the possession order is suspended, the order should be in Form N27(2).[118]

Long lessees and service charges

Particular considerations apply when defending long lessees who face forfeiture proceedings based on alleged arrears of service charges.[119] This is an increasing problem. Many people who would traditionally have occupied private sector rented accommodation have bought their own flats, sometimes with insufficient income, only to find that they face the kinds of problems associated with rented accommodation – disrepair, lack of proper management, over-charging and possession proceedings.

The mere fact that a freeholder or managing agent has served a demand for service charges does not mean that the amounts claimed are automatically payable. Advisers should always make the following checks:

First, has the landlord complied with the provisions of the lease relating to recovery of service charges? The lease almost certainly specifies in detail what items can be included in service charge demands, the manner in which such costs can be recovered and the way they are to be calculated. These provisions must be strictly complied with. For example if a lease does not say that a lessor can charge for a particular type of service, charges are not recoverable unless there is a wide 'catch all' clause.[120] Also it may be necessary for the landlord to serve a demand for service charges in a particular form if they are to be recoverable. Some leases provide that a landlord must actually incur expenditure before it is recoverable, whereas other leases provide that a landlord may recover service charges in advance.[121] Check whether the apportionment between the lessees has been made on the correct basis and that a particular lessee is not paying too high a percentage of the total. Careful reading of a lease may show that the freeholder or landlord is not entitled to the sums claimed and that the lessee has a complete defence to forfeiture proceedings.

Secondly, has the landlord complied with the consultation procedure in the Landlord and Tenant Act? The Landlord and Tenant Act 1985 s20 requires landlords to submit estimates and to consult with lessees before carrying out major works. This provision applies where the amount which a landlord intends to spend is more than £1,000 or £50

---

118 See Part V, precedent 17.
119 See eg *The Leaseholder's Rights Guide* (SHAC 1986).
120 For example, *Boldmark Ltd v Cohen and Cohen* (1985) 19 HLR 135.
121 But see Landlord and Tenant Act 1985 s19(2).

multiplied by the number of flats, whichever is greater.[122] If s20 applies, the landlord has to serve a notice describing the works, giving two estimates of the cost and inviting comments from the lessees. Unless they are 'urgently required', works should not start within one month of service of the notice and the landlord should 'have regard to any observations received'.[123] The general rule is that a landlord who fails to comply with this procedure is not entitled to recover the service charges in question, although the court has power to dispense with this requirement if it is 'satisfied that the landlord acted reasonably'.[124]

Thirdly, have the expenses been reasonably incurred and are works or services carried out to a reasonable standard?   Landlord and Tenant Act 1985 s19 provides that costs included in service charge demands can only be taken into account if they are 'reasonably incurred' and where 'services or works are of a reasonable standard'. Even if landlords comply with the terms of leases and the consultation procedure, and spend money on works or services, lessees have a defence to a claim for service charges if the sums were not reasonably incurred or if works or services are poorly carried out. Courts may decide that a proportion of charges are reasonably incurred and that the remainder are not.[125]

One problem in advising long lessees about service charges is the difficulty of predicting whether or not a court will decide that a landlord has acted reasonably. The provisions of the Landlord and Tenant Act 1985 give the courts a good deal of discretion and there have been no reported cases since these requirements were adopted to illustrate what is reasonable.[126]

Fourthly, has the landlord supplied the information required by the Landlord and Tenant Act 1987?   Section 47 provides that any written demand for rent or service charges must contain the name and address of the landlord and, if the address is outside England and Wales, an address inside England and Wales where notices may be served. If the landlord fails to comply with this requirement, 'any part of the amount demanded which consists of a service charge . . . shall be treated for all purposes as not being due from the tenant to the landlord at any time before that information is furnished by the landlord'.[127]

Lastly, were any costs included in the claim for service charges incurred

---

122 Service Charge (Estimates and Consultation) Order 1988 SI No 1285.
123 S20(3)(d) and (e).
124 S20(5).
125 *Yorkbrook Investments Ltd v Batten* (1985) 276 EG 493, CA.
126 Cf *Finchbourne Ltd v Rodrigues* [1976] 3 All ER 581, decided prior to the implementation of HA 1980 Sch 19, the forerunner of ss19 and 20.
127 See *Dallhold Estate (UK) Pty Ltd v Lindsay Trading Properties Inc.* [1992] EGCS 29, Ch D and *Hussain v Singh* (1992) *Independent* 6 October, CA.

more than 18 months before payment was demanded? Has a local authority grant been approved in respect of any works for which a proportion of the expenditure is claimed?   If the answer to either of these questions is 'yes', the proportion of the service charges is irrecoverable.[128]

128 See Landlord and Tenant Act 1985 s20B, inserted by Landlord and Tenant Act 1987
    Sch 2, para 4 and Landlord and Tenant Act s20A, inserted by Housing and Planning
    Act 1986 Sch 5, para 9.

CHAPTER 10

Statutory Tenants Ceasing to Reside

General principles

After a contractual RA protected tenancy has been determined, the tenant becomes a statutory tenant with continuing RA protection provided that s/he occupies the premises 'as his or her residence'. Although there is no requirement in the Act that a contractual tenant should occupy premises as his or her residence, this is crucial for statutory tenants.

If a statutory tenant ceases to reside in the premises, RA protection is lost completely and a landlord bringing possession proceedings need prove only ownership of the premises, the termination of the contractual tenancy and that the tenant no longer resides in the premises.[1] On the other hand, if a statutory tenant does not give up possession and cease to live in the premises, the only way in which the landlord can repossess is to prove one of the RA grounds for possession, and if appropriate, that it is reasonable to make an order for possession.[2]

RA 1977 s 2 provides for the creation of statutory tenancies:

> 2.—(1)   Subject to this Part of this Act—
>
> (a) after the termination of a protected tenancy of a dwelling-house the person who, immediately before that termination, was the protected tenant of the dwelling-house shall, if and so long as he occupies the dwelling-house as his residence, be the statutory tenant of it; and
>
> (b) Part I of Schedule 1 to this Act shall have effect for determining what person (if any) is the statutory tenant of a dwelling-house at any time after the death of a person who, immediately before his death, was either a protected tenant of the dwelling-house or the statutory tenant of it by virtue of paragraph (a) above.
>
> (2)   In this Act a dwelling-house is referred to as subject to a statutory tenancy when there is a statutory tenant of it.

---

1   There is no need in these circumstances to prove a RA ground for possession or that it is reasonable to make an order for possession.

2   *Boyer v Warbey* [1953] 1 QB 234; *Brown v Draper* [1944] 1 All ER 246.

(3) In subsection (1)(*a*) above and in Part I of Schedule 1, the phrase 'if and so long as he occupies the dwelling-house as his residence' shall be construed as it was immediately before the commencement of this Act (that is to say, in accordance with section 3(2) of the RA 1968).

(4) A person who becomes a statutory tenant of a dwelling-house as mentioned in subsection (1)(*a*) above is, in this Act, referred to as a statutory tenant by virtue of his previous protected tenancy.

(5) A person who becomes a statutory tenant as mentioned in subsection (1)(*b*) above is, in this Act, referred to as a statutory tenant by succession.

There was no express requirement in the first RAs[3] that a statutory tenant reside in the premises. However, in a series of cases it was decided that the protection given to a statutory tenant is 'a personal privilege which ceases when the tenant goes out of occupation'.[4] The object of the Acts was to protect tenants who occupied premises as their home,[5] not absentee tenants. The continuing importance of this principle is recognised by s2(3).

In determining whether or not a tenant occupies premises as his or her residence, the first material date is the date of termination of the contractual tenancy.[6] Whether or not the tenant was living in the premises prior to the termination of the contractual tenancy is irrelevant. However, if the tenant is not residing in the premises when the contractual tenancy is terminated, a statutory tenancy cannot arise.[7] Even if a former protected tenant resumes residence after the termination of the contractual tenancy, it is impossible to reinstate RA protection as a statutory tenant; it is lost forever.[8] In addition, the tenant must remain in residential occupation throughout the statutory tenancy. Accordingly, if the tenant sublets the whole of premises which s/he rents, the protection of a statutory tenancy is lost because it is impossible for him or her to be in residential occupation.[9] However, it is not necessary for the tenant to reside in all parts of the premises all of the time. A landlord cannot claim that a tenant has ceased to be a statutory tenant of one part only of premises and recover session of that part.[10] Accordingly, a tenant who sublets parts of the

---

3   For example, the Increase of Rent and Mortgage Interest (War Restrictions) Act 1915 and the Increase of Rent and Mortgage (Restrictions) Act 1920.
4   *Middleton v Baldock (TW)* [1950] 1 All ER 708.
5   *Skinner v Geary* [1931] 2 KB 546.
6   Ibid; *John Brown v Bestwick* [1950] 2 All ER 338; *Colin Smith Music v Ridge* [1975] 1 WLR 463.
7   *Brown v Bestwick* n6, cf *Francis Jackson Developments v Hall* [1951] 2 KB 488.
8   *Brown v Bestwick* n6.
9   Ibid. See too case 6 below and *Regalian Securities Ltd v Ramsden* [1981] 2 All ER 65, HL at 74.
10   *Berkeley v Papadoyannis* [1954] 2 QB 149.

premises from time to time, with a general intention to live in the future in the parts which are sublet, retains the statutory tenancy.[11]

'Residence' is not, however, interpreted in a narrow sense.[12] A statutory tenant need not occupy premises 24 hours a day, 365 days a year. It is accepted that tenants may be in residence for the purpose of the RA even though they have been physically absent from premises for prolonged periods of 'temporary absence'. Similarly, it is well established that a tenant may maintain residence in two homes at the same time.

Temporary absence

A tenant must show two things to establish that s/he is still occupying, as a residence, premises from which s/he is temporarily absent.[13]

a) Some kind of physical presence.[14] It is not enough merely to keep an inward intention to return. This intention must be clothed by an outward and visible sign of the intention to return.[15] A tenant must leave behind deliberate symbols of his or her occupation and preserve the premises for his or her ultimate homecoming.[16] In some cases this requirement has been satisfied by the tenant leaving behind furniture,[17] a caretaker to look after the premises[18] or relatives.[19] In practice, tenants intending to be absent for any length of time would be well advised to leave behind some personal items such as books, records, clothes, crockery and cutlery as well as furniture.

b) The tenant must at all times retain a definite intention to return.[20] There must be a real hope on the tenant's part that s/he will return, coupled with the practical possibility of its fulfilment within a reasonable time.[21] It is not enough for this intention to be dependent on something else happening, such as the death of a parent.[22] The

11   Ibid and *Herbert v Byrne* [1964] 1 All ER 882.
12   *Skinner v Geary* n5.
13   *Brown v Brash* [1948] 2 KB 247.
14   'Corpus possessionis'.
15   *Brown v Brash* n13.
16   Ibid.
17   *Gofor Investments Ltd v Roberts* (1975) 29 P & CR 366; *Brown v Draper* n2; *Hallwood Estates v Flack* (1950) 66 TLR (Pt 2) 368; *Dixon v Tommis* [1952] 1 All ER 725.
18   *Brown v Brash* n13.
19   *Dixon v Tommis* n17; *Roland House Gardens v Cravitz* (1974) 29 P & CR 432; *Warriner Ltd v Wood* (1944) 144 EG 81.
20   'Animus possidendi', *Cove v Flick* [1954] 2 All ER 441.
21   *Tickner v Hearn* [1960] 1 WLR 1406.
22   *Cove v Flick* n20.

reasons for a tenant's absence may be relevant and it is far easier to prove an intention to return if the initial absence is due to 'some sudden calamity' such as a sentence of imprisonment[23] or a flood.[24] Other reasons given for temporary absence have been illness,[25] illness of relatives[26] and disrepair coupled with the pregnancy of the tenant's wife.[27] It is possible that a tenant's intention to return may override a purported assignment of the tenancy which is a nullity.[28]

It is a question of fact and degree in each case as to whether a tenant's absence is such that s/he has ceased to occupy premises as a residence. The burden of proof initially lies on the landlord to show that the tenant is absent. Once a landlord has established this, it is for the tenant to show that s/he has maintained a physical presence in the premises and an intention to return.[29]

The following cases illustrate how long 'temporary absence' can be:

Wigley v Leigh[30] – tenant's absence from 1940 to 1949. Initially she stayed with relatives because her husband was at war but she was then prevented from returning because she suffered from tuberculosis.

Dixon v Tommis[31] – at the time of the hearing the tenant had been absent for six months and did not intend to return for three years. He left his furniture in the premises while his son and his son's family lived there.

Gofor Investments v Roberts[32] – at the time of the hearing the tenants had been absent for five years and intended to return within 'three to five years'. They had been living in Morocco and Malta and had left their furniture and two sons in the premises.

Richards v Green[33] – the tenant had been absent for two and a half years. He had been living at a house owned by his parents, initially because they had been ill, but after their death because he was clearing up the house and arranging for it to be sold.

23   *Brown v Brash* n13.
24   *Bushford v Falco* [1954] 1 All ER 957.
25   *Tickner v Hearn* n21.
26   *Richards v Green* (1983) 268 EG 443; (1984) 11 HLR 1, CA.
27   *Atyeo v Fardoe* (1978) 37 P & CR 494.
28   *Bushford v Falco* n24.
29   *Roland House v Cravitz* n19.
30   [1950] 1 All ER 73.
31   See n17.
32   Ibid.
33   See n26.

Tickner v Hearn[34] – absence of five and a half years by tenant who was in a mental hospital suffering from schizophrenia. The mere fact that she was 'mentally unsound' did not mean that she was incapable of forming an intention to return to the premises.[35]

On the other hand, in *DJ Crocker Securities (Portsmouth) Ltd v Johal*[36] the Court of Appeal refused to overturn a judge's finding that a tenant had ceased to occupy a flat as his home. The tenant had returned to look after his father in Malaysia in 1977. Since then he had lived and worked in Malaysia with his wife and children, and since 1980 had only spent between nine and 26 days in the flat.

Occupation through other people

Although the presence of friends and relatives living in premises may be evidence of the tenant's intention to return,[37] it is not, as a general rule, possible for a tenant to maintain RA protection through the residence of other people if s/he has no intention of returning.[38] However, an exception was that a husband was deemed to be continuing to occupy premises as a residence even if he did not intend to return, if his wife was still living in the premises.[39] It was not, however, possible for a tenant who was a wife to maintain her own RA protection by leaving her husband living in the premises.[40] This position has been changed by the Matrimonial Homes Act 1983 s1(6),[41] which provides:

> A spouse's occupation by virtue of this section shall for the purpose of the Rent (Agriculture) Act 1976, and of the Rent Act 1977 (other than Part V and sections 103 to 106), be treated as possession by the other spouse and for the purposes of Part IV of the Housing Act 1985 and Part I of the Housing Act 1988 be treated as occupation by the other spouse.

If the spouse who is the tenant moves out and the statutory tenancy

34 See n21.
35 Compare, however, *Duke v Porter* (1986) 280 EG 633, CA – absence of 10 years. Held tenant had ceased to occupy as a resident.
36 (1989) 42 EG 103.
37 *Dixon v Tommis* n17; *Roland House v Cravitz* n19.
38 *Collins v Claughton* [1959] 1 All ER 95.
39 *Old Gate Estates v Alexander* [1949] 2 All ER 822; *Wabe v Taylor* [1952] 2 All ER 420; *Brown v Draper* n2; *Middleton v Baldock (TW)* n4.
40 *Collins v Claughton* n38.
41 Formerly Matrimonial Homes Act 1967 s1. Note that s1(6) of the 1983 Act is of no assistance unless at some time both spouses have lived in the premises as a matrimonial home – *Hall v King* (1987) 19 HLR 440, CA.

continues as a result of the non-tenant spouse's residence, the actual tenant remains liable for the rent, unless an order is made in accordance with the Matrimonial Homes Act 1983 s1(3)(c).[42]

RA protection cannot, however, be maintained by the continuing occupation of a divorced ex-spouse of the tenant,[43] although the Matrimonial Homes Act 1983 does provide for the transfer of tenancies from one spouse to another.[44] Obviously none of these problems of continuing occupation applies if the tenancy was originally granted in joint names.

A Rent Act protected tenancy does not rest in the trustee in bankruptcy if the tenant is made bankrupt. Accordingly there is nothing to prevent a statutory tenancy arising in the ordinary way.[45]

Residence in two homes

It has been recognised since the early days of the RAs[46] that it is possible for a tenant to occupy two premises as residences at the same time. A tenant may maintain RA protection in both homes or alternatively may maintain protection in one while owning the other. The classic example is of a tenant who has one home in the town and another in the country.[47] The question 'to be answered by ordinary common-sense standards, is whether the particular premises are in the personal occupation of the tenant as his or her home, or, if the tenant has more than one home, as one of his or her homes. Occupation merely as a convenience for . . .

42   *Griffiths v Renfree* (1989) 21 HLR 338, [1989] 2 EGLR 46, CA.
43   *Heath Estates v Burchell* (1980) 130 NLJ 548; *Metropolitan Properties Co Ltd v Cronan* (1982) 262 EG 1077 and *Crago v Julian* [1992] 1 All ER 744, (1991) Times 4 December, [1991] EGCS 124, CA.
44   Matrimonial Homes Act 1983 s7 and Sch 1. See too Matrimonial Causes Act 1973 s24. It is important that any application for a transfer of the tenancy is made promptly if the tenant spouse is not actually residing in the premises and the tenancy is a statutory tenancy. Occupation by a non-tenant spouse ceases to count as residence by the tenant on the making of the decree absolute (Matrimonial Homes Act 1983 s1(10)) unless the contrary is specifically ordered. In these circumstances the making of the decree absolute may terminate the statutory tenancy unless the order transferring the tenancy is made simultaneously. The court's power to transfer a statutory tenancy to another spouse is restricted to cases where the statutory tenancy is in existence at the date of the application for the transfer (*Lewis v Lewis* [1985] 2 WLR 962).
45   Insolvency Act 1986 s283(3)(a), overruling *Smalley v Quarrier* [1975] 2 All ER 688; *Eyre v Hall* (1986) 280 EG 193; (1986) 18 HLR 509.
46   For example, *Skinner v Geary* n5.
47   For example, *Langford Property Co v Athanassoglou* [1948] 2 All ER 722.

occasional visits'[48] is not sufficient. It is not merely a question of what a tenant does in particular premises; the court should look at all the circumstances and the way in which the tenant leads his or her life.[49] Comparatively small amounts of occupation may be sufficient, as in *Langford Property Co v Athanassoglou*[50] where a tenant slept in his 'town house' twice a week and rarely ate there, and *Bevington v Crawford*[51] where tenants lived mainly in Cannes and spent approximately two or three months each year in their rented accommodation in Harrow.

It is more difficult for a tenant to claim to occupy separate premises as residences when they are close together.[52] For example, in *Hampstead Way Investment v Lewis-Weare*[53] a tenant rented a flat half a mile from a house which he owned and in which his wife lived. He slept most nights in the rented accommodation but the House of Lords held that he did not occupy it as a residence. Similarly, the RA does not provide protection for premises which are occupied only occasionally when the tenant is on holiday.[54] The tenant may occupy two homes as residences where s/he is in the course of moving from one home to another.[55]

48 *Beck v Scholz* [1953] 1 All ER 814 at 816.
49 *Regalian Securities Ltd v Scheuer* (1982) 263 EG 973.
50 See n47.
51 (1974) 232 EG 191.
52 *Regalian v Scheuer* n49. See too *Swanbrae Ltd v Elliott* (1987) 19 HLR 86.
53 [1985] 1 All ER 564, HL; cf, though, *Palmer v McNamara* (1990) 23 HLR 168, (1991) 17 EG 88 CA, (comparable 'occupation as a residence' under Rent Act 1977 s12 satisfied even though no cooker and landlord did not sleep in premises).
54 *Walker v Ogilvy* (1974) 28 P & CR 288.
55 *Herbert v Byrne* n11.

CHAPTER 11

Grounds for Possession against Rent Act Protected Tenants

The starting point for all grounds of possession is RA 1977 s98, which provides:

98.—(1)   Subject to this Part of this Act, a court shall not make an order for possession of a dwelling-house which is for the time being let on a protected tenancy or subject to a statutory tenancy unless the court considers it reasonable to make such an order and either—

(a)   the court is satisfied that suitable alternative accommodation is available for the tenant or will be available for him when the order in question takes effect, or

(b)   the circumstances are as specified in any of the Cases in Part I of Schedule 15 to this Act.

(2)   If, apart from subsection (1) above, the landlord would be entitled to recover possession of a dwelling-house which is for the time being let on or subject to a regulated tenancy, the court shall make an order for possession if the circumstances of the case are as specified in any of the Cases in Part II of Schedule 15.

The main distinction between the various grounds for possession is that if a landlord is relying on one of the so-called 'discretionary' grounds, s/he must prove not only the existence of the ground for possession but also that it is reasonable to make an order for possession (see below).

The discretionary grounds are those set out in Cases 1 to 10 and in s98(1)(a) (ie, that 'suitable alternative accommodation' is available). The 'mandatory grounds' are those set out in Cases 11 to 20 and statutory overcrowding:[1] in these cases the landlord has to prove only that the contractual tenancy has been terminated and that a ground for possession is satisfied.

---

1   RA 1977 s101.

Suitable alternative accommodation

This ground is fulfilled if 'the court is satisfied that suitable alternative accommodation is available for the tenant or will be available for him when the order in question takes effect'.[2]

Further guidance is given in Sch 15 Pt IV, which provides:

3.   For the purposes of section 98(1)(*a*) of this Act, a certificate of the [local] housing authority for the district in which the dwelling-house in question is situated, certifying that the authority will provide suitable alternative accommodation for the tenant by a date specified in the certificate, shall be conclusive evidence that suitable alternative accommodation will be available for him by that date.

4.   Where no such certificate as mentioned in paragraph 3 above is produced to the court, accommodation shall be deemed to be suitable for the purposes of section 98(1)(*a*) of this Act if it consists of either—

(*a*)   premises which are to be let as a separate dwelling such that they will then be let on a protected tenancy, (other than one under which the landlord might recover possession of the dwelling-house under one of the Cases in Part II of this Schedule) or

(*b*)   premises to be let as a separate dwelling on terms which will, in the opinion of the court, afford to the tenant security of tenure reasonably equivalent to the security afforded by Part VII of this Act in the case of a protected tenancy of a kind mentioned in paragraph (*a*) above,

and, in the opinion of the court, the accommodation fulfils the relevant conditions as defined in paragraph 5 below.

5.—(1)   For the purposes of paragraph 4 above, the relevant conditions are that the accommodation is reasonably suitable to the needs of the tenant and his family as regards proximity to place of work, and either—

(*a*)   similar as regards rental and extent to the accommodation afforded by dwelling-houses provided in the neighbourhood by any local housing authority for persons whose needs as regards extent are, in the opinion of the court, similar to those of the tenant and of his family; or

(*b*)   reasonably suitable to the means of the tenant and to the needs of the tenant and his family as regards extent and character; and

that if any furniture was provided for use under the protected or statutory tenancy in question, furniture is provided for use in the accommodation which is either similar to that so provided or is reasonably suitable to the needs of the tenant and his family.

(2)   For the purposes of sub-paragraph (1)(*a*) above, a certificate of a [local] housing authority stating—

(*a*)   the extent of the accommodation afforded by dwelling-houses

---

2   Ibid s98(1)(a).

provided by the authority to meet the needs of tenants with families of such number as may be specified in the certificate, and

(b)   the amount of the rent charged by the authority for dwelling-houses affording accommodation of that extent,

shall be conclusive evidence of the facts so stated.

6.   Accommodation shall not be deemed to be suitable to the needs of the tenant and his family if the result of their occupation of the accommodation would be that it would be an overcrowded dwelling-house for the purposes of Part X of the Housing Act 1985.

7.   Any document purporting to be a certificate of a local housing authority named therein issued for the purposes of this Schedule and to be signed by the proper officer of that authority shall be received in evidence and, unless the contrary is shown, shall be deemed to be such a certificate without further proof.

8.   In this Part 'local housing authority' and 'district' in relation to such an authority have the same meaning as in the Housing Act 1985.

A landlord may thus prove that alternative accommodation is suitable either by obtaining a certificate that the local authority will provide accommodation or by satisfying the various criteria set out in Sch 15 Pt IV.

Local authority certificate that accommodation available

Schedule 15 Pt IV para 3 provides that a certificate from a local authority housing department confirming that it will provide suitable alternative accommodation for the tenant is conclusive evidence that suitable alternative accommodation will be available[3] at the date specified in the certificate. The certificate must be from the housing authority in which the relevant premises are situated, otherwise it is totally ineffective.[4] It seems that there is no requirement that the certificate provide details of the address or size of the suitable alternative accommodation. If, after issuing a certificate, a local authority failed to provide suitable alternative accommodation, the court would have power under s100(2) to stay execution of the order on an application by the tenant. There is no requirement that the certificate be in any particular form: a signed letter will suffice.

In view of the shortage of local authority accommodation, it is rare for local authorities to provide certificates under para 3. Accordingly, whether or not suitable accommodation is available is usually decided in the light of the guidelines in paras 4 to 8.

3   *Wallasey v Pritchard* (1936) 3 LJNCCR 35.
4   *Sills v Watkins* [1956] 1 QB 250.

No local authority certificate that accommodation available

If there is no local authority certificate the landlord must prove that the requirements set out below are satisfied.

Equivalent security of tenure

> . . . premises which are to be let as a separate dwelling . . . on a protected tenancy (other tha one under which the landlord might recover possession . . . under one of the Cases in Part II of this Schedule) or . . . let as a separate dwelling on terms which will . . . afford to the tenant security of tenure reasonably equivalent to . . . a protected tenancy . . .

It is clear that the accommodation offered must be in a single building: accommodation offered in two separate houses cannot be suitable.[5] Similarly, the requirement is not satisfied if the premises offered consist of two separate parts of a building which are separated by another flat[6] or if the alternative accommodation involves sharing a kitchen.[7]

Problems may arise where alternative accommodation is to be let on a sub-tenancy. It will be sufficient to meet the requirements if it is a protected sub-tenancy, even if the head tenancy contains a prohibition against subletting. In such circumstances, however, someone who has moved to the alternative accommodation and has become a sub-tenant may face possession proceedings brought by a superior landlord and find that s/he has no security of tenure as against that superior landlord. Tenants faced with offers of suitable alternative accommodation should, therefore, always ascertain the interest in the premises of the person who will be letting the accommodation to them. Even though accommodation offered in breach of terms in a lease may still be 'suitable alternative accommodation', it would clearly not be reasonable for the court to make an order for possession.[8] Often it is prudent to obtain office copy entries from the Land Registry to check the ownership of the property offered and, in particular, to find out whether the property is subject to any mortgage.[9] If it is, consent to the proposed tenancy should be obtained from the mortgagee to ensure that the lender is bound by the tenancy and to avoid the risk of eviction if the landlord fails to keep up with mortgage payments. (See p313 below.)

---

5 *Sheehan v Cutler* [1946] KB 339.
6 *Selwyn v Hamill* [1948] 1 All ER 70.
7 *Cookson v Walsh* (1954) 163 EG 486.
8 See N Madge 'Unsuitable Alternative Accommodation' November 1983 *LAG Bulletin* 140.
9 Use Land Registry forms 96 and 109.

Schedule 15 Pt IV para 4(b) provides that accommodation may be suitable even if it is not let on a protected tenancy, if the security of tenure provided is 'reasonably equivalent' to full RA protection. In determining this it is necessary to look strictly at the rights which the landlord of the alternative accommodation has to terminate the tenancy and not at common practice or the assurances given by the new landlord.[10] What is 'reasonably equivalent' security will depend on the facts. In one case an unprotected fixed-term tenancy of 16 years was held to provide reasonably equivalent security.[11] In another, an unprotected fixed-term tenancy of 10 years offered to a tenant aged 57 and her husband aged 58 was held to provide reasonably equivalent security.[12] It is not necessary for the alternative accommodation to be let by the same landlord – it is enough that it is available and suitable.

If the tenant against whom possession is sought occupies premises as a sole tenant, a joint tenancy or even joint ownership of a house cannot be suitable alternative accommodation since the other joint tenant or joint owner may unilaterally terminate the tenancy or force a sale.[13] It is not clear whether other premises owned by the tenant can amount to suitable alternative accommodation.[14]

The HA 1988 s34 provides that in possession procedings against a protected or statutory tenant based on the availability of suitable alternative accommodation, the court should consider whether the grant of an assured tenancy (see chapter 14) would provide reasonably equivalent security. If 'in the circumstances, the grant of an assured tenancy would not afford the required security' the court may direct that the tenancy of the suitable alternative accommodation should be held on a protected tenancy. The grounds for possession against assured tenants are much wider than those against RA protected tenants (eg, if the landlord wishes to demolish or reconstruct) and so tenants' representatives should try to persuade the court to direct that any new tenancy should be a protected tenancy. It may also be in the tenant's interest to argue that rents under assured tenancies are likely to be higher (see p177 below).

10   For example, *Sills v Watkins* n4, where the offer of alternative accommodation was a pre-1980 HA council tenancy with no security of tenure. Although in practice the council did not evict tenants without reason this offer did not comply with the statutory requirements.

11   *Fulford v Turpin* [1955] CLY 2324.

12   *Edwards v Cohen* (1958) 108 LJ 556.

13   *Barnard v Towers* [1953] 2 All ER 877, CA; *Greenwich LBC v McGrady* (1982) 6 HLR 36; *LB Hammersmith and Fulham v Monk* (1992) 39 EG 135, (1992) 24 HLR 203, HL.

14   See the conflicting dicta in *Barnard v Towers* n13 and *Standingford v Probert* [1950] 1 KB 377, CA.

Closeness to workplace

> The accommodation is reasonably suitable to the needs of the tenant and his
> family as regards proximity to place of work . . .

A 'place of work' need not be a factory or an office. It can be an area or
the location in which the tenant's work is based.[15] The court should
consider not only distance from work, but also the time which it would
take to travel, the means of transport available and any inconvenience
which would be caused.[16] The work may be unpaid.[17]

When considering the workplaces of other members of the tenant's
family, the court can consider only those members actually residing with
the tenant. The phrase 'member of family' is given its ordinary meaning as
understood by an ordinary person.[18] It has been held to include, a son,
daughter-in-law[19] and mother-in-law.[20] It is possible that a lodger may be
counted as a member of the family.[21]

Rental and size

> . . . the accommodation is similar as regards rental and extent to the
> accommodation afforded by dwelling-houses provided in the neighbourhood
> by any local housing authority for persons whose needs as regards extent are
> . . . similar to those of the tenant and his family or . . . reasonably suitable to
> the means of the tenant and to the needs of the tenant and his family as
> regards extent and character.

The landlord can satisfy this test in either of two ways. First, the
landlord may produce a certificate from the local authority for the area in
which the tenant rents his or her current accommodation setting out the
kind of accommodation which would be provided for people of similar
needs. The certificate should probably state the number of rooms which
would be provided and give some indication as to the dimensions of such
rooms.[22] A certificate which stated that local authority rents would be
more than twice as high as the alternative accommodation offered did not

15 *Yewbright Properties Ltd v Stone* (1980) 40 P & CR 402.
16 Ibid. See too *Minchburn Ltd v Fernandez* May 1985 *Legal Action* 66 where
    alternative accommodation was held not to be suitable because it would have
    doubled the tenant's 30-minute walk to work to one hour. The needs of the particular
    tenant count, not those of a reasonable tenant.
17 *Dakyns v Pace* [1948] 1 KB 22.
18 *Standingford v Probert* n14; *Scrace v Windust* [1955] 1 WLR 475.
19 *Standingford v Probert* n14.
20 *Scrace v Windust* n18.
21 *Standingford v Probert* n14; cf *Stewart v Mackay* [1947] SLT 250.
22 Per Edmund Davies LJ in *MacDonnell v Daly* [1969] 1 WLR 1482; cf *Wallasey v
    Pritchard* n3.

show that the accommodation offered was similar as regards rental.[23] It is for a judge to decide, after considering the certificate, whether or not the accommodation offered is similar to that which the local authority would provide. In *Jones v Cook*[24] the Court of Appeal set aside a possession order where a judge had simply accepted the contents of a certificate which had stated that the property offered by the landlord was 'similar in extent to council-owned dwelling-houses which may be provided in the neighbourhood for families consisting of husband, wife and three children'.

If there is no local authority certificate (and it is comparatively rare for a landlord to obtain such a certificate), the court should consider whether the property offered is reasonably suitable. Accommodation may be suitable even though it is inferior to the accommodation currently occupied by the tenant.[25] It may also be suitable even though it is considerably smaller.[26] Part only of the accommodation currently rented by the tenant may amount to suitable alternative accommodation if at the time of the hearing the tenant is not occupying all of the accommodation let (eg because part is sublet[27]) or because it is larger than the tenant requires.[28]

When the court considers the 'needs' of the tenant and the tenant's family, it should primarily consider their housing needs and not incidental advantages such as the use of a stable and paddock.[29] The court may, however, take into account a tenant's professional needs, such as an artist using a room as a studio[30] or the need for a tenant to entertain business associates.[31] Accommodation may be unsuitable if it is too large[32], if it is

23   *Turner v Keiller* [1950] SC 43 and *Robert Thackeray's Estate Ltd v Kaye* (1989) 21 HLR 160, CA.

24   (1990) 22 HLR 319, CA.

25   Per Lord Asquith in *Warren v Austen* [1947] 2 All ER 185.

26   *Quick v Fifield* (1982) 132 NLJ 140 (less than half the size) and *Hill v Rochard* [1983] 1 WLR 478.

27   *Parmee v Mitchell* [1950] 2 KB 199; *Thompson v Rolls* [1926] All ER 257 and *Yoland v Reddington* (1982) 263 EG 157.

28   *MacDonnell v Daly* n21 (two out of three rooms); *Mykolyshyn v Noah* [1970] 1 WLR 1271 (current accommodation less sitting room).

29   *Hill v Rochard* n26, although such matters will be relevant when considering reasonableness. On tenants' 'needs' generally, see HW Wilkinson 'What does a tenant need?' (1985) 135 NLJ 933 where there is a summary of the facts of some of the cases noted in the following footnotes.

30   *MacDonnell v Daly* n22.

31   *De Markozoff v Craig* (1949) 93 SJ 693; cf *Stewart v Mackay* n21 (tenant's inability to take in lodgers); *Wilcock v Booth* (1920) 122 LT 678 (loss of off-licence) and *Warren v Austen* n25 (unreasonable to make order where alternative accommodation not large enough to enable tenant to continue to take lodgers).

32   *LB Islington v Metcalfe and Peacock* (1983) unreported; noted at August 1983 *LAG Bulletin* 105.

in disrepair[33], if it lacks a bathroom and toilet[34], if it means the tenant living with his estranged wife[35] or if it does not have a garden in which the tenant's children can play.[36] Accommodation in a shared house may be unsuitable for a tenant currently living alone.[37]

The court should take into account environmental factors. For example, in *Redspring Limited v Francis*[38] the alternative accommodation was on a busy traffic thoroughfare, had no garden, was next door to a fish shop and was near to a hospital, cinema and public house with the result that there were people 'coming and going' at all hours of the day and night, whereas the tenant's current accommodation was in a quiet and secluded residential street. However, environmental factors can be taken into account only so far as they relate to the character of the property. The proximity of the tenants' friends and cultural interests are not relevant here, although they clearly are relevant when the court comes to consider reasonableness.[39]

So far as rent is concerned, tenants' representatives should bear in mind that if the new tenancy is being offered on an assured tenancy there will be minimal rent control and after a year or the termination of any fixed-term tenancy, the landlord will be able to seek a market rent (HA 1988 s13). Accordingly it may be necessary to adduce evidence about market rents or rents for assured tenancies determined by rent assessment committees in the area. Alternatively, a landlord may be persuaded to consent to a direction that the alternative accommodation should be held on a protected tenancy (HA 1988 s34).

Furniture

if any furniture was provided for use under the protected or statutory tenancy in question, furniture is provided for use in the accommodation which is either similar to that so provided or is reasonably suitable to the needs of the tenant and his family.

Availability

accommodation is available for the tenant or will be available for him when the order in question takes effect

33   If there is any question of disrepair in the alternative accommodation it is always wise for the tenant to obtain a full survey report.
34   *Esposito v Ware* (1950) 155 EG 383.
35   *Heglibiston Establishments v Heyman* (1977) 246 EG 567.
36   *De Markozoff v Craig* n31; cf in the public sector *Enfield LBC v French* (1984) 17 HLR 211.
37   *Barnard v Towers* n13.
38   [1973] 1 WLR 134.
39   *Siddiqui v Rashid* [1980] 1 WLR 1018.

The suitable alternative accommodation must be available for the particular tenant.[40] In determining whether it is available, accommodation which was previously available is completely irrelevant,[41] although refusals by the tenant of previous offers of other accommodation may be considered when the court decides the question of reasonableness. It is sufficient for the landlord to show that such accommodation is available even if it is to be rented from another person.

Overcrowding

> Accommodation shall not be deemed to be suitable to the needs of the tenant and his family if the result of their occupation of the accommodation would be that it would be an overcrowded dwelling-house for the purpose of Part X of the Housing Act 1985.[42]

For the definition of overcrowding, see p157 below.

It should be remembered that even if the court is satisfied that suitable alternative accommodation exists, the court must still consider whether it is reasonable to make a possession order. Failure to do this makes the possession order a nullity.[43] It is important to remember that if the court does make an order for possession, the new tenancy will be a Housing Act assured tenancy, without the protection given by Rent Act rent regulation, unless the court directs that the tenancy should be held on a protected tenancy. See p75.

Discretionary Grounds

Case 1: Rent arrears or breach of obligations of tenancy

> Where any rent lawfully due from the tenant has not been paid, or any obligation of the protected or statutory tenancy which arises under this Act, or—
>
> (a)   in the case of a protected tenancy, any other obligation of the tenancy, in so far as is consistent with the provisions of Part VII of this Act, or
>
> (b)   in the case of a statutory tenancy, any other obligation of the previous protected tenancy which is applicable to the statutory tenancy,
>
> has been broken or not performed.

This is the most common ground for possession used by landlords. They

40   *Topping v Hughes* [1925] NI 90.
41   *Kimpson v Markham* [1921] 1 KB 207.
42   RA 1977 Sch 15 para 6.
43   See chapter 12 and *Minchburn Estates v Fernandez (No 2)* (1986) 19 HLR 29, CA.

must prove that either there are rent arrears or that there has been a breach of a term or other obligation of the tenancy.

Rent arrears

A landlord must prove two things, first that rent was lawfully due from the tenant and second that some rent remained unpaid, at the date of issue of the summons.[44] This applies only to rent which is due from the actual tenant against whom possession is claimed and not to that due from a predecessor of the present tenant.[45] Rent becomes lawfully due at midnight on the day when it is payable.[46] If rent has been tendered to the landlord on a regular basis when it has become due, but has not been accepted by the landlord, there is a complete defence to the proceedings based on alleged rent arrears if the tenant pays into court all the rent which is due.[47] Accordingly, if a landlord refuses to accept rent, it is important that the tenant continues to tender rent regularly (for example by sending cheques by recorded delivery) and maintains a separate bank or building society account so that the rent can be paid as soon as court proceedings are issued. If the tenant has not tendered rent regularly and there are arrears outstanding when proceedings are issued, the mere fact that the tenant pays all the rent arrears and fixed costs into court before the hearing date does not deprive the landlord of the grounds for possession under Case 1[48], but it is unlikely that the court will consider it reasonable to make an order for possession (see p161 below).

Failure to provide a rent book does not disentitle the landlord from claiming that rent is lawfully due.[49]

When advising a tenant who faces a claim for possession based on rent arrears, it is important to check exactly what rent is lawfully recoverable, and, in particular, whether the landlord has been claiming too much rent. This may happen where:

a) a landlord has been charging more than a 'fair rent' registered by the rent officer.[50] A rent registration for furnished premises is binding even if a later tenancy of the same premises is unfurnished, and vice-versa.

---

44   *Bird v Hildage* [1948] 1 KB 91.
45   *Tickner v Clifton* [1929] 1 KB 207.
46   *Aspinall v Aspinall* [1961] Ch 526.
47   *Bird v Hildage* n44.
48   Ibid.
49   *Shaw v Groom* [1970] 2 QB 504.
50   RA 1977 ss 44, 45 and 57. *Kakhit v Carty* [1990] 2 WLR 1107. Cf *Metrobarn v Gehring* [1976] 1 WLR 776, *Kent v Millmead Properties Ltd* (1982) 10 HLR 13 and *Cheniston Investments Ltd v Waddock* (1990) 20 HLR 652, CA.

Tenants who have paid more than the registered rent may claim back the difference for a period of up to two years before the claim; or
b) a landlord has increased the rent without complying with RA 1977 s51. In general, any agreement between a landlord and a RA protected tenant to increase the rent must comply with the provisions of s51. Any such agreement must be in writing and contain wording pointing out that a tenant's security of tenure is not affected by refusing to enter into the agreement and referring to the tenant's right to apply to the rent officer. If a landlord unilaterally increases the rent or if an agreement does not comply with s51, the increase is irrecoverable and the tenant can claim back the difference for a period of one year; or
c) a landlord has failed to serve a valid notice of increase. In some situations (eg, where a landlord wants to increase the rent following a new rent regisration) a landlord must serve a formal notice of increase. Failure to do so means that the increase is not legally recoverable;
d) a landlord has failed to furnish the tenant with an address at which notices may be served. In such circumstances the Landlord and Tenant Act 1987 s48 provides that any rent which would otherwise be due is to be treated as not being due before the landlord has rectified the failure.[51]

These provisions may mean that a landlord claiming rent arrears in fact owes the tenant money rather than vice versa. In such a situation a tenant may reclaim the balance by suing (or if proceedings have already been issued, by counterclaiming) or by withholding rent until all sums due have been recovered.[52]

Advisers should also check whether there is any possibility of a counterclaim for breach of repairing obligations (see p226), or whether there has been any failure by the relevant authorities to make payments of housing benefit (see p268).

Breach of any other tenancy obligation

The original provisions of the contractual tenancy continue to bind a statutory tenant so far as they are consistent with the provisions of the RA.[53] Breach of such obligations is a ground for possession, but see 'Waiver' below. However, the obligation must be one which is binding upon tenants in their capacity as tenants and not one of a personal nature

---

51   See *Dallhold Estate (UK) Pty Ltd v Lindsay Trading Properties Inc* [1992] EGCS 29 Ch D.
52   RA 1977 ss54 and 57.
53   Ibid s3(1).

or collateral to the agreement.[54] This can be determined by asking whether the obligation would be equally applicable if the tenancy were assigned to another person. For example an obligation to remain in the employment of the landlord is a personal one, and breach of it cannot give rise to grounds for possession under Case 1. Similarly, a covenant that the tenant should give up possession by a particular date cannot be relied upon by a landlord since it is inconsistent with the provisions of the RA.[55] A court can make an order for possession provided that there has been a breach of an obligation under the tenancy agreement, even if it no longer exists at the date of the hearing: it is not confined to considering breaches which are existing at the time of the hearing.[56]

It is outside the scope of this book to consider in detail the meaning of covenants which may be found in tenancy agreements. The following brief points should however be noted.

a) *Covenants against subletting.* The exact wording of the covenant is important because the three forms of phraseology frequently used have different meanings. A 'covenant against subletting' without any further qualification is merely a prohibition against subletting the whole of the premises which are let.[57] It does not prohibit subletting of part or sharing the premises with licensees. A 'covenant against subletting the whole or any part of the premises' does prohibit the subletting of the whole or any part of the premises, but does not cover taking in lodgers or sharing the premises with anyone else who is not a formal sub-tenant. A covenant which is wide enough to cover all of these activities is one to the effect that the tenant 'cannot sublet the whole or any part of the premises or share occupation with any other person', or that 'the tenant can only use the premises as a private residence in his sole occupation.'[58] A tenant who has friends, who share living expenses, staying in the premises is not in breach of a covenant against parting with possession, taking lodgers or using premises for business purposes.[59] The mere fact that a name other than that of the tenant appears on the electoral register relating to the premises is not by itself evidence that anyone other than the tenant is living in the accommodation.[60]

54   *RMR Housing Society v Combs* [1951] 1 All ER 16.
55   *Barton v Fincham* [1921] 2 KB 291; *Hunt v Bliss* (1919) 89 LJKB 174 and *Artizans, Labourers and General Dwellings Company Ltd v Whitaker* [1919] 2 KB 301.
56   *Brown v Davies* [1957] 3 All ER 401.
57   *Cook v Shoesmith* [1951] 1 KB 752.
58   *Falgor Commercial SA v Alsabahia* (1985) 18 HLR 123, CA.
59   *Heglibiston v Heyman* n35.
60   *Metropolitan Properties Co Ltd v Griffiths* (1982) 43 P & CR 138.

b) A *covenant against user for immoral purposes* is basically designed to prevent prostitution. It does not prohibit two unmarried people living together.[61]

c) A *covenant against business user* can have a wide meaning. It may include the carrying out of the activities of a political organisation on the premises[62] and the taking in of two paying lodgers.[63]

Waiver   The acceptance of rent by a landlord who has knowledge of a breach of covenant may amount to a waiver of that breach and thus prevent the landlord from relying upon Case 1.[64] If the tenancy is contractual, acceptance of rent is a complete waiver of a breach even if the acceptance is qualified. However, if the tenancy is statutory, it is a question of fact in each case as to whether the breach has been waived.[65] A qualified acceptance of rent from a statutory tenant (for example acceptance 'without prejudice') may mean that the landlord is still entitled to rely on the breach of covenant[66], but an unqualified acceptance of rent by the landlord of a statutory tenant is as much a waiver of the breach as if it were a payment by a contractual tenant.[67] Acceptance of rent by landlords' agents who have knowledge of a breach of covenant amounts to waiver.[68] Thus the knowledge of a porter that there is someone other than a tenant living in the premises amounts to knowledge of the landlord.[69]

Case 2: Nuisance or annoyance, user for immoral or illegal purposes

> Where the tenant or any person residing or lodging with him or any sub-tenant of his has been guilty of conduct which is a nuisance or annoyance to adjoining occupiers, or has been convicted of using the dwelling-house or allowing the dwelling-house to be used for immoral or illegal purposes.

Nuisance or annoyance

'Nuisance' and 'annoyance' are both used in the natural sense of the

---

61   *Heglibiston v Heyman* n35.
62   *Florent v Horez* (1983) 268 EG 807.
63   *Tendler v Sproule* [1947] 1 All ER 193; cf *Lewis v Weldcrest Ltd* (1978) 247 EG 211.
64   *Carter v Green* [1950] 1 All ER 627.
65   *Oak Property Co Ltd v Chapman* [1947] 2 All ER 1; *Trustees of Smith's (Henry) Charity v Willson* [1983] 1 All ER 73.
66   Ibid.
67   *Carter v Green* n64; cf *Henry Smith's Charity v Willson* n65.
68   *Hyde v Pimley* [1952] 2 All ER 102.
69   *Metropolitan Properties Co Ltd v Cordery* (1979) 251 EG 567.

words. This ground may be satisfied by drunkenness, abusive behaviour, noise, obstructive behaviour towards other occupiers or violence.[70] Unknown people coming to the premises at all hours of the day and night may amount to an annoyance.[71] It is not necessary that the act which lead to the annoyance should have taken place on the premises. For example, a married tenant who exercised 'undue familiarity' with the landlord's daughter in an alley some 200 yards away from the premises let was held to be guilty of 'annoyance'.[72] It is possible for the court to infer that annoyance or nuisance has been caused to adjoining occupants without direct evidence from them[73], but it is more usual for the landlord to call adjoining occupants to give evidence. The word 'adjoining' does not mean that the premises must be physically touching the tenant's premises: it means that the persons affected by nuisance or annoyance must live near enough to be affected by the tenant's conduct, because, for example, they share a common entrance.[74]

Immoral or illegal purposes

'Immoral purposes' is the statutory formula for prostitution.[75]

The mere fact that a tenant has been convicted of a crime which took place on the premises may not be sufficient to establish this limb of the ground for possession. It must be shown that 'for the purpose of committing the crime, the premises have been used. . . . [It is] not enough that the tenant has been convicted of a crime with which the premises have nothing to do beyond merely being the scene of its commission'.[76] However, the ground may be satisfied even though a tenant has been convicted of an offence which does not specifically refer to 'using premises'.[77] Depending on the circumstances, a conviction for possession of cannabis or some other unlawful drug on the premises may amount to a ground for possession. There is, however, a difference between tenants having drugs in their immediate possession on the premises (for example in a pocket or a handbag) and using the premises as a storage or hiding place.[78] Examples of other activities which may satisfy this ground for

70   Per Wood J in *Cobstone Investments Ltd v Maxim* [1984] 2 All ER 635.
71   *Florent v Horez* n62.
72   *Whitbread v Ward* (1952) 159 EG 494.
73   *Platts (Frederick) Co v Grigor* [1950] 1 All ER 941, CA.
74   *Cobstone v Maxim* n70.
75   *Yates v Morris* [1951] 1 KB 77.
76   Per Scrutton LJ in *Schneiders & Sons v Abrahams* [1925] 1 KB 301 at 311.
77   *Abrahams v Wilson* [1971] 2 QB 88.
78   Ibid per Widgery LJ.

possession are using premises as a coiner's den or as a deposit for stolen goods.[79]

Case 3: Neglect of or damage to premises

> Where the condition of the dwelling-house has, in the opinion of the court, deteriorated owing to acts of waste by, or the neglect or default of, the tenant or any person residing or lodging with him or any sub-tenant of his and, in the case of any act of waste by, or the neglect or default of, a person lodging with the tenant or a sub-tenant of his, where the court is satisfied that the tenant has not, before the making of the order in question, taken such steps as he ought reasonably to have taken for the removal of the lodger or sub-tenant, as the case may be.

This ground for possession may apply even though there has been no breach of any term of the tenancy or of any common law duty.[80] The court should however take into account only neglect or waste which has taken place since the tenant became tenant of the premises. For example where a son who was living with aged parents became a statutory tenant by succession after their death, it was wrong for the court to take into account his failure to do any works in the garden before their death.[81] There is no need for a landlord to give advance warning of an intention to issue proceedings relying on this ground,[82] although failure to do so may be relevant when the court considers reasonableness and costs.

Case 4: Ill treatment of furniture

> Where the condition of any furniture provided for use under the tenancy has, in the opinion of the court, deteriorated owing to ill-treatment by the tenant or any person residing or lodging with him or any sub-tenant of his and, in the case of any ill-treatment by a person lodging with the tenant or a sub-tenant of his, where the court is satisfied that the tenant has not, before the making of the order in question, taken such steps as he ought reasonably to have taken for the removal of the lodger or sub-tenant, as the case may be."

See notes under Case 3 above.

---

79   *Schneiders v Abrahams* n76; *Everett v Stevens* [1957] CLY 3062.
80   *Lowe v Lendrum* (1950) 159 EG 423 where it was also said that 'neglect' is used in the context of tenant-like conduct.
81   *Holloway v Povey* (1984) 15 HLR 104.
82   See n80.

Case 5: Notice to quit by tenant

Where the tenant has given notice to quit and, in consequence of that notice the landlord has contracted to sell or let the dwelling-house or has taken any other steps as the result of which he would, in the opinion of the court, be seriously prejudiced if he could not obtain possession.

There must be a valid notice to quit before a landlord can rely on this ground for possession.[83] The words 'notice to quit' have their normal technical meaning (see p86 above) and the disappearance of a tenant followed by a return by him of the keys did not amount to 'notice to quit'.[84] Similarly an agreement to move out is not sufficient.[85]

There are no recent cases on the meaning of 'serious prejudice'. In an old case decided on a section with different wording, it was held that there was no prejudice to a landlord where a proposed sale of the premises 'went off' without any liability for damages on the part of the landlord.[86]

Case 6: Subletting without the landlord's consent

Where, without the consent of the landlord, the tenant has, at any time after:
(a)   [. . .]
(b)   22nd March 1973, in the case of a tenancy which became a regulated tenancy by virtue of section 14 of the Counter-Inflation Act 1973;
(bb) the commencement of section 73 of the Housing Act 1980, in the case of a tenancy which became a regulated tenancy by virtue of that section;
(c)   14th August 1974, in the case of a regulated furnished tenancy; or
(d)   8th December 1965, in the case of any other tenancy,
assigned or sublet the whole of the dwelling-house or sublet part of the dwelling-house, the remainder being already sublet.

This ground gives protection to a landlord against the risk of finding someone totally unknown to him or her irremovably installed in the property.[87] The ground applies even if there is no prohibition against assigning or subletting in the tenancy agreement and covers a vesting

83   *De Vries v Sparks* (1927) 137 LT 441. Cf the differing views of the learned authors referred to in Arden 'Grounds for Possession: 4' January 1979 *LAG Bulletin* 15 at footnote 29.
84   *Standingford v Bruce* [1926] 1 KB 466.
85   *De Vries v Sparks* n83.
86   *Hunt v Bliss* n55.
87   *Hyde v Pimley* n68.

assent (that is, a transfer of a lease made to implement the terms of a will) made by executors of a deceased tenant which takes effect as an assignment.[88] It does not however apply unless all of the premises rented have been disposed of by assigning or subletting. In practice the ground normally applies only to subletting or assignment by a contractual tenant. If a statutory tenant sublets the whole of premises, RA protection is lost because the tenant can no longer occupy the premises as his or her residence.[89] It is not possible to assign a statutory tenancy (see above).

Consent to a subletting or assignment may be given implicitly[90], for example by accepting rent for some time after acquiring knowledge of the subletting.[91] Consent may be given after the subletting or assignment, at any time up to the issue of proceedings.[92] If the tenancy agreement contains a provision that the tenant cannot assign or sublet without the permission of the landlord, there is an implied proviso that consent cannot be withheld unreasonably.[93]

It is not necessary for a landlord to prove that a sub-tenancy or sub-tenancies have continued to exist right up to the date when proceedings were issued. It is enough that a tenant has at any time sublet or assigned the whole of the premises.[94] However, there are likely to be strong grounds for arguing that it is unreasonable to make an order for possession if there is no subsisting sub-tenancy at the time when proceedings are issued. This ground for possession can enable a landlord to obtain possession against both the tenant and sub-tenant (notwithstanding the effect of s137 (see p206)) provided that the court is satisfied that it is reasonable to make the order.[95]

Only tenants who have sublet after the various dates specified in Case 6 are caught by this ground. Sub-paragraph (a) related to controlled tenancies and was repealed by HA 1980. Sub-paragraph (b) relates to tenancies which were brought into RA protection by amendments to s4 which provides the maximum rateable values for dwelling-houses falling within full RA protection. Sub-paragraph (bb) relates to tenancies from

---

88   *Pazgate Ltd v McGrath* (1984) 17 HLR 127. See however chapter 19 below.
89   See p111 above. See too *Poland v Cadogan (Earl)* [1980] 3 All ER 544 dealing with similar provisions in the Leasehold Reform Act 1967 where the comparable wording is slightly different. It seems unlikely that statutory tenants who enjoy only personal rights in premises are able to create sub-tenancies of the whole, but cf comments of Ormrod LJ in *Henry Smith's Charity v Willson* n65.
90   *Regional Properties Ltd v Frankenschwerth* [1951] 1 All ER 178.
91   *Hyde v Pimley* n68.
92   Ibid.
93   Landlord and Tenant Act 1927 s19 and Landlord and Tenant Act 1988 s1.
94   *Finkle v Strzelczyk* [1961] 3 All ER 409.
95   *Leith Properties Ltd v Springer* [1982] 3 All ER 731, CA.

the Crown Estates Commission which were brought into full RA protection by HA 1980.

Case 7

Case 7 was repealed by HA 1980 s152 and Sch 26. It related to controlled off-licences.

Case 8: Former employees

Where the dwelling-house is reasonably required by the landlord for occupation as a residence for some person engaged in his whole-time employment, or in the whole-time employment of some tenant from him or with whom, conditional on housing being provided, a contract for such employment has been entered into, and the tenant was in the employment of the landlord or a former landlord, and the dwelling-house was let to him in consequence of that employment and he has ceased to be in that employment.

In order to succeed under this ground a landlord must prove that[96]:

a) the tenant was in the employment of the landlord or a former landlord at the time when the premises were let.[97] 'Tenant' refers to the original contractual tenant. For example if the son of the original tenant becomes a statutory tenant by succession[98], the landlord can rely on this ground for possession if the father was in the landlord's employment at the beginning of that contractual tenancy;[99]

b) premises were let in consequence of that employment. This is a question of fact in each case.[100] The questions to be asked are: 'What was the reason for the landlord letting the premises to the tenant?' 'What was in the mind of the person who let the premises?' 'Was it let because of the tenant's employment or was there another reason?'[101] It is possible for premises to be let in consequence of employment even if there is no reference to the premises in the employee's contract of employment. If premises are let some time after an employee originally took the job, the letting may be in consequence of the employment or

---

96   *Munro v Daw* [1947] 2 All ER 360; *Benninga (Mitcham) Ltd v Bijstra* [1945] 2 All ER 433.
97   *Fuggle (RF) Ltd v Gadsden* [1948] 2 KB 236.
98   RA 1977 Sch 1.
99   *Bolsover Colliery Co Ltd v Abbott* [1946] KB 8.
100   *Long Eaton Co-op v Smith* [1949] 1 All ER 633 considering agricultural wages legislation.
101   *Benninga v Bijstra* n96; cf *Queen's Club Gardens v Bignell* [1924] 1 KB 117.

it may be treated as a separate 'independent' transaction.[102] If a former employer grants a new contractual tenancy after the tenant has stopped working for him or her, the new tenancy cannot be in consequence of that employment.[103] It is not necessary for it to be shown that the tenancy was granted as a result of any particular type of employment, only that it was in consequence of the relationship of employer and employee.[104] It is not possible for landlord and tenant to agree that a particular tenancy was not created in consequence of employment when the facts show clearly that the opposite was the case[105];

c) employment has ceased. A tenant who has changed jobs (for example from a farm worker to a laundry machine operator) but who is still employed by the same employer has not ceased to be in employment;[106] and

d) the premises are reasonably required by the landlord for occupation as a residence by someone engaged in the whole-time employment of the landlord or someone with whom a contract of employment has been entered into which is conditional on housing being provided. When the court considers whether or not the proposed new occupant is employed or whether a contract of employment has been entered into, the relevant date is the date of the court hearing.[107] Note that the premises must be reasonably required.[108]

A tenant may be entitled to compensation if a landlord obtains an order for possession under Case 8 by deceit. See p141 below.

Case 9: Premises required for occupation by a landlord or landlord's family

Where the dwelling-house is reasonably required by the landlord for occupation as a residence for—

    (a)   himself, or

    (b)   any son or daughter of his over 18 years of age, or

    (c)   his father or mother, or

    (d)   if the dwelling-house is let on or subject to a regulated tenancy, the father or mother of his wife or husband,

---

102 *Long Eaton Co-op v Smith* n100.
103 *Lever Brothers v Caton* (1921) 37 TLR 664.
104 *Munro v Daw* n96.
105 *Harvard v Shears* (1967) 111 SJ 683.
106 *Duncan v Hay* [1956] 1 WLR 1329.
107 *Benninga v Bijstra* n96.
108 See comments on similar wording in Case 9 at p136.

and the landlord did not become landlord by purchasing the dwelling-house
or any interest therein after—

(i)   7th November 1956, in the case of a tenancy which was then a
      controlled tenancy;

(ii) 8th March 1973, in the case of a tenancy which became a regulated
      tenancy by virtue of section 14 of the Counter-Inflation Act 1973;

(iii) 24th May 1974, in the case of a regulated furnished tenancy; or

(iv) 23rd March 1965, in the case of any other tenancy.

This ground for possession has to be read in conjunction with Sch 15 Pt
III para 1, which provides:

> A court shall not make an order for possession of a dwelling-house by reason
> only that the circumstances of the case fall within Case 9 in Part I of this
> Schedule if the court is satisfied that, having regard to all the circumstances of
> the case, including the question whether other accommodation is available
> for the landlord or the tenant, greater hardship would be caused by granting
> the order than by refusing to grant it.

'Reasonably required'

Case 9 applies where the premises are reasonably required as a residence by
the landlord or certain specified members of the landlord's family. The
words 'reasonably required' mean more than a 'desire' on the landlord's
part, but less than 'absolute necessity'.[109] The court should consider
whether this requirement is reasonable on the landlord's part, and in
doing so the tenant's interests are not relevant.[110] The tenant's interests
should be taken into account when the overall question of reasonableness
is considered (see below). Matters which are relevant when considering
whether the landlord's requirements are reasonable are, for example, the
nature and place of the landlord's business, the size of his or her family,
their actual residence or lack of it, their health, and 'innumerable other
possible factors'.[111] The requirement need not be an immediate
requirement.[112] It is perfectly proper for a landlord to seek possession
under case 9 where the need for accommodation will exist in the
ascertainable but not too far distant future.[113] However, possession has
been refused in a case where a landlord stated that he required a basement

---

109 *Aitken v Shaw* 1933 SLT 21; *Kennealy v Dunne* [1977] QB 837.
110 *Funnell v Armstrong* [1962] EGD 319.
111 *Chandler v Strevett* [1947] 1 All ER 164 per Bucknill LJ.
112 Cf *Aitken v Shaw* n109.
113 *Kidder v Birch* (1983) 265 EG 773. See too *Alexander v Mohamadzadeh* (1985) 276
     EG 1258 (relevant date for deciding whether premises are required is date of hearing,
     not date of issue of proceedings).

for his daughter to live in on her marriage which might take place in two years' time,[114] and in a case where the trial judge had found that premises let to five surveyors were 'an investment property' which was not required by the landlord.[115] The landlord must need the premises 'with a view to living there for some reasonable period, definite or indefinite', and not for the purpose of sale[116] or for temporary accommodation while repairs are carried out in the landlord's own accommodation.[117] A landlord does, however, come within this ground for possession even if only part of the premises is required.[118]

The premises must be required for the landlord, or for the landlord's children, the landlord's parents or parents-in-law.[119] It has been said that this includes 'all normal emanations of' the landlord,[120] including a housekeeper who lived in the same household as the landlord and was paid to look after children after the landlord had separated from his wife.[121] It has also included the illegitimate son of a landlord's wife, even though he was not the landlord's son and the landlord had not adopted him.[122] It does not, however, include someone who would occupy premises as a separate household and not as part of the landlord's household, for example, where it was intended that a couple should live in a separate self-contained flat in the same building as the landlord, in order to look after him.[123] Where premises are owned by joint landlords they must reasonably be required as a residence for *all* the joint landlords.[124] Personal representatives of the deceased landlord may be a 'landlord' for the purposes of Case 9. Normally it will be necessary for the personal representatives to have a beneficial interest in the premises in order to come within this ground for possession, otherwise they would be acting in breach of trust. However, in exceptional cases personal representatives who do not have a beneficial interest may reasonably require possession,

114 *Kissias v Lehany* [1979] CLY 1625.
115 *Ghelani v Bowie* [1988] 42 EG 119, CA.
116 *Rowe v Truelove* (1976) 241 EG 533.
117 *Johnson-Sneddon v Harper* May 1977 LAG Bulletin 114.
118 *Kelley v Goodwin* [1947] 1 All ER 810.
119 But not step-children: *Towns v Hole* [1956] CLY 7493 and *Harty v Greenwich LB and Done* [1956] CLY 7494.
120 *Richter v Wilson* [1963] 2 QB 426.
121 *Smith v Penny* [1947] KB 230.
122 *Theodotou v Potsos* (1991) 23 HLR 356, CA.
123 *Richter v Wilson* n120; *Bloomfield v Westley* [1963] 2 All ER 337.
124 *Baker v Lewis* [1946] 2 All ER 592; *McIntyre v Hardcastle* [1948] 2 KB 82; but see *Bostock v Tacher de la Pagerie* (1987) 282 EG 999, CA; (1987) 19 HLR 358 (legal estate owned by father who sought possession as residence for daughter who was equitable tenant in common of beneficial interest). Cf also *Tilling v Whiteman* [1980] AC 1 (on Case 11).

for example, so that children of the original, deceased landlord may live in the premises.[125]

Landlord by purchase

A landlord is not entitled to rely on Case 9 if s/he became the landlord by purchasing the premises after specified dates.[126] (The Counter-Inflation Act 1973 s14 (in sub-paragraph (ii)) is a reference to tenancies which came within full RA protection when the rateable value limits in the RA 1977 s4 were increased.) This is to prevent an outsider buying up tenanted property and then evicting the tenant.[127] In this connection the word 'purchasing' means 'buying'.[128] It does not include 'inheriting'[129], acquiring through a family settlement,[130] a transfer to a family member 'in consideration of mutual love and affection'[131] or the granting of an intermediate lease with no premium.[132] A tenant will have a defence to proceedings under Case 9 if his or her tenancy was in existence at the date when the premises were bought. The relevant date is the date of exchange of contracts, and not the date of completion.[133] However, an owner is entitled to rely on Case 9 if s/he bought the property with vacant possession and subsequently let to the tenant[134], or if s/he bought premises with one sitting tenant who left and was then replaced by another tenant.[135] If a landlord has become a 'landlord by purchase' s/he does not acquire the right to bring proceedings under Case 9 even if a new

125 *Patel v Patel* [1982] 1 All ER 68; cf *Sharpe v Nicholls* [1945] 2 All ER 55 and *Parker v Rosenberg* [1947] 1 All ER 87.
126 See p137 above. In some circumstances it may still be necessary to determine whether a tenancy is furnished or unfurnished (see s14 sub paras (iii) and (iv)) in which case note *Woodward v Docherty* [1974] 2 All ER 844 and *Mann v Cornella* (1980) 254 EG 403 – a tenancy is unfurnished if the value attributable to furniture is not substantial.
127 *Fowle v Bell* [1946] 2 All ER 668; *Epps v Rothnie* [1946] 1 All ER 146.
128 *Powell v Cleland* [1947] 2 All ER 672.
129 *Baker v Lewis* n124. Note, though, that where an owner said, before she died, that she wished her executors to offer a property for sale to the plaintiff, who then bought it, he was 'a landlord by purchase' and was not entitled to possession. *Ammadio v Dalton* (1991) 22 HLR 332.
130 *Thomas v Fryer* [1970] 2 All ER 1, even though money was paid by one beneficiary under the will to the others.
131 *Mansukhani v Stanley* (1992) *Times* 17 April.
132 *Powell v Cleland* n128.
133 *Emberson v Robinson* [1953] 1 WLR 1129; *Newton and Wife v Biggs* [1953] 1 All ER 99.
134 *Epps v Rothnie* n127.
135 *Fowle v Bell* n127. See too *Newton and Wife v Biggs* n133 where the former owner sold premises to the plaintiff on condition that he was granted a tenancy. The new landlord was not a landlord by purchase.

contractual tenancy on different terms is created or there are minor changes in the subject matter of the tenancy, for example by the addition or deduction of rooms.[136] Similarly if a 'landlord by purchase' dies, the person to whom the property is transferred acquires no greater right under case 9 than the original landlord by purchase.[137]

'Greater hardship'

Tenants have a complete defence to possession proceedings brought under Case 9 if they can prove that greater hardship would be caused to them by a possession order than would be caused to the landlord by refusing to grant the possession order. The burden of proving this lies on the tenant.[138] The court should consider how the balance of hardship will operate at the time when a possession order would take effect.[139] The 'greater hardship test' gives the court a very wide discretion to take into account all factors which may affect both landlord and tenant.[140] Matters which may be taken into consideration include:

- The availability of other accommodation for both landlord and tenant. Judges can apply their own knowledge of the difficulty in finding accommodation[141] but it is always advisable for tenants to be able to give evidence about the unsuccessful attempts which they have made to find other accommodation and any particular local accommodation difficulties. The fact that a tenant has taken no steps to look for other accommodation may be prejudicial.[142]
- The financial means of both parties – for example the ability or inability of a tenant to buy a house.[143]
- The health of the parties both physical and mental and the nearness of relatives.[144]
- Hardship which may occur in the future, as well as present hardship.[145]
- The need for a tenant to sell or to store furniture on moving.[146]

---

136 *Wright v Walford* [1955] 1 All ER 207.
137 *Littlechild v Holt* [1949] 1 All ER 933.
138 *Smith v Penny* n121; *Sims v Wilson* [1946] 2 All ER 261; *Kelley v Goodwin* n118; *Kidder v Birch* n113; *Robinson v Donovan* [1946] 2 All ER 731; *Chandler v Strevett* n111; *Manaton v Edwards* (1985) 276 EG 1256; (1985) 18 HLR 116, CA.
139 *Wheeler v Evans* [1948] 1 KB 459; *Kidder v Birch* n113.
140 *Robinson v Donovan* n138.
141 *King v Taylor* [1954] 3 All ER 373; *Bassett v Fraser* (1981) 9 HLR 105. See too *Manaton v Edwards* n138.
142 *Kelley v Goodwin* n118; *Alexander v Mohamadzadeh* n113.
143 *Kelley v Goodwin* n118.
144 *Thomas v Fryer* n130; *King v Taylor* n141.
145 *Sims v Wilson* n138; *Wheeler v Evans* n139; *Bumstead v Wood* (1946) 175 LT 149.
146 *Sims v Wilson* n138.

- Hardship which may be caused to all people who may be affected by the grant or refusal of an order for possession including 'relatives, dependants, lodgers, guests and the stranger within the gates – but [the court] should weigh such hardship with due regard to the status of the persons affected and their 'proximity' to the tenant or landlord'.[147]

The court should not however take into account trivial things such as 'the absence of a view of a neighbouring hill, river, tree or something pleasant of that kind'.[148]

There is a 'convention' that where the only issues before a court are questions of greater hardship and reasonableness, no order for costs should be made against the party who loses.[149]

It is hard for a landlord or tenant who is dissatisfied with a trial judge's finding in relation to greater hardship to succeed on appeal. The Court of Appeal takes the view that in all but exceptional cases greater hardship is a matter for the trial judge, and his or her findings should not be upset.[150] Generally inferences made by judges about greater hardship are based on their findings of fact and no appeal can be made against a judge's findings of fact. There have, however, been successful appeals where tenants argued that the judge's inferences drawn from the facts were wrong and where the judge failed to consider the question of greater hardship properly. It appears that, contrary to the normal rule[151], the Court of Appeal may be able to take into account material changes in circumstances which have occurred since the original hearing.[152]

Compensation for misrepresentation or concealment

Section 102 provides:

> Where, in such circumstances as are specified in Case 8 or Case 9 in Schedule 15 to this Act, a landlord obtains an order for possession of a dwelling-house let on a protected tenancy or subject to a statutory tenancy and it is subsequently made to appear to the court that the order was obtained by misrepresentation or concealment of material facts, the court may order the landlord to pay to the former tenant such sum as appears sufficient as compensation for damage or loss sustained by the tenant as a result of the order.

Generally a landlord who deprives a tenant of a RA protected tenancy by

---

147 *Harte v Frampton* [1947] 2 All ER 604.
148 *Coplans v King* [1947] 2 All ER 393.
149 *Funnell v Armstrong* n110.
150 *Coplans v King* n142 and *Hodges v Blee* (1987) 283 EG 1215.
151 *Goldthorpe v Bain* [1952] 2 All ER 23.
152 *King v Taylor* n141.

deceit is liable to a claim for damages[153], and the tenant may be able to apply to set aside the possession order. This section, however, provides additional remedies where a landlord has obtained possession under Case 8 or 9 by misrepresentation or concealment. Section 102 applies not only to misrepresentations made during the course of the hearing, but also to any made earlier which result in a tenant consenting to a possession order.[154]

There are few reported cases dealing with the quantum of damages. In *Neil v Kingsnorth*[155] a landlord converted a property into four flats and sold them off immediately after obtaining a possession order under Case 9. The tenant, who had found better accommodation by the date of the court hearing, obtained special damages of £180, general damages of £750 for worry and inconvenience and exemplary damages of £5,000. It seems that, unlike a claim founded in deceit, the court may, unless exemplary or aggravated damages are awarded, be limited by the wording of the section to considering the loss suffered by the tenant, and not any benefit accruing to the landlord, although tenants' advisers should bear in mind Lord Denning's comments that a statutory tenancy is a valuable asset[156] and the decision in *Murray v Lloyd*[157] where, in another context, damages for the loss of a statutory tenancy were assessed at a quarter of the vacant possession freehold value of the premises.

Case 10: Overcharging of sub-tenant

Where the court is satisfied that the rent charged by the tenant—

(a) for any sublet part of the dwelling-house which is a dwelling-house let on a protected tenancy or subject to a statutory tenancy is or was in excess of the maximum rent for the time being recoverable for that part, having regard to [. . .] Part III of this Act, or

(b) for any sublet part of the dwelling-house which is subject to a restricted contract is or was in excess of the maximum (if any) which it is lawful for the lessor, within the meaning of Part V of this Act to require or receive having regard to the provisions of that Part.

153 Under the tort of deceit. See *Mafo v Adams* [1970] 1 QB 548, CA.
154 *Thorne v Smith* [1947] 1 All ER 39.
155 (1987) 9 December (unreported), Shoreditch County Court, noted at March 1988 *Legal Action* 21.
156 See remarks by Lawton LJ in *Drane v Evangelou* [1978] 2 All ER 437 at 443, that to deprive a tenant of the roof over his head is one of the most serious torts imaginable. See too Clayton and Tomlinson 'Damages for loss of a RA tenancy' January 1986 *Legal Action* 10.
157 [1989] 1 WLR 1060, [1990] 1 EGLR 274, 21 HLR 525, Ch D.

Case 10 applies where a tenant overcharges a sub-tenant. It may come about in a number of ways, for example by charging more than the registered rent[158], where there has been a failure to comply with the statutory provisions relating to agreed increases in rent[159] or where the tenant has charged a sub-tenant who enjoys a restricted contract more than the rent registered by a rent tribunal.[160] This ground for possession does not apply where the interest of the sub-occupant is outside the protection of the RA or where there is merely an arrangement to share the premises with other people.[161] If a sub-tenant is overcharged, the court may make an order for possession of the whole of the premises rented by the tenant or just that part to which the overcharging relates.[162]

There appears to be no reported authority on the position of a sub-tenant when a landlord has established that there has been overcharging within the meaning of Case 10. In ordinary circumstances an order for possession against a tenant also operates against a sub-tenant, but it would seem that if the sub-tenancy is lawful, the sub-tenant would become a direct tenant of the landlord as a result of s137.[163]

Mandatory Grounds

Case 11: Returning owner-occupier

[Where a person (in this Case referred to as 'the owner-occupier') who let the dwelling-house on a regulated tenancy had, at any time before the letting, occupied it as his residence] and—

    (a)   not later than the relevant date the landlord gave notice in writing to the tenant that possession might be recovered under this Case, and

    (b)   the dwelling-house has not, since—

        (i) 22nd March 1973, in the case of a tenancy which became a regulated tenancy by virtue of section 14 of the Counter-Inflation Act 1973;

---

158 RA 1977 ss44 and 45.
159 Ibid s51.
160 Ibid s88.
161 *Kenyon v Walker* [1946] 2 All ER 595.
162 *Boulton v Sutherland* [1938] 1 All ER 488.
163 See p205 below. It is debatable whether or not a landlord would be able to rely on this ground against the sub-tenant – cf *Leith Properties Ltd v Springer* n95, where it was held that a landlord was entitled to rely on case 6 against a sub-tenant notwithstanding the effect of s137. Even if that reasoning does apply to proceedings under case 10, it is hard to imagine circumstances where it would be reasonable for the court to make an order against the sub-tenant.

(ii)   14th August 1974, in the case of a regulated furnished tenancy; or
(iii)   8th December 1965, in the case of any other tenancy,
been let by the owner-occupier on a protected tenancy with respect to which the condition mentioned in paragraph (a) above was not satisfied, and
[(c)   the court is of the opinion that of the conditions set out in Part V of this Schedule one of those in paragraphs (a) and (c) to (f) is satisfied.]

If the court is of the opinion that, notwithstanding that the condition in paragraphs (a) or (b) above is not complied with, it is just and equitable to make an order for possession of the dwelling-house, the court may dispense with the requirements of either or both of those paragraphs as the case may require.

The giving of a notice before 14th August 1974 under section 79 of the Rent Act 1968 shall be treated, in the case of a regulated furnished tenancy, as compliance with paragraph (a) of this Case.

[Where the dwelling-house has been let by the owner-occupier on a protected tenancy (in this paragraph referred to as 'the earlier tenancy') granted on or after 16th November 1984 but not later than the end of the period of two months beginning with the commencement of the Rent (Amendment) Act 1985 and either—
(i)   the earlier tenancy was granted for a term certain (whether or not to be followed by a further term or to continue thereafter from year to year or some other period) and was during that term a protected shorthold tenancy as defined in section 52 of the Housing Act 1980, or
(ii)   the conditions mentioned in paragraphs (a) to (c) of Case 20 were satisfied with respect to the dwelling-house and the earlier tenancy,
then for the purposes of paragraph (b) above the condition in paragraph (a) above is to be treated as having been satisfied with respect to the earlier tenancy.]

This ground for possession has been amended twice since the 1977 Act, first by HA 1980 s66(1) which inserted sub-paragraph (c) and second by the Rent (Amendment) Act 1985 which inserted the provisions in brackets at the beginning and end of the case. Like Cases 12 and 20 it should be read in conjunction with Sch 15 Pt V, which was inserted by HA 1980 s66(3) and Sch 7 and which provides:

Provisions applying to Cases 11, 12 and 20
    1.   In this Part of this Schedule—
'mortgage' includes a charge and 'mortgagee' shall be construed accordingly;
'owner' means, in relation to Case 11, the owner-occupier; and

'successor in title' means any person deriving title from the owner, other than a purchaser for value or a person deriving title from a purchaser for value.

2.   The conditions referred to in paragraph (*c*) in each of Cases 11 and 12 and in paragraph (*e*)(ii) of Case 20 are that—

(*a*)   the dwelling-house is required as a residence for the owner or any member of his family who resided with the owner when he last occupied the dwelling-house as a residence;

(*b*)   the owner has retired from regular employment and requires the dwelling-house as a residence;

(*c*)   the owner has died and the dwelling-house is required as a residence for a member of his family who was residing with him at the time of his death;

(*d*)   the owner has died and the dwelling-house is required by a successor in title as his residence or for the purpose of disposing of it with vacant possession;

(*e*)   the dwelling-house is subject to a mortgage, made by deed and granted before the tenancy, and the mortgagee—

(i)   is entitled to exercise a power of sale conferred on him by the mortgage or by section 101 of the Law of Property Act 1925; and

(ii)   requires the dwelling-house for the purpose of disposing of it with vacant possession in exercise of that power; and

(*f*)   the dwelling-house is not reasonably suitable to the needs of the owner, having regard to his place of work, and he requires it for the purpose of disposing of it with vacant possession and of using the proceeds of that disposal in acquiring, as his residence, a dwelling-house which is more suitable to those needs.

In Case 11, as with all the other grounds for possession in Sch 15 Pt II (ie, Cases 11 to 20) the phrase 'relevant date' is defined by Sch 15 Pt III para 2, which provides:

2.   Any reference in Part II of this Schedule to the relevant date shall be construed as follows:—

(*a*)   except in a case falling within paragraph (*b*) or (*c*) below, if the protected tenancy, or, in the case of a statutory tenancy, the previous contractual tenancy, was created before 8th December 1965, the relevant date means 7th June 1966; and

(*b*)   except in a case falling within paragraph (*c*) below, if the tenancy became a regulated tenancy by virtue of section 14 of the Counter-Inflation Act 1973 and the tenancy or, in the case of a statutory tenancy, the previous contractual tenancy, was created before 22nd March 1973, the relevant date means 22nd September 1973; and

(*c*)   in the case of a regulated furnished tenancy, if the tenancy or, in the case of a statutory furnished tenancy, the previous contractual tenancy was created before 14th August 1974, the relevant date means 13th February 1975; and

(d)   in any other case, the relevant date means the date of the commencement of the regulated tenancy in question.

The purpose of Case 11 is to allow owner-occupiers who intend to go away and then to return to their home, to let the premises while they are away.[164] To rely on Case 11 a landlord must prove:

a)   that prior to the granting of the tenancy in question, the landlord has at some time in the past occupied the premises as his or her residence. The effect of the Rent (Amendment) Act 1985 is that it is no longer necessary for landlords to prove that they occupied the premises immediately before the granting of the tenancy.[165] Residence at any time in the past is sufficient. It is sufficient for such previous residence to have been temporary and intermittent, although visits to a house by a landlord to stay with a girlfriend who lives there do not count as 'occupation as a residence'.[166] The landlord must previously have occupied the same premises as those which are let to the tenant whom the landlord is seeking to evict: it is not sufficient for the landlord to have lived in other rooms in the same building;

b)   in most cases that notice of his or her intention to rely on Case 11 was given before the commencement of the tenancy. The schedule provides that such notice must be in writing, although no particular form is necessary. It has been said that it is 'of the utmost importance to a tenant that he should appreciate when he takes rented property whether or not he is obtaining security of tenure'.[167] Such notice must actually be received by the tenant, otherwise it has not been given in accordance with the terms of the schedule. It is not enough for the landlord merely to say that it was sent to the tenant if a tenant's evidence that s/he did not receive the notice is believed.[168] However, the schedule provides that the requirement for written notice may be dispensed with if the court considers that 'it is just and equitable to

---

164   Griffiths LJ in *Bradshaw and Martin v Baldwin-Wiseman* (1985) 17 HLR 260 at 264.

165   Reversing the effect of *Pocock v Steel* [1985] 1 WLR 229. The Rent (Amendment) Act 1985 operates retrospectively and applies to tenancies created before it received the Royal Assent: *Hewitt v Lewis* [1986] 1 All ER 927, CA.

166   *Naish v Curzon* (1984) 17 HLR 220, CA; *Mistry v Isidore* (1990) 22 HLR 281, [1990] 2 EGLR 97, CA, and *Ibie v Trubshaw* (1990) 22 HLR 191, CA.

167   See n164.

168   *Minay v Sentongo* (1983) 45 P & CR 190.

make an order for possession of the dwelling-house'. These words have 'a very wide importance' and mean that the court should take into account all of the circumstances, including questions of greater hardship, and not just the circumstances which surround a failure to give written notice.[169] They include circumstances affecting the landlord, the landlord's successors in title, the tenant's circumstances and the effect of the failure to give notice.[170] Where, prior to the granting of a tenancy, tenants are told orally that the premises are the landlord's home, that the landlord will be returning and there is no misunderstanding about this, the court is likely to consider that oral notice is just as effective as written notice and so dispense with the formal requirements.[171] However, if no formal notice was given at the beginning of the tenancy because at that time the landlord had no intention of creating a 'Case 11 tenancy' it cannot be just and equitable to dispense with the requirement.[172] The fact that the parties signed what purported (wrongly) to be a temporary 'licence' agreement is not enough to make it 'just and equitable' to dispense with the need for a notice[173];

c) that all tenants to whom the premises have previously been let since the dates specified in Case 11 have been given written notice. Again there is a provision which entitles the court to dispense with this requirement if it is considered just and equitable; and

d) that one of the requirements in sub-paragraphs (a), (c), (d), (e) or (f) in Sch 15 Pt V is satisfied. The most important of these is that the premises are 'required as a residence'. All that is required is that the landlord 'bona fide wants' or 'genuinely has the immediate intention' of occupying the premises.[174] The landlord need not require the premises as a permanent residence and fairly intermittent residence will be sufficient.[175] This is a question of fact in each case. It is sufficient if only one of two joint landlords requires the premises as a residence.[176] Another important use of Case 11 would be where a landlord's place of work has changed and s/he wishes to sell the house with vacant possession in order to buy a new house which is more

---

169 *Bradshaw v Baldwin-Wiseman* n164; *Fernandes v Parvardin* (1982) 264 EG 49.
170 *Bradshaw v Baldwin-Wiseman* n164.
171 *Fernandes v Parvardin* n169.
172 *Bradshaw v Baldwin-Wiseman* n164.
173 *Ibie v Trubshaw* (1990) 22 HLR 191, CA.
174 *Kennealy v Dunne* n109; cf *Ghelani v Bowie* (1988) 42 EG 119, CA.
175 *Naish v Curzon* (1984) 17 HLR 220 where it was argued by the tenant that the landlord required the premises only for holidays and short visits, and *Davies v Peterson* (1989) 21 HLR 63, [1989] 06 EG 130, CA.
176 *Tilling v Whiteman* n124.

suitable, bearing in mind his or her place of work.[177] The other situations in which possession may be obtained under Case 11 arise following the death of the landlord or relate to rights which a mortgagee has.

The Rent Act (County Court Proceedings for Possession) Rules 1981[178], provide a speedy procedure for landlords who wish to obtain possession relying on Case 11. These rules can be used even if in fact no proper Case 11 notice has been given before the commencement of the tenancy if the landlord believes that it was given.[179] They provide that possession proceedings based on case 11 and the other mandatory grounds for possession may be started by originating application (rather than by particulars of claim) with an affidavit in support. The main advantage for landlords is that the time between service of proceedings and the hearing date need be only seven days[180], as opposed to the usual period of 21 days. A tenant wishing to defend proceedings under the Rent Act (County Court Proceedings for Possession) Rules should serve an affidavit in reply setting out the basis upon which the claim is defended as quickly as possible. It may also be necessary to make an application for discovery of relevant documents (eg, all previous tenancy agreements and Case 11 notices) and for an adjournment. Often court listing officers allow very little time for the hearing of cases brought under this speedy procedure, and so the court may not be able to deal with a fully contested case, even if the judge wishes to do so. Practice varies between courts, and advisers should not rely upon courts being willing to adjourn this kind of case. Unless the landlord or any solicitors instructed agree to an adjournment, the tenant should be prepared for a full hearing on the date of the hearing on the originating application.

Case 12: Retirement homes

Where the landlord (in this Case referred to as 'the owner') intends to occupy the dwelling-house as his residence at such time as he might retire from regular employment and has let it on a regulated tenancy before he has so retired and—

(a)   not later than the relevant date the landlord gave notice in writing

---

177   There must be a connection within a reasonable time between the proposed sale and purchase: *Bissessar v Ghosn* (1986) 18 HLR 486, CA.
178   SI No 139.
179   *Minay v Sentongo* n168.
180   The period is seven days for such proceedings brought under Cases 11, 12 and 20 but 14 days for proceedings brought under the other mandatory grounds.

to the tenant that possession might be recovered under this Case; and

(*b*)   the dwelling-house has not, since 14th August 1974, been let by the owner on a protected tenancy with respect to which the condition mentioned in paragraph (*a*) above was not satisfied; and

(*c*)   the court is of the opinion that of the conditions set out in Part V of this Schedule one of those paragraphs (*b*) to (*e*) is satisfied.

If the court is of the opinion that, notwithstanding that the condition in paragraph (*a*) or (*b*) above is not complied with, it is just and equitable to make an order for possession of the dwelling-house, the court may dispense with the requirements of either or both those paragraphs, as the case may require.

This ground for possession is similar in format to Case 11. For the definition of 'relevant date' see Sch 15 Pt III para 2 at p145 above. Provisions as to the giving of written notice and the circumstances in which notice may be dispensed with are also similar to those relating to Case 11.

Case 12 may be relied upon if:

a)   the owner has retired and requires the premises as 'a retirement home'; or

b)   the owner has died and the premises are required as a residence for a member of the family. 'Member of the family' is not defined and is wider than the definition in Case 9; or

c)   the owner has died and a successor in title either requires the premises as a residence or wishes to dispose of them with vacant possession; or

d)   in some circumstances a mortgagee requires the premises for the purpose of disposing of them with vacant possession.

A landlord seeking possession under this ground may use the quicker procedure provided by the Rent Act (County Court Proceedings for Possession) Rules 1981 (see above). The minimum period of time between service and the hearing is seven days.

Case 13: Out of season holiday lets

Where the dwelling-house is let under a tenancy for a term of years certain not exceeding 8 months and—

(*a*)   not later than the relevant date the landlord gave notice in writing to the tenant that possession might be recovered under this Case; and

(*b*)   the dwelling-house was, at some time within the period of 12 months ending on the relevant date, occupied under a right to occupy it for a holiday.

For the purposes of this Case a tenancy shall be treated as being for a term of years certain notwithstanding that it is liable to determination by re-entry or on the happening of any event other than the giving of notice by the landlord to determine the term.

This ground was designed to enable landlords who let premises on holiday lets during, for example, the summer, to be able to recover possession if they let them on longer lets during the winter. However, the case as enacted operates in far wider circumstances than that. To rely on Case 13, a landlord must prove that:

a) the premises were occupied at some time during the last 12 months for the purpose of 'a holiday'. Even if a landlord produces a copy of a 'holiday let agreement' relating to such a period, it may be possible for the tenant to prove that that agreement was 'a sham' or 'did not reflect the intention of the parties' to it.[181] However, it should be remembered that the burden of proving this lies on the tenant;

b) the relevant tenancy was granted for a fixed period of not more than eight months. It would, however, appear that case 13 is available even where a tenant who initially agreed to rent the premises for eight months has held over and occupied the premises for a far longer period; and

c) not later than the commencement of the tenancy the landlord gave written notice to the tenant that this ground for possession might be relied upon. It is important to note that, unlike Cases 11 and 12, the court has no power to dispense with this requirement.[182]

If a landlord uses the Rent Act (County Court Proceedings for Possession) Rules 1981, the minimum period between service and the hearing is 14 days (see p148 above).

Case 14: Educational institutions

Where the dwelling-house is let under a tenancy for a term of years certain not exceeding 12 months and—

(a)   not later than the relevant date the landlord gave notice in writing to the tenant that possession might be recovered under this Case; and

(b)   at some time within the period of 12 months ending on the relevant date, the dwelling-house was subject to such a tenancy as is referred to in section 8(1) of this Act.

---

181 See p82 above and *Buchmann v May* [1978] 2 All ER 993 and *R v Rent Officer for Camden ex parte Plant* (1980) 257 EG 713.
182 Cf *Fowler v Minchin* (1987) 19 HLR 224, CA.

For the purposes of this Case a tenancy shall be treated as being for a term of years certain notwithstanding that it is liable to determination by re-entry or on the happening of any event other than the giving of notice by the landlord to determine the term.

This ground applies to any premises which, during the period of 12 months preceding the current tenancy, were let by a specified educational institution[183] to a student who was pursuing or intended to pursue a course of study provided by that institution or by another specified educational institution.[184] The term 'specified educational institution' includes universities, any other publicly-funded instition providing further education, and a number of associations and companies which have been specifically designated as such for Rent Act and Housing Act purposes. Again, notice in writing must have been given to the current tenant and the court has no power to dispense with service of that notice.

If the landlord uses the Rent Act (County Court Proceedings for Possession) Rules 1981, the minimum period between service and the hearing is 14 days (cf p148 above).

Case 15: Ministers of religion

Where the dwelling-house is held for the purpose of being available for occupation by a minister of religion as a residence from which to perform the duties of his office and—

(a)   not later than the relevant date the tenant was given notice in writing that possession might be recovered under this Case, and

(b)   the court is satisfied that the dwelling-house is required for occupation by a minister of religion as such a residence.

Case 16: Agricultural employees

Where the dwelling-house was at any time occupied by a person under the terms of his employment as a person employed in agriculture, and

a)   the tenant neither is nor at any time was so employed by the landlord and is not the widow of a person who was so employed, and

b)   not later than the relevant date, the tenant was given notice in writing that possession might be recovered under this Case, and

---

183   Assured and Protected Tenancies (Lettings to Students) Regulations 1988 SI No 2236, and the Assured and Protected Tenancies (Lettings to Students) (Amendment) Regulations 1990 SI No 1825 and the Assured and Protected Tenancies (Lettings to Students) (Amendments) Regulations 1991 SI No 233.
184   See RA 1977 s8.

    c)   the court is satisfied that the dwelling-house is required for occupation by a person employed, or to be employed, by the landlord in agriculture.

For the purposes of this Case 'employed', 'employment' and 'agriculture' have the same meanings as in the Agricultural Wages Act 1948.

The court cannot dispense with the requirement that notice must be served prior to the commencement of the tenancy. A term in a tenancy agreement that the tenant will vacate on 28 days' notice if the premises are required for another farm worker is not sufficient,[185] but a certificate of a fair rent which was handed to the tenant before the commencement of the tenancy and which stated that the tenancy was to be subject to Case 16 has been held to be sufficient.[186]

Case 17: Redundant farmhouses

Where proposals for amalgamation, approved for the purposes of a scheme under section 26 of the Agriculture Act 1967, have been carried out and, at the time when the proposals were submitted, the dwelling-house was occupied by a person responsible (whether as owner, tenant, or servant or agent of another) for the control of the farming of any part of the land comprised in the amalgamation and

    (a)   after the carrying out of the proposals, the dwelling-house was let on a regulated tenancy otherwise than to, or to the widow of, either a person ceasing to be so responsible as part of the amalgamation or a person who is, or at any time was, employed by the landlord in agriculture, and

    (b)   not later than the relevant date the tenant was given notice in writing that possession might be recovered under this Case, and

    (c)   the court is satisfied that the dwelling-house is required for occupation by a person employed, or to be employed, by the landlord in agriculture, and

    (d)   the proceedings for possession are commenced by the landlord at any time during the period of 5 years beginning with the date on which the proposals for the amalgamation were approved or, if occupation of the dwelling-house after the amalgamation continued in, or was first taken by, a person ceasing to be responsible as mentioned in paragraph *(a)* above or his widow, during a period expiring 3 years after the date on which the dwelling-house next became unoccupied.

For the purposes of this Case 'employed' and 'agriculture' have the same meanings as in the Agricultural Wages Act 1948 and 'amalgamation' has the same meaning as in Part II of the Agriculture Act 1967.

185 See *Fowler v Minchin* (1987) 19 HLR 224, CA where a possession order was refused.
186 *Springfield Investments v Bell* (1990) 22 HLR 440, CA.

Case 18: More redundant farmhouses

Where—
- (a) the last occupier of the dwelling-house before the relevant date was a person, or the widow of a person, who was at some time during his occupation responsible (whether as owner, tenant, or servant or agent of another) for the control of the farming of land which formed, together with the dwelling-house, an agricultural unit within the meaning of the Agriculture Act 1947, and
- (b) the tenant is neither—
  - (i) a person, or the widow of a person, who is or has at any time been responsible for the control of the farming of any part of the said land, nor
  - (ii) a person, or the widow of a person, who is or at any time was employed by the landlord in agriculture, and
- (c) the creation of the tenancy was not preceded by the carrying out in connection with any of the said land of an amalgamation approved for the purposes of a scheme under section 26 of the Agriculture Act 1967, and
- (d) not later than the relevant date the tenant was given notice in writing that possession might be recovered under this Case, and
- (e) the court is satisfied that the dwelling-house is required for occupation either by a person responsible or to be responsible (whether as owner, tenant, or servant or agent of another) for the control of the farming of any part of the said land or by a person employed or to be employed by the landlord in agriculture, and
- (f) in a case where the relevant date was before 9th August 1972, the proceedings for possession are commenced by the landlord before the expiry of 5 years from the date on which the occupier referred to in paragraph (a) above went out of occupation.

For the purposes of this Case 'employed' and 'agriculture' have the same meanings as in the Agricultural Wages Act 1948 and 'amalgamation' has the same meaning as in Part II of the Agriculture Act 1967.

Case 19: Protected shorthold tenancies

Where the dwelling-house was let under a protected shorthold tenancy (or is treated under section 55 of the Housing Act 1980 as having been so let) and—
- (a) there either has been no grant of a further tenancy of the dwelling-house since the end of the protected shorthold tenancy or, if there was such a grant, it was to a person who immediately before the grant was in possession of the dwelling-house as a protected or statutory tenant; and
- (b) the proceedings for possession were commenced after appropriate notice by the landlord to the tenant and not later than 3 months after the expiry of the notice.

A notice is appropriate for this Case if—
- (i) it is in writing and states that proceedings for possession under this Case may be brought after its expiry; and
- (ii) it expires not earlier than 3 months after it is served nor, if, when it is served, the tenancy is a periodic tenancy, before that periodic tenancy could be brought to an end by a notice to quit served by the landlord on the same day;
- (iii) it is served—
    - (a) in the period of 3 months immediately preceding the date on which the protected shorthold tenancy comes to an end; or
    - (b) if that date has passed, in the period of 3 months immediately preceding any anniversary of that date; and
- (iv) in a case where a previous notice has been served by the landlord on the tenant in respect of the dwelling-house, and that notice was an appropriate notice, it is served not earlier than 3 months after the expiry of the previous notice.

The creation of 'protected' shorthold tenancies was covered by HA 1980 s52. They should not be confused with assured shorthold tenancies.[187] No further protected shorthold tenancies can be granted since 15 January 1989. Protected shorthold tenancies had to comply with the provisions which were necessary to create a protected tenancy within the meaning of the RA 1977 s1 and had to be for a fixed period of not less than one year and not more than five years. If the tenancy included a 'break clause' which allowed the landlord to bring it to an end before the fixed period for any reason other than non-payment of rent or breach of any other obligations in the tenancy, the tenancy was not a protected shorthold tenancy. Similarly there was no valid protected shorthold tenancy if the tenancy was granted to an existing protected or statutory tenant of the same premises. Until 1 December 1981 outside London and until 4 May 1987 in Greater London, there was a requirement that there should be either a registered rent or a certificate of fair rent in existence before a valid shorthold tenancy could be created. After these dates, those requirements were abolished, and landlords could create shorthold tenancies without registering a fair rent.[188] In addition, the landlord had to give a notice in the prescribed form to the tenant before the creation of the tenancy stating that the tenancy would be a shorthold tenancy and that the landlord had the right to possession on the expiry of the fixed term.[189] There are now

---

187 See HA 1988 ss20–23 and p199 below.
188 See Protected Shorthold Tenancies (Rent Registration) Order 1981 SI No 1578 and Protected Shorthold Tenancies (Rent Registration) Order 1987 SI No 265.
189 Protected Shorthold Tenancies (Notice to Tenant) Regulations 1980 SI No 1707. The court does have power to dispense with this requirement – see Case 19.

relatively few tenants with protected shorthold tenancies. Most were originally granted for the minimum permissable term of one year and, after the implementation of the Housing Act 1988, most landlords granted new tenancies which automatically became assured shorthold tenancies (see p199 below).[190]

So far as possession proceedings are concerned, different provisions apply depending on whether the landlord is seeking to terminate the tenancy before the expiry of the fixed period or at the end of that fixed period. The former can be done only if there is a provision allowing the landlord to forfeit the tenancy and if there are either rent arrears or the tenant has breached some other obligation within the tenancy. In this case the usual provisions relating to forfeiture apply (see above). In addition the landlord must claim possession under Case 1 and satisfy the court that it is reasonable to make an order for possession (see above).

If the landlord wishes to bring possession proceedings at the end of or after the end of the fixed period of the tenancy s/he must begin court proceedings not more than three months after the expiry of a notice given in accordance with Case 19.[191] Such a notice must be in writing and served within the period of three months immediately before the end of the fixed period of the tenancy, or, if the fixed period has already expired, in the period of three months immediately before the anniversary of the expiry date of the fixed period. The notice itself must give at least three months' notice, but if the tenancy has become periodic, it must give at least the equivalent notice which would be required in a notice to quit. If these conditions are complied with the landlord has an automatic ground for possession. The court has no power to dispense with the requirement that a notice be served before possession proceedings are brought.

If the landlord uses the Rent Act (County Court Proceedings for Possession) Rules 1981, the minimum period between service and the hearing date is 14 days (cf p148 above).

Case 20: Lettings by armed forces personnel

Where the dwelling-house was let by a person (in this Case referred to as 'the owner') at any time after the commencement of section 67 of the Housing Act 1980 and—

(a)   at the time when the owner acquired the dwelling-house he was a member of the regular armed forces of the Crown;

190 See Housing Act 1988 s34(3).
191 Failure to do so will give the tenant a complete defence to proceedings and the landlord will have to serve a new notice before bringing further proceedings: *Ridehalgh v Horsefield* [1992] EGCS 45, CA.

(b)   at the relevant date the owner was a member of the regular armed forces of the Crown;

(c)   not later than the relevant date the owner gave notice in writing to the tenant that possession might be recovered under this Case;

(d)   the dwelling-house has not, since the commencement of section 67 of the Act of 1980 been let by the owner on a protected tenancy with respect to which the condition mentioned in paragraph (c) above was not satisfied; and

(e)   the court is of the opinion that—

(i)   the dwelling-house is required as a residence for the owner; or

(ii)   of the conditions set out in Part V of this Schedule one of those in paragraphs (c) to (f) is satisfied.

If the court is of the opinion that, notwithstanding that the condition in paragraph (c) or (d) above is not complied with, it is just and equitable to make an order for possession of the dwelling-house, the court may dispense with the requirements of either or both of these paragraphs, as the case may require.

For the purposes of this Case 'regular armed forces of the Crown' has the same meaning as in section 1 of the House of Commons Disqualification Act 1975.

A member of the regular armed forces may rely on this ground for possession only if s/he was a member of the forces at the time when s/he acquired the premises and at the date when the tenancy began. The provisions relating to the giving of notice are similar to those in Case 11. See p145 for reasons in sub-paragraphs (c) to (f) which may found a claim for possession. The procedure set out in the Rent Act (County Court Proceedings for Possession) Rules 1981 may be used for possession proceedings brought under this case (see p148 above). The minimum period between service of proceedings and the hearing date is seven days.

Other grounds

Statutory overcrowding

Section 101 concerns overcrowded dwelling-houses.

101.   At any time when a dwelling-house is overcrowded, within the meaning of Part X of the Housing Act 1985, in such circumstances as to render the occupier guilty of an offence, nothing in this Part of this Act shall prevent the immediate landlord of the occupier from obtaining possession of the dwelling-house.

This section in effect provides an additional mandatory ground for possession. Statutory overcrowding is defined by HA 1985 Pt X, which provides:

Definition of overcrowding

324. A dwelling is overcrowded for the purposes of this Part when the number of persons sleeping in the dwelling is such as to contravene—

(a) the standard specified in section 325 (the room standard), or

(a) the standard specified in section 326 (the space standard).

325.—(1) The room standard is contravened when the number of persons sleeping in a dwelling and the number of rooms available as sleeping accommodation is such that two persons of opposite sexes who are not living together as husband and wife must sleep in the same room.

(2) For this purpose—

(a) children under the age of ten shall be left out of account, and

(b) a room is available as sleeping accommodation if it is of a type normally used in the locality either as a bedroom or as a living room.

326.—(1) The space standard is contravened when the number of persons sleeping in a dwelling is in excess of the permitted number, having regard to the number and floor area of the rooms of the dwelling available as sleeping accommodation.

(2) For this purpose—

(a) no account shall be taken of a child under the age of one and a child aged one or over but under ten shall be reckoned as one-half of a unit, and

(b) a room is available as sleeping accommodation if it is of a type normally used in the locality either as a living room or as a bedroom.

(3) The permitted number of persons in relation to a dwelling is whichever is the less of—

(a) the number specified in Table I in relation to the number of rooms in the dwelling available as sleeping accommodation, and

(b) the aggregate for all such rooms in the dwelling of the numbers specified in column 2 of Table II in relation to each room of the floor area specified in column 1.

No account shall be taken for the purposes of either Table of a room having a floor area of less than 50 square feet.

TABLE I

Number of rooms	Number of persons
1	2
2	3
3	5
4	7½
5 or more	2 for each room

TABLE II

Floor area of room	Number of persons
110 sq. ft. or more	2
90 sq. ft. or more but less than 110 sq. ft.	1½
70 sq. ft. or more but less than 90 sq. ft.	1
50 sq. ft. or more but less than 70 sq. ft.	½

(4)   The Secretary of State may by regulations prescribe the manner in which the floor area of a room is to be ascertained for the purpose of this section; and the regulations may provide for the exclusion from computation, or the bringing into computation at a reduced figure, of floor space in a part of the room which is of less than a specified height not exceeding eight feet.

(5)   Regulations under subsection (4) shall be made by statutory instrument which shall be subject to annulment in pursuance of a resolution of either House of Parliament.

(6)   A certificate of the local housing authority stating the number and floor areas of the rooms in a dwelling, and that the floor areas have been ascertained in the prescribed manner, is prima facie evidence for the purposes of legal proceedings of the facts stated in it.

Responsibility of occupier

327.—(1)   The occupier of a dwelling who causes or permits it to be overcrowded commits a summary offence, subject to sub-section (2).

(2)   The occupier is not guilty of an offence—

(a)   if the overcrowding is within the exceptions specified in section 328 or 329 (children attaining age of 10 or visiting relatives), or

(b)   by reason of anything done under the authority of, and in accordance with any conditions specified in, a licence granted by the local housing authority under section 330.

(3)   A person committing an offence under this section is liable on conviction to a fine not exceeding level 2 on the standard scale and to a further fine not exceeding one-tenth of the amount corresponding to that level in respect of every day subsequent to the date on which he is convicted on which the offence continues.

328.—(1)   Where a dwelling which would not otherwise be overcrowded becomes overcrowded by reason of a child attaining the age of one or ten, then if the occupier—

(a)   applies to the local housing authority for suitable alternative accommodation, or

(b)   has so applied before the date when the child attained the age in question,

he does not commit an offence under section 327 (occupier causing or permitting overcrowding), so long as the condition in subsection (2) is met and the occupier does not fail to take action in the circumstances specified in subsection (3).

(2)   The condition is that all the persons sleeping in the dwelling are persons who were living there when the child attained that age and thereafter continuously live there, or children born after that date of any of those persons.

(3)   The exception provided by this section ceases to apply if—

(a)   suitable alternative accommodation is offered to the occupier on or after the date on which the child attains that age, or, if he has applied before that date, is offered at any time after the application, and he fails to accept it, or

(b)   the removal from the dwelling of some person not a member of the occupier's family is on that date or thereafter becomes reasonably practicable having regard to all the circumstances (including the availability of suitable alternative accommodation for that person), and the occupier fails to require his removal.

329.   Where the persons sleeping in an overcrowded dwelling include a member of the occupier's family who does not live there but is sleeping there temporarily, the occupier is not guilty of an offence under section 327 (occupier causing or permitting overcrowding) unless the circumstances are such that he would be so guilty if that member of his family were not sleeping there.

It has been held that a room with no natural lighting or ventilation was not a room generally used in the locality as a living or a bedroom,[192] and so it could not be taken into account when determining the number of rooms.

A 'room' is a room which can be used for living or sleeping in.[193] The relevant date when overcrowding must exist is the date of the trial and so a tenant will have a complete defence if overcrowding has ceased by the time of the court hearing.[194] It seems that it is not necessary for there to be a conviction before a landlord can rely on this 'ground'.[195] All that a landlord need to do is to prove that the circumstances are such that a conviction for overcrowding could be obtained and that any contractual tenancy has been validly determined – normally by serving a notice to quit.

Closing orders etc

A tenant is not entitled to rely upon the protection of the RA when a closing order[196] or a demolition order[197] is in force in relation to the

---

192   *Patel v Godal* [1979] CLY 1620.
193   Ibid.
194   *Zbytniewski v Broughton* [1956] 3 All ER 348.
195   Ibid.
196   HA 1985 s276.
197   HA 1985 s270(5) (recovery of possession after the making of a demolition order) and *Marela v Machorowski* [1953] 1 QB 565.

premises.[198] The effect of a closing order or a demolition order is to remove security of tenure. They do not, however, provide landlords with an automatic right to possession. Any tenancy must still be terminated in the normal way (eg, by notice to quit).[199] A local authority does, however, have a statutory duty to rehouse residential occupiers who have been displaced from residential accommodation as a result of a closing order, irrespective of whether they come within the category of 'priority need' within the meaning of the HA 1985 s59.[200]

It should, however, be noted that HA 1985 s582 restricts the recovery of possession of premises which have been compulsorily purchased by a local authority. Any possession order may be suspended for a period of three years after the making of the CPO.

198 See too s264(5) (recovery of possession after landlord has given an undertaking to the local authority in relation to unfit premises).
199 *Aslan v Murphy (No 2)* (1989) *Times* 10 July, 139 NLJ 936, CA.
200 Land Compensation Act 1973 s39(1).

CHAPTER 12

Reasonableness

If a landlord is seeking possession on the grounds that suitable alternative
accommodation is available or on one of grounds 1 to 10, s/he, as well as
proving the ground for possession, must satisfy the court that it is
reasonable to make an order for possession. The same applies if a landlord
is seeking possession against an assured tenant on any of the discretionary
grounds in HA 1988 Sch 2 (see chapter 14). The question of reasonableness, which is an 'overriding requirement'[1], gives the court a very wide
discretion.[2] Reasonableness must always be considered where a landlord
has pleaded one of the discretionary grounds, so it is inappropriate for
judgment to be entered in default in such cases.[3] Failure to consider
reasonableness means that the judgment is a nullity[4], even where the
tenant consents to the possession order.[5] If the case is appealed because the
county court judge failed to consider the question of 'reasonableness', it
should be sent back to the county court for a new trial.[6] In *Cumming v
Danson* Lord Greene MR said:

> in considering reasonableness . . . it is, in my opinion, perfectly clear that the
> duty of the Judge is to take into account all relevant circumstances as they
> exist at the date of the hearing. That he must do in what I venture to call a

---

1 See Megarry *The Rent Acts* (Stevens 11th edn 1988) p387 and *Smith v McGoldrick*
   (1976) 242 EG 1047.
2 *Bell London and Provincial Properties Ltd v Reuben* [1946] 2 All ER 547 and
   Plaschkes v Jones (1982) 9 HLR 110.
3 *Peachey Property Corporation Ltd v Robinson* [1967] 2 QB 543; *Smith v Poulter*
   [1947] KB 339 and *Salter v Lask (No 1)* [1925] 1 KB 584.
4 *Shrimpton v Rabbits* (1924) 131 LT 478. *Minchburn v Fernandez (No 2)* (1986) 19
   HLR 29, CA, and *Verrilli v Idigoras* [1990] EGCS 3, CA.
5 See p254 below and *R v Bloomsbury and Marylebone County Court ex parte
   Blackburne* (1985) 275 EG 1273, CA, where a tenant consented to an order for
   possession in return for a payment of £11,000. The order was set aside because the
   judge had not considered the question of reasonableness.
6 *Smith v McGoldrick* n1.

broad common-sense way as a man of the world, and come to his conclusion giving such weight as he thinks right to the various factors in the situation. Some factors may have little or no weight, others may be decisive, but it is quite wrong for him to exclude from his consideration matters which he ought to take into account.[7]

There are many examples of circumstances which can be relevant:

a) *The financial position of the parties.* For example, a financial gain which the landlord would receive from a possession order and the financial loss resulting to the tenant,[8] the fact that the landlord's only motive is pecuniary gain,[9] loss of income to the tenant from subletting[10] or from taking paying guests.[11]

b) *Hardship to people living with either party.* For example, over-crowding affecting the landlord's invalid sister and refugees living with them[12], although the court may enquire as to the cause of such overcrowding.[13]

c) *The length of time the tenant has lived in the premises.*[14]

d) *The landlord's reasons for wishing to obtain possession.*[15]

e) *The health of the parties and their relatives.*[16]

f) *The age of the parties.*[17]

g) *The loss of amenities.* For example, a garden[18], the importance of leisure activities and spiritual needs.[19]

h) *The public interest.* For example, the use by the landlord of possession proceedings to defeat the legislation[20] or even the need of the landlord to widen a road for the public safety.[21]

i) *The conduct of the parties.* For example, a tenant's past failure

---

7   [1942] 2 All ER 653 at 655.
8   *Cresswell v Hodgson* [1951] 1 All ER 710; *Williamson v Pallant* [1924] All ER 623.
9   *Battlespring Ltd v Gates* (1983) 268 EG 355.
10 *Yoland v Reddington* (1982) 263 EG 157.
11 *Warren v Austen* [1947] 2 All ER 185.
12 *Cumming v Danson* [1942] 2 All ER 653. See too *Rhodes v Cornford* [1947] 2 All ER 601.
13 *Wint v Monk* (1981) 259 EG 45. See too *Hardie v Frediani* [1958] 1 WLR 318.
14 *Battlespring v Gates* n9; *Minchburn v Fernandez (No 2)* n4.
15 *Minchburn v Fernandez (No 2)* n4.
16 *Briddon v George* [1946] 1 All ER 609; *Hensman v McIntoch* (1954) 163 EG 322; *Williamson v Pallant* n8.
17 *Battlespring v Gates* n9.
18 *Warren v Austen* n11.
19 *Siddiqui v Rashid* [1980] 1 WLR 1018.
20 *Cresswell v Hodgson* n8.
21 *Wallasey v Pritchard* (1936) 3 LJNCCR 35.

to decorate or tend the garden,[22] or lies told by parties in court to substantiate their claim.[23]

Particular factors relating to reasonableness apply to the various grounds for possession. For example in proceedings based on rent arrears, in practice it is rare for the court to consider it reasonable to make an absolute order for possession unless there are substantial arrears. See for example *Woodspring DC v Taylor*[24] on p26 above. It is very unusual for any order for possession to be made if all the arrears have been paid into court before the hearing or if the arrears are very low[25] although it may be reasonable to make an order if the tenant has a bad history of payment and in particular if summonses based on rent arrears have been issued in the past.[26] The possibility of payments of 'rent direct' by the local authority paying HB to the landlord may be an important factor when a tenant argues that it is not reasonable to make a possession order.[27] If arrears are in the region of a few hundred pounds, it is usual for a suspended order for possession to be made[28] although some judges have a tendency to make an absolute order even if the arrears are fairly low, if the tenant fails to appear in court. If a tenant has withheld rent because s/he believed that s/he had a counterclaim based on breach of the landlord's repairing obligations (see below), but at court the tenant loses on that issue, it is normally not reasonable for the court to make an absolute order without giving the tenant the opportunity to pay the arrears, although the position may be different if the tenant fails to make any offer to pay off the arrears and has a history of non-payment.[29]

If possession proceedings are brought on the grounds of breach of an obligation in the tenancy, much depends on the seriousness of the breach and the tenant's intention. For example if there is a breach which is 'trivial' and which 'cannot injure the plaintiff in any way at all' it will not be reasonable to make any order.[30] The same applies if a breach is committed in innocence, with the tenant believing that s/he was not

22   *Brown v Davies* [1957] 3 All ER 401.
23   *Yelland v Taylor* [1957] 1 All ER 627.
24   (1982) 4 HLR 95.
25   *Hayman v Rowlands* [1957] 1 All ER 321; *Sopwith v Stutchbury* (1983) 17 HLR 50, but see *Lee-Steere v Jennings* (1988) 20 HLR 1, CA.
26   *Dellenty v Pellow* [1951] 2 All ER 716.
27   Cf *Second WRVS Housing Society v Blair* (1987) 19 HLR 104, CA.
28   See p201 below. Suspended possession orders are described by Lord Denning MR as the 'everyday practice' in *Hayman v Rowlands* n25.
29   *Lal v Nakum* (1982) 1 HLR 50. See too *Lombard Realty Co v Shailer* [1955] CLY 2366 and *LB Harringey v Stewart* [1991] 2 EGLR 252, 23 HLR 557.
30   *Upjohn v MacFarlane* [1922] 2 Ch 256.

committing any breach.[31] It may even be unreasonable for the court to make an order for possession if the tenant says that s/he intends to continue breaking the covenant, even if the covenant itself is reasonable.[32] Usually, however, the tenant indicates that s/he will not breach the particular covenant in future and, if the past breach has not been serious, the court makes an order which is suspended on condition that the tenant does not commit further breaches. The main exception to this practice is where there has been breach of a covenant against immoral user (ie, prostitution) where it has been held that it is prima facie reasonable to make an order for possession.[33] Where allegations that the tenant has neglected premises have been substantiated, it may be unreasonable to make an order for possession without giving the tenant an opportunity to put matters right.[34]

In proceedings brought under Case 9, the overriding question of reasonableness has to be considered separately and independently from the question of whether or not the premises are reasonably required by the landlord (see above). The mere fact that it has been found that the landlord reasonably requires the premises does not mean that it is reasonable to make an order for possession: 'because a wish is reasonable, it does not follow that it is reasonable in a court to gratify it'.[35]

Reasonableness is above all a question of fact based on the particular circumstances of each case. It is generally difficult for a party who is dissatisfied with a judge's determination in respect of reasonableness to succeed on appeal[36] unless it can be shown that:

- there was no evidence to support the judge's determination; or
- the judge took into account irrelevant considerations; or
- the judge failed to take into account relevant considerations; or
- no reasonable judge could have made such a finding.[37]

Where evidence has been given in a county court hearing which is relevant to the question of reasonableness, the Court of Appeal assumes that the

---

31   Ibid.
32   *Bell London and Provincial v Reuben* n2 and *Metropolitan Properties v Crawford and Wetherill* March 1987 *Legal Action* 20, CC. See too *Tideway Investment and Property Holdings Ltd v Wellwood* [1952] 2 All ER 514.
33   *Yates v Morris* [1951] 1 KB 77.
34   *Holloway v Povey* (1984) 15 HLR 104.
35   *Shrimpton v Rabbits* n4.
36   Eg *Pazgate Ltd v McGrath* (1984) 17 HLR 127 at 134; and *Lee-Steere v Jennings* n25 and *LB Haringey v Stewart* [1991] 2 EGLR 252, 23 HLR 557; cf *Mathews v Ahmed* (1985) CAT No 2 noted at (1985) 7 CL 3. See too County Courts Act 1984 s77(6).
37   *Yoland v Reddington* n10.

judge had that evidence in mind when making an order even if it was not expressly referred to.[38]

38   *Tendler v Sproule*]1947] 1 All ER 193. See *Rhodes v Cornford* n12, but cf *Minchburn v Fernandez (No 2)* n4.

CHAPTER 13

Restricted Contracts

A tenant or licensee[1] who moved into premises before 15 January 1989 and who does not enjoy full RA protection may occupy premises under a restricted contract.[2] Many, but not all, tenants or licensees of resident landlords whose interests were created before 15 January 1989 and who were deprived of full RA protection,[3] had restricted contracts. The other principal classes of tenants who had restricted contracts were those who were excluded from RA protection because their tenancies provide for the provision of substantial attendances or small quantities of board.[4]

The RA when dealing with restricted contracts[5] refers to occupiers acquiring 'security of tenure'. This is an inaccurate description because the only rights of this kind which restricted contract occupants have are to delay for relatively short periods the time when a landlord is able to obtain an order for possession.

Nowadays there are, however, relatively few tenants or licensees remaining with restricted contracts. The Housing Act 1988 s36 not only provided that no new restricted contracts could be created on or after 15 January 1989, but also stipulated that if the rent under a restricted contract was varied by agreement, it should be treated as a new contract, and could therefore no longer be a restricted contract. Accordingly, only tenants or licensees whose interests were created before 15 January 1989

---

1 Although RA 1977 s19(2) includes a reference to rent, it is clear that the term 'restricted contract' includes licensees with exclusive occupation of premises – *Luganda v Service Hotels Ltd* [1969] 2 All ER 692 (room occupied for three years in large hotel); *R v Battersea, Wandsworth, Mitcham and Wimbledon Rent Tribunal ex parte Parikh* [1957] 1 All ER 352 (occupant described by landlord as 'paying guest'); but cf *R v Paddington and St Marylebone Rent Tribunal ex parte Walston Hotels Ltd* (1948) 152 EG 449 (no exclusive occupation) and *R v South West London Rent Tribunal ex parte Beswick* (1976) 32 P & CR 67 (a room in a YWCA hostel).
2 See RA 1977 s19.
3 Ibid s12 and Sch 2.
4 Ibid ss7 and 19.
5 Ibid ss102A to 106.

and whose rents have not been varied by agreement can have restricted contracts. (A registration of a rent by a rent tribunal does not count as a variation by agreement.)

The rights of occupants with restricted contracts depend on whether the restricted contract was created before or after 28 November 1980 when amendments made by HA 1980[6] came into operation. Pre-1980 HA restricted contract occupiers have the right to apply to the rent tribunal to delay the operation of any notice to quit. After the matter has been considered by the rent tribunal, the county court is unlikely to delay the making of a possession order for long.[7] Post-1980 HA restricted contract occupiers have no right to apply to the rent tribunal to delay the operation of notices to quit, but when possession proceedings are issued against them, they may apply to the judge at the hearing for a period of up to three months' further residence.[8]

Pre-1980 Housing Act restricted contracts

The relevant sections of the RA 1977 are ss103 to 106, which provide:

> *Notice to quit served after reference of contract to Rent Tribunal*
> **103.**—(1)   If, after a restricted contract has been referred to a rent tribunal by the lessee under section 77 or 80 of this Act, a notice to quit the dwelling to which the contract relates is served by the lessor on the lessee at any time before the decision of the tribunal is given or within the period of 6 months thereafter, then, subject to sections 105 and 106 of this Act, the notice shall not take effect before the expiry of that period.
> (2)   In a case falling within subsection (1) above,—
> (a)   the rent tribunal may, if they think fit, direct that a shorter period shall be substituted for the period of 6 months specified in that subsection; and
> (b)   if the reference to the rent tribunal is withdrawn, the period during which the notice to quit is not to take effect shall end on the expiry of 7 days from the withdrawal of the reference.

---

6   Ibid s69(3).
7   It seems that neither RA 1977 nor HA 1980 contain provisions stating how long the giving up of possession can be delayed after the making of the order. HA 1980 s89 does not apply to restricted contracts (HA 1980 s89(2)(d)) and RA 1977 s106A applies only to post-1980 HA restricted contracts. It would seem that *pre*-1980 HA restricted contracts are the only type of tenancy or licence for which judges retain their common law power to delay the making of a possession order for a 'reasonable period' – see *Air Ministry v Harris* [1951] 2 All ER 862; *Sheffield Corporation v Luxford* [1929] 2 KB 180 and *Jones v Savery* [1951] 1 All ER 820.
8   RA 1977 s106A.

Application to Tribunal for security of tenure where notice to quit is served
104.—(1)   Subject to sections 105 and 106(3) of this Act, where—
  (a)   a notice to quit a dwelling the subject of a restricted contract has been served, and
  (b)   the restricted contract has been referred to a rent tribunal under section 77 or 80 of this Act (whether before or after the service of the notice to quit) and the reference has not been withdrawn, and
  (c)   the period at the end of which the notice to quit takes effect (whether by virtue of the contract, of section 103 of this Act or of this section) has not expired,
the lessee may apply to the rent tribunal for the extension of that period.

(2)   Where an application is made under this section, the notice to quit to which the application relates shall not have effect before the determination of the application unless the application is withdrawn.

(3)   On an application under this section, the rent tribunal, after making such inquiry as they think fit and giving to each party an opportunity of being heard or, at his option, of submitting representations in writing, may direct that the notice to quit shall not have effect until the end of such period, not exceeding 6 months from the date on which the notice to quit would have effect apart from the direction, as may be specified in the direction.

(4)   If the rent tribunal refuse to give a direction under this section,—
  (a)   the notice to quit shall not have effect before the expiry of 7 days from the determination of the application; and
  (b)   no subsequent application under this section shall be made in relation to the same notice to quit.

(5)   On coming to a determination on an application under this section, the rent tribunal shall notify the parties of their determination.

Notices to quit served by owner occupiers
105.   Where a person who has occupied a dwelling as a residence (in this section referred to as 'the owner-occupier') has, by virtue of a restricted contract, granted the right to occupy the dwelling to another person and—
  (a)   at or before the time when the right was granted (or, if it was granted before 8th December 1965, not later than 7th June 1966) the owner-occupier has given notice in writing to that other person that he is the owner-occupier within the meaning of this section, and
  (b)   if the dwelling is part of a house, the owner-occupier does not occupy any other part of the house as his residence,
neither section 103 nor 104 of this Act shall apply where a notice to quit the dwelling is served if, at the time the notice is to take effect, the dwelling is required as a residence for the owner-occupier or any member of his family who resided with him when he last occupied the dwelling as a residence.
106.—(1)   Subsections (2) and (3) below apply where a restricted contract has been referred to a rent tribunal and the period at the end of which a notice

to quit will take effect has been determined by virtue of section 103 of this Act or extended under section 104.

(2)   If, in a case where this subsection applies, it appears to the rent tribunal, on an application made by the lessor for a direction under this section,—

(a)   that the lessee has not complied with the terms of the contract, or

(b)   that the lessee or any person residing or lodging with him has been guilty of conduct which is a nuisance or annoyance to adjoining occupiers or has been convicted of using the dwelling, or allowing the dwelling to be used, for an immoral or illegal purpose, or

(c)   that the condition of the dwelling has deteriorated owing to any act or neglect of the lessee or any person residing or lodging with him, or

(d)   that the condition of any furniture provided for the use of the lessee under the contract has deteriorated owing to any ill-treatment by the lessee or any person residing or lodging with him,

the rent tribunal may direct that the period referred to in subsection (1) above shall be reduced so as to end at a date specified in the direction.

(3)   No application may be made under section 104 of this Act with respect to a notice to quit if a direction has been given under subsection (2) above reducing the period at the end of which the notice is to take effect.

(4)   In any case where—

(a)   a notice to quit a dwelling which is the subject of a restricted contract has been served, and

(b)   the period at the end of which the notice to quit takes effect is for the time being extended by virtue of section 103 or 104 of this Act, and

(c)   at some time during that period the lessor institutes proceedings in the county court for the recovery of possession of the dwelling, and

(d)   in those proceedings the county court is satisfied that any of paragraphs (a) to (d) of subsection (2) above applies,

the court may direct that the period referred to in paragraph (b) above shall be reduced so as to end at a date specified in the direction.

Rent tribunals

Rent tribunals were set up by the post-war Attlee government with the main purpose of fixing reasonable rents for furnished premises which were then outside full RA protection. As an adjunct to their rent-fixing role, rent tribunals were given the power to delay the operation of notices to quit in order to prevent landlords from evicting tenants immediately after a reduced rent had been registered. Over the years the power to delay the operation of notices to quit became their more important role because few occupants saw any point in applying for the rent to be reduced when the almost inevitable consequence of such a reduction would be eviction approximately six months later. However, even prior to HA 1988, the significance of rent tribunals had been reduced greatly by two legislative changes. First, the RA 1974, which gave full security of tenure to the vast majority of furnished tenants, removed a large proportion of tenancies from rent tribunal jurisdiction. Second, HA 1980 s69 (see p173 below) removed the power of rent tribunals to delay the operation of notices to quit served on all post-1980 HA restricted contracts. The number of applications to rent tribunals has dropped accordingly, and they are now used very little. In 1981 there were 2,260 applications but this had dropped to 1,219 in 1983. (It should also be noted that the constitution of rent tribunals was changed by HA 1980 s72 which abolished rent tribunals[9] but stated that rent assessment committees (RACs) would carry out all the functions previously carried out by rent tribunals, and that when doing so RACs would be called rent tribunals.)

There are two situations in which a rent tribunal may defer the operation of a notice to quit:

a) if an occupant has already made an application to the rent tribunal to register a rent and the landlord then serves a notice to quit. Section 103 provides that in these circumstances the notice to quit will normally not take effect until six months after a decision by the rent tribunal relating to the rent. However, s103(2) gives the rent tribunal power to direct a shorter period than six months 'if they think fit'. If the application to the rent tribunal is withdrawn, the notice to quit takes effect either seven days after the withdrawal or at the time when the notice to quit would normally take effect, whichever is later[10];

b) if a notice to quit is served and the occupant then applies to a rent tribunal, s104 provides that the tribunal may defer the operation of the notice to quit for a period of up to six months. It is vital that any application to the rent tribunal is made *before* the expiry of the notice to quit. If the application is made *after* the notice to quit has expired there is no subsisting restricted contract and the tribunal accordingly has no jurisdiction.[11] Similarly, rent tribunals have no jurisdiction to delay possession proceedings where there is a fixed-term tenancy, because such tenancies expire by effluxion of time without the need for service of any notice to quit and these powers of rent tribunals only come into operation following a notice to quit.

9   Repealing ibid s76.
10   Ibid s103(2)(b).
11   *R v Paddington and St Marylebone Rent Tribunal ex parte Haines* [1961] 3 All ER 1047, but cf *R v South West London Rent Tribunal ex parte Gravesande* (1966) 200 EG 1092.

Application to a rent tribunal

There is no specified form of application to the rent tribunal. The Rent Assessment Committees (England and Wales) (Rent Tribunal) Regulations 1980[12] merely provide that the application should be in writing and specify the address of the premises, the names of the lessor and lessee and the lessor's address. In practice, standard forms of application can be obtained from the office of the local RAC. Such an application may either be delivered by hand, in which case it is deemed to have reached the tribunal on the day when it was delivered, or alternatively posted, in which case it is deemed to have reached the tribunal on the day when it would 'be delivered in the ordinary course of the post'.[13] If there are joint occupiers all the tenants or licensees must make the application together. An application by one joint occupier alone is invalid.[14] After receiving an application the rent tribunal gives notice to both parties that an oral hearing will be arranged if one of the parties so requests.[15] Each party is entitled to not less than seven clear days' notice of the time and place of the hearing.[16]

There is little guidance as to the principles which should be used by a rent tribunal when deciding for how long the operation of a notice to quit should be delayed. 'There is a complete discretion in the tribunal – a discretion which must, of course, be judicially exercised – to substitute a shorter period than the 6 months' period.'[17] Matters which tribunals commonly take into account are why the landlord wants possession, the conduct of both parties, and the ability of the occupant to find other accommodation. A rent tribunal cannot intentionally extend a notice to quit until such time as a tenant becomes a regulated tenant (for example during the period after the death of a resident landlord[18]), but this may be achieved incidentally.[19]

---

12 SI No 1700.
13 Para 3 of the Regulations. For 'ordinary course of the post' see *Practice Direction* [1985] 1 All ER 889 (two working days for first class, four working days for second class).
14 *Turley v Panton* (1975) 29 P & CR 397, but see *Featherstone v Staples* [1986] 2 All ER 461, CA; *Howson v Buxton* (1928) 97 LJKB 749 and *Lloyd v Sadler* [1978] QB 774.
15 Para 4 of the Regulations.
16 Ibid para 5. See too *R v Devon and Cornwall Rent Tribunal ex parte West* (1974) 29 P & CR 316 and *R v Kensington and Chelsea Rent Tribunal ex parte MacFarlane* [1974] 3 All ER 390.
17 *R v West London Rent Tribunal ex parte Saliterman* (1969) 20 P & CR 776. See too *Campbell v Daramola* (1974) 235 EG 687 and *Preston and Area Rent Tribunal v Pickavance* [1953] AC 562.
18 *Landau v Sloane* [1981] 2 WLR 349.
19 *Williams v Mate* (1982) 4 HLR 15.

Further applications can be made by the occupant before the expiry of the period of 'security' given by the rent tribunal and in theory a rent tribunal could give unlimited further periods of six months,[20] but in practice prolonged extensions are rare.

Problems may arise where what appears to be an invalid notice to quit has been served or where a tenant claims to be a protected tenant but the landlord claims that the circumstances are such that there is only a restricted contract – for example because the landlord claims to reside in the premises. In these circumstances the wisest course of action for the occupant is to make an application to the rent tribunal but to send a covering letter stating that the application is made 'without prejudice' to the occupant's contention that the notice to quit is invalid or s/he is a fully protected tenant. A rent tribunal then has an obligation to enquire into its jurisdiction[21] and to decide whether it should go ahead and register a rent and defer the operation of the notice to quit. In considering such questions the rent tribunal should hear evidence from both parties.[22] It should also be noted that any view which the rent tribunal forms is not conclusive, since a final decision as to the occupant's status can only be made by a court of competent jurisdiction – for example the county court.[23]

Section 105 excludes the rent tribunal's jurisdiction to defer the operation of a notice to quit where a returning 'owner-occupier' wishes to regain possession. This section is largely redundant since most landlords in this situation did not create a restricted contract but instead a protected tenancy subject to the right to recover possession under Case 11 (see above).

Section 106 gives rent tribunals or the court power to reduce a period of delay before the operation of the notice to quit on the grounds of the tenant's misbehaviour. The 'grounds' are similar to Cases 1 to 4 in Sch 15 (see above), but this section is rarely used. No form is prescribed: a letter will suffice.

Even after the expiry of a deferred notice to quit, a landlord must obtain a possession order before evicting a tenant or licensee. Any attempt

20   See *R v Paddington South Rent Tribunal ex parte Millard* [1955] 1 All ER 691; *Preston Rent Tribunal v Pickavance* n17.
21   *R v City of London Rent Tribunal ex parte Honig* [1951] 1 All ER 195; *R v Fulham, Hammersmith and Kensington Rent Tribunal ex parte Zerek* [1951] 1 All ER 482; *R v Sheffield Area Rent Tribunal ex parte Pushouse* (1957) 121 JP 553; *R v Croydon and South West London Rent Tribunal ex parte Ryzewska* [1977] 1 All ER 312; *R v Rent Officer for Kensington and Chelsea ex parte Noel* [1977] 1 All ER 356 and *R v Rent Officer for Camden ex parte Ebiri* [1981] 1 All ER 950.
22   *R v Fulham etc Rent Tribunal ex parte Zerek* n21.
23   *R v Rent Officer for Camden ex parte Ebiri* n21.

to evict without getting a court order is a criminal offence under the Protection from Eviction Act 1977 s1. That section now extends to all tenancies and licences which are not statutorily protected, provided that they are not 'excluded' as a result of amendments to Protection from Eviction Act 1977 s5 made by HA 1988 s32. See p88 above.

When proceedings are issued, the landlord need only prove ownership or an interest in the premises and that the contract has been terminated, by the expiry of either a notice to quit or a fixed-term contract. The court must make an order for possession but it seems that in these circumstances the court retains its common law power to decide on what date the possession order will take effect.[24] This is normally 14 or 28 days after the hearing.

Post-1980 Housing Act restricted contracts

Rent tribunals have no jurisdiction to delay the operation of notices to quit in respect of restricted contracts entered into after 28 November 1980. Section 106A[25] gives the county court a limited discretion and provides:

> *Discretion of court in certain proceedings for possession*
> **106A.**—(1)   This section applies to any dwelling-house which is the subject of a restricted contract entered into after the commencement of section 69 of the Housing Act 1980.
> (2)   On the making of an order for possession of such a dwelling-house, or at any time before the execution of such an order, the court may—
> (*a*)   stay or suspend execution of the order, or
> (*b*)   postpone the date of possession,
> for such period or periods as, subject to subsection (3) below, the court thinks fit.
> (3)   Where a court makes an order for possession of such a dwelling-house, the giving up of possession shall not be postponed (whether by the order or any variation, suspension or stay of execution) to a date later than 3 months after the making of the order.
> (4)   On any such stay, suspension or postponement as is referred to in subsection (2) above, the court shall, unless it considers that to do so would cause exceptional hardship to the lessee or would otherwise be unreasonable, impose conditions with regard to payment by the lessee of arrears of rent (if

24   The restrictions imposed by HA 1980 s89 do not apply to restricted contracts at all and RA 1977 s106A (see below) applies only to post-1980 restricted contracts. As to the court's common law powers, see the cases referred to in n1 on p248 below. The court may take into account any time already obtained by the rent tribunal's delaying operation of the notice to quit.

25   Inserted by HA 1980 s69(2).

any) and rent or payments in respect of occupation after termination of the tenancy (mesne profits) and may impose such other conditions as it thinks fit.

(5)   Subsection (6) below applies in any case where—

(a)   proceedings are brought for possession of such a dwelling-house;

(b)   the lessee's spouse or former spouse, having rights of occupation under the Matrimonial Homes Act 1967, is then in occupation of the dwelling-house; and

(c)   the restricted contract is terminated as a result of those proceedings.

(6)   In any case to which this subsection applies, the spouse or former spouse shall, so long as he or she remains in occupation, have the same rights in relation to, or in connection with, any such stay, suspension or postponement as is referred to in subsection (2) above, as he or she would have if those rights of occupation were not affected by the termination of the restricted contract.

This section applies to restricted contracts created between 28 November 1980 and 14 January 1989. Restricted contracts could only be granted after 14 January 1989 if they were granted in pursuance of a contract entered into before that date (HA 1988 s36) and in that case, this section applies.

It is a criminal offence for a landlord to recover or attempt to recover possession of premises which were occupied under a restricted contract without issuing proceedings.[26] In the case of a restricted contract created after 28 November 1980 the offence applies both to restricted contract tenancies and restricted contract licences which have been determined.[27]

However, the court's powers when dealing with such possession proceedings are very limited. The court may delay the operation of a possession order for up to three months, but no more.[28] Section 106A gives no guidance as to the principles to be exercised by the court when deciding when such a possession order should take effect. However, as with rent tribunals' corresponding powers in relation to pre-1980 HA restricted contracts, courts commonly take into account the landlord's reason for requiring possession, the conduct of the parties and the ability of the occupant to find other accommodation. In delaying the operation of possession orders the court must impose conditions relating to the payment of arrears of rent and current sums which become due, unless to do so would cause 'exceptional hardship'. There is no definition of 'exceptional hardship'.

---

26   Protection from Eviction Act 1977 ss1 and 3.

27   Ibid s3(2A) as inserted by HA 1980 s69(1).

28   *Bryant v Best* (1987) 283 EG 843, CA.

Tenancies created on or after 15 January 1989

Almost all new residential tenancies created on or after 15 January 1989 are assured or assured shorthold tenancies.[1]

HA 1988 s34 provides that no new protected tenancies can be created after the Act came into force (ie, 15 January 1989), unless one of three exceptions applies:

- the tenancy is entered into in pursuance of a contract made before the Act came into force; or
- the tenancy is granted to an existing protected or statutory tenant by the same landlord. If there are joint tenants or joint landlords, it is sufficient for only one of the joint tenants to have been a protected tenant and for only one of the joint landlords to have been the landlord of the existing tenant or tenants. Although the wording of this section is not very clear, it is plain that Parliament's intention was that this exception should apply even if the tenant has moved from other accommodation[2]; or
- before the grant of the new tenancy an order for possession was made on the ground of suitable alternative accommodation against a protected or statutory tenant[3] and in the possession proceedings relating to the earlier tenancy, the court directed that the tenancy of the suitable alternative accommodation should be held on a protected tenancy. The court should consider whether an assured tenancy would 'afford the required security'. If it would not, it may direct that the suitable alternative accommodation should be held on a protected tenancy. It is obviously important that representatives of tenants in suitable alternative accommodation cases do all they can to ensure that

1 Occupiers of agricultural accommodation may enjoy a new 'assured agricultural occupancy' status.
2 See *Kotecha v Rimington* (1991) 16 January, Leicester County Court, March 1991 *Legal Action* 15.
3 Under RA 1977 s98(1)(a) or Sch 16 Case 1 or Rent (Agriculture) Act 1976 Sch 4 Case 1.

the court directs that the new tenancy should be held on a protected tenancy. The higher rent which would be recoverable under an assured tenancy may mean that the alternative accommodation would not be suitable 'to the means of the tenant' and/or it would be unreasonable to make a possession order.

CHAPTER 14

Assured Tenancies

Introduction

Assured tenancies are a new form of tenancy and bear no similarities to the assured tenancies which were created by HA 1980 s56. For example, there is no requirement that lettings should be by 'approved bodies' or that landlords should be certified as such by the Secretary of State. It has been impossible to create the old, 1980 HA type of assured tenancies since the 1988 Act came into force. Old-style assured tenancies were automatically converted into the new form of assured tenancies (HA 1988 s1(3)). Any new tenancy granted to an existing assured tenant following an application to the court under Landlord and Tenant Act 1954 s24 also becomes a new assured tenancy (HA 1988 s37).

The new assured tenancies are lettings at market rents with security of tenure. There is no control over the rents at which such tenancies are initially let and subsequent rent regulation is minimal. The security of tenure provided is different from RA protection and the grounds for possession are more widely drafted.

Statutory references are to the HA 1988 unless otherwise stated, throughout Section B (chapters 14 and 15).

Definition of 'assured tenancy'

Section 1 contains three prerequisites for the creation of an assured tenancy.

- *The dwelling-house must be let as a separate dwelling* This is the well-known phrase which appears in RA 1977 s1. If a tenancy comprises two or more separate units of accommodation which are let together to a tenant, there can be no assured tenancy.[1] Section 3 provides that if a tenant enjoys exclusive occupation of some rented accommodation, with a right to share other accommodation with other people, apart from the landlord, the mere fact that the other accommodation is shared, does not prevent the tenant from occupying the accommodation which is not shared as a separate dwelling.

- *The tenant or, if there are joint tenants, each of the joint tenants, must be individuals*   A genuine letting to a company cannot be an assured tenancy.[2] In such cases, the tenancy is unprotected and may be terminated either by effluxion of time or by service of a notice to quit. If this is done, a landlord who brings possession proceedings is automatically entitled to possession without having to prove any ground.

- *The tenant or, if there are joint tenants, at least one of them, must occupy the premises as his or her only or principal home*   This is the same wording as HA 1985 s81, the 'tenant condition', which applies to secure tenancies. It is a more restrictive definition than the comparable provision in RA 1977 s2(1)(a). Although it is possible for tenants to occupy more than one home at the same time, an assured tenancy can continue only in respect of the tenant's principal home. There is no reason why an assured tenant should not be temporarily absent from the premises in question, provided that they remain his or her main home.[3] If an assured tenant moves out permanently, the tenancy becomes unprotected and can be terminated by notice to quit.

A tenancy cannot be an assured tenancy if any of the exceptions listed in Sch 1 applies. Many of these exceptions are similar to those set out in RA 1977 Pt I.[4] They include:

- premises with high rateable values (ie, over £1,500 in Greater London

1   See, eg, *Horford Investments Ltd v Lambert* [1976] Ch 39; *St Catherine's College v Dorling* [1980] 1 WLR 66; *Kavanagh v Lyroudias* [1985] 1 All ER 560 and Megarry *The Rent Acts* (Stevens 11th edn 1988) pp87–117.
2   *Hiller v United Dairies* [1934] 1 KB 57; *Hilton v Plustitle Ltd and Rose* [1988] 3 All ER 1051 and *Kaye v Massbetter Ltd and Kanter* (1991) 39 EG 129, (1992) 24 HLR 28, CA. However the court may decide that a letting to a company fails to represent the substance and reality of the transaction, is an artificial transaction or that the company is merely a nominee. See dicta in *Cove v Flick* [1954] 2 All ER 441; *Firstcross v East West Ltd* (1980) 7 HLR 577 and *Gisborne v Burton* (1988) 38 EG 129 and the passages in *AG Securities v Vaughan* [1988] 3 All ER 1058, HL; February 1989 *Legal Action* 21 concerning 'artificiality' and 'pretence'.
3   *Crawley BC v Sawyer* (1987) 20 HLR 98; *Sutton LB v Swann* (1985) 17 HLR 140.
4   See in particular RA 1977 ss4, 5, 8, 9, 10, 11, 12 (and Sch 2), 13 and 14.

and over £750 elsewhere) or, if granted after 1 April 1990, with a high rent (ie, a rent of more than £25,000 per annum)[5];
– tenancies at a low rent (ie, rent free or less than two-thirds of the rateable value) or, if granted after 1 April 1990, at a rent of less than £1,000 per annum in London or less than £250 per annum elsewhere[6];
– business premises which are protected under Landlord and Tenant Act 1954 Pt II;
– licensed premises such as public houses;
– agricultural land or holdings;
– lettings to students by specified educational institutions[7];
– holiday lettings where the tenant merely has 'the right to occupy the dwelling-house for a holiday'[8];
– resident landlords. This exception does not apply to purpose-built blocks of flats. For the exception to apply, the tenancy must have been granted by a landlord who, both at the time of the grant of the tenancy and at all times since, has had his or her 'only or principal home' elsewhere in the building. The schedule, like RA 1977 Sch 2, provides that existing assured tenants cannot be deprived of security of tenure by accepting a new tenancy or moving to another part of the same building after a landlord has become a resident landlord. Similarly there are periods of disregard after the sale of premises or the death of a landlord when the fact that there is no resident landlord living in the building does not mean that the 'resident landlord' exception ceases to apply;
– Crown tenancies, but not premises managed by the Crown Estate Commissioners;
– local authority tenancies, or tenancies granted by the Commission for New Towns, the Development Board for Rural Wales, development corporations, fully mutual housing associations or housing action trusts; and
– tenancies granted by private sector landlords as a result of arrangements with local authorities to provide temporary accommodation for homeless people under the Housing Act 1985 ss63, 65(3) and 69(1), unless tenants are notified that they are to be assured tenants or one year has passed since receipt of a s64 notification[9].

5   References to Rating (Housing) Regulations 1990 SI No 434.
6   References to Rating (Housing) Regulations 1990 SI No 434.
7   See the Assured and Protected Tenancies (Lettings to Students) (Amendment) Regulations 1990 SI No 1825 summarised on p151.
8   But note *Buchmann v May* [1978] 2 All ER 993 and *R v Rent Officer for Camden ex parte Plant* (1980) 257 EG 713 where tenancies which were not genuine 'holiday lets' were found to be protected tenancies.
9   Housing Act 1988 s1(6).

If one of these exceptions applies, the tenant has no security of tenure. Once a notice to quit has been served and has expired, the tenant has no statutory protection, except, in some cases, Protection from Eviction Act 1977 s3 which provides that it is unlawful for a landlord to evict such a tenant without taking court proceedings. The landlord has to prove only that the contractual tenancy has been terminated.

Termination of Assured Tenancies

Security of tenure

Section 5 provides:

5.—(1)   An assured tenancy cannot be brought to an end by the landlord except by obtaining an order of the court in accordance with the following provisions of this Chapter or Chapter II below or, in the case of a fixed term tenancy which contains power for the landlord to determine the tenancy in certain circumstances, by the exercise of that power and, accordingly, the service by the landlord of a notice to quit shall be of no effect in relation to a periodic assured tenancy.

(2)   If an assured tenancy which is a fixed term tenancy comes to an end otherwise than by virtue of—

(a)   an order of the court, or

(b)   a surrender or other action on the part of the tenant,

then, subject to section 7 and Chapter II below, the tenant shall be entitled to remain in possession of the dwelling-house let under that tenancy and, subject to subsection (4) below, his right to possession shall depend upon a periodic tenancy arising by virtue of this section.

(3)   The periodic tenancy referred to in subsection (2) above is one—

(a)   taking effect in possession immediately on the coming to an end of the fixed term tenancy;

(b)   deemed to have been granted by the person who was the landlord under the fixed term tenancy immediately before it came to an end to the person who was then the tenant under that tenancy;

(c)   under which the premises which are let are the same dwelling-house as was let under the fixed term tenancy;

(d)   under which the periods of the tenancy are the same as those for which rent was last payable under the fixed term tenancy; and

(e)   under which, subject to the following provisions of this Part of this Act, the other terms are the same as those of the fixed term tenancy immediately before it came to an end, except that any term which makes provision for determination by the landlord or the tenant shall not have effect while the tenancy remains an assured tenancy.

(4)   The periodic tenancy referred to in subsection (2) above shall not

arise if, on the coming to an end of the fixed term tenancy, the tenant is entitled, by virtue of the grant of another tenancy, to possession of the same or substantially the same dwelling-house as was let to him under the fixed term tenancy.

(5)   If, on or before the date on which a tenancy is entered into or is deemed to have been granted as mentioned in subsection (3)(b) above, the person who is to be the tenant under that tenancy—

(a)   enters into an obligation to do any act which (apart from this subsection) will cause the tenancy to come to an end at a time when it is an assured tenancy, or

(b)   executes, signs or gives any surrender, notice to quit or other document which (apart from this subsection) has the effect of bringing the tenancy to an end at a time when it is an assured tenancy,

the obligation referred to in paragraph (a) above shall not be enforceable or, as the case may be, the surrender, notice to quit or other document referred to in paragraph (b) above shall be of no effect.

(6)   If, by virtue of any provision of this Part of this Act, Part I of Schedule 1 to this Act has effect in relation to a fixed term tenancy as if it consisted only of paragraphs 11 and 12, that Part shall have the like effect in relation to any periodic tenancy which arises by virtue of this section on the coming to an end of the fixed term tenancy.

(7)   Any reference in this Part of this Act to a statutory periodic tenancy is a reference to a periodic tenancy arising by virtue of this section.

Section 5 provides that a periodic assured tenancy can be brought to an end by a landlord only by means of an order of the court. Section 5(1) makes it clear that notices to quit served by landlords have no effect upon periodic assured tenancies. However, a notice to quit served by a tenant terminates the assured tenancy and the tenant's security of tenure.

If a contractual, fixed-term assured tenancy is brought to an end, other than by an order of a court or by surrender, a periodic assured tenancy (called a 'statutory periodic tenancy') will generally come into existence immediately after the fixed-term tenancy has come to an end. In some ways this is similar to a RA statutory tenancy,[10] but there are significant differences. The most important of these is the provision for fixing the terms of the statutory periodic tenancy. The basic rule is that the terms will be the same as for the former contractual assured tenancy (s5(3)(d) and (e)). However, s6 provides a mechanism by which landlords and tenants may propose new terms.

10   RA 1977 s2.

Notice of intention to bring possession proceedings

Section 8 provides:

8.—(1) The court shall not entertain proceedings for possession of a dwelling-house let on an assured tenancy unless—
  (a)   the landlord or, in the case of joint landlords, at least one of them has served on the tenant a notice in accordance with this section and the proceedings are begun within the time limits stated in the notice in accordance with subsections (3) and (4) below; or
  (b)   the court considers it just and equitable to dispense with the requirement of such a notice.

  (2)   The court shall not make an order for possession on any of the grounds in Schedule 2 to this Act unless that ground and particulars of it are specified in the notice under this section; but the grounds specified in such a notice may be altered or added to with the leave of the court.

  (3)   A notice under this section is one in the prescribed form informing the tenant that—
  (a)   the landlord intends to begin proceedings for possession of the dwelling-house on one or more of the grounds specified in the notice; and
  (b)   those proceedings will not begin earlier than a date specified in the notice which, without prejudice to any additional limitation under subsection (4) below, shall not be earlier than the expiry of the period of two weeks from the date of service of the notice; and
  (c)   those proceedings will not begin later than twelve months from the date of service of the notice.

  (4)   If a notice under this section specifies, in accordance with subsection (3)(a) above, any of Grounds 1, 2, 5 to 7, 9 and 16 in Schedule 2 to this Act (whether with or without other grounds), the date specified in the notice as mentioned in subsection (3)(b) above shall not be earlier than—
  (a)   two months from the date of service of the notice; and
  (b)   if the tenancy is a periodic tenancy, the earliest date on which, apart from section 5(1) above, the tenancy could be brought to an end by a notice to quit given by the landlord on the same date as the date of service of the notice under this section.

  (5)   The court may not exercise the power conferred by subsection (1)(b) above if the landlord seeks to recover possession on Ground 8 of Schedule 2 to this Act.

  (6)   Where a notice under this section—
  (a)   is served at a time when the dwelling-house is let on a fixed term tenancy, or

(b)   is served after a fixed term tenancy has come to an end but relates (in whole or in part) to events occurring during that tenancy,

the notice shall have effect notwithstanding that the tenant becomes or has become tenant under a statutory periodic tenancy arising on the coming to an end of the fixed term tenancy.

A landlord wishing to bring possession proceedings against an assured tenant should first serve a notice, in prescribed form, informing the tenant that it is the landlord's intention to bring proceedings on one or more grounds specified in the notice. The form of the notices, which are similar to NSPs used against public sector secure tenancies, is specified by the Assured Tenancies and Agricultural Occupancies (Forms) Regulations 1988. See p368. Particulars of the grounds relied upon have to be included, as well as reference to the ground itself. For example, if proceedings are to be issued under ground 11, it is not enough for the notice merely to state 'persistent rent arrears', without giving figures of arrears and dates of late payment.[11] The court has power to alter or add to the grounds specified in the notice (s8(2)). Schedule 2, Pt IV makes it clear that it is sufficient if just one out of two or more joint landlords gives notice.

Usually, notices of intention to bring possession proceedings against assured tenants have to give two weeks' notice, but in the case of grounds 1, 2, 5, 6, 7, 9 and 16 at least two months' notice or notice equivalent to the contractual period of the tenancy, whichever is longer, must be given. Proceedings must be begun within 12 months of service of the notice, otherwise a new notice must be served. There is no need for a landlord of an assured tenant to serve a notice to quit as well as a notice of intention to bring proceedings.[12]

It should be noted that the court (except in relation to ground 8 – ie, 13 weeks' arrears) has power to dispense with service of a notice prior to the institution of possession proceedings if it considers it 'just and equitable' to do so. This phrase is used in RA 1977 Sch 15 Pt II also (see p146 above), but it is hard to predict when the courts will exercise this discretion. It is likely to be interpreted as a wide discretion giving the courts power to review all factors which may affect or prejudice both the landlord and tenant.[13] It may be that if a landlord has given written notice which does not comply with the regulations prescribing its form, or if oral

---

11   *Torridge DC v Jones* (1985) 18 HLR 107 (arrears of rent) and *South Bucks DC v Francis* [1985] CLY 1900 (various acts of nuisance); but cf *Dudley MBC v Bailey* (1990) 22 HLR 424, CA.

12   Section 5(1).

13   Cf *Bradshaw v Baldwin-Wiseman* (1985) 17 HLR 260 and *Fernandes v Parvardin* (1982) 264 EG 49 (RA 1977 Sch 15 Case 11 cases).

notice is given, the court will consider that the tenant has not been prejudiced, and that it is 'just and equitable' to dispense with the requirement. On the other hand it may not be just and equitable if the tenant had no notification at all.

Forefeiture

A fixed-term assured or assured shorthold tenancy can be terminated during the fixed term if the landlord can prove that any of grounds 2, 8, 10, 11, 12, 13, 14 or 15 exists and provided that the tenancy contains a provision entitling the landord to do so (see HA 1988 s7(6)). In the past a landlord wishing to determine a fixed-term tenancy would generally have relied on a forfeiture clause and the tenants would have been able to seek relief from forfeiture (eg, under County Court Act 1984 s138 or Law of Property Act 1925 s146 – see p103). Some commentators have assumed that fixed-term assured and assured shorthold tenants wuld be entitled to seek relief from forfeiture in the normal way. On the other hand, it may be argued that s45(4), when read in conjunction with s5(1) and 7(6), means that proceedings brought against a fixed-term tenant during the currency of the fixed term are not forfeiture proceedings, and that accordingly the tenant is not entitled to seek relief from forfeiture.[14]

Grounds for possession

Section 7 provides:

7.—(1)   The court shall not make an order for possession of a dwelling-house let on an assured tenancy except on one or more of the grounds set out in Schedule 2 to this Act; but nothing in this Part of this Act relates to proceedings for possession of such a dwelling-house which are brought by a mortgagee, within the meaning of the Law of Property Act 1925, who has lent money on the security of the assured tenancy.

(2)   The following provisions of this section have effect, subject to section 8 below, in relation to proceedings for the recovery of possession of a dwelling-house let on an assured tenancy.

(3)   If the court is satisfied that any of the grounds in Part I of Schedule 2 to this Act is established then, subject to subsection (6) below, the court shall make an order for possession.

(4)   If the court is satisfied that any of the grounds in Part II of Schedule 2

---

14   See (1989) 139 NLJ 376 (17 March) and authors' corrigendum to Sweet & Maxwell's *Annotated Housing Act 1988*. Compare (1989) 139 NLJ 74 (20 January) and 104 (27 January), but note *Patel v Sullivan* (1991) 28 June, Wandsworth County Court, noted at September 1991 *Legal Action* 17.

to this Act is established, then, subject to subsection (6) below, the court may make an order for possession if it considers it reasonable to do so.

(5)   Part III of Schedule 2 to this Act shall have effect for supplementing Ground 9 in that Schedule and Part IV of that Schedule shall have effect in relation to notices given as mentioned in Grounds 1 to 5 of that Schedule.

(6)   The court shall not make an order for possession of a dwelling-house to take effect at a time when it is let on an assured fixed term tenancy unless—

(a)   the ground for possession is Ground 2 or Ground 8 in Part I of Schedule 2 to this Act or any of the grounds in Part II of that Schedule, other than Ground 9 or Ground 16; and

(b)   the terms of the tenancy make provisions for it to be brought to an end on the ground in question (whether that provision takes the form of a provision for re-entry, for forfeiture, for determination by notice or otherwise).

(7)   Subject to the preceding provisions of this section, the court may make an order for possession of a dwelling-house on grounds relating to a fixed term tenancy which has come to an end; and where an order is made in such circumstances, any statutory periodic tenancy which has arisen on the ending of the fixed term tenancy shall end (without any notice and regardless of the period) on the day on which the order takes effect.

As well as serving a notice of intention to bring proceedings, or persuading the court to dispense with such a notice, a landlord must also satisfy the court that one of the grounds for possession set out in Sch 2 exists. Some of the grounds are similar in form to existing RA and HA grounds[15], but others are new. As in the RA 1977 and HA 1985, some grounds for possession are mandatory, whereas others are discretionary, with a requirement that the landlord must convince the court that it is reasonable to make an order for possession as well as satisfying the ground for possession.

Mandatory grounds for possession

Ground 1: Owner-occupiers

Not later than the beginning of the tenancy the landlord gave notice in writing to the tenant that possession might be recovered on this ground or the court is of the opinion that it is just and equitable to dispense with the requirement of notice and (in either case)—

(a)   at some time before the beginning of the tenancy, the landlord who is seeking possession or, in the case of joint landlords seeking possession, at least one of them occupied the dwelling-house as his only or principal home; or

15   See pp22 and 126.

(b)   the landlord who is seeking possession or, in the case of joint landlords seeking possession, at least one of them requires the dwelling-house as his or his spouse's only or principal home and neither the landlord (or, in the case of joint landlords, any one of them) nor any other person who, as landlord, derived title under the landlord who gave the notice mentioned above acquired the reversion on the tenancy for money or money's worth.

This ground is similar to Case 11 in RA 1977 Sch 15 (see p143), but much wider in its ambit. A landlord must prove:

- at, or before, the grant of the tenancy the landlord gave notice in writing that possession might be recovered on this ground. The notice need not be in any particular form and may be included as a recital in any tenancy agreement provided that the agreement does not operate retrospectively. The court has power to dispense with such a notice if it considers this just and equitable;[16] and either
- at some time before the grant of the tenancy, the landlord, or if there are joint landlords, at least one of them, has occupied the dwelling-house as his or her only or principal residence.[17] A landlord's previous occupation may suffice even if it was only temporary or intermittent.[18] To satisfy this limb, the landlord need not give any reason for requiring possession; or
- the landlord (or at least one of them) 'requires the dwelling-house as his or his spouse's only or principal home'. The landlord need not show that the premises are 'reasonably' required, merely that the landlord 'bona fide wants' or 'genuinely has the immediate intention' of occupying the premises.[19] Premises need not be required as a permanent residence and fairly intermittent residence will be sufficient.[20]

This ground for possession is not available to a new landlord who acquired the premises 'for money or money's worth' from an original landlord who gave a notice that possession might be recovered under this ground. (See the explanation of the equivalent provision in RA 1977 Sch 15 Case 9 on p136.)

---

16   See Bradshaw and Fernandes n13 and Minay v Sentongo (1983) 45 P&CR 190.
17   Note the contrast with the wording under RA 1977 Sch 15 Case 11. For the meaning of 'only or principal residence' see pp7 and 20.
18   Naish v Curzon (1984) 17 HLR 220, CA; Mistry v Isidore (1990) 22 HLR 281, [1990] 2 EGLR 97, CA, and Ibie v Trubshaw (1990) 22 HLR 191, CA.
19   Cf RA 1977 Sch 15 Case 9. See Kennealy v Dunne [1977] QB 837.
20   Naish v Curzon (1984) 17 HLR 220 and Davies v Peterson (1989) 21 HLR 63, [1989] 06 EG 130, CA.

Ground 2: Mortgagees

The dwelling-house is subject to a mortgage granted before the beginning of the tenancy and—

(a)   the mortgagee is entitled to exercise a power of sale conferred on him by the mortgage or by section 101 of the Law of Property Act 1925; and

(b)   the mortgagee requires possession of the dwelling-house for the purpose of disposing of it with vacant possession in exercise of that power; and

(c)   either notice was given as mentioned in Ground 1 above or the court is satisfied that it is just and equitable to dispense with the requirement of notice;

and for the purposes of this ground 'mortgage' includes a charge and 'mortgagee' shall be construed accordingly.

This ground applies if, for example, the mortgagor has defaulted on instalments of the mortgage. It seems that the purpose of this ground is to enable a mortgagee, who has consented to a former owner-occupier letting or whose mortgage deed does not prohibit letting, to obtain the full, vacant possession value when exercising a power of sale. Note, though, the suggestion by Lord Denning MR that the court's equitable powers may prevent a lender from obtaining possession, 'except when it is sought bona fide and reasonably for the purpose of enforcing the security'.[21]

Ground 3: Tenancy preceded by 'holiday let'

The tenancy is a fixed term tenancy for a term not exceeding eight months and—

(a)   not later than the beginning of the tenancy the landlord gave notice in writing to the tenant that possession might be recovered on this ground; and

(b)   at some time within the period of twelve months ending with the beginning of the tenancy, the dwelling-house was occupied under a right to occupy it for a holiday.

This ground is almost identical to RA 1977 Sch 15 case 13 (see p149).[22]

The court has no power to dispense with service of the notice required prior to the grant of the tenancy.[23]

---

21   *Quennel v Maltby* [1979] 1 WLR 318, CA.

22   See n8.

23   Cf *Fowler v Minchin* (1987) 19 HLR 224, cf *Springfield Investmetns v Bell* (1990) 22 HLR 440, CA.

Ground 4: Educational institutions

The tenancy is a fixed term tenancy for a term not exceeding twelve months and—

(a)   not later than the beginning of the tenancy the landlord gave notice in writing to the tenant that possession might be recovered on this ground; and

(b)   at some time within the period of twelve months ending with the beginning of the tenancy, the dwelling-house was let on a tenancy falling within paragraph 8 of Schedule 1 to this Act.

This ground applies where, during the 12 months preceding the tenancy, premises were let by a specified educational institution.[24] As with ground 3, notice stating that this ground may be relied upon has to be served before the commencement of the tenancy. It is almost identical to RA 1977 Sch 15, Case 14 (see p150).

Ground 5: Ministers of religion

The dwelling-house is held for the purpose of being available for occupation by a minister of religion as a residence from which to perform the duties of his office and—

(a)   not later than the beginning of the tenancy the landlord gave notice in writing to the tenant that possession might be recovered on this ground; and

(b)   the court is satisfied that the dwelling-house is required for occupation by a minister of religion as such a residence.

This ground apples to premises which are 'held for the purpose of being available for occupation by a minister of religion as a residence from which to perform the duties of his office'. Notice that possession might be required must be served before the grant of the tenancy, and the landlord must satisfy the court that the property is required for occupation by a minister of religion as a residence. It is similar to RA 1977 Sch 15 Case 15.[25]

Ground 6: Demolition or reconstruction

The landlord who is seeking possession or, if that landlord is a registered housing association or charitable housing trust, a superior landlord intends to

24   See Assured and Protected Tenancies (Lettings to Students) Regulations 1988 SI No 2236, and Assured and Protected Tenancies (Lettings to Students) (Amendment) Regulations 1990 SI No 1825 and Assured and Protected Tenancies (Lettings to Students) (Amendment) Regulations 1991 SI No 233.

25   Cf RA 1977 Sch 15 Case 15, p151.

demolish or reconstruct the whole or a substantial part of the dwelling-house or to carry out substantial works on the dwelling-house or any part thereof or any building of which it forms part and the following conditions are fulfilled—

(a) the intended work cannot reasonably be carried out without the tenant giving up possession of the dwelling-house because—

   (i) the tenant is not willing to agree to such a variation of the terms of the tenancy as would give such access and other facilities as would permit the intended work to be carried out, or

   (ii) the nature of the intended work is such that no such variation is practicable, or

   (iii) the tenant is not willing to accept an assured tenancy of such part only of the dwelling-house (in this sub-paragraph referred to as 'the reduced part') as would leave in the possession of his landlord so much of the dwelling-house as would be reasonable to enable the intended work to be carried out and, where appropriate, as would give such access and other facilities over the reduced part as would permit the intended work to be carried out, or

   (iv) the nature of the intended work is such that such a tenancy is not practicable; and

(b) either the landlord seeking possession acquired his interest in the dwelling-house before the grant of the tenancy or that interest was in existence at the time of that grant and neither that landlord (or, in the case of joint landlords, any of them) nor any other person who, alone or jointly with others, has acquired that interest since that time acquired it for money or money's worth; and

(c) the assured tenancy on which the dwelling-house is let did not come into being by virtue of any provision of Schedule 1 to the Rent Act 1977, as amended by Part I of Schedule 4 to this Act or, as the case may be, section 4 of the Rent (Agriculture) Act 1976, as amended by Part II of that Schedule.

For the purposes of this ground if, immediately before the grant of the tenancy, the tenant to whom it was granted or, if it was granted to joint tenants, any of them was the tenant or one of the joint tenants under an earlier assured tenancy of the dwelling-house concerned, any reference in paragraph (b) above to the grant of the tenancy is a reference to the grant of that earlier assured tenancy.

For the purposes of this ground 'registered housing association' has the same meaning as in the Housing Associations Act 1985 and 'charitable housing trust' means a housing trust, within the meaning of that Act, which is a charity, within the meaning of the Charities Act 1960.

This ground is available for a landlord who 'intends to demolish or reconstruct the whole or a substantial part of the dwelling-house or to carry out substantial works'. It is very similar to Landlord and Tenant Act 1954 s30(1)(f), which allows landlords of business tenants to oppose the grant of a new tenancy in similar circumstances.

It has been held that 'reconstruction' means 'a substantial interference with the structure of the premises and then a rebuilding, in probably a different form, of such part of the premises as has been demolished by reason of the interference with the structure'.[26]

The landlord must show that the intention to demolish or reconstruct will be fulfilled shortly after the date of the hearing.[27] There are two elements to the concept of intention – first, a genuine desire that the result will come about and, secondly, a reasonable prospect of bringing about that result. For example, in *Edwards v Thompson*[28] the landlord failed to prevent the grant of a new tenancy because she had not found a developer at the time of the hearing and 'there was a real possibility that [she] would not be in a position to carry out the entire development on the termination of the current tenancy . . . She had failed to show that she had the means and ability; she had not established the necessary intention.' A landlord's case is stronger if planning permission has been obtained in advance of the institution of possession proceedings, but this is not essential if it can be shown that there is a reasonable prospect of getting consent.[29]

The landlord must also show that, because of one of four specified reasons, the intended work cannot reasonably be carried out without the tenant giving up possession of the premises. 'Possession' means 'putting and end to legal rights of possession' and not merely access. For example, in *Heath v Drown*[30] a business tenant successfully defeated the landlord's claim even though the front wall of the premises had to be entirely rebuilt and it would not be possible to occupy the premises while such work was carried out.

This ground for possession is not available to a landlord who has acquired his or her interest in the property by purchasing it after the grant of the tenancy.

When a possession order is made under this ground the landlord must pay a sum equal to the tenant's reasonable removal expenses (s11(1) – see below).

---

26   *Joel v Swaddle* [1957] 3 All ER 325 at 329 (removal of internal walls and replacement with RSJs amounted to reconstruction of a substantial part). See too *Barth v Pritchard* [1990] 20 EG 65 and *Cook v Mott* (1961) 178 EG 637, CA.
27   *Betty's Cafe v Phillips* [1958] 1 All ER 607, HL.
28   [1990] 29 EG 41. See too *Capocci v Goble* (1987) 284 EG 230, CA.
29   *Gregson v Cyril Lord* [1962] 3 All ER 907.
30   [1972] 2 All ER 561 and see HA 1988 s16.

Ground 7: Death of the tenant

The tenancy is a periodic tenancy (including a statutory periodic tenancy) which has devolved under the will or intestacy of the former tenant and the proceedings for the recovery of possession are begun not later than twelve months after the death of the former tenant or, if the court so directs, after the date on which, in the opinion of the court, the landlord or, in the case of joint landlords, any one of them became aware of the former tenant's death.

For the purposes of this ground, the acceptance by the landlord of rent from a new tenant after the death of the former tenant shall not be regarded as creating a new periodic tenancy, unless the landlord agrees in writing to a change (as compared with the tenancy before the death) in the amount of the rent, the period of the tenancy, the premises which are let or any other term of the tenancy.

Although an assured tenancy may pass by will or on intestacy after the death of the tenant, the landlord may obtain possession if proceedings are brought within 12 months of the death of the tenant or the date upon which the landlord became aware of the death. No other reason for seeking possession need be given. This ground does not apply if a spouse or person living with the tenant 'as his or her wife or husband' succeeds to the tenancy as a result of the statutory succession provisions in s17. The Act specifies that acceptance of rent after the death of the former tenant should not be regarded as creating a new tenancy unless the landlord has agreed in writing to a change in the terms of the tenancy, such as an increase in rent.

Ground 8: Three months' rent arrears

Both at the date of the service of the notice under section 8 of this Act relating to the proceedings for possession and at the date of the hearing—
(a) if rent is payable weekly or fortnightly, at least thirteen weeks' rent is unpaid;
(b) if rent is payable monthly, at least three months' rent is unpaid;
(c) if rent is payable quarterly, at least one quarter's rent is more than three months in arrears; and
(d) if rent is payable yearly, at least three months' rent is more than three months in arrears;
and for the purpose of this ground 'rent' means rent lawfully due from the tenant.

This is the first of three distinct grounds for possession based on rent arrears, although it is likely that in practice some landlords will plead all three in the alternative. Under ground 8, three months' rent arrears (or 13 weeks' arrears in the case of a weekly tenancy) give a landlord an automatic right to a possession order. However the landlord must prove that there were three months' arrears, both at the time when the notice of the landlord's intention to bring proceedings was served and at the date of the hearing. It should be borne in mind that not even delays on the part of a local authority or the DSS in making HB payments provide a defence to proceedings brought under ground 8.

If there are HB problems, the best tactic is to seek an adjournment in the hope that they will be resolved and the arrears cleared or significantly reduced before the case comes back to court. In cases where arrears have been caused by delays in paying HB, it is worth considering applying for leave to issue a third-party notice against the local authority or, if the DSS is at fault, the Secretary of State.

As with all rent arrears grounds, it is important for advisers to consider whether or not there has been any breach of repairing obligations on the landlord's part. If there has, any damages awarded on a counterclaim based on the disrepair are set off against arrears of rent and may result in the arrears being wiped out or reduced below the level of three months' arrears.[31]

It is also important to check that the plaintiff has complied with the provisions of Landlord and Tenant Act 1987 ss47 and 48, which require demands for rent to include the landlord's name and address, and that landlords supply tenants with a notice giving details of an address in England and Wales where notices may be served. If landlords fail to comply with these provisions, rent is not due until the failure has been rectified.[32]

Discretionary Grounds for Possession

Ground 9: Suitable alternative accommodation

> Suitable alternative accommodation is available for the tenant or will be available for him when the order for possession takes effect.

As with the RA 1977,[33] the availability of suitable alternative accommodation, either at the time of the hearing or when the order is to

---

31 Check any express terms. NB Landlord and Tenant Act 1985 s11, and Defective Premises Act 1972. See *British Anzani (Felixstowe) v International Marine Management* [1980] 1 QB 137, *Chiodi v De Marney* [1988] 41 EG 80, CA, and *Davies v Peterson* (1989) 21 HLR 63, CA.
32 See *Dallhold Estate (UK) Pty Lrd v Lindsay Trading Properties Inc* [1992] EGCS 29, Ch D and *Hussain v Singh* (1992) *Independent* 6 October, CA.
33 Section 98(1)(a).

take effect, is a ground for possession. Schedule 2 Pt III[34] gives further clarification as to the matters to be taken into account when determining whether or not accommodation is suitable.

1.   For the purposes of ground 9 above, a certificate of the local housing authority for the district in which the dwelling-house in question is situated, certifying that the authority will provide suitable alternative accommodation for the tenant by a date specified in the certificate, shall be conclusive evidence that suitable alternative accommodation will be available for him by that date.

2.   Where no such certificate as is mentioned in paragraph 1 above is produced to the court, accommodation shall be deemed to be suitable for the purposes of ground 9 above if it consists of either—
(a)   premises which are to be let as a separate dwelling such that they will then be let on an assured tenancy, other than—
   (i)   a tenancy in respect of which notice is given not later than the beginning of the tenancy that possession might be recovered on any of grounds 1 to 5 above, or
   (ii)   an assured shorthold tenancy, within the meaning of Chapter II of Part 1 of this Act, or
(b)   premises to be let as a separate dwelling on terms which will, in the opinion of the court, afford to the tenant security of tenure reasonably equivalent to the security afforded by Chapter I of Part I of this Act in the case of an assured tenancy of a kind mentioned in subparagraph (a) above,
and, in the opinion of the court, the accommodation fulfils the relevant conditions as defined in paragraph 3 below.

3.—(1)   For the purposes of paragraph 2 above, the relevant conditions are that the accommodation is reasonably suitable to the needs of the tenant and his family as regards proximity to place of work, and either—
(a)   similar as regards rental and extent to the accommodation afforded by dwelling-houses provided in the neighbourhood by any local housing authority for persons whose needs as regards extent are, in the opinion of the court, similar to those of the tenant and his family; or
(b)   reasonably suitable to the means of the tenant and to the needs of the tenant and his family as regards extent and character; and
that if any furniture was provided for use under the assured tenancy in question, furniture is provided for use in the accommodation which is either similar to that so provided or is reasonably suitable to the needs of the tenant and his family.

---

34   Cf RA 1977 Sch 15 Pt IV. Part III of Sch 2 of HA 1988 is very similar to the comparable RA provisions, although the alternative accommodation should be let on an assured tenancy, rather than on a protected tenancy.

(2)   For the purposes of subparagraph (1)(a) above, a certificate of a local housing authority stating—

(a)   the extent of the accommodation afforded by dwelling-houses provided by the authority to meet the needs of tenants with families of such number as may be specified in the certificate, and

(b)   the amount of the rent charged by the authority for dwelling houses affording accommodation of that extent,

shall be conclusive evidence of the facts so stated.

4.   Accommodation shall not be deemed to be suitable to the needs of the tenant and his family if the result of their occupation of the accommodation would be that it would be an overcrowded dwelling-house for the purposes of Part X of the Housing Act 1985.

5.   Any document purporting to be a certificate of a local housing authority named therein issued for the purposes of this Part of this Schedule and to be signed by the proper officer of that authority shall be received in evidence and, unless the contrary is shown, shall be deemed to be such a certificate without further proof.

6.   In this Part of this Schedule 'local housing authority' and 'district' in relation to such an authority, have the same meaning as in the Housing Act 1985.

When a possession order is made under this ground, the landlord must pay a sum equal to the tenant's reasonable removal expenses (s11(1) – see below).

Ground 10: Rent arrears

Some rent lawfully due from the tenant—

(a)   is unpaid on the date on which the proceedings for possession are begun; and

(b)   except where subsection (1)(b) of section 8 of this Act applies, was in arrears at the date of the service of the notice under that section relating to those proceedings.

A landlord must prove that there were rent arrears both at the date when proceedings were begun and – unless the court considers it 'just and equitable' to dispense with service of a notice prior to issue – when the notice was served. This is the ground for possession which is most similar to Case 1 in Sch 15 to the RA 1977. In theory, a possession order may be made even if the arrears are paid off before the hearing, although in most circumstances there would be strong grounds for arguing that it would not be reasonable to make an order.[35]

---

35   *Hayman v Rowlands* [1957] 1 All ER 321; *Sopwith v Stutchbury* (1983) 17 HLR 50; but see *Lee-Steere v Jennings* (1988) 20 HLR 1, CA.

Ground 11: Persistent delay in paying rent

Whether or not any rent is in arrears on the date on which proceedings for possession are begun, the tenant has persistently delayed paying rent which has become lawfully due.

Even if there are no arrears on the date when possession proceedings are issued, persistent delay in paying rent that is due is a ground for possession. The phrase 'persistent delay' is not defined but is likely to have the same meaning as in Landlord and Tenant Act 1954 s30(1)(b)–ie, one instalment of rent has been in arrears for a significant period of time or instalments have persistently been paid late, or both.[36]

Ground 12: Breach of any obligation

Any obligation of the tenancy (other than one related to the payment of rent) has been broken or not performed.

This ground for possession is similar to the second limb of Case 1 in RA 1977 Sch 15 (see p126).

Ground 13: Waste or neglect

The condition of the dwelling-house or any of the common parts has deteriorated owing to acts of waste by, or the neglect or default of, the tenant or any other person residing in the dwelling-house and, in the case of an act of waste by, or the neglect or default of, a person lodging with the tenant or a sub-tenant of his, the tenant has not taken such steps as he ought reasonably to have taken for the removal of the lodger or sub-tenant.

For the purposes of this ground, 'common parts' means any part of a building comprising the dwelling-house and any other premises which the tenant is entitled under the terms of the tenancy to use in common with the occupiers of other dwelling-houses in which the landlord has an estate or interest.

This ground is similar to Case 3 in RA 1977 Sch 15 (see p132), but slightly wider, in that it applies not only to the premises let, but also to common parts.

Ground 14: Nuisance or annoyance or conviction for illegal or immoral user

The tenant or any other person residing in the dwelling-house has been guilty of conduct which is a nuisance or annoyance to adjoining occupiers, or has

---

36   See *Hopcutt v Carver* (1969) 209 EG 1069 and *Horowitz v Ferrand* [1956] CLY 4843.

been convicted of using the dwelling-house or allowing the dwelling-house to be used for immoral or illegal purposes.

This ground is almost exactly the same as Case 2 in RA 1977 Sch 15 (see p130).

Ground 15: Deterioration of furniture

The condition of any furniture provided for use under the tenancy has, in the opinion of the court, deteriorated owing to ill-treatment by the tenant or any other person residing in the dwelling-house and, in the case of ill-treatment by a person lodging with the tenant or by a sub-tenant of his, the tenant has not taken such steps as he ought reasonably to have taken for the removal of the lodger or sub-tenant.

This ground is almost exactly the same as Case 4 in RA 1977 Sch 15 (see p132).

Ground 16: Premises let to employees

The dwelling-house was let to the tenant in consequence of his employment by the landlord seeking possession or a previous landlord under the tenancy and the tenant has ceased to be in that employment.

This ground for possession is wider than Case 8, the comparable RA ground (see p135). It applies whether or not the employer requires the premises for another employee. Normally the employer and the landlord have to be the same person. However if health service employees are employed by a health service body (eg a health authority) but live in premises owned by the Department of Health, the Secretary of State, when bringing possession proceedings, may rely upon Ground 16.[37]

Reasonableness

The criteria for establishing whether or not it is reasonable to make an order for possession against an assured tenant are the same as those used in proceedings against RA protected tenants or secure tenants (see p161).

Although all of these grounds for possession can apply to periodic assured tenancies, grounds 1, 3, 4, 5, 6, 7, 9 and 16 cannot be used against fixed-term assured tenants whose tenancies have not expired by effluxion of time (s7(6)).

---

37   National Health and Community Care Act 1990 s60(6) and Sch 8, para 10.

Other court orders

Removal expenses

Section 11 provides:

> 11.—(1)   Where a court makes an order for possession of a dwelling-house let on an assured tenancy on Ground 6 or Ground 9 in Schedule 2 to this Act (but not on any other ground), the landlord shall pay to the tenant a sum equal to the reasonable expenses likely to be incurred by the tenant in removing from the dwelling-house.
>
> (2)   Any question as to the amount of the sum referred to in subsection (1) above shall be determined by agreement between the landlord and the tenant or, in default of agreement, by the court.
>
> (3)   Any sum payable to a tenant by virtue of this section shall be recoverable as a civil debt due from the landlord.

A landlord can only be compelled to pay removal expenses where possession is obtained on the grounds that the landlord wishes to demolish or reconstruct premises or where suitable alternative accommodation is available.

Misrepresentation and concealment

If, after a possesion order has been made, the court is satisfied that the landlord obtained the order 'by misrepresentation or concealment of material facts', the court may order the landlord to pay 'such sum as appears sufficient as compensation for damage or loss sustained . . . as a result of the order' (s12). This provision is similar to RA 1977 s102 (see p141), but, unlike s102, applies to all the grounds for possession.

Adjournment, stays and suspension

Section 9 provides:

> 9.—(1)   Subject to subsection (6) below, the court may adjourn for such period or periods as it thinks fit proceedings for possession of a dwelling-house let on an assured tenancy.
>
> (2)   On the making of an order for possession of a dwelling-house let on an assured tenancy or at any time before the execution of such an order, the court, subject to subsection (6) below, may—
>
> (a)   stay or suspend execution of the order, or
> (b)   postpone the date of possession,
> for such period or periods as the court thinks just.
>
> (3)   On any such adjournment as is referred to in subsection (1) above or on any such stay, suspension or postponement as is referred to in subsection

(2) above, the court, unless it considers that to do so would cause exceptional hardship to the tenant or would otherwise be unreasonable, shall impose conditions with regard to payment by the tenant of arrears of rent (if any) and rent or payments in respect of occupation after the termination of the tenancy (mesne profits) and may impose such other conditions as it thinks fit.

(4)   If any such conditions as are referred to in subsection (3) above are complied with, the court may, if it thinks fit, discharge or rescind any such order as is referred to in subsection (2) above.

(5)   In any case where—

   (a)   at a time when proceedings are brought for possession of a dwelling-house let on an assured tenancy, the tenant's spouse or former spouse, having rights of occupation under the Matrimonial Homes Act 1983, is in occupation of the dwelling-house, and

   (b)   the assured tenancy is terminated as a result of those proceedings,

the spouse or former spouse, so long as he or she remains in occupation, shall have the same rights in relation to, or in connection with, any such adjournment as is referred to in subsection (1) above or any such stay, suspension or postponement as is referred to in subsection (2) above, as he or she would have if those rights of occupation were not affected by the termination of the tenancy.

(6)   This section does not apply if the court is satisfied that the landlord is entitled to possession of the dwelling-house—

   (a)   on any of the grounds in Part I of Schedule 2 to this Act; or

   (b)   by virtue of subsection (1) or subsection (4) of section 21 below.

If a court is satisfied that one of the mandatory grounds for possession applies, it has only the very limited power to adjourn, stay or suspend an order for possession which is provided for by HA 1980 s89(1) – ie, for 14 days, unless exceptional hardship would be caused, in which case the time for giving up possession may be delayed for up to six weeks. Otherwise s9 gives the court a discretion to adjourn proceedings, stay or suspend the execution of any order or postpone the date of possession for such period or periods as the court thinks fit, although when doing so the court must impose conditions relating to the payment of rent or rent arrears unless doing so would 'cause exceptional hardship . . . or would otherwise be unreasonable'. This means that if a landlord satisfies the court that one of the discretionary grounds is proved, the court has exactly the same discretion as it has when making an order against a tenant enjoying the protection of RA 1977 or HA 1985.

A spouse or former spouse who remains in occupation has the same rights in relation to adjournments, stays and suspensions as the tenant.

CHAPTER 15

Assured Shorthold Tenancies

Assured shorthold tenancies provide no long-term security of tenure and are subject to minimal rent control. Although, legally, they are a kind of assured tenancy, the lack of security of tenure means that, from a tenant's point of view, the adjective 'assured' is something of a misnomer.

Most private sector lettings since January 1989 have been assured shorthold tenancies.

Definition of 'assured shorthold tenancy'

The HA 1988 s20 stipulates four requirements for the creation of an assured shorthold tenancy:

- It must be for a fixed term of not less than six months.
- It must not contain any provision enabling the landlord to terminate the tenancy within six months of the beginning of the tenancy. Section 45(4) provides that a power of re-entry or forfeiture for breach of condition does not count as a provision enabling the landlord to determine the tenancy for this purpose.
- Notice in the prescribed form must be served before the commencement of the tenancy stating that the tenancy will be an assured shorthold tenancy. The court has no power to dispense with service of this notice. The form of the notice is prescribed by the Assured Tenancies and Agricultural Occupancies (Forms) Regulations 1988.[1] The omission of certain words from the prescribed form may render the notice invalid.[2]
- It would be an assured tenancy but for these three requirements being satisfied.[3]

1   1 SI No 2203.
2   *London and Quadrant Housing v Robertson* (1991) 4 July, Bromley County Court, September 1991 *Legal Action* 17.
3   This is analogous to HA 1980 s52 which referred to 'a protected shorthold tenancy' as being 'a protected tenancy' which satisfied certain criteria.

A further tenancy of the same or substantially the same premises granted to a former assured shorthold tenant will also be an assured shorthold tenancy even if any of the first three requirements is no longer satisfied.

Section 20(3) makes it impossible for a landlord to grant an assured shorthold tenancy to anyone who, immediately before the grant of a new tenancy, was an assured tenant of the same landlord. This is the case even if the premises in question are different.

Possession proceedings

Section 21 provides:

21.—(1)   Without prejudice to any right of the landlord under an assured shorthold tenancy to recover possession of the dwelling-house let on the tenancy in accordance with Chapter I above, on or after the coming to an end of an assured shorthold tenancy which was a fixed term tenancy, a court shall make an order for possession of the dwelling-house if it is satisfied—

(a)   that the assured shorthold tenancy has come to an end and no further assured tenancy (whether shorthold or not) is for the time being in existence, other than a statutory periodic tenancy; and

(b)   the landlord or, in the case of joint landlords, at least one of them has given to the tenant not less than two months' notice stating that he requires possession of the dwelling-house.

(2)   A notice under paragraph (b) of subsection (1) above may be given before or on the day on which the tenancy comes to an end; and that subsection shall have effect notwithstanding that on the coming to an end of the fixed term tenancy a statutory periodic tenancy arises.

(3)   Where a court makes an order for possession of a dwelling-house by virtue of subsection (1) above, any statutory periodic tenancy which has arisen on the coming to an end of the assured shorthold tenancy shall end (without further notice and regardless of the period) on the day on which the order takes effect.

(4)   Without prejudice to any such right as is referred to in subsection (1) above, a court shall make an order for possession of a dwelling-house let on an assured shorthold tenancy which is a periodic tenancy if the court is satisfied—

(a)   that the landlord or, in the case of joint landlords, at least one of them has given to the tenant a notice stating that, after a date specified in the notice, being the last day of a period of the tenancy and not earlier than two months after the date the notice was given, possession of the dwelling-house is required by virtue of this section; and

(b)   that the date specified in the notice under paragraph (a) above is not earlier than the earliest day on which, apart from section 5(1) above, the tenancy could be brought to an end by a notice to quit given by the landlord on the same date as the notice under paragraph (a) above.

The ability of a landlord to recover possession against an assured shorthold tenant depends upon whether or not the fixed term had expired.

During the fixed term

The normal grounds for possession against assured tenants apply. Although the wording of the Act is far from clear, it seems that:

- the tenancy must contain a term allowing the landlord to re-enter or terminate the tenancy for breach of any covenant in the tenancy or if one of the grounds for possession against assured tenants exists; and
- the landlord must serve notice of proceedings for possession in accordance with s8 (see p182); and
- the landlord must prove the existence of any of the following grounds for possession, namely 2, 8, 10, 11, 12, 13, 14 or 15 (ie, essentially 'tenants default' grounds), and, if appropriate, that it is reasonable for an order to be made.

The tenant may be able to apply for relief from forfeiture.[4]

After expiry of the fixed term

Most landlords grant assured shorthold tenancies for the minimum of six months, but then allow the tenant to 'hold over' after the end of that period. In those circumstances, if the tenant continues to occupy premises as his or her only or principal home, a statutory periodic tenancy arises, but it lacks security of tenure. All that a landlord need do to recover possession is to:

a) prove that the tenancy has come to an end and that no new tenancy has been granted; and

b) give at least two months' notice to the tenant that the landlord requires possession. (More then two months' notice is required only where there is an express provision requiring a longer period of notice or the rental period is longer than two months, eg, where there is a quarterly tenancy, in which case three months' notice would have to be given.) Notice may be given before the fixed term expires. There are no requirements as to the form of the notice – the only indication that it has even to be in writing is the reference to notice being 'served'. There

4   See p102 above and *Patel v Sullivan* (1991) 28 June, Wandsworth County Court, September 1991 *Legal Action* 17.

is no power to dispense with service of the notice. A notice is valid even if given by only one of several joint landlords;

c) take court proceedings.

If landlords comply with these requirements, they are automatically entitled to possession. The court has no power to suspend possession orders, apart from Housing Act 1980 s89(1).

It should be noted that there are proposals in a Lord Chancellor's Department Consultation Paper *Housing Cases in the County Courts* for a new type of possession action to enable landlords to recover possession against assured shorthold tenants quickly, perhaps without hearings.[5]

5   See September 1992 *Legal Action* 18.

Private sector tenancies: general

CHAPTER 16

Sub-tenants

The relationship between a mesne (ie, intermediate) tenant and sub-tenant is in most respects the same as the relationship between any landlord and tenant. The RA 1977 s152 expressly provides that ' "Tenant" . . . includes "sub-tenant" ' and that ' "tenancy" includes 'sub-tenancy" '. The HA 1988 s45 contains a similar provision in relation to assured or assured shorthold tenancies. Possession proceedings may be brought by a mesne tenant against a sub-tenant in exactly the same way that a freeholder may bring proceedings against a tenant. Even if, as against the head landlord, the sub-tenancy is illegal in that it is in breach of a covenant against subletting, this has no effect on the relationship between mesne tenant and sub-tenant.[1]

The position may, however, be more complicated if in some way the head tenancy comes to an end. If the mesne tenant surrenders his or her interest the sub-tenant becomes a direct tenant of the head landlord[2] even if there is a covenant against subletting.[3] The same applies if the head tenancy is brought to an end by a notice to quit served by the mesne tenant on the landlord.[4] However, if the head tenancy is determined in any other way (for example by a landlord's notice to quit, forfeiture, effluxion of time or a possession order) the common law rule is that the sub-tenancy comes to an end at the same time, leaving the sub-tenant with no rights as against the head landlord.[5] However, this common law rule is

1 *Critchley v Clifford* [1961] 3 All ER 288.
2 *Mellor v Watkins* (1874) LR 9 QB 400; but not, it seems, if it was a statutory tenant who purported to grant the sub-tenancy – *Solomon v Orwell* [1954] 1 All ER 874.
3 *Parker v Jones* [1910] 2 KB 32.
4 *Mellor v Watkins* n2.
5 *Critchley v Clifford* n1 at 293 and 296; *Sherwood (Baron) v Moody* [1952] 1 All ER 389; *Cow v Casey* [1949] 1 All ER 197 (the latter two cases were decided under sections with different wording from the current s137). A sub-tenant in this situation is in effect a trespasser as against the head landlord (*Cow v Casey*) and speedy proceedings for possession under CCR Ord 24 or RSC Ord 113 (see below) can be used – *Moore Properties Ltd v McKeon* [1976] 1 WLR 1278. Note, however, that if a landlord is seeking to determine the head tenancy by forfeiture proceedings, a sub-tenant can apply for relief against forfeiture (see pp102–108 above) even if s137 provides no protection – Law of Property Act 1925 s146(4) and *Factors (Sundries) Ltd v Miller* [1952] 2 All ER 630.

modified in relation to lawful RA sub-tenancies by RA 1977 s137 which provides:

137.—(1)   If a court makes an order for possession of a dwelling-house from—

    (a)   a protected or statutory tenant, or

    (b)   a protected occupier or statutory tenant as defined in the Rent (Agriculture) Act 1976,

and the order is made by virtue of section 98(1) or 99(2) of this Act or, as the case may be, under Part I of Schedule 4 to that Act, nothing in the order shall affect the right of any sub-tenant to whom the dwelling-house or any part of it has been lawfully sublet before the commencement of the proceedings to retain possession by virtue of this Act, nor shall the order operate to give a right to possession against any such sub-tenant.

(2)   Where a statutorily protected tenancy of a dwelling-house is determined, either as a result of an order for possession or for any other reason, any sub-tenant to whom the dwelling-house or any part of it has been lawfully sublet shall, subject to this Act, be deemed to become the tenant of the landlord on the same terms as if the tenant's statutorily protected tenancy had continued.

(3)   Where a dwelling-house—

    (a)   forms part of premises which have been let as a whole on a superior tenancy but do not constitute a dwelling-house let on a statutorily protected tenancy; and

    (b)   is itself subject to a protected or statutory tenancy,

then, from the coming to an end of the superior tenancy, this Act shall apply in relation to the dwelling-house as if, in lieu of the superior tenancy, there had been separate tenancies of the dwelling-house and of the remainder of the premises, for the like purposes as under the superior tenancy, and at rents equal to the just proportion of the rent under the superior tenancy.

In this subsection 'premises' includes, if the sub-tenancy in question is a protected or statutory tenancy to which section 99 of this Act applies, an agricultural holding within the meaning of the Agricultural Holdings Act 1948.

(4)   In subsection (2) and (3) above 'statutorily protected tenancy' means—

    (a)   a protected or statutory tenancy;

    (b)   a protected occupancy or statutory tenancy as defined in the Rent (Agriculture) Act 1976; or

    (c)   if the sub-tenancy in question is a protected or statutory tenancy to which section 99 of this Act applies, a tenancy of an agricultural holding within the meaning of the Agricultural Holdings Act 1948.

(5)   Subject to subsection (6) below, a long tenancy of a dwelling-house which is also a tenancy at a low rent but which, had it not been a tenancy at a low rent, would have been a protected tenancy or an assured tenancy, within

the meaning of Part I of the Housing Act 1988, shall be treated for the purposes of subsection (2) above as a statutorily protected tenancy.

(6) Notwithstanding anything in subsection (5) above, subsection (2) above shall not have effect where the sub-tenancy in question was created (whether immediately or derivatively) out of a long tenancy falling within subsection (5) above and, at the time of the creation of the sub-tenancy—

(a) a notice to terminate the long tenancy had been given under section 4(1) of the Landlord and Tenant Act 1954 or, as the case may be, served under paragraph 4(1) of Schedule 10 to the Local Government and Housing Act 1989; or

(b) the long tenancy was being continued by section 3(1) of the said Act of 1954 or, as the case may be, paragraph 3 of the said Schedule 10;

unless the sub-tenancy was created with the consent in writing of the person who at the time when it was created was the landlord, within the meaning of Part I of the said Act of 1954 or, as the case may be, paragraph 3 of the said schedule 10.

(7) This section shall apply equally where a protected occupier of a dwelling-house, or part of a dwelling-house, has a relevant licence as defined in the Rent (Agriculture) Act 1976, and in this section 'tenancy' and all cognate expressions shall be construed accordingly.

The construction of this section is 'unusually difficult'.[6] In brief, the effect of subsections (1) and (2) is that if a protected or statutory head tenancy is determined, any lawful[7] sub-tenant or lawful assignee[8] becomes a direct tenant of the landlord on the same terms enjoyed under his or her sub-tenancy.[9] If the head tenancy is not a protected or statutory tenancy (for example because the premises were not let as a separate dwelling but as a building containing several units intended for individual occupation[10]), subsection (3) enables a lawful sub-tenant to become a direct tenant of the part sublet when the head tenancy is determined.[11] Section 137(3) is, however, of no help to a sub-tenant if the head lease is a business tenancy.

6 Per Lord Reid in *Maunsell v Olins* [1975] 1 All ER 16 at 17.
7 There is no question of s137 applying if the sub-tenancy is in breach of a covenant against subletting or a required consent is not obtained – *Drive Yourself Hire Co (London) Ltd v Strutt* [1953] 2 All ER 1475 and *Trustees of Henry Smith's Charity v Willson* [1983] 1 All ER 73. As to consent to subletting see comments on Case 6 above. The relevant time at which to consider whether consent has been given is the date of issue of proceedings – *Oak Property Co Ltd v Chapman* [1947] 2 All ER 1.
8 *Drive Yourself v Strutt* n7.
9 However, if proceedings are brought under Case 6 (subletting of the whole without consent), the landlord may be entitled to an order for possession against the sub-tenant notwithstanding s137 if the court considers it reasonable to make such an order – *Leith Properties Ltd v Springer* [1982] 3 All ER 731, CA.
10 See RA 1977 s1 and *Horford Investments v Lambert* [1973] 3 WLR 872.
11 See, eg, *Cadogan (Earl) v Henthorne* [1956] 3 All ER 851.

In those circumstances it is unlikely that a sub-tenant will be successful in defending possession proceedings brought by the freeholder if the head tenancy has been determined.[12] Section 138 contains provisions which apply if the head tenancy is unfurnished but the sub-tenancy is furnished. There is no equivalent to RA 1977 s137 in the HA 1988. If the whole of premises which are let on an assured tenancy are sublet, the dwelling can no longer be the tenant's 'only or principal home' and accordingly the tenancy ceases to be assured. If it is a periodic tenancy, it can be determined by notice to quit. If the notice to quit is valid, the landlord is then entitled to possession both against the tenant and the sub-tenant.

12   See *Maunsell v Olins* [1975] AC 373, HL; *Pittalis v Grant* [1989] QB 605, [1989] 2 All ER 622, (1989) 21 HLR 368, CA; *Bromley Park Gardens v George* (1991) 36 EG 139, 23 HLR 441, CA, and (in different circumstances) *Grosvenor Estate Belgravia v Cochren* [1991] 44 EG 169, CA.

CHAPTER 17

Unprotected Tenants and Licensees

If the tenant does not come within one of the forms of statutory protection described above, a landlord seeking possession need only commence proceedings and prove that s/he has some interest in the premises and that the contractual tenancy has been determined. It is likely that the only defence available in the short term to such a tenant is to allege that the contractual tenancy had not been determined at the date when proceedings were issued, for example because a notice to quit was defective.

Protection from Eviction Act 1977 s3 makes it unlawful for landlords of many unprotected tenants and licensees to enforce their right to recover possession 'otherwise than by proceedings in the court'. Landlords who fail to comply with s3 commit a criminal offence contrary to s1(2) and are liable to a claim for damages in tort. Section 3 has been amended by HA 1980 s69(1) and by HA 1988 ss30 and 31. It now applies to all non-statutorily protected tenancies and licences apart from excluded tenancies and excluded licences created on or after 15 January 1989. The categories of tenancies and licences which are 'excluded' are defined by HA 1988 s31 (see p9). In brief, they are tenancies or licences in hostels where accommodation is shared with a landlord or landlord's family, where the occupier is a former trespasser, where occupation is for a holiday and where occupation is rent free.

A licensee has a complete defence to possession proceedings if the licence has not been terminated by the time that proceedings are issued,[1] or if a further licence has been created. A licence may simply be a temporary agreement that someone may be or stay on premises. In *Thomas v Sorrell* Vaughan CJ stated 'a dispensation or licence properly passeth no interest nor alters or transfers property in anything but only makes an action lawful, which without it has been unlawful'.[2] It may be hard to draw the line between an owner who says 'you can stay on the premises' and one

---

1   *GLC v Jenkins* [1975] 1 All ER 354.
2   (1673) Vaugh 330.

who says 'I do not agree to you staying on the premises, but I will refrain from evicting you until a certain date'.

If the licensee is a contractual licensee, the owner must observe the contractual provisions which the licence contains relating to termination. Whether or not there are contractual provisions in the licence, a licensee must be given reasonable notice[3]: there is no need for the notice itself to specify the particular time or indeed a reasonable time. But a reasonable time must have elapsed between the giving of the notice and the issue of court proceedings.[4] The notice determines the licence immediately on service,[5] but does not become operative until the expiry of such a reasonable time, even if the notice contains a specified period of time which is too short. There are no set rules as to what is reasonable. The length of time depends on the circumstances in any particular case, and factors which may be taken into account are the length of time that the licensee has resided in the premises and the periods for which payments are made. A notice to terminate a licence must now comply with Protection from Eviction Act 1977 s5, as amended, unless the licence is 'excluded'. If a licence is excluded, notice may be given orally.[6] If there are joint owners, notice may be given by one of them acting alone.[7]

A former licensee whose licence has been determined but who remains on the premises is a trespasser. Accordingly, the owner is entitled to damages for trespass without bringing evidence that s/he could or would have re-let the property if the trespasser had not been there. The measure of damages is usually the value to the trespasser of the use of the property for the period during which s/he has trespassed, and in a normal case this is the ordinary letting value of the property.[8]

3   Minister of Health v Bellotti [1944] 1 All ER 238.
4   Ibid.
5   Ibid.
6   Crane v Morris [1965] 3 All ER 77. Section 5 has been amended by HA 1988 s32.
7   Annen v Rattee (1985) 273 EG 503.
8   Swordheath Properties Ltd v Tabet [1979] 1 All ER 240. See chapter 26.

CHAPTER 18

Premises Occupied by Employees

Employees who occupy residential premises owned by their employers (ie service occupiers) may be either tenants or licensees. Where it is necessary for the employee to live in the premises for the better performance of his or her job or where the employee is required to live in premises as a term of his or her contract of employment, it is likely that the employee is merely a licensee of those premises.[1] If this is not the case, the employee is a tenant.[2] If the tenancy satisfies the normal RA requirements[3] the tenant will have full RA protection, subject only to the possibility of possession proceedings brought under case 8 (see above). If the tenancy satisfies the usual requirements in HA 1988, the tenant will have an assured tenancy, subject only to the possibility of possession proceedings brought under ground 16 (see above). If however the employee is a licensee, s/he has no security of tenure. A service licensee has only the limited protection that the employer must bring court proceedings to evict him or her. The Protection from Eviction Act 1977 s8(2) provides:

> For the purposes of Part I of this Act a person who, under the term of his employment, had exclusive possession of the premises other than as a tenant shall have been deemed to have been a tenant and the expressions 'let' and 'tenancy' shall be construed accordingly.

This means that ss1 (unlawful eviction and harassment of occupier) and 3 (prohibition of eviction without due process of law) apply. The employer need prove only that s/he owns or has an interest in the premises and that the rights of the employee (or ex-employee) to reside in the premises have been determined, in accordance with either the contract of employment or

1   *Smith v Seghill Overseers* (1875) LR 10 QB 422; *Fox v Dalby* (1874) LR 10 CP 285 and *Glasgow Corporation v Johnstone* [1965] AC 609.
2   *Royal Philanthropic Society v County* (1985) 276 EG 1068.
3   See RA 1977 s1. One particular problem which tenants who are employees sometimes face is that there is no rent payable and accordingly the tenancy is outside full RA protection due to s5. See *Heslop v Burns* [1974] 1 WLR 1241 and *Montagu v Browning* [1954] 1 WLR 1039.

any other agreement relating to the premises. A notice to terminate a service licence must now comply with the requirements of the Protection from Eviction Act s5 unless it is an "excluded licence".[4] In some circumstances, where occupation of a licensee is expressed to be contemporaneous with employment if the licensee's employment has come to an end no notice at all is necessary.[5]

If a service licensee considers that s/he has been unfairly dismissed, an application may be made to the industrial tribunal. Although the industrial tribunal may recommend reinstatement, this is of little assistance in defending possession proceedings for tied accommodation. The industrial tribunal cannot *order* reinstatement and the court considering possession proceedings is generally interested only in ascertaining whether or not the contract has been terminated, not whether it has been terminated fairly or unfairly. Applications for adjournments of such possession proceedings pending the hearing of an application to an industrial tribunal are generally unsuccessful.[6]

---

4   HA 1988 ss30–31, p88 above.
5   *Doe d Hughes v Derry* (1840) 9 C & P 494, *Ivory v Palmer* [1975] ICR 840, CA, and *Norris v Checksfield* (1991) 23 HLR 425, CA.
6   See, eg, *Whitbread West Pennines Ltd v Reedy* (1988) 20 HLR 642, CA (manager of public house dismissed).

CHAPTER 19
Death

A contractual tenancy does not terminate on the tenant's death unless the tenancy expressly so provides.[1] If the tenant leaves a will, the tenancy passes to the tenant's executors. If the tenant dies intestate the tenancy passes to the President of the Family Division until such time as letters of administration are taken out.[2] This applies to contractual RA tenancies and assured and assured shorthold tenancies, but not to RA statutory tenancies.

If a landlord wishes to terminate a contractual tenancy vested in executors or administrators by serving a notice to quit, that notice must be served on the executors or administrators as the case may be. If letters of administration have not been taken out, the notice must be served on the President of the Family Division c/o The Treasury Solicitor, Queen Anne's Chambers, 28 Broadway, London SW1H 9JS.[3] It is possible to find out whether such notice has been served by telephoning the Treasury Solicitor's Department on 071-210 3000. If a deceased tenant's contractual tenancy is not determined in this way, any sub-occupiers have a complete defence to possession proceedings which are issued before the tenancy has been determined.[4] In the long term, however, there is nothing to stop the landowner serving a valid notice to quit and then bringing new proceedings.

In the ordinary course of events, a RA statutory tenancy comes to an end on the death of the tenant since s/he can no longer occupy the premises as a residence.[5] As a statutory tenancy is only a personal right it cannot be left to another person through the deceased tenant's will.[6] However RA 1977 s2(1)(b) and Sch 1 Pt I, as amended by HA 1988 s39, provide that a

1 *Youngmin v Heath* [1974] 1 WLR 135.
2 Administration of Estates Act 1925 s9.
3 *Practice Direction* [1985] 1 All ER 832.
4 *Wirral BC v Smith* (1982) 43 P & CR 312.
5 RA 1977 s2. See pp111-17 above and *Skinner v Geary* [1931] 2 KB 546.
6 *John Lovibond and Sons Ltd v Vincent* [1929] 1 KB 687.

spouse who was living with the tenant at the time of his or her death or, if there was no such spouse, a member of the tenant's family who had been living with him or her for two years immediately before the death, can succeed to the tenancy. A spouse who 'inherits' a tenancy in this way is called a 'statutory tenant by succession' and acquires a statutory tenancy. 'Spouse' is defined by HA 1988 Sch 4 as including any person living with the deceased tenant as wife or husband. Any other member of the family who succeeds to a tenancy as a result of the death of a tenant on or after 15 January 1989 acquires an assured tenancy (see chapter 14). The succession provisions apply to both contractual and statutory tenancies.[7] RA 1977 Sch 1 provides that any tenancy can be passed on twice in this way.

Any spouse or member of the original tenant's family who acquires a tenancy in this way takes over the tenancy with all the rights and obligations which existed on the tenant's death – for example rent arrears or a suspended possession order.[8]

It is possible for a tenant to leave his or her contractual tenancy in a will to one person, but for another to be entitled to succeed to the tenancy in accordance with RA 1977 Sch 1. In this situation any person who would be entitled to succeed to the tenancy acquires a statutory tenancy by succession and the contractual tenancy goes into 'abeyance' until the statutory tenancy comes to an end.[9]

Although assured and assured shorthold tenancies can be inherited by will or on intestacy, the death of an assured tenant gives the landlord a ground for possession against anyone other than the deceased tenant's spouse or anyone living with the 'original tenant as his or her wife or husband'.[10]

7   Moodie v Hosegood [1951] 2 All ER 582, HL.
8   Sherrin v Brand [1956] 1 QB 403.
9   Moodie v Hosegood n7, overruling Smith v Mather [1948] 1 All ER 704 and Thynne v Salmon [1948] 1 All ER 49.
10   HA 1988 Sch 4 para 2. See also HA 1988 Sch 2 ground 7 – see p191 above.

CHAPTER 20

Rental Purchase Agreements

Generally

Rental purchase agreements[1] are happily now of restricted application. The true rental purchase agreement is in essence a contract for the sale of a property with the purchaser allowed into possession paying the purchase price by instalments and with completion of the sale taking place, if ever, only following payment of the last instalment. It is inaccurate to describe the arrangement as a rental agreement as the purchaser is usually allowed into possession under the terms of the agreement for sale, not as tenant, but as licensee.

Normally such agreements will be in written form often of a pro forma nature. It is essential to study the document carefully as the terms can differ quite widely. The agreement will provide for a specified sum to be paid before completion can be called for. It will usually also specify the interest rate to be charged on the outstanding capital. A fixed weekly or monthly sum is generally specified which will either go directly towards repaying the capital borrowed or go towards satisfying the accruing interest, buildings insurance and other outgoings, with only part going towards repayment of the capital. Some agreements provide for completion to take place before payment of the whole capital sum but with the vendor granting a mortgage at the date of completion of the sale for the sum outstanding at the time. There are many permutations.

---

1 See generally B Hoggett 'Houses on the never-never: some legal aspects of rental purchase' (1972) 36 *Conv* 325; 'Houses on the never-never – some recent developments" (1975) 39 *Conv* 343; 'How to help the rental purchaser' June 1976 *LAG Bulletin* 133; L Burrows and R Murphy 'Rental Purchase – The Case for Change' (1990), Shelter and National Consumer Council 'Buying a Home on Rental Purchase; A Consumer View' (1989).

Rental purchase and Rent Act evasion

Many ostensible rental purchase agreements were prepared not with the intention of selling the property to a willing purchaser but with the sole intention of avoiding the RA by seeking not to create a tenancy. Following *Street v Mountford*[2] it was thought that, where there was a bona fide rental purchase intended by the parties, no landlord/tenant relationship would be established. However, after *Bretherton v Paton*[3] it seems that entering into possession even with the intention of purchasing the property does not bar the application of the *Street* principle where the occupier has exclusive possession paying a specified periodic payment. Normally in such circumstances the tenancy will be protected under the RA or be an assured tenancy under HA 1988.

Where it is felt that an arrangement is not caught by the principle in *Street* and it proves necessary to consider whether an arrangement is a bona fide rental purchase, advisers should consider the following points.

a) Was there any expectation that the occupier would in fact purchase the property? If not, then this is likely to be decisive. It will be necessary to check the dealings between the parties *before* the document was signed. How was the property advertised, what conversation took place, did the owner really want to sell the property?

b) Was the sale price inflated above market value or was the interest rate specified in the agreement inflated as compared to the then current mortgage rate?

c) Is the term of repayment unduly long, either in itself or when compared with the length of any leasehold interest granted?

d) Are there any clauses inconsistent with a bona fide contract for sale, for example a prohibition against assigning, subletting or parting with possession in the agreement?

e) Was there the usual investigation of title and the property as is normal before a purchase/sale?

f) Have the parties' actions since the date of the agreement been more consistent with a tenancy than a bona fide sale?

g) Were solicitors instructed by the occupier before entering into the agreement?

Where an occupier wishes to dispute his or her description in the agreement s/he can either apply for a declaration by the county court that

---

2   [1985] 2 WLR 877; [1985] 2 All ER 289, HL.
3   (1986) 18 HLR 257, CA; cf *Sharp v McArthur* (1987) 19 HLR 364, see also *Martin v Davies* (1952) 7 HLR 119, CA and *Francis Jackson Developments Ltd v Stemp* [1943] 2 All ER 601, CA.

s/he is a protected tenant[4] or raise that proposition as a defence to possession proceedings.

It is, however, important to bear in mind that it may be to the occupier's advantage to accept the apparent status of rental purchaser if, for example, the specified sale price is at or below the true market value or if the periodic payments are below a fair or market rent level.

Statutory and equitable protection

Assuming that the agreement in question is a bona fide rental purchase agreement the court has a statutory discretion to protect the occupier from eviction under the HA 1980 s88:

> **88.**—(1)   Where, under the terms of a rental purchase agreement, a person has been let into possession of a dwelling-house and, on the termination of the agreement or of his right to possession under it, proceedings are brought for the possession of the dwelling-house, the court may—
>
>   (*a*)   adjourn the proceedings; or
>   (*b*)   on making an order for the possession of the dwelling-house, stay or suspend execution of the order or postpone the date of possession;
> for such period or periods as the court thinks fit.

This is broadly similar to the protection given to mortgagors in default although there is no requirement that the occupier clear the arrears within a reasonable period.

The court can, but is not obliged to, grant relief on the condition that the occupier makes payments towards the arrears:

> (2)   On any such adjournment, stay, suspension or postponement the court may impose such conditions with regard to payments by the person in possession in respect of his continued occupation of the dwelling-house and such other conditions as the court thinks fit.[5]

The court has specific power to revoke or vary any condition which it has imposed.[6]

The definition of 'rental purchase agreement' is quite widely defined:

> (4)   In this section 'rental purchase agreement' means an agreement for the purchase of a dwelling-house (whether freehold or leasehold property) under which the whole or part of the purchase price is to be paid in three or

---

4   RA 1977 s141.
5   Ibid s88(2).
6   Ibid s88(3).

more instalments and the completion of the purchase is deferred until the whole or a specified part of the purchase price has been paid.[7]

The definition requires the purchase price to be paid in at least three instalments so as not to protect purchasers who are allowed into possession in the more usual transaction after exchange of contracts when normally a 10 per cent deposit is paid but before completion when the second and final instalment is made.

The court has some limited equitable jurisdiction to grant relief against forfeiture for breach of any terms of the agreement although the statutory discretion is much more extensive.[8]

Necessity for possession proceedings

Where a person is let into possession under a rental purchase agreement (as defined above) and continues to reside in the property after termination of the agreement or his or her right to possession under the agreement, then the provisions of the Protection from Eviction Act 1977 will usually apply so as to require the owner to regain possession by court order.[9] An additional prohibition against eviction without court order is contained in the Consumer Credit Act 1974 in respect of regulated conditional sale agreements where credit of less than £15,000 is afforded to the occupier.[10]

Other Points

Payments under 'an agreement for the purchase of a dwelling under which the whole or part of the purchase price is to be paid in more than one instalment and the completion of the purchase is deferred until the whole or a specified part of the purchase price has been paid' qualify as 'rent' for the purpose of the occupier qualifying for HB.[11]

Occupiers under rental purchase agreements appear eligible for tax relief on the interest paid as if they were mortgagors.[12] A specific claim for relief will be necessary as the owners of properties subject to rental purchase agreements in favour of the occupiers are not likely to be prescribed mortgagees for the purpose of the MIRAS scheme. In principle it would seem that an occupier might be eligible to both tax relief and HB.

7   Ibid s88(4).
8   See references at n1 and note at (1974) 37 MLR 705.
9   HA 1980 Sch 25 para 61.
10   Consumer Credit Act 1974 ss8, 92(2) and 189.
11   Housing Benefit (General) Regulations 1987 SI No 1971 reg 10(1).
12   Income and Corporation Taxes Act 1988 ss354 and 367(3).

CHAPTER 21

Shared Ownership

The last decade has seen attempts to blur the edges between owner-occupation and renting. There is every reason to believe that the blurring will continue. Great efforts have been made to ease people into owner-occupation by use of shared ownership schemes. These allow the occupier progressively to buy tranches of the home that s/he occupies until the property is owned outright, or at least owned subject to a mortgage.

There are particular problems which face occupiers under such schemes, the principal one being that where part is owned subject to a mortgage and part is rented, there are potentially two separate claims for possession if the occupier defaults. It will be necessary to service both debts simultaneously in order to retain possession.

Under a typical shared ownership scheme a freeholder agrees to grant a long lease to the occupier in return for a premium representing (say) a quarter or half of the capital value of the property. The premium is raised by way of a mortgage from an institutional lender, or even from the freeholder. The occupier moves into the property and pays rent calculated by reference to the outstanding element not yet purchased.

Example: P agrees to buy a one-third share of a 99-year lease on a flat renovated by a housing association which has a market value of £90,000. The market rent for the flat is £600 per month. P takes a 99-year lease and borrows £30,000 from a bank, secured by way of legal charge on the leasehold title. P then makes mortgage repayments on the £30,000 borrowed and rent at the rate of £400 per month. Subsequently P agrees to purchase a further one-third share. P borrows an additional £30,000, and as a result the rent paid to the association is reduced to £200 per month but the mortgage repayments double. On buying the last third P will then cease paying rent to the association and will continue to pay the mortgage repayments until the end of the term agreed with the bank at the time of the taking of the lease.

In this example the occupier will be an assured tenant since s/he does not prima facie fall within any of the exceptions in HA 88 Sch 1. Only where the rent payable under the tenancy is over £25,000 per annum or below £250 per annum (£1,000 in London) would the tenancy fall outside the HA 88 assured tenancy regime on grounds of rent level (see p179). As such s/he will be liable to possession proceedings under all the grounds in HA 88 Sch 2.

Additionally, since in purchasing the lease the purchaser executed a legal charge, s/he is also liable to possession proceedings in the event of default under that agreement.

Occupiers under shared ownership agreements which fall within scope of the HA 88 and the Administration of Justice Acts will be entitled to claim relief under either legislative regime in the event of possession proceedings being brought by the relevant plaintiff.

Advisers will need to consider the particular agreement entered into by the individual being advised, as there are many differing forms of the shared ownership agreement.

Part III

Possession Procedure

CHAPTER 22

Procedure in Possession Proceedings

The need for possession proceedings

It is normal for a landlord who wishes to evict an occupier to take possession procdings through the court. In many circumstances a landlord who takes the law into his or her own hands by evicting someone without first obtaining a court order risks a prosecution under Protection from Eviction Act 1977, with a fine and/or imprisonment and/or a claim for substantial damages, for breach of covenant for quiet enjoyment, trespass and/or unlawful eviction under Housing Act 1988 ss27 and 28. However, there are exceptions which advisers should bear in mind.

Trespassers

See chapter 24.

Excluded licences and tenancies (see chapter 17)

Housing Act 1988 s30 and 31 created categories of 'excluded tenancies and licences' and amended Protection from Eviction Act 1977 s3 (prohibition of eviction without due process of law). The combined effect of these sections is that if there is an excluded tenancy or licence, a landlord who evicts may not be committing a criminal offence under Protection from Eviction Act s1 (unlawful eviction and harassment), and if the tenancy or licence has been properly terminated (eg, by service of a valid notice to quit), the occupant has no civil redress.

A tenancy or licence is excluded if:

a) under its items the occupier shares any accommodation with the landlord or licensor and the landlord or licensor occupies as his or her only or principal home 'premises of which the whole or part of the shared accommodation formed part';

b) the tenant or licensee shares accommodation with a member of the

family of the landlord or licensor and the landlord or licensor has his or
her only or principal home in the building where the shared accommodation is situated;

c) the tenant or licensee was oringinally a trespasser of premises but was
   granted a tenancy or licence as a temporary expedient;
d) it confers on the tenant or licensee the right to occupy premises for a
   holiday only;
e) it is granted otherwise than for money or money's worth;
f) the premises are in a hostel provided by a public sector landlord.

From the point of view of landlords, it may be wise to take possession
proceedings even if they believe that there is an excluded tenancy or
licence. There is not only the risk that the tenancy or licence may not in
fact be excluded, but also, if the occupants are on the premises at the time
of eviction, the possibility of a prosecution under Criminal Law Act 1977
s6 (using or threatening violence to secure entry). Prosecutions can be
brought under s6 even if the occupants are trespassers. An offence may be
committed under s6 'whether the violence in question is directed against
the person or against property'.[1]

If a landlord is threatening to evict without obtaining a possession
order and the occupants believe that they enjoy some form of security of
tenure, the safest course of action is to seek an injunction without delay,
pending an application for a declaration.

Commencement

Possession proceedings will usually be started in the county court. Indeed,
certain landlords who initiate proceedings in the High Court may be
prohibited from recovering some or all of their costs (HA 1985 s110(3),
RA 1977 s141(4) and HA 1988 s40(4)). The appropriate county court
will be that for the area in which the premises are situated (CCR Ord 4
r3). Apart from that geographical limitation, the county court has
jurisdiction to hear and determine all actions for the recovery of land
(County Courts Act 1984 s21), previous limitations made by reference to
rateable value having been repealed in 1991.

The landlord will submit to the county court office particulars of
claim in writing, often in standard form (for the particulars required see
Ord 6 r3). The proceedings then take the form of a fixed date action (Ord
3 r2). The court office will issue a summons to be served on the occupier
either personally or by post (Ord 7 r10(1)) at least 21 days before the

1   Section 6(4)(a).

return date (Ord 7 r10(5)). Shorter periods will apply where possession is sought under Ord 24 (trespassers) or for certain mandatory RA grounds (see p148). For personal and substituted service see Ord 7 r15.

Usually, the date given for hearing will be one upon which a large number of similar actions are listed. Theoretically, each case will be separately tried on that date. However, given the matters which are required to be proved before possession may be granted there is unlikely to be court time for a full trial of an action if both parties are legally represented. If the particulars of claim seek relief other than a possession order/mesne profits/rent arrears and the action is defended, the first appointed day will usually be used for a pre-trial review (Ord 3 r3(3), (4)).

The requirements for an action against squatters and certain other unauthorised occupiers under Ord 24 are substantially different and are detailed at pp235–44.

Particulars of claim in the usual form are reproduced in the precedents in Part V below.

Adjournments

In many county courts the date set for hearing may be reached not long after the occupier receives the summons. Time will be needed to react to the situation, get legal advice, apply for legal aid where necessary (see p230), and prepare a defence. To secure additional time, an application should be made to the court for an adjournment of the hearing. The court has power to adjourn the hearing (Ord 13 r3(1); but see RA 1977 s100; HA 1985 s85 and HA 1988 s9) and to give directions for the future conduct of the case (Ord 13 r2(1)). The application should be made on county court prescribed Form N244 and the plaintiff should be given at least two days' notice (Ord 13 r1(2)). In an emergency this will not be possible and the court should be asked to abridge the notice so that the application may be heard on the return day of the fixed date summons (Ord 13 r4(1)).

The adviser should telephone the plaintiff and request agreement to an adjournment, giving details of the defence and the reason for the delay in the occupier seeking advice. S/he should suggest that the hearing date be vacated (which the court office can organise without a hearing) or that the hearing be treated as a pre-trial review (Ords 1 r3 and 17 r1). The plaintiff may be more likely to agree to the initial hearing being treated as a pre-trial review or to the date being vacated if a defence has already been filed. If necessary, a solicitor can use a green form for the preparation of a short-form defence. If emergency legal aid has been granted, the plaintiff must be informed and advised that an order for costs will be sought if the adjournment is refused by the plaintiff but granted by the court. This telephone call should be followed by a letter, delivered by hand if necessary, confirming the content of the telephone conversation. The adviser should attend court, and, if no agreement has been reached, negotiate outside the court (see above). If the plaintiff still refuses to agree to an adjournment, an application must be made to the judge for an adjournment (Ord 13 r3; but see RA 1977 s100; HA 1985 s85 and HA 1988 s9) and for directions giving time to file a defence (Ord 13 r2). The tenant and adviser should be available to give oral evidence as to the reasons for the delay (eg, that no reply has been received to an application for emergency legal aid (see p232)). If this is not possible, an affidavit must be filed. The judge will also require an outline of the defence. If a tenant cannot attend because of illness, a doctor's certificate should be submitted to the judge.[2] It will not be a miscarriage of justice if an adjournment is refused where the occupier has not substantiated his or her claim that s/he had a valid defence by either giving oral evidence or making an affidavit of what the defence was.[3] However, where the adjournment ought properly to have been granted, the order for possession will be overturned on appeal.[4]

If the adviser has been instructed literally at the door of the court, reference should be made to the procedure suggested at pp54–6.

Defences and counterclaims

The main text of this work sets out the substantive and technical defences which may be raised in response to an action for possession of residential property. The reader should refer to the main text for consideration of the issues which must always be reviewed in planning the defences.

The form of defence must be in writing and submitted at the office of the county court (Ord 9 r2(1)). A simple form of admission/defence is issued to the defendant for such purposes and is enclosed with the summons. The defence should usually be submitted within 14 days of service of the summons (Ord 9 r2(1)). In practice, provided that the defence is filed and served before the trial date, no formal application for more time is usually made (Ord 9 r9(1)). Where the adviser has been instructed at a late stage or there have been delays in obtaining legal aid, it may be necessary to take a hastily drafted defence to the hearing on the return day (with copies for the plaintiff and court). The defendant must

---

2   *Dick v Piller* [1943] KB 497; notes in *County Court Practice* to Ord 13 r3.
3   *Fryer v Brook* (1984) 81 LS Gaz 2856, CA.
4   *Janstan Investments Ltd v Corregor* (1973) 21 November (unreported), CA and *Spitaliotis v Morgan* (1985) 277 EG 750.

be allowed to defend even if the defence is put in at this very late stage: Ord 9 r9(2). The defence should answer each of the substantive points raised in the particulars of claim, as failure to respond to a point made is taken as admission of it. Moreover, the defence and counterclaim must be sufficiently accurately drafted to withstand the test of a full trial. Any short-form defence will accordingly need substantial amendment before full trial.

Often the defendant will wish to raise a grievance arising from the breach of some duty or misconduct on the part of the landlord/owner. Most frequently this occurs in cases of disrepair and harassment. As such a complaint arises out of the subject matter of the proceedings, that is the tenancy (or other tenure), it may be raised by way of counterclaim. For the details of the law applicable to counterclaims for disrepair, readers are referred to Luba *Repairs: Tenants' Rights* (LAG) and for counterclaims for harassment to Arden and Partington *Quiet Enjoyment* (LAG). However, it should be noted that the following heads appear most commonly in counterclaims to possession proceedings (particularly those brought for rent arrears):

Disrepair
- breach of an express repairing covenant in the tenancy agreement (see the terms of the tenancy agreement);
- failure to repair the structure or exterior of the premises or the common parts (Landlord and Tenant Act 1985 s11 as amended);
- failure to repair (or maintain in proper working order) installations in the dwelling or serving the dwelling (LTA 1985 s11 as amended);
- failure to take reasonable care of the tenant and the tenant's property to prevent injury to either (Defective Premises Act 1972 s4);
- negligence in construction of the dwelling, performance of repairing works or treatment of infestation etc;
- nuisance (where the disrepair is caused by a problem emanating from property retained by the landlord).

Harassment
- trespass to land/trespass to the person/trespass to goods (tort);
- breach of the covenant of quiet enjoyment (contract);
- breach of Protection from Eviction Act 1977 s3 (for unprotected tenants);
- intimidation (tort).

The counterclaim must be put in writing and delivered at the court office (Ord 9 r2(1)), and it must contain full particulars of the matters complained of.

It is usual for the counterclaim to be included in the same document as the defence. If the defendant recovers damages on his or her counterclaim these may be set off, so as to reduce in whole or in part monies claimed by the plaintiff. In the case of counterclaims for disrepair, the application of a full set-off will amount to a complete defence to an action for arrears of rent. Accordingly, the body of the defence itself should plead the set-off, even though it may seek to set off an as yet unliquidated claim for damages in the counterclaim.[5]

An example of a defence (including counterclaims as appropriate) is given on p355 below.

Payment into court

As in all civil actions which include a money claim, it is possible for defendants in certain possession proceedings to make payments into court prior to the date set for trial. If the claim for possession is based on non-payment of rent, and some or all of the arrears are admitted, the tenant might be advised to make a payment on account into court before the hearing (Ord 11 r1(1)). Payment or tendering of rent after the action is started does not deprive the court of jurisdiction, but in practice such action will render it unreasonable for the court to make an order for possession unless there is a long history of default.[6] Where there are arrears which cannot be paid before the hearing, it is likely that any adjournment will be granted only on condition that current rent is paid in future and (if appropriate) arrears paid by lump sum or instalments (Ord 13 r1(8); RA 1977 s100(3); HA 1985 s85(2); HA 1988 s9(3)). Obviously, payment into court on account should not be considered as an option where any part of the money claim is disputed, eg, where the tenant asserts the sum claimed is overpaid HB and not rent.

Interim rent

While awaiting trial of the action for possession, a landlord may apply for an order for interim rent (Ord 13 r12). The tenant will often respond with an undertaking to pay current rent pending trial. No such order should be made, however, if there is a genuine dispute as to the sum due or if a counterclaim is being pursued.[7] It should also be noted that the court

5   *British Anzani (Felixstowe) v International Marine Management (UK) Ltd* [1980] QB 137.
6   *Dellenty v Pellow* [1951] 2 All ER 716, CA.
7   *Old Grovebury Manor Farm v Seymour* [1979] 1 All ER 573.

cannot order that a tenant's defence be struck out merely because of failure to comply with an order to pay interim rent.[8] The only methods by which interim orders for payment of rent can be enforced are those which apply to judgments in general.[9]

It would only be in an exceptional case that the court would accept a landlord's application for an interlocutory injunction and order the tenant to pay HB into court, rather than require an application from the landlord for interim payments in the usual way.[10]

Appeals

Appeals may be entered against the making of any possession order in the county court. If the order was made by the district judge, appeal lies to the circuit judge (Ord 37 r6). On the other hand, an appeal against an order for possession made by the circuit judge lies to the Court of Appeal (County Courts Act 1984 s77(1)). In neither case is leave to appeal required. If, however, the judge was hearing the matter in an appellate capacity (ie, on appeal from the district judge), leave of the judge or Court of Appeal is required to pursue a further appeal (County Court Appeals Order 1991 Ord 2(1)(b)).

Pending any appeal an application should be made in the county court for a stay of the order for possession, as the mere lodging of an appeal does not act as a stay (RSC Ord 59 r19(5)). If a stay is refused by the circuit judge, application for a stay may be made in the Court of Appeal.

The general right of appeal is qualified in certain possession cases. There is no right of appeal on any question of fact if the court could only grant possession on being satisfied it was reasonable to do so (County Courts Act 1984 s77(6) and RA 1977 s99 as it applies to Cases 1–6 and 9; HA 1985 s84(2)(a) and HA 1988 s7 as it applies to grounds 9–16). As indicated in the text relating to each of the main schemes for security of tenure (see p45 and p164), it is exceptionally difficult to overturn on a point of law any order where the issue is whether it was reasonable to award possession to the plaintiff.

8   *HH Property Co Ltd v Rahim* (1986) *Times* 8 November; (1986) 282 EG 455, CA.
9   See RSC Ord 45.
10   *Berg v Markhill* (1985) 17 HLR 455.

CHAPTER 23

Legal Aid

Generally[1]

The Legal Aid Board has power to grant legal aid to defendants in all kinds of possession proceedings in courts, but full legal aid is not available to provide representation for restricted contract occupiers in applications to defer the operation of notices to quit.[2] In deciding whether or not to grant legal aid, the legal aid area office considers the financial eligibility of the defendant[3] and the merits of the case. Two criteria to be applied when considering the merits are set out in the Legal Aid Act 1988 s15 which provides:

(2) A person shall not be granted representation for the purposes of any proceedings unless he satisfies the Board that he has reasonable grounds for taking, defending or being a party to the proceedings.

(3) A person may be refused representation for the purposes of any proceedings if, in the particular circumstances of the case, it appears to the Board—

(a) unreasonable that he should be granted representation under this Part, or

(b) more appropriate that he should receive assistance by way of representation under Part III;

and regulations may prescribe the criteria for determining any questions arising under paragraph (b) above.

The importance of representation for defendants in possession proceedings was recognised by the Law Society (which, prior to 1 April 1989, used to administer legal aid). Former 'Note for Guidance No 9 (criteria for the grant of legal aid)', published by the Law Society, provided:

1 For more detailed treatment of legal aid see O Hansen *Legal Aid in Practice* (Legal Action Group 3rd edn 1993).
2 See p171 above. Solicitors can however advise and assist at rent tribunal hearings under the provisions of the green form scheme.
3 See the tables published each April in *Legal Action*.

Another case which arises under the second criteria involves possession proceedings, usually because of rent arrears. Tenants of local authorities, most housing associations and most private tenants have security of tenure under the Housing Act 1985 or the Rent Act 1977. In considering a claim for possession where rent arrears are involved the court *shall only* make an order where it considers it reasonable to do so (s.84(2)(*a*), Housing Act 1985: s.98(1), Rent Act 1977). Thus there is a potential defence in a rent arrears case.

Even if an order is made the court has the discretion to stay or suspend execution of the order or postpone the date of possession (s.85(2)(*a*) and (*b*), Housing Act 1985; s.100(2)(*a*) and (*b*), Rent Act 1977). When suspending an order the court is required to order payments of the arrears and current rent or occupation charges, but if such payments would cause exceptional hardship or be otherwise unreasonable no order for payments need be made (s.85(3), Housing Act 1985; s.100(3), Rent Act 1977 as amended).

When considering whether to grant a certificate, and bearing in mind the formality of court proceedings and the seriousness to the tenant of possible homelessness, it will be particularly important to examine the background to the application to determine whether the applicant has reasonable grounds for, for example, asking the court not to make an order, or to suspend it on reasonable terms.'[4]

These paragraphs no longer appear in the current Notes for Guidance published by the Legal Aid Board, but they summarise accurately the attitude which the Legal Aid Board should take when considering applications for legal aid to defend possession proceedings.

In the 1992 *Legal Aid Handbook*, the main reference to possession proceedings in the Notes for Guidance is in the section[5] dealing with refusal of legal aid where it is unreasonable to have representation because the proceedings are not 'likely to be cost effective'. One example given where proceedings may not be cost effective is 'where the arrears are not in dispute and it is unlikely that an immediate order for possession would be made, and the only issue appears to be the terms on which a suspended order would be made'. The Notes also state, however, that:

the cost effectiveness factor may be outweighed by other matters – the importance of the case to the applicants . . . the possibility in rent arrears cases that the client may be able to persuade the court not to make any order at all if it is unreasonable or would cause hardship. It is for the solicitor on behalf of the applicant, to satisfy the area office that such factors exist and outweigh the lack of cost effectiveness.

---

4   *Legal Aid Handbook 1986* p220. See also (1984) 81 LS Gaz 1508 and June 1984 *Legal Action* 5.
5   Para 6–07, pages 48–49.

A note in the 1990 *Legal Aid Handbook* to the effect that it would not be reasonable to grant legal aid to defend mortgage possession proceedings, has now been altered to state that it may be unreasonable to grant legal aid where 'a solicitor would not normally be employed in such proceedings, eg, arithmetical calculations in . . . mortgage arrears or application to suspend warrant of possession or execution'. (The wording is not clear, but it is arguable that the wording 'arithmetical calculations' does not just refer to mortgage arrears, but also to applications to suspend warrants etc.) It is, however, 'up to the solicitor to satisfy the area officer that in the particular circumstances it is necessary for a solicitor to be employed'.[6]

If there are problems in obtaining a legal aid certificate in a case where there is a prospect of defending proceedings successfully, avoiding an outright possession order or setting aside a possession order which has already been made, the risk of homelessness should be stressed. There are not many things of greater importance to tenants than avoiding homelessness.

Emergency legal aid

In almost all cases involving possession proceedings it is necessary to make an application for *emergency* legal aid since the routine financial assessment carried out by the Department of Social Security and the legal aid administration of ordinary applications commonly means that it takes weeks if not months for legal aid to be granted. When considering applications for emergency legal aid the area office should consider both the applicant's likely financial eligibility and whether 'it is in the interests of justice that the applicant should, as a matter of urgency, be granted legal aid'.[7] It is always vital that emergency applications are submitted as quickly as possible since many legal aid area offices treat delay in submitting an application as a reason not to grant an emergency certificate. It is also a good idea before submitting an emergency application to telephone the solicitors for the plaintiff to notify them that such an application is being made and to ask whether or not they are prepared to agree to an adjournment of the hearing. It is very unlikely that they will agree to such a request, but if their refusal is noted on the emergency legal aid application form, it provides added force to the tenant's solicitor's argument that emergency legal aid should be granted, and prevents the area office from refusing to grant a certificate with a suggestion that the

6   *Legal Aid Handbook*, 1992, pp49–50.
7   Civil Legal Aid (General) Regulations 1989 SI No 339 reg 19.

tenant's solicitor should ask the landlord's solicitors for an adjournment. There is a provision for payment out of the legal aid fund for urgent work done by a solicitor outside normal office hours immediately prior to the issue of an emergency certificate if the solicitor applies for an emergency certificate at the first available opportunity and the application is granted.[8] All correspondence relating to applications for emergency certificates should be marked 'URGENT'.

Although legal aid may be granted over the telephone, it is only in very rare cases that this is appropriate when defending possession proceedings. Applications should be submitted on Forms CLA1, CLA3 and CLA4A or CLA4B. Some area offices now fax a note to solicitors within 48 hours to indicate whether or not an emergency certificate has been granted, but if such a note is not received it is wise for the tenant's solicitor to telephone the area office to enquire about the progress of the application. Not only is this likely to mean that the application will be granted more quickly, but also that the solicitor will know immediately when the application is granted, rather than waiting the week or fortnight which it often takes the area office to type up and send out the emergency certificate.

When advising tenants about emergency legal aid applications, it is important to bear in mind and discuss with them the amount of any contribution which they may have to make and to explain the effect of the requirement that legal aid applicants co-operate with the DSS in relation to assessment of their means. This latter requirement can create difficulties for employees whose employers do not deduct tax and for some self-employed people who do not have accounts properly drawn up and who subsequently find that their emergency legal aid certificates have been revoked because they have been unable to provide accounts for the previous year to the DSS. It should also be remembered, particularly in mortgage possession proceedings, that the statutory charge[9] (the Legal Aid Board's right to set any unrecovered solicitors' charges against any property preserved or recovered in proceedings) may apply if the defendant is successful and not all of his or her solicitor's costs are recovered.[10] It is theoretically possible that the statutory charge may apply to a contractual tenancy[11] (though not to a statutory tenancy which is merely a personal right (see p111 above)) but in most cases there would clearly be no practical possibility of the Legal Aid Board enforcing the statutory charge in such circumstances.

It should be remembered that the green form scheme can be used for all

8   Ibid reg 103(6).
9   Legal Aid Act 1988 s16.
10   *Curling v The Law Society* [1985] 1 All ER 705.
11   See, eg, 'Legal aid – More about the statutory charge' (1985) 82 LS Gaz 1214.

steps apart from representation which are taken before a legal aid certificate is granted unless leave has specifically been granted for representation. In particular, if for example the tenant has delayed in instructing a solicitor, or if there are delays in the granting of an emergency legal aid certificate, it may be wise for the tenant's solicitors to draft a defence under the green form scheme and for it to be filed at the court in the tenant's own name.[12]

If there are several defendants in possession proceedings or several joint tenants, it is important for all to apply for legal aid if possible. Consideration should also be given in the circumstances to the regulation[13] which provides that the Legal Aid Board may call for contributions from non-legally aided persons if they are 'concerned jointly with or having the same interest as the applicant'.

12   In such circumstances it is unwise for a solicitor formally to go on to the record until legal aid is granted. It may be possible to obtain an extension to the green form to allow a solicitor to attend court as a 'McKenzie' adviser (*McKenzie v McKenzie* [1970] 3 All ER 1034 and January 1989 *Legal Action* 5). It should also be noted that the Legal Advice and Assistance (Scope) Regulations 1989 SI No 550 provide that a judge may give approval for advice by way of representation where a party to proceedings is eligible for green form advice and the solicitor wishing to represent him or her is already present in the court on another matter.
13   Civil Legal Aid (General) Regulations 1989 reg 32.

CHAPTER 24
Trespassers and Orders 24 and 113

Generally

Strictly speaking there used to be no need for landowners to bring court proceedings to evict trespassers. They were entitled to use 'self help' and to evict trespassers without a court order.[1] However, to use the words of Lord Denning, this was a course 'not to be recommended' to landlords because of the 'possible disturbance' which might be caused.[2] Additionally, a landowner now risks prosecution under the Criminal Law Act 1977 s6 if violence is used or threatened for the purpose of securing entry to premises when there is someone present on those premises. Also if the trespassers are former licensees who are entitled to rely on Protection from Eviction Act s3 as amended[3], a landlord using self help risks a prosecution. Advisers should however note the Criminal Law Act 1977 s7 which creates criminal offences where a trespasser fails to leave the premises if required to do so by or on behalf of a displaced residential occupier or a protected intending occupier of those premises.[4]

In possession proceedings against trespassers, landowners need prove only their title and an intention to regain possession.[5] If occupiers wish to claim some right of occupation which amounts to a defence (for example a continuing licence or tenancy) the burden of proving its existence lies on them. The main defences likely to be advanced by people who face possession proceedings brought by a landowner who claims that they are trespassers are:

- they have a tenancy or licence which has not been determined. Neither

---

1   *R v Blankley* [1979] Crim LR 166; *McPhail v Persons Unknown* [1973] 3 All ER 393.
2   *McPhail* n1 per Lord Denning MR at 396.
3   Protection from Eviction Act 1977 as amended by HA 1988 ss30 and 31. See pp88 and 209.
4   See Suzanne Tarlin 'Squatting and the criminal law' December 1977 *LAG Bulletin* 285.
5   *Portland Managements Ltd v Harte* [1976] 1 All ER 225.

CCR Ord 24 nor RSC Ord 113 (see below) can be used if there is or was a tenancy. As to termination of licences, see chapter 15 above;

- although the people in occupation of land do not themselves have a tenancy or licence, someone else, other than the landowner, has a tenancy or licence which has not been determined. Landowners are not entitled to orders for possession unless they can prove that they have an immediate right to possession. This is not the case if there is an intermediate undetermined tenancy or licence. This situation most commonly arises where a tenant moves away or dies and someone else moves into the property without the landowner's permission (see p240 below);

- the landowner has failed to comply with the necessary procedural requirements, eg, as to service of proceedings (see p241 below). Sometimes this may succeed in delaying matters, giving occupiers time to find other accommodation, but is unlikely to provide a long-term defence;

- the decision by a public body, such as a local authority, to bring possession proceedings can be challenged on administrative law grounds, eg, that it has failed to take into account relevant factors or has misdirected itself in law. Particular factors apply where the occupiers are gypsies or travellers. Usually it will be necessary to seek an adjournment and apply for judicial review to quash the decision to bring proceedings (see p243 below);

- trespassers have acquired possessory title as a result of 12 years' adverse possession. If land or premises have been occupied by trespassers for a period of 12 years, the landowner loses the ability to obtain a possession order. The claim becomes statute barred by virtue of the Limitation Act 1980 s15.[6]

Proceedings may be issued as an ordinary possession summons claiming possession on the ground that the defendants are trespassers. However, it is far more common for landlords to use either the County Court Rules Ord 24[7] or the Rules of the Supreme Court Ord 113. These rules were introduced in 1970 to provide quicker and easier procedures for landlords who wished to evict squatters. However, the scope of the rules is wider than this, and the procedure can be used against some classes of occupiers who are not squatters. Order 24 provides:

---

6   It is impossible in this book to deal in detail with the law relating to adverse possession. See, eg, Megarry and Wade Law of Real Property (Sweet & Maxwell 5th edn 1984) pp1030–1050 and Arden and Partington Housing Law (Sweet & Maxwell 1983) pp79–91.

7   Formerly Ord 26.

Summary proceedings for the recovery of land or rent

Proceedings to be by originating application

1. Where a person claims possession of land which he alleges is occupied solely by a person or persons (not being a tenant or tenants holding over after the termination of the tenancy) who entered into or remained in occupation without his licence or consent or that of any predecessor in title of his, the proceedings may be brought by originating application in accordance with the provisions of this Order.

Affidavit in support

2.—(1) The applicant shall file in support of the originating application an affidavit stating—

(a) his interest in the land;

(b) the circumstances in which the land has been occupied without licence or consent and in which his claim to possession arises; and

(c) that he does not know the name of any person occupying the land who is not named in the originating application.

(2) Where the applicant considers that service in accordance with rule 3(2)(b) may be necessary, he shall provide, together with the originating application, sufficient stakes and sealable transparent envelopes for such service.

Service of originating application

3.—(1) Where any person in occupation of the land is named in the originating application, the application shall be served on him—

(a) by delivering to him personally a copy of the originating application, together with the notice of the return day required by Order 3, rule 4(4)(b), and a copy of the affidavit in support, or

(b) by an officer of the court leaving the documents mentioned in subparagraph (a), or sending them to him, at the premises, or

(c) in accordance with Order 7, rule 11, as applied to originating applications by Order 3, rule 4(6), or

(d) in such other manner as the court may direct.

(2) Where any person not named as a respondent is in occupation of the land, the originating application shall be served (whether or not it is also required to be served in accordance with paragraph (1)), unless the court otherwise directs, by—

(a) affixing a copy of each of the documents mentioned in paragraph (1)(a) to the main door or other conspicuous part of the premises and, if practicable, inserting through the letter-box at the premises a copy of those documents enclosed in a sealed transparent envelope addressed to 'the occupiers', or

(b) placing stakes in the ground at conspicuous parts of the occupied land, to each of which shall be affixed a sealed transparent envelope addressed to 'the occupiers' and containing a copy of each of the documents mentioned in paragraph (1)(a).

Application by occupier to be made a party

4. Without prejudice to Order 15, rule 1, any person not named as a respondent who is in occupation of the land and wishes to be heard on the question whether an order for possession should be made may apply at any stage of the proceedings to be joined as respondent, and the notice of the return day required by Order 3, rule 4(4)(b), shall contain a notice to that effect.

Hearing of originating application

5.—(1) Except in case of urgency and by leave of the court, the day fixed for the hearing of the originating application shall not be less than five days after the day of service.

(2) Notwithstanding anything in Order 21, rule 5, no order for possession shall be made on the originating application except by the judge or, with the leave of the judge, by the registrar.

(3) An order for possession in proceedings under this Order shall be to the effect that the plaintiff do recover possession of the land mentioned in the originating application.

(4) Nothing in this Order shall prevent the court from ordering possession to be given on a specified date, in the exercise of any power which could have been exercised if the proceedings had been brought by action.

Warrant of possession

6.—(1) Subject to paragraphs (2) and (3), a warrant of possession to enforce an order for possession under this Order may be issued at any time after the making of the order and subject to the provisions of Order 26, rule 17, a warrant of restitution may be issued in aid of the warrant of possession.

(2) No warrant of possession shall be issued after the expiry of 3 months from the date of the order without the leave of the court, and an application for such leave may be made ex parte unless the court otherwise directs.

(3) Nothing in this rule shall authorise the issue of a warrant of possession before the date on which possession is ordered to be given.

Setting aside order

7. The judge may, on such terms as he thinks just, set aside or vary any order made in proceedings under this Order.

Orders 24 and 113 may be used both against people who entered premises as trespassers and against people who were licensees but whose licences have been terminated.[8] However, neither Ord 24 nor Ord 113 can be used against licensees if the licence had not been terminated by the date on which proceedings were issued.[9] They can also be used against unlawful

---

8   Ord 24 r1, Ord 113 r1. *GLC v Jenkins* [1975] 1 All ER 354; cf *McPhail v Persons Unknown* n1 above.
9   *GLC v Jenkins* n8.

sub-tenants where the head tenancy has been terminated,[10] for example by effluxion of time, but not against a tenant or a former tenant. In addition, sub-occupiers, whether occupying by consent or otherwise, have a complete defence to the proceedings if a head tenancy has not been terminated. For example in *Wirral Borough Council v Smith*[11] a local authority landlord was unable to evict friends of a dead tenant because it had failed to serve a notice to quit on the President of the Family Division.[12] In *Preston Borough Council v Fairclough*[13] the landlord was unable to evict friends of tenants who had abandoned the premises leaving rent arrears. The Court of Appeal held that there was no implied surrender (see p94 above) and that the head tenancy had not been terminated in any other way. (See chapter 5 above for public sector sub-occupiers.)

Orders 24 and 113 can be used by tenants against other people who have entered their rented premises without their permission, even if such people have the consent of the head landlord.[14] It makes no difference whether the tenant is a contractual tenant or a statutory tenant.[15] It is unclear whether a licensee of premises (such as a short-life housing association) may use these speedy proceedings against trespassers.[16] If there is convincing evidence that there is a real danger that squatters may move onto land adjoining that already occupied, the order may be made to extend to that adjoining land.[17]

If landlords seek to use these procedures, all that they can claim is an order for possession and costs. They cannot make any claim for mesne profits or damages, and if they attempt to do so in the summons or originating application, the judge may dismiss the entire proceedings.[18]

---

10   *Moore Properties (Ilford) Ltd v McKeon* [1976] 1 WLR 1278.
11   (1982) 43 P & CR 312.
12   She had died intestate. See p213 above and Administration of Estates Act 1925 s9.
13   (1983) 8 HLR 70; cf, though, *R v LB Croydon ex parte Toth* (1986) 18 HLR 493.
14   *Borg v Rogers* [1981] CAT 330 (UB), N Madge 'Curtailing short cuts in possession proceedings' April 1983 *LAG Bulletin* 53.
15   See pp85 and 111 above and *Thompson v Ward* [1953] 1 All ER 1169.
16   Cf *West Hampstead Housing Association v Church and Others* (1983) 27 October (unreported), QBD (Goulding J) and *Family Housing Association v Gedge* December 1988 *Legal Action* 17. Query though whether the *West Hampstead* case is correct in view of the comments made by Lord Templeman in *Street v Mountford*. But see *Harper v Charlesworth* (1825) 4 B & C 574.
17   See *University of Essex v Djemal* [1980] 1 WLR 1301 and *Ministry of Agriculture v Hayman* (1990) 59 P&CR 48.
18   *Westminster City Council v Monahan* [1981] 1 All ER 1050.

Use of summary procedure

Difficulties may arise where the landowners claim that occupants are trespassers, but the occupants themselves claim that they have a complete defence to the proceedings and raise a triable issue. In *Henderson v Law*[19] Griffiths LJ stated:

> there will obviously be cases in which, although proceedings are started by way of a summary procedure, it quickly becomes apparent that a substantial issue has to be tried. If it was apparent to the applicant that a serious issue was bound to arise as to whether a tenancy or a holding-over existed, no doubt the judge would regard the use of a summary procedure as inappropriate, or even in an extreme case as an abuse of the process, and dismiss the application: but I would expect such cases to be rare, because I would not anticipate that solicitors would seek to steal a march by using inappropriate procedures. From time to time there are bound to be cases such as this where, from the applicant's point of view, an unexpected issue surfaces which raises a question of a tenancy or a holding-over. In such cases, the judge must exercise his discretion and decide whether it is wise to continue the summary hearing, or to adjourn it for a further hearing after the parties have a chance to reconsider the position or possibly to dismiss the application and leave the applicant to have the issues determined in a subsequent action. But merely because a respondent chooses, without warning, to assert that there is either a tenancy or holding-over cannot of itself be a sufficient reason to say that the use of Order 24 was an inappropriate procedure.

In *Filemart Ltd v Avery*,[20] Woolf LJ indicated that in view of the fact that CCR Ord 24 and RSC Ord 113 are summary procedures which could 'result in a defendant's being deprived of possession of property without the normal trial which takes place in contested proceedings . . . it is in only a limited number of cases that it is appropriate to dispose of the matter' without a full hearing.

In other cases it has been held that the summary procedure is inappropriate to deal with cases involving the distinction between leases and licences[21] and complicated title claims.[22] If a triable issue is raised, judges have a wide discretion. They may either dismiss the application, order the filing of pleadings and discovery, allow the affidavits which have already been filed to stand as pleadings or try the case by hearing oral evidence.[23] If occupants wish to raise triable issues it is important for these

---

19 (1984) 17 HLR 237 at 241. See too *Cooper v Varzdari* (1986) 18 HLR 299.
20 [1989] 46 EG 92, CA.
21 *Islamic Republic of Pakistan v Ghani* 1976 CAT 426A and see N Madge n14.
22 *Cudworth v Masefield* (1984) *Times* 16 May. See too *Baker v Hoerdt* July 1978 *LAG Bulletin* 166 and *Phserowsky & Stanton v Phillips* July 1978 *LAG Bulletin* 166.
23 *Filemart Ltd v Avery* [1989] 46 EG 92, CA.

to be summarised in an affidavit which should be available for the initial hearing.

One of the main differences between summary and ordinary possession proceedings is that it is not necessary for the landowner to know the names of the defendants. It is possible to sue 'persons unknown'. In many cases one set of possession proceedings under Ord 24 or Ord 113 is issued against one or several named defendants and 'persons unknown'.[24] However, if a landlord does know the name of someone in occupation of premises, that person must be sued as a named defendant. Failure to do this may provide a defence to the proceedings.[25]

Service

Both rules set out in detail how proceedings should be served.[26] If personal service is to be effected by anyone other than an officer of the court, each named defendant must be served.[27] So far as the other methods of service are concerned, it is arguable that, as these are summary proceedings, the provisions as to service should be strictly complied with[28] but sometimes landowners succeed in obtaining possession orders despite minor irregularities if they can show that no one has been prejudiced and no injustice caused.[29] If it can be shown that the originating summons or originating application came to the attention of everyone in occupation of the premises, irregularity in service may not amount to a defence.

There should be five clear days between service and the hearing of proceedings relating to residential premises unless it is a case of urgency.[30] Applications by landowners for shorter periods should be made to the

---

24 Ord 113 r3(c) and Ord 24 r2(c).
25 *Downey v Persons in Occupation of 29 Broadhurst Gardens* (1978) 25 January, Ch D (noted at April 1978 *LAG Bulletin* 94).
26 Ord 24 r3 and Ord 113 r4. In respect of 'open land' note the amendments made by the County Court (Amendment) Rules 1987 SI No 493 and the Rules of the Supreme Court (Amendment No 3) Order 1986 SI No 2289.
27 *GLC v Tully* (1976) 120 SJ 555 where large numbers of bundles containing documents were affixed to doors, window sills and barricades, but none was addressed to any of the named defendants.
28 See Supreme Court Practice 113/1–8/4 and *re 9 Orpen Road, Stoke Newington* [1971] 1 All ER 944 and *Wiltshire CC v Frazer and Others* (1984) 47 P & CR 69 at 72.
29 For example, *Westminster City Council v Chapman* [1975] 2 All ER 1103 where the only attempt at service was to place one envelope containing court papers through the letter box, and *Burston Finance v Wilkins and Persons Unknown* (1975) *Times* 17 July.
30 Ord 113 r6 and Ord 24 r5. Only two days is necessary for open land.

judge who hears the case.[31] If the judge decides that it is not an urgent case and that less than five days' notice has been given, the proper course is to adjourn the proceedings to a later date, thus giving the necessary five days' notice.[32] In the High Court, hearings are now normally before a master in chambers but proceedings may be dealt with by a judge in open court. In the county court, proceedings may be dealt with by either a circuit judge or a district judge in open court.[33] At the hearing, anybody who is not a named party to the proceedings may apply to be joined and added as a defendant.[34] Unless occupants have a defence to the proceedings, there is no point in applying to be joined as a defendant since it merely opens up the likelihood of an order for costs. Orders for costs cannot be made against 'persons unknown', only against named defendants.

The summary procedure is not appropriate in cases where a mortgagee is seeking an order for possession against an occupier who, it is alleged, is a tenant of the mortgagor with no right to remain as against the mortgagee. The correct course is to proceed by way of summons.[35]

When dealing with proceedings against trespassers courts should normally make an order for possession to take effect 'forthwith' (ie, immediately).[36] Although the rules refer to making an order for possession to take effect on a specified later date,[37] the court can do this only if all parties consent, or if the defendants are former restricted contract licensees,[38] former service occupiers[39] or licensees under a rental purchase agreement (see p250 below).

In summary proceedings for possession, orders for possession cannot be made in respect of part only of the premises claimed in the originating application or originating summons.[40] However, it is possible for a landowner to claim possession of all of the premises owned by him or her even if only parts are subject to occupation by trespassers.[41]

Once an order for possession has been made, the landowner can apply

31   *Westminster City Council v Monahan* n18.
32   Ibid. See too *Mercy v Persons Unknown* (1974) 231 EG 1159 (only two days' notice of hearing, landlord wanted to sell flats, held no particular urgency, order for possession set aside by Court of Appeal).
33   Ord 24 r5(2), as amended.
34   Ord 24 r4 and Ord 113 r5.
35   *London Goldhawk Building Society v Eminer* (1977) 242 EG 462 and chapter 35.
36   *McPhail v Persons Unknown* n1; *Swordheath Properties Ltd v Floydd* [1978] 1 All ER 721 and *Mayor and Burgesses of Camden LB v Persons Unknown* [1987] CLY 2183, CA; June 1987 *Legal Action* 19.
37   Ord 113 r6 and Ord 24 r5(4).
38   RA 1977 s106A.
39   *McPhail v Persons Unknown* n1.
40   *Baker v Hoerdt* n22.
41   *University of Essex v Djemal* [1980] 2 All ER 742.

ex parte for a writ of possession to be enforced by the sheriff, or, in the county court, a warrant to be enforced by the bailiff.[42] There are specific powers in both Orders for judges to set aside orders for possession.[43] It will generally be necessary for someone seeking to have the order set aside to show in an affidavit why s/he failed to attend the original hearing and a defence on the merits to the proceedings (see p257 below).

If a landowner does not use summary proceedings for possession, but issues an ordinary possession summons against people who are trespassers, s/he is entitled to seek an order for damages for trespass. There is no need for the landlord to prove that s/he would have re-let the premises. Damages are assessed at the value of the premises to the trespassers, and in the absence of other evidence, this will normally be the ordinary letting value.[44]

Administrative law defences

Decisions of public bodies, such as local authorities, may be challenged in the courts on the ground that:

- the decision is so unreasonable that no reasonable local authority could have come to the decision;
- the local authority failed to take into account relevant material when reaching its decision;
- the local authority took into account irrelevant material in coming to the decision;
- in making the decision the local authority misdirected itself in law;
- it has fettered its discretion by adopting a blanket policy without regard to the facts of the individual case.

The usual method of challenging a decision for any of these reasons is to make an application to the Divisional Court for judicial review, for an order of certiorari and/or mandamus to compel the local authority to comply with its obligations.

A tenant with contractual rights may challenge the decision to bring proceedings relying on these administrative law grounds in the possession proceedings themselves.[45] However, where the defendant is a trespasser with no private law or contractual rights, the proper course of action is to make an application for judicial review and seek an adjournment of the possession proceedings pending the outcome of the application for

42   Housing Act 1980 s88.
43   Ord 24 r7 and Ord 113 r7.
44   *Swordheath Properties v Tabet* [1979] 1 All ER 240, CA. See chapter 26.
45   *LB Wandsworth v Winder* [1985] AC 461, HL; *Bristol DC v Clark* [1975] 1 WLR 1443; *Cannock Chase Council v Kelly* [1978] 1 WLR 1 and p51 above.

judicial review.[46] Courts dealing with possession proceedings are unlikely to be sympathetic to such applications for adjournments unless it can be shown that there is a real possibility of obtaining leave for judicial review[47] and that steps are being taken expeditiously to obtain leave. Courts are particularly reluctant to allow squatters to use such tactics merely to delay proceedings. Trespassers should make applications for emergency legal aid for judicial review as quickly as possible after it is known that a decision to take proceedings has been made. In some circumstances it may be possible to do this even before possession proceedings are served. Separate applications for emergency legal aid will be needed for judicial review and the possession proceedings.

The fact that a local authority is in breach of its statutory obligations (eg, to provide accommodation to homeless people under HA 1985 Pt III or to provide sites for gypsies under Caravan Sites Act 1968 s6) does not automatically provide a defence to possession proceedings.[48] However, breach of such statutory obligations may be extremely important when trying to prove that a local authority has been acting unreasonably. For example, in *West Glamorgan CC v Rafferty*,[49] the Court of Appeal held that a decision by a local authority, which had for a long time been in breach of its statutory duty to provide sites for gypsies, to evict travellers without making any arrangements whatever for the provision of alternative accommodation was so unreasonable that it was perverse. The Court of Appeal dismissed the local authority's appeal against an order dismissing its claim for possession. Similarly, in *R v LB Brent ex parte McDonagh*,[50] gypsies who were occupying an unauthorised site were given a letter informing them that they would not be evicted by the local authority until they had been provided with a suitable alternative site. The local authority's subsequent decision to evict them without giving them any notification or reasons was quashed because the gypsies had been given a legitimate expectation and because Brent had failed to take into account Department of the Environment Circulars 28/77 and 44/78 which refer to the hardship which may be caused by indiscriminate evictions.

46   *Avon CC v Buscott and Others* [1988] 1 All ER 841 and *Waverley BC v Hilden* [1988] 1 All ER 807. See too *R v LB Southwark ex parte Borrow* December 1988 *Legal Action* 17.
47   RSC Ord 53 r3.
48   *Southwark LBC v Williams* [1971] Ch 734, *RB Kensington and Chelsea v Wells* (1973) 72 LGR 289 and *R v LB Barnet ex parte Grumbridge* (1992) *Times* 7 February, DC.
49   (1986) 18 HLR 375.
50   (1989) 21 HLR 494, DC.

CHAPTER 25

Costs

As a general rule a judge has a complete discretion, provided that it is exercised judicially, to award costs against either party or not to award costs at all. The County Court Rules Ord 38 r1(2) provides:

> (2)   The costs of and incidental to all proceedings in a county court shall be in the discretion of the court.[1]

There are no fixed rules about the award of costs,[2] but in the absence of special circumstances it is normal that a successful party should receive costs from the unsuccessful party.[3] An example of such a special circumstance occurred in *Ottway v Jones*[4] where the plaintiff landlord established grounds for possession based on nuisance and annoyance but failed to convince the court that it was reasonable to make an order for possession, with the result that judgment on the claim was entered for the defendant. However, in view of the finding of nuisance the judge held that the successful defendant should pay the plaintiff's costs and this order was not disturbed by the Court of Appeal. It should also be noted that in proceedings under RA Case 9 (see above), where the only issue decided by the court is the question of 'greater hardship' there is a convention that each side should bear its own costs.[5]

It is common for judges when making a possession order against a defendant who is legally aided with a nil contribution, either to make no order for costs or to make an order for costs but to provide that that order should not be enforced without leave of the court. Similarly, where an unsuccessful defendant has legal aid but subject to a contribution, an order for costs may be made but limited to the amount of the defendant's

---

1   See RSC Ord 62, and notes in *Supreme Court Practice 1992* at 62/2/34 dealing with appeals from county court orders for costs.
2   *Lewis v Haverfordwest RDC* [1953] 2 All ER 1599.
3   *Brown v Sparrow* [1982] 1 WLR 1269.
4   [1955] 2 All ER 585.
5   *Funnell v Armstrong* [1962] EGD 319.

contribution towards the legal aid fund. A legal aid certificate may thus be some protection against an order for costs but there is no absolute rule.

The usual procedure is for costs either to be taxed or to be assessed. Where there has been only one hearing and both parties agree to costs being assessed[6] the judge may order that a fixed sum of costs be paid. This normally includes the plaint fee and fixed solicitors' costs for issuing the summons.[7] Where a county court makes a suspended possession order with terms for payment of arrears of rent and the defendant has neither delivered a defence, admission or counterclaim, nor otherwise denied liability, there are fixed costs for attendance of a solicitor or barrister at the hearing. Part II of Appendix B to Ord 38 provides that these are (in 1992) as follows:

sum claimed £600 or less	£31.00
sum claimed more than £600, but less than £3,000	£46.00
sum claimed exceeding £3,000	£57.00

These sums are in addition to the plaint fee and any solicitors' costs on the summons for the issue of proceedings.

Where proceedings have been more prolonged or one party does not agree to costs being assessed, costs are taxed by the district judge. Costs may be ordered to be taxed on either scale 1 or scale 2. It is possible for a judge to order costs to be taxed on a particular scale but to limit the costs to a maximum figure.[8] In forfeiture proceedings, landlords' represent-atives may submit that costs should be awarded on an indemnity basis. In *Billson v Residential Apartments Ltd*,[9] Lord Templeman stated that this practice was 'ripe for reconsideration'.

If proceedings are issued in the High Court against a RA protected tenant, a HA assured tenant or a HA secure tenant, a landlord is not entitled to recover any costs.[10]

Taxation should usually be avoided if the occupier is to pay the costs, as a taxing fee of five per cent of the bill of costs is recoverable in addition to the landlord's costs. This is by way of reimbursement of the taxing fee which the landlord has to pay the court.

For a discussion of the very different position relating to costs in mortgage possession actions, see chapter 35 below.

---

6   Costs cannot be assessed in this way if the parties do not agree—*Golding v Smith* [1910] 1 KB 462.
7   In 1992 the normal plaint fee for possession proceedings was £43. Solicitors' fixed costs for issuing proceedings were £55.50. Assessed costs in possession proceedings dealt with on the first hearing are often in the region of £110 to £200, including the fixed costs.
8   *Brown v Sparrow* n3.
9   [1992] 01 EG 91, HL; see too *Copall v Fryxell* (1991) *Times* 31 December, QBD.
10   RA 1977 s141, HA 1985 s110 and HA 1988 s40.

CHAPTER 26
Mesne Profits and Damages for Trespass

If a possession order is made after a tenancy has been terminated, a landlord is entitled to seek mesne profits from the termination of the tenancy until possession is given up. Mesne profits are calculated according to the 'fair value of the premises: when the rent represents that fair value the assessment is according to the amount of the rent, but if the fair value is higher than the rent the assessment is by reference to that higher value.'[1] However, according to Woodfall[2] the court will usually not award more than the registered rent for the premises.

If the person in occupation has never been a tenant, a landlord may be entitled to damages for trespass. The amount awarded should reflect the value of the premises to a tenant. It is not necessary for a landlord to prove that s/he would have re-let the premises if the defendant had not been on the premises.[3] Damages for trespass cannot be claimed if a landlord is seeking possession under Ord 24 or Ord 113.

1 Woodfall *Law of Landlord and Tenant* (Sweet & Maxwell 28th edn 1978) 1–2158.
2 Ibid.
3 *Swordheath Properties v Tabet* [1979] 1 All ER 240.

CHAPTER 27

Possession Orders

Occupier without full Rent Act or Housing Act protection

At common law judges had a discretion to allow occupiers a reasonable time before a possession order took effect even if they had no security of tenure under the RA.[1] However, this discretion was largely taken away by the HA 1980. Apart from various exceptions, county court orders for possession must now take effect not later than 14 days after the making of the order unless it would cause exceptional hardship, in which case the order can be postponed to a date which is not more than six weeks after the making of the order. The HA 1980 s89 provides:

Restriction on discretion of court in making orders for possession of land
89.—(1)   Where a court makes an order for the possession of any land in a case not falling within the exceptions mentioned in subsection (2) below, the giving up of possession shall not be postponed (whether by the order or any variation, suspension or stay of execution) to a date later than fourteen days after the making of the order unless it appears to the court that exceptional hardship would be caused by requiring possession to be given up by that date; and shall not in any event be postponed to a date later than six weeks after the making of the order.
    (2)   The restrictions in subsection (1) above do not apply if—
    (*a*)   the order is made in an action by a mortgagee for possession; or
    (*b*)   the order is made in an action for forfeiture of a lease; or
    (*c*)   the court had power to make the order only if it considered it reasonable to make it; or
    (*d*)   the order relates to a dwelling-house which is the subject of a restricted contract (within the meaning of section 19 of the 1977 Act); or
    (*e*)   the order is made in proceedings brought as mentioned in section 88(1) above.

---

1   *Air Ministry v Harris* [1951] 2 All ER 862 (six months too long); *Sheffield Corp v Luxford* [1929] 2 KB 180 (one year too long); *Jones v Savery* [1951] 1 All ER 820 (one month reasonable).

It should be noted that this section applies only to county court orders for possession. The discretion of, for example, High Court judges sitting in the Chancery Division, is not affected.[2]

Gathering together all possible variations (including those not referred to in s89) the position is as follows:

Trespassers

The courts must make an order to take effect immediately unless the trespassers are former restricted contract licensees, former service occupiers or both parties consent to a longer period (see above p243 Ord 24 or Ord 113).

Proceedings are brought by a mortgagee for possession

The court has a wide discretion to suspend or postpone the order (see p280 below). For discussion of general procedure in mortgage possession actions, see chapters 33 and 34 below.

Forfeiture of a lease

In rent arrears cases any order forfeiting a lease must be suspended for at least 28 days. In proceedings for forfeiture based on other breaches of covenant, the court has a wide discretion to grant relief from forfeiture or to suspend the order (see pp97–110 above).

The discretionary grounds within RA 1977, HA 1980 and HA 1988

The court has a wide discretion to suspend or postpone the order (see below), although the court should not make a totally indeterminate order.[3]

Restricted contracts

If the restricted contract was created after 28 November 1980 the court may delay the order for possession by up to three months. The total time allowed cannot exceed three months.[4] In the case of a pre-1980 HA restricted contract, it seems that whether or not the rent tribunal has exercised its power to delay the operation of any notice to quit, in possession proceedings the court retains its common law powers to allow a reasonable period.[5]

2 *Bain & Co v Church Commissioners* (1988) *Independent* 18 July; (1988) 21 HLR 29.
3 *Kidder v Birch* (1983) 265 EG 773 (no date given for possession, but statement that warrant should lie in the court office until the death of landlady's mother. Held, order bad and varied so that it would become operable only if the landlady's mother died within 12 months).
4 *Bryant v Best* (1987) 283 EG 843, CA.
5 See, eg, *Air Ministry v Harris, Sheffield Corp v Luxford* and *Jones v Savery* all at n1.

Rental purchase agreements

A wide discretion to adjourn, stay or suspend (see p215 above).

Mandatory grounds for possession against assured tenants and proceedings against assured shorthold tenants

If the court is satisfied that a landlord is entitled to possession on one of the mandatory grounds or because an assured shorthold tenancy has expired and notice has been given, the court must make a possession order to take effect within 14 days unless exceptional hardship would be caused, in which case six weeks may be allowed (HA 1988 s9(6)). See p185.

In all other cases

The county court's discretion is limited by s89 to a maximum of 14 days unless exceptional hardship would be caused. There is no definition of exceptional hardship.

Occupier with security of tenure

Even if a landlord of a protected, statutory or assured tenant in the private sector or a secure occupier in the public sector proves that one of the discretionary grounds for possession exists, the court may consider that it is not reasonable to make any order for possession.[6] For example, in rent arrears cases, if the arrears are low, the court may merely make a money judgment order with a direction that the tenant pay off the arrears by instalments. However, to date, the most common form of order, particularly in rent arrears cases, has been a suspended possession order.[7] RA 1977 s100, HA 1985 s85 and HA 1988 s9(2), which are in almost identical terms, give the court a wide discretion to postpone the date on which possession should be given or to stay or suspend the execution of an order.[8]

RA 1977 s100, as amended, provides:

Extended discretion of court in claims for possession of certain dwelling-houses

100.—(1)   Subject to subsection (5) below, a court may adjourn, for such period as it thinks fit, proceedings for possession of a dwelling-house which is let on a protected tenancy or subject to a statutory tenancy.

(2)   On the making of an order for possession of such a dwelling-house, or at any time before the execution of such an order (whether made before or

6   See p161 above, and for example, *Woodspring DC v Taylor* [1982] 4 HLR 95, CA.
7   County Court Form N28.
8   For an example of the court's common law power to adjourn see *R v A Circuit Judge ex parte Wathen* (1976) 33 P & CR 423.

after the commencement of this Act), the court, subject to subsection (5) below, may—

(a)   stay or suspend execution of the order, or

(b)   postpone the date of possession

for such period or periods as the court thinks fit.

(3)   On any such adjournment as is referred to in subsection (1) above or any such stay, suspension or postponement as is referred to in subsection (2) above, the court shall, unless it considers that to do so would cause exceptional hardship to the tenant or would otherwise be unreasonable, impose conditions with regard to payment by the tenant of arrears of rent (if any) and rent or payments in respect of occupation after termination of the tenancy (mesne profits) and may impose such other conditions as it thinks fit.

(4)   If any such conditions as are referred to in subsection (3) above are complied with, the court may, if it thinks fit, discharge or rescind any such order as is referred to in subsection (2) above.

(4A)   Subsection (4B) below applies in any case where—

(a)   proceedings are brought for possession of a dwelling-house which is let on a protected tenancy or subject to a statutory tenancy;

(b)   the tenant's spouse or former spouse, having rights of occupation under the Matrimonial Homes Act 1967, is then in occupation of the dwelling-house; and

(c)   the tenancy is terminated as a result of those proceedings.

(4B)   In any case to which this subsection applies, the spouse or former spouse shall, so long as he or she remains in occupation, have the same rights in relation to, or in connection with, any such adjournment as is referred to in subsection (1) above or any such stay, suspension or postponement as is referred to in subsection (2) above, as he or she would have if those rights of occupation were not affected by the termination of the tenancy.

(5)   This section shall not apply if the circumstances are as specified in any of the Cases in Part II of Schedule 15.

When postponing, suspending or delaying possession orders against protected, statutory, assured or secure tenants, the court must impose conditions with regard to the repayment of arrears (if any) unless this would cause exceptional hardship or would otherwise be unreasonable. The court may impose such other conditions as it thinks fit.[9] The court may, either when it makes the initial order[10] or at any later time, discharge or rescind the order if the conditions originally imposed have been complied with.[11] Spouses of tenants (who are not joint tenants) have the same rights as the actual tenants to seek the suspension or postponement

---

9   RA 1977 s100(3) as inserted by HA 1980 ss75 and 87(3).

10   See county court Form N28 and *Vandermolen v Toma* (1981) 9 HLR 91.

11   RA 1977 s100(4), HA 1980 s87(4). See too *Haymills Houses v Blake* [1955] 1 All ER 592.

of orders until the making of a decree absolute provided that they are still living in the premises.

Criteria for suspending possession orders

It is clear that the court's powers under RA 1977 s100(2), HA 1985 s85(2) and HA 1988 s9(2) must be exercised judicially, but (except in cases of immoral user, where, prima facie, the court's discretion to suspend should not be exercised[12]) there is little guidance as to circumstances in which orders should be suspended, or the factors to be taken into account. In practice, unless there are large rent arrears, on the first occasion that a tenant is brought to court for arrears, it is usual, *if the grant of an order is appropriate at all,* for a possession order to be suspended on condition that the tenant pays the current rent when due *and* a regular amount towards the arrears. Even if rent arrears are high, the court may take the view that the landlord is to some extent to blame in allowing large arrears to accrue without taking any action and that accordingly the tenant should be given the chance to pay off the arrears by instalments under a suspended possession order, although it should be remembered that if an assured tenant owes three months' rent, ground 8 is mandatory. It is not uncommon for courts to make suspended orders which provide for arrears to be paid off over a few years. Some courts take the realistic view that if a possession order is suspended, there is some likelihood of the landlord recovering arrears, whereas if an absolute possession order is obtained, practically, it is unlikely that the landlord will ever recover the arrears. Often though, courts are more prepared to suspend an order against a tenant with substantial arrears if the landlord is a local authority, rather than a private individual.

When considering what form of possession order should be made, the time the defendants have been tenants, their previous conduct, their age and health are all relevant factors.[13] The court should also take into account the level of arrears and the tenant's income and expenditure. Again there is little guidance about the size of such payments, but there is a strong argument where a tenant is receiving income support that no suspended order should require the tenant to pay more than five per cent[14] of the personal allowance for a single claimant aged 25 or over towards the arrears. This is the limit of the amount which a benefit officer can deduct from the claimant's benefit and pay direct to the landlord towards

---

12   *Yates v Morris* [1950] 2 All ER 577, although in *Yates* the order was suspended.
13   *Woodspring DC v Taylor* n6.
14   From April 1992, £2.15 per week.

satisfaction of arrears.[15] The basis of the argument is that since those drafting the regulations, taking into account the needs of claimants and the level of their benefit, consider that it is not reasonable for more than five per cent to be deducted when direct payments are made to the landlord, it would be unreasonable and contrary to RA 1977 s100(3), HA 1985 s85(3) and HA 1988 s9(3) for the court to order the deduction of a greater sum. Indeed, if the DSS is already making deductions to go towards the arrears, it may well be unreasonable for the court to make any possession order at all because the landlord's interests are already being adequately protected.[16]

There is a tendency for advisers to view a suspended possession order as a victory, but it should be remembered that it is still a possession order and that if a tenant subsequently fails to comply with conditions imposed it can be difficult to argue that those conditions were not reasonable: also costs will usually be awarded. So it is particularly important to ensure that a tenant will be able to afford to make any proposed payments before agreeing to particular amounts. For the particular dangers inherent in a suspended possession order made against a secure occupier see p52 above.

Particular problems are caused when suspended possession orders are made against secure tenants (see pp52 and 53 above). In view of the wording of Housing Act 1985 s82(2) and the Court of Appeal decision in *Thompson v Elmbridge DC*,[17] one breach of the terms of a suspended possession order results in the termination of the tenancy. Accordingly, one payment of rent or one contribution towards the arrears which is made one day late means that the rights which go with the tenancy (eg, succession, rights under the Matrimonial Homes Act, the right to buy, repairing obligations on the landlord's part, etc) are lost. If a tenant is in receipt of benefits, this is particularly serious, because the practice of the DSS is to forward contributions taken from income support towards rent arrears quarterly in arrears – resulting in the automatic breach of the terms of any suspended possession order. In these circumstances it is particularly important to try to persuade the court to make an order adjourning the case on terms. (See p52.[18])

---

15 Social Security (Claims and Payments) Regulations 1987 SI No 1968, as amended, Sch 9 para 5(3).
16 *Woodspring DC v Taylor* n6 and *Second WRVS Housing Society v Blair* (1986) 19 HLR 104.
17 (1987) 19 HLR 526. See too *Leicester CC v Aldwinkle* (1992) 24 HLR 40 and *R v Sheffield CC ex parte Creaser and Jarvis*, September 1991 *Legal Action* 15, QBD.
18 See too Suspended Possession Orders (1991) 141 NLJ 853 (June 21).

Consent orders

It is a well-established principle that landlords and tenants cannot 'contract out' of the statutory protection provided by RA 1977, HA 1985 and HA 1988.[19] This rule can have important consequences where protected occupiers decide to compromise possession proceedings by agreeing to a 'consent order'. The court cannot make a 'consent order' against a protected or secure tenant unless there is either a concession by express admission that RA or HA protection does not apply or, alternatively, it is established that a ground for possession exists and, if appropriate, it is reasonable to make an order for possession.[20] Any order made without such a concession or without the establishment of a ground for possession and consideration of reasonableness, is a nullity and can be challenged by judicial review, even if both parties were legally represented and consented to it.[21] It may well be that a 'consent order' could be set aside at a later date if it were established that a concession that statutory protection did not apply was not made bona fide.[22]

In *R v Bloomsbury and Marylebone County Court ex parte Blackburne*[23] possession proceedings based on rent arrears were settled on the basis that the tenant would consent to a possession order in return for payment of £11,000 plus costs. Both parties were legally represented. Subsequently the tenant changed his mind and successfully applied for an order of certiorari to quash the possession order.

In *Plaschkes v Jones*[24] an unrepresented tenant went to court intending to defend possession proceedings. However, at court he agreed to a possession order, being under the impression that he would be able to obtain a council house. He later found that he was not able to get a council house and the Court of Appeal allowed his subsequent appeal because the county court had not considered the question of reasonableness.

19   *Barton v Fincham* [1921] 2 KB 291; *Mouat-Balthasar v Murphy* [1966] 3 All ER 477; *Kenyon v Walker* [1946] 2 All ER 595.
20   *R v Bloomsbury and Marylebone County Court ex parte Blackburne* (1985) 275 EG 1273, CA; *R v Newcastle upon Tyne County Court ex parte Thompson* (1988) 20 HLR 430, CA and *Wandsworth LBC v Fadayomi* (1987) 19 HLR 512; [1987] 3 All ER 474, CA.
21   *Blackburne* n20.
22   See, eg, Atkins LJ's references to bona fides in *Barton v Fincham*, n19, at 299.
23   See n20.
24   (1982) 9 HLR 110.

Variation of terms of possession orders

The County Court Rules provide that any debtor who is subject to an order which provides for the repayment of money may apply to the court on notice to vary the order so that payments can be made by smaller amounts if the debtor is unable to pay at the existing rate.[25] The Rules also give the court power to extend the time within which a person is required by any order or judgment to do anything.[26] This includes the time which a tenant has for payment of rent arrears under a suspended possession order. Such an application can be made even after the time when the money should have been paid[27] provided that a warrant has not been executed, but it is obviously best for the application to be made as soon as it is clear that the tenant cannot comply with the order. County courts also have wide powers to set aside orders made under CCR Ord 24 and in any proceedings where a party has failed to attend a hearing.[28]

In addition, the court's statutory power to stay, suspend or postpone the execution of a possession order against a protected or secure tenant (see above) can be exercised at any time prior to execution, even if an absolute order for possession was made at the original hearing,[29] or if the original order was made 'by consent'.[30] Such an application cannot, however, be used to obtain a complete rehearing of the case.[31] Where the court has made an absolute order under, for example, RA 1977 Case 8 or Case 9 (see above), the power can be used to delay possession so that the tenant has more time to find other accommodation, but it cannot be used to delay indefinitely the date when possession should be given up, even if the circumstances of landlord and tenant have changed.[32]

In view of the references to 'period or periods', it is clear that more than one application under HA 1988 s9(2), HA 1985 s85(2) or RA 1977 s100(2) can be made.[33]

An application to vary or suspend an order should be made on notice

---

25 Ord 22 r10.
26 Ord 13 r4.
27 *R v Bloomsbury and Marylebone County Court ex parte Villerwest* [1976] 1 All ER 897; *Vandermolen v Toma* n10.
28 See CCR Ords 24 r7 and 37 r2.
29 *Payne v Cooper* [1957] 3 All ER 335.
30 *Rossiter v Langley* [1925] 1 KB 741; cf *Leicester CC v Aldwinkle* (1992) 24 HLR 40, CA.
31 *Goldthorpe v Bain* [1952] 2 All ER 23 at 25.
32 Ibid.
33 *Sherrin v Brand* [1956] 1 All ER 194 at 204 (per Birkett LJ) and *Vandermolen v Toma* n10.

by a notice of application[34] supported by an affidavit setting out the grounds relied upon. See p360 for a precedent.

Status of tenancy after possession order

An order for possession which is suspended does not end a statutory tenancy, an assured tenancy or a secure tenancy. For example, a spouse living with a tenant who dies may be entitled to become the statutory tenant by succession despite a suspended order against the tenant.[35] Similarly, tenants enjoy the normal right to bring an action for breach of repairing covenants, whether express or implied and protected or statutory tenants can apply to the rent officer. However, a breach of the terms of a suspended possession order automatically brings a secure tenancy to an end (see p53).[36]

An absolute order for possession terminates the tenancy, even if the operation of that order has been delayed for a fixed period. In this situation the occupant is no longer a tenant, once the date stated for the delivery up of possession has passed. 'He has nothing left but the limited interest granted to him by what may be described as the indulgence of the court pursuant to Section 100(2). In effect he has a period of grace.'[37]

Execution of warrant for possession

If a tenant fails to give up possession as required by an absolute order, the landlord's remedy is to apply for a warrant of possession.[38] In the county court a landlord follows the same procedure if s/he wishes to enforce a suspended order for possession on a tenant's failure to comply with the terms of that order. An application for a warrant of possession is made by the landlord completing a form.[39] It seems that a landlord cannot enforce a suspended possession order, if a tenant fails to comply with the terms of the suspension, without making an application for a warrant,[40] but (unless the original order specified that no warrant was to be issued without the leave of the court) a warrant in the county court is issued without any prior notice to the tenant and without a hearing. In this

34   Form N244 or N245.
35   *Sherrin v Brand* n33; *Kyriacou v Pandeli* [1980] CLY 1648.
36   *Thompson v Elmbridge BC* (1987) 19 HLR 526.
37   *American Economic Laundry v Little* [1950] 2 All ER 1186 at 1190. See too *Mills v Allen* [1953] 2 All ER 634 at 641.
38   Ord 26 r17.
39   Form N325.
40   *R v Ilkeston County Court ex parte Kruza* (1985) 17 HLR 539.

respect the county court procedure differs from that in the High Court where leave to issue execution on a suspended order for possession on the grounds of an alleged breach of the terms of that order must not be given without allowing a tenant the opportunity to be heard.[41] The sheriff's duty, on receiving a writ of possession, is to enforce it 'as soon as . . . reasonably practicable', not 'at once'.[42]

Although tenants are not notified in advance of landlords' applications for warrants of possession in the county court, the bailiffs often notify occupiers of the time and date when they propose to call to evict them. Even at this stage tenants who have protected, statutory, assured or secure tenancies can apply to suspend the warrant, relying on RA 1977 s100(2), HA 1985 s85(2) or HA 1988 s9(2).[43] On such an application, tenants can either claim that there has been no breach of the terms of the suspended order or submit that for other reasons the warrant should not be enforced. The county court also has a discretion by virtue of the County Courts Act 1984 s88 to stay any execution (eg, a warrant for possession) for such time and on such terms as the court thinks fit, if it appears to the satisfaction of the court that a party to proceedings is unable to pay any sum or instalment. An application to stay execution can be made using Forms N244 or N245 and it is best for it to be supported by an affidavit (see p362 for precedents). The application can be filed at any time before execution by the bailiffs. Filing of the application may prevent the bailiffs from evicting the tenants, but it is important to ensure that the bailiffs are notified of the application, and to find out whether they still intend to continue with the eviction. If they refuse to call off the eviction, an ex parte application should be made to the judge. Some bailiffs agree not to execute warrants even if no application has been filed if an assurance is given that the tenants will make such an application.

Unless an application is made in accordance with Ord 37 to set aside the original judgment (see below), the judge hearing the application will usually not be prepared to reconsider the original order and the court's attitude will depend on the seriousness of the breach and, if the tenant is in arrears with payments, the reason for this. If the amount of money which the tenant has failed to pay is sizeable and there is no good reason for this, the court is unlikely to be sympathetic unless the tenant can pay a lump

---

41   RSC Ords 45 and 46. *Fleet Mortgage and Investment Co Ltd v Lower Maisonette 46 Eaton Place Ltd* [1972] 2 All ER 737 and *Practice Direction* [1972] 1 All ER 576, *Supreme Court Practice 1985* 46/4/2 and RSC Ord 13 r4. For criticism of the county court procedure, see comments by the Court of Appeal in *Leicester CC v Aldwinkle* (1992) 24 HLR 40, CA.

42   *Six Arlington Street Investments v Persons Unknown* (1986) *Times* 31 March.

43   *R v Ilkeston County Court ex parte Kruza* n40.

sum before the hearing. Other reasons for refusing such an application are unreasonable delay in applying to the court and the prejudicial effect on third parties, such as a new tenant to whom the premises have been re-let.[44]

One cause of tenants' failures to comply with the financial provisions of suspended orders may be delays in receiving HB. It may be that the service of a witness summons (CCR Ord 20 r12) on a senior official responsible for administering the scheme (in the local authority) compelling him or her to attend at the application and to explain the cause of the delay will not only be of assistance in making the application, but will also cause any benefit due to be paid rather rapidly.

Tenants outside the protection of the RA, the HA 1985 and the HA 1988 cannot apply to suspend the execution of a warrant for possession once it has been issued.[45]

When the bailiffs come to execute a county court warrant or the sheriffs a High Court warrant, they can evict anyone they find on the premises, even if they were not a party to the possession proceedings or moved in after the possession order was made.[46] The only remedy for someone in the premises who was not a party to possession proceedings is to apply to be joined to the action and to set aside the order for possession. Obviously such a course of action is likely to be successful only if there would have been a defence to the proceedings and if there is a good reason why the applicant did not attend at the hearing.

A county court or High Court warrant can be executed at any time within one year after it has been issued. If a landlord wants to rely on a warrant after that period s/he must apply for it to be renewed.[47] For a discussion of warrants for possession in mortgage actions, see chapter 35 below.

After eviction by the bailiff

If an eviction follows the forfeiture of a lease, the former lessee may still apply for relief against forfeiture in accordance with the provisions of the Administration of Justice Act 1985 s55 (county court), or the Common Law Procedure Act 1852 s210 (High Court), provided that such an application is made within six months of execution of the order or the

---

44   *Rhodes Trust v Khan* (1979) 123 SJ 719, CA.
45   *Moore v Lambeth County Court Registrar* [1969] 1 All ER 782.
46   *R v Wandsworth County Court ex parte Wandsworth LBC* [1975] 3 All ER 390.
47   County Courts Act 1984 s111(2) and CCR Ord 26 r17 and r6. Cf though, Ords 24 and 113 (chapter 24 above).

time when the landlord regained possession (see pp102–7 above).[48] Otherwise, if eviction has taken place, the only possibility open to a former tenant is to apply to set aside the original possession order. Although courts have power to set aside any order obtained by deceit and any order made in summary possession proceedings,[49] the most common way of applying to set aside an order is to rely on the provisions of CCR Ord 37. Order 37 r2 allows the court to set aside any judgment obtained in a party's absence. Order 37 r3 provides for the setting aside of judgments made where there has been a failure of postal service and notice of any hearing did not come to the defendant's attention in time. Order 37 r5 gives the court a discretion to set aside any judgment where there has been a failure to comply with the court rules. It may also be possible to make an application under Ord 37 r1 for a rehearing where there has been misconduct by the plaintiff or where fresh evidence is available, but, since such an application has to be served on the other party not more than 14 days after trial, it will normally be necessary to make an application for an extension of time pursuant to Ord 13 r4. Any application under Ord 37 should be made as soon as possible and should be supported by an affidavit.

Applications under Ord 37 can be made after execution.[50] In *LB Tower Hamlets v Abadie*[51] a possession order had been made against a secure tenant under ground 8 (repossession of temporary accommodation where original home available after improvement work). After a long delay the tenant, who was not present at the original hearing, applied to set aside the order. His application was granted by the registrar, but reversed on appeal by the circuit judge and the order for possession executed. However, the tenant appealed and the Court of Appeal held that the order could be set aside even after it had been executed. They found that, despite the delay, the council had not actually been prejudiced and that the tenant had an arguable defence to the claim for possession.

Sometimes, particularly in squatting cases, occupiers move into premises after a warrant has been executed or the landlord has in some other way regained possession in accordance with the provisions of an order for possession. It seems that unless there is some connection between the new occupiers and the people who were originally evicted, the

48   See too Law of Property Act 1925 s146 and *Billson v Residential Apartments* [1992] 01 EG 91, HL.
49   See Ord 24 r7.
50   *Governors of Peabody Donation Fund v Hay* (1987) 19 HLR 145, CA; *Grimshaw v Dunbar* [1953] 1 All ER 350; *Hayman v Rowlands* [1957] 1 All ER 321 and *Ladup Ltd v Siu* (1983) *Times* 24 November, CA.
51   [1990] EGCS 4, (1990) 22 HLR 264, CA.

landlord cannot apply for a further warrant in the same proceedings, but must issue further proceedings for possession. Once an order has been executed the proceedings are over and cannot be reactivated.[52]

The position is different if there is a 'close nexus' between the new occupiers and any people who were dispossessed in earlier proceedings. If the further occupation is 'part and parcel of the same transaction'[53] the landlord is entitled to apply ex parte for a writ of restitution.[54] The effect of a writ of restitution is to enable the bailiff or sheriff to evict any person in unlawful occupation of premises again without the landowner having to issue new proceedings. A writ of restitution may be issued even though not all of the new occupiers of the land were among the original defendants.[55] It is theoretically possible for a landowner to apply to court to commit for contempt a person who has re-entered premises unlawfully after an earlier eviction, but such an order should only be made in the most exceptional circumstances.[56]

---

52   *Thomas v Metropolitan Housing Corp* [1936] 1 All ER 210; *Ratcliffe v Tait* (1664) 1 Keble 216; *Lovelace v Ratcliffe* (1664) 1 Keble 785; *Doe d Pait v Roe* (1807) 1 Taunton 55; *Clissold v Cratchley* [1910] 2 KB 244 and *Brighton BC v Persons Unknown* (1991) 14 January, Brighton county court, June 1991 *Legal Action* 13.
53   *Wiltshire County Council v Frazer (No 2)* [1986] 1 All ER 65 per Simon Brown J.
54   CCR Ord 26 r17(4) and RSC Ord 46 r3.
55   *Wiltshire CC v Frazer (No 2)* n53.
56   *Alliance Building Society v Austen* [1951] 2 All ER 1068 where such an order was in fact granted.

CHAPTER 28

Domestic Relationship Breakdown

Often possession proceedings will arise at the same time as or shortly after a breakdown in domestic relationships between occupiers. One partner may have moved out leaving the other in financial difficulties. Or failure to communicate between partners may have allowed arrears to accumulate without the knowledge of one of them.

Where the landlord has not yet threatened possession proceedings there will be time to get advice about immediate rights to remain in the property or secure a transfer of tenancy, occupancy or ownership. The special position of those who are the partners of mortgage defaulters is dealt with in chapter 37.

For information where urgent action is needed (eg, to prevent violence or sale of the property by a departing owner) the reader is referred to LAG's *Debt and Housing Emergency Procedures*.[1] For a review of the respective rights of partners where the property is a public sector tenancy see April and September 1981 *LAG Bulletin* 82 and 211, January and February 1983 *LAG Bulletin* 12 and 27, and May/June 1983 *Roof* 15.

If possession proceedings are in the offing, cohabitees should take urgent independent advice on their position. At present, statute makes provision for only *spouses* to intervene in possession proceedings taken against their partners: for private sector tenancies see p115 and p251, for the public sector pp19–20 and for the spouses of mortgagors p319.

If the possession proceedings are based on failure by the partner who has left 'to occupy the premises as his or her home' the other spouse will be able to defend successfully on the basis that s/he continues to occupy 'on behalf of' the tenant. The Matrimonial Homes Act 1983 s1(6) provides that the occupation by the remaining spouse maintains a statutory, assured or secure tenancy notwithstanding the absence of the tenant, usually up to the date of any decree absolute of divorce. The position arising where a cohabitee is left in occupation is considerably more complex.[2]

---

1 (Legal Action Group, 3rd edn due 1993).
2 See further, eg, S Parker *Cohabitees* (Longman 3rd edn 1991).

If possession proceedings are based on one of the grounds which requires the court to be satisfied that suitable alternative accommodation is available, this may involve the provision of separate units of housing for the tenant and his or her partner. Any spouse or cohabitee anxious that s/he should be adequately housed if possession is ordered against the tenant in these circumstances should apply to be joined as a party to the proceedings (CCR Ord 15 r3).[3]

3   *Wandsworth LBC v Fadayomi* (1987) 19 HLR 512; [1987] 3 All ER 474, CA.

CHAPTER 29

Homelessness

A full description of the law relating to homelessness is beyond the scope of this book and readers seeking a detailed summary are accordingly referred to *Homeless Persons – Arden's Guide to the Housing Act 1985 Part III* (LAG 4th edn 1992). However, the following notes may be of assistance with the respects in which homelessness law affects those subject to actual or potential possession proceedings. For consideration of homelessness in the context of mortgage possession proceedings see chapter 39 below. All references in this chapter are to the Housing Act 1985 unless otherwise stated.

Threatened homelessness

All those against whom possession proceedings are initiated ultimately run the risk of homelessness. Local authorities have a statutory duty to assist persons who are being 'threatened with homelessness'. For the strict duty to arise it must be likely that a person will become homeless within 28 days (s58(4)). However, authorities are directed to take action at an earlier stage where possible. The Code of Guidance issued by the Secretary of State under s71 (third edition) provides at paragraph 5.10 that:

> Someone is defined as 'threatened with homelessness' if s/he is likely to become homeless within 28 days (s58(4)). Authorities should, however, be ready to advise and assist people where the possibility of their becoming homeless is known to the authority more than 28 days in advance. With homelessness, as with most things, prevention is very much better than cure and authorities should therefore aim to take early action. The earlier action can be taken, the greater is the likelihood that measures to avert homelessness can be effective . . . . Authorities will wish to avoid adding the stress of uncertainty to existing stresses and should therefore keep applicants up to date with arrangements that will be made to assist them.

It is for the authority to decide whether the occupier is threatened with homelessness within the meaning of s58(4). In calculating whether the occupier is within 28 days of homelessness, it is often necessary to remind authorities that they must work back from the date on which any possession order is to take effect rather than from some hypothetical future date on which the occupier may actually be evicted. Some authorities are not prepared to accept that those faced with possession proceedings on mandatory grounds or an inevitable possession order in other circumstances, are threatened with homelessness. This is expressly contrary to the Code of Guidance which provides (para 10.12) that:

> Local authorities should not require tenants to fight a possession action where the landlord has a certain prospect of success, such as an action for recovery of property let on an assured shorthold tenancy, on the ground that the fixed term has ended. Authorities need only be satisfied that proper notice has been served of the intention to proceed, eg, a copy of the proper notice served on the tenant claiming repossession.

Once the occupier is accepted as threatened with homelessness the authority must either 'take reasonable steps to secure that accommodation does not cease to be available for his occupation' (where the occupier is in priority need and not intentionally threatened with homelessness) or 'furnish advice and assistance' to help maintain accommodation (where the occupier is not in priority need or became threatened with homelessness intentionally): s66(2) and (3). The first of these duties is usually interpreted as a duty to secure alternative accommodation.

Where the possession proceedings are taken or threatened by a private owner or housing association, the advice and assistance which an authority is required to provide by s66 might include: legal advice on the merits of the claim; possible defences; other legal advice; the provision of representation in court by the council's own lawyers (Local Government Act 1972 s222); counselling; financial assistance; welfare benefits advice and much else besides.

If the possession proceedings have been initiated by the local authority, the occupier can at least seek some assistance as to what steps should be taken if a possession order is made (see final sentence of para 2.11 of the Code and also para A1.16).

Homelessness

There are three situations in which an occupier involved in possession proceedings may in fact be statutorily homeless and therefore entitled to some immediate assistance from the local authority.

Squatters

All squatters (ie, those occupying property without authorisation of the owner) are homeless persons within the meaning of s58. The fact that the owner has chosen to evict them by court proceedings rather than by physically dispossessing them does not alter their status.

Unreasonable to remain

Occupiers are homeless unless the authority is satisfied that it is reasonable for them to continue in occupation of their accommodation (s58(2A)).[1] The authority might accept that it is not reasonable to continue in occupation if faced by a strong case for mandatory possession and the risk of court costs (Code para 10.12).

Possession order expired

A person against whom a possession order has been made becomes homeless on the date it takes effect. Thus in the case of an order for 'possession in 28 days', the defendant will be homeless on the 29th day.[2] However, some authorities wrongly refuse to accept applicants as homeless until the order is executed by bailiffs. It is suggested however that the legal position is clear. Once the possession order itself becomes effective the former tenant becomes a trespasser and is homeless.[2A]

The type of assistance the authority must provide to a homeless person varies depending upon whether the applicant is in priority need (s59) and/or intentionally homeless (s60).

Intentional homelessness

Where a court finds in possession proceedings that a 'fault ground' (eg, rent arrears or nuisance) is established and an order for possession is made, it is likely that a person rendered homeless by such an order will wrongly be automatically treated as intentionally homeless by the local housing authority. The homeless (including those in priority need) will not be accepted immediately for *permanent* rehousing if they are classified as intentionally homeless (s65(3)). They would at most receive temporary accommodation.

Three points of importance arise. First, it will be obvious that any form of consent order should be avoided in possession proceedings (even if

---

1 *Hammell v RB Kensington and Chelsea* (1988) 20 HLR 666, CA.
2 *R v Mole Valley DC ex parte Minnett* (1983) 12 HLR 49.
2A *R v Inverness DC ex p Stewart* (1991) unreported, noted at September 1991 *Legal Action* 16.

it is possible for such an order to be made – see p254) since this will at least raise the inference for the authority that the homeless person has brought about his or her own homelessness.[3]

Second, it does not automatically follow that an occupier against whom an adverse possession order has been made is intentionally homeless; the authority is required to make its own enquiries (s62) and to satisfy itself as to the true facts of the case. For example, if the ground on which possession was granted was nuisance, the authority must itself investigate who caused or was responsible for the nuisance.[4] The council cannot fetter its discretion in the application of the definition of intentionality (s60) by slavishly adopting the findings of the court which dealt with the possession action.

Third, occupiers not infrequently panic and quit the premises before they are required to do so – either at the stage at which possession proceedings are threatened or under way, or before the time allowed by the possession order has expired. If in quitting they have brought to an end their interest in the property (eg, by notice to quit or surrender) they will have become homeless. In such circumstances it is open to a local authority to find that, notwithstanding that the family would have become homeless in due course, they are 'intentionally homeless' because it would have been reasonable for them to have remained in the property as at the date they left it.[5] Consideration should be given to the possibility of challenging such a finding. The authority could usefully be referred to the Code of Guidance (para 7.4(c)) which provides that there should not be a finding of intentional homelessness in respect of an owner occupier 'who is faced with foreclosure or possession proceedings to which there is no defence' and leaves.

A more acute illustration of the same problem arises where the local authority has actually advised the tenant to resist the possession proceedings. Although the authority cannot properly advise defending in hopeless cases,[6] it may assert that a person renders him or herself intentionally homeless as a result of ignoring appropriate advice.[7]

If presented with a decision of 'intentionally homeless' the applicant should be immediately referred to an adviser specialising in housing law.

3   R v Wandsworth LBC ex parte Henderson (1986) 18 HLR 522; noted at September 1986 Legal Action 124.
4   Devenport v Salford CC (1983) 8 HLR 57, CA.
5   Din v Wandsworth LB (1982) 1 HLR 73, HL.
6   R v Portsmouth CC ex parte Knight (1983) 10 HLR 115 and R v Surrey Heath BC ex parte Li (1984) 16 HLR 79.
7   R v Penwith DC ex parte Hughes (1980) unreported; noted at August 1980 LAG Bulletin 187.

Deemed applications

In order to be considered for rehousing as homeless, persons displaced by possession proceedings must apply to the local authority. If those persons make an application at a stage where they are actually homeless and in priority need they must be accommodated by the authority while enquiries are made into the circumstances of their homelessness etc (s63). In order to avoid even this interim housing duty to the homeless, some local authorities have created the device of a 'deemed application' as a bluff to use against secure occupiers whom they subject to possession proceedings. The usual phrasing runs (after reciting the threat of proceedings) ' . . . and at the same time we will treat you as having applied for rehousing as a person threatened with homelessness. Despite being in priority need you will be classified as intentionally homeless and will be accommodated at your present address only until the date ordered by the judge in the possession order. Thereafter no application for accommodation by you will be accepted and you will be homeless'.

Faced with this sort of quite improper conduct, the tenant should take the matter up with a councillor and/or the local ombudsman. The 'deemed' application is a nullity[8] and the person eventually threatened with homelessness or made homeless should apply to the authority for assistance in the ordinary way.

Protection of property

It is important to note that local authority duties towards the homeless extend to the protection of property and powers are available to assist the non-priority homeless (s70). Assistance should be sought once loss of possession has become inevitable. The effect of a possession order will be that the defendant loses a home – s70 prevents loss of all the belongings too.

Housed as homeless

Local authorities may seek recovery of possession of accommodation into which a homeless person has been temporarily placed. For the 'security of tenure' of such occupiers see p59.

8   *R v East Northamptonshire DC ex parte Spruce* (1988) 20 HLR 508.

CHAPTER 30

Housing Benefit

Many residents threatened with possession proceedings will be in that situation as a result of failure to make rental or other payments to the landlord. The housing benefit scheme is designed to assist those on low incomes in meeting their liabilities for housing costs. The benefit is claimed from and payable by the local authority for the area in which the property is situated. Indeed, precisely in order to avoid homelessness resulting from rent arrears, local authorities are supposed to 'inform people of their entitlement' (Homelessness Code of Guidance para 10.7, 3rd edn).

In outline, the scheme provides[1] that recipients of income support will be eligible for assistance with up to 100 per cent of rent, and others on low income receive proportionate help. This book does not allow scope for a full description of the workings of housing benefit (HB), for which see Zebedee and Ward *Guide to Housing Benefit and Community Charge Benefit* (SHAC). However, there are a number of aspects of the HB scheme which touch directly on possession proceedings.

Maximising HB to clear arrears

If there are rent arrears and the occupier is presently (or has recently been) on a low income the starting point will be to check that HB is in payment and that the correct amount is being and has been received. A separate legal aid green form can be completed for this purpose. Once the appropriate HB entitlement has been established the HB scheme may help to make useful inroads into the outstanding arrears.

First, *backdating* should be considered. If there has been some entitlement in the past which the occupier failed to claim, application should be made for backdating of the current award of benefit. This will

---

1 Social Security Act 1986 and Housing Benefit (General) Regulations 1987 (HB Regulations 1987) SI No 1971.

produce a lump sum of arrears of HB which can be applied to meeting the rent debt. The local authority has power to backdate up to 12 months if good cause is shown for not having initiated a claim at an earlier date.[2] 'Good cause' is undefined and might be established by a variety of circumstances ranging from ill health to earlier inaccurate advice. The adviser should not hesitate to present the individual claimant's explanation as one amounting to good cause.

Second, the possibility of *enhancing* HB above the amount previously or currently in payment should be considered. Even if full entitlement to HB has been paid, those not on income support may nevertheless be in hardship making up any residual rent liability. The scheme provides local authorities with power to pay more than normal entitlement to HB up to a maximum of 100 per cent of rent (reg 69(8)). Advisers should ensure that this enhancement is sought in arrears cases as it will produce additional cash to help protect the occupier from eviction for arrears. Some initial resistance can be expected from the local authority, as the extra amount paid under this provision does not attract the usual HB subsidy and the maximum extra payable in any one year is limited to 0.1 per cent of its overall HB expenditure (Social Security Act 1986 s28(9)). The adviser should counter with the assertions:

- the 'claimant's circumstances are exceptional' and therefore reg 69(8) applies;
- the extra monies will attract grant subsidy in place of HB subsidy;
- if the authority is approaching the maximum 0.1 per cent limit, the case should be referred to the HB Review Board which is not bound by that limit.

There is no statutory definition as to what might amount to 'exceptional' circumstances. Obviously, low income alone will not suffice as HB claimants are, by definition, on low incomes. Advisers should draw particular attention to family size, disablement, any other reasons for higher than average outgoings, severe indebtedness, domestic breakdown etc.

If proceedings have already been started they should be adjourned pending the outcome of applications for backdating or enhancement of HB.

Paper 'arrears'

Not infrequently, public sector landlords initiate possession proceedings

2   HB Regulations 1987 reg 72(15).

based on arrears which, upon examination, turn out to be entirely related to payment or otherwise of HB. This arises in two sets of circumstances.

Delayed or late payment

Once the occupier has claimed HB from the local authority, the latter should, within 14 days, start paying HB towards the resident's rent liability.[3] If this is delayed or wrongly calculated 'paper arrears' can result, simply from failure to pay the appropriate HB. Where the plaintiff is the local authority, the resident may properly be advised to respond to possession proceedings based on such arrears either by inviting the court to strike out the proceedings as an abuse of process or by entering a defence and counterclaiming for breach of statutory duty. Where the plaintiff is a private landlord or housing association the local authority could be joined as a third party (CCR Ord 12) or the senior officer responsible summonsed to give evidence (CCR Ord 20 r12 and Form N286), in order to prompt the authority into payment of the correct benefit and a lump sum of arrears.

Overpayment

The second species of paper arrears arises from HB overpayments. Typically, a local authority pays HB to its own tenants by way of credit to the rent account. The rent due is directly 'paid'[4] in this way in whole or in part and the occupier's rent liability met. Inevitably, there are mistakes and tenants are paid too much benefit or paid benefit to which they are not entitled. The regulations prescribe careful procedures to restrict recovery and ensure notification in such cases.[5] However, local authorities, on discovering an overpayment, not infrequently seize back from the occupier's rent account the benefit overpaid and then issue statements showing tenants 'in arrears' by that amount. The activity is wholly improper for (inter alia) the following reasons:

- many overpayments are irrecoverable (reg 99(2)) and the authority has a discretion as to whether to recover any overpayment (reg 100);
- the authority is obliged to issue written notification of the decision that there has been an overpayment, that it should be recovered and as to the method selected for recovery (reg 77 and Sch 6 para 14);

---

3 Ibid regs 76(3) and 88(3).
4 See the definition of 'payment' in Social Security Act 1986 s28(1A)(c) inserted with retrospective effect by Social Security Act 1989.
5 HB Regulations 1987 regs 98–105.

- the permitted methods of recovery of overpaid HB do not include the unilateral plundering of the occupier's rent account.

If possession proceedings are initiated against an occupier for such 'paper arrears' the defence should be that the amount alleged is not 'rent lawfully due' but HB (see p25), and that the county court in possession proceedings is not the appropriate venue for recovery.

Similar difficulties occur when HB payments are made direct to private and housing association landlords (see below) and are subsequently discovered to have been overpayments. If a local authority exercises its power to seek recovery from the landlord (reg 101), the tenant's adviser needs to guard against any attempt to count monies voluntarily repaid by the landlord as 'arrears'.

Direct payments of housing benefit

The HB scheme contains a series of provisions (described below) under which benefit can be paid directly to a private or housing association landlord. These are directly relevant to possession proceedings because:

- failure by a landlord to apply for the direct payment facility may be helpful in establishing that it is not 'reasonable in all the circumstances' for the court to make a possession order in proceedings based on rent arrears (see p26 (secure occupiers), p163 (RA occupiers), p194 (assured tenants));
- an offer to the landlord for future HB to be paid direct may encourage a compromise in the proceedings;
- an undertaking by the occupier to the court to apply for direct payments to meet future rent might persuade the court to grant any necessary adjournment;
- where a direct payment scheme has been operating but the landlord has been overpaid, the landlord might repay the authority and claim that the occupier is 'in arrears' (see below).

These provisions are in addition to those permitting direct payments toward rent arrears (up to £2.15 pw (in 1992/93)) to be made by the DSS on behalf of income support and other social security claimants.[6]

The local authority *must* pay HB direct to the landlord where (reg 93):

(1) direct deductions are already being made from income support by the DSS towards rent arrears; or

---

6   Social Security (Claims and Payments) Regulations 1987 SI No 1968 Sch 9.

(2) eight or more weeks' worth of rent is outstanding (except where it is in the overriding interest of the claimant for direct payments not to be made).

Additionally, the authority *may* agree to pay HB direct where (reg 94):

(3) the claimant requests direct payments; or
(4) the landlord requests direct payments and the claimant agrees; or
(5) payment direct is in the interests of the claimant and his or her family; or
(6) the tenant has left owing rent arrears and there is an outstanding payment of HB attributable to that accommodation.

Where direct payments are to be made, both the occupier and the landlord are informed in writing (reg 77 and Sch 6 para 11).

Usually upon receipt of the direct payment the landlord applies the HB in satisfaction of all or part of the occupier's rent liability. Difficulties can arise if subsequently it is discovered that the amount of HB has been overpaid. In these circumstances, if the local authority determines that the overpayment is recoverable (reg 99) and should be recovered (reg 100) it may seek recovery from the landlord to whom it was paid as an alternative to recovery from the claimant (reg 101(1)(b)). The landlord (often a housing association) may agree to repay. Regrettably, the landlord may then wrongly seek to 'adjust' the tenant's rent account or record book and claim that 'arrears' are due in the sum repaid to the authority. Whatever the precise legal interrelationship between the three parties concerning the overpaid sum it is clearly not 'arrears of rent' upon which the landlord can or should mount proceedings for possession.

Part IV

Mortgages

CHAPTER 31

Mortgages

In 1904 an appeal judge said, 'no one, I am sure, by the light of nature ever understood an English mortgage of real estate'.[1] In 1986 the Law Commission in more reserved tone, commented in its introduction to Working Paper No 99 on reform of land mortgages:[2]

> The English law of land mortgages is notoriously difficult. It has never been subjected to systematic statutory reform, and over several centuries of gradual evolution it has acquired a multi-layered structure that is historically fascinating but inappropriately and sometimes unnecessarily complicated.

It is clear that the current state of English law is inadequate. This is recognised by the Law Commission, which in November 1991 published its recommendations for the reform of the law regulating land mortgages.[3] The defects in the law are all the more important given the great social impact of its subject matter. Between 1979 and 1987 the owner-occupied share of the residential market increased from 54.6 per cent to 64 per cent[4] and is still increasing. Many of these properties are subject to one or more mortgages. Between 1980 and 1990 the number of mortgage possession actions started in the county courts in England and Wales rose from 27,105 to 186,649.[5] The number of repossessions by members of the Council of Mortgage Lenders (which comprises all the

1 *Samuel v Jarrah Timber and Woodparing Corporation* [1904] AC 323 per Lord MacNaughten at 326.
2 Law Commission Working Paper No 99 *Land Mortgages* (HMSO 1986).
3 Law Commission 'Transfer of Land – Land Mortgages' Law Com No 204 HC5 (HMSO 1991).
4 J Doling, V Khan and B Stafford 'How far can privatization go? Owner-occupation and mortgage default' *National Westminster Bank Quarterly Review* August 1985 and Building Societies Association *Building Society News* Vol 8 No 5 May 1988.
5 Lord Chancellor's Department, *Judicial Statistics: Annual Report 1991* (Cm 1990) and *Civil Justice Review – A Report of the Review Body on Civil Justice* (Cm 394, HMSO, 1988).

major lenders) in 1991 came to 75,540 and at the end of June 1992 there were 191,280 mortgage borrowers more than six months in arrears.[6]

It is against this backdrop that this chapter is written, to try to explain the law and practice of mortgage possession actions and how advisers can help prevent loss of occupation by borrowers and their families.

Nature of legal mortgages

A lender who has secured the loan on property has a considerable advantage over an unsecured lender and is not solely dependent on the solvency of the borrower to recover the money lent. A mortgagee (ie, lender) has a number of options open as methods of enforcing the security. The lender may sue the borrower on the personal covenant in the mortgage deed, may appoint a receiver to collect rent due from any tenants in the property or seek a foreclosure order from the court. However, in practice, large institutional lenders will usually seek to obtain possession of the property and sell with vacant possession to recover the money owed to them. Part IV of this book will primarily deal with the law and practice related to this last method of enforcement. Throughout, the terms 'lender' and 'borrower' will be used in place respectively of the more technical terms 'mortgagee' and 'mortgagor', except where a term of art is to be used. The lender will, of course, almost invariably be a building society, bank or similar institution rather than an individual.

Since 1925, legal mortgages can only be effected in one of two ways.[7] The first is by the granting of a lease by the freehold owner to the lender for a term of 3,000 years. Where the property is leasehold, the lease granted in favour of the lender will be for a term equivalent to the owner's interest, less one day. In both cases there is included a provision for 'cesser on redemption'—that is for the lease to terminate on redemption of the loan. The second and much more usual way is by a charge by deed expressed to be by way of legal mortgage. This is commonly known as a legal charge. Although the borrower remains the holder of the legal estate, with the lender obtaining no legal term as such, the lender is by statute given the same powers and remedies as a lender whose loan is protected by the creation of a lease in the lender's favour.[8]

In practice, modern institutional lenders invariably rely on mortgages by way of legal charge as they are simpler to use. The legal charge is an agreement whereby a particular property is used as security to ensure that a

---

6   Council of Mortgage Lenders *Mortgage Monthly* Vol 12 no 8, August 1992.
7   Law of Property Act 1925 ss85(1), 86(1).
8   Ibid s87(1).

borrower complies with the terms of a loan from the lender without the transfer of possession or title by the borrower to the lender. In default by the borrower the lender is given various statutory powers in respect of the property and generally additional contractual powers are reserved to the lender in the mortgage deed. The borrower is usually made responsible in the charge deed for the maintenance and insurance of the building, and is made personally liable for the payment of the mortgage money and the lender's legal costs and expenses in enforcing the security. Advisers should look at the terms of the charge deed and any collateral agreement for the details in each case. In the case of loans from fringe banks and similar lenders it is essential to obtain a copy of the loan agreement as well as the legal charge so that all the terms of the loan are clear. Usually this will be forthcoming on demand.

Types of mortgage

There are commonly two different forms of modern mortgage used by individuals for the securing of a loan—whether originally for the purchase of a property or for a subsequent loan—and it is important for advisers to clarify which the borrower has entered into. Perhaps the more common (although this is changing because of encouragement from many of the financial institutions) is the capital repayment (or annuity) mortgage. This usually requires a monthly repayment to the lender, part of which is repayment of the capital borrowed and the balance of which is interest. In this way the capital is repaid gradually over the term of the loan. The other common form of mortgage is the endowment mortgage in which two monthly payments are required: one is to the lender comprising interest on the capital borrowed and the second is the premium on a life insurance policy which is paid to the insurance company. This policy is designed to mature at the end of the term agreed with the lender. During the term the benefit of the policy is assigned to the lender and it is a condition of the loan that the premiums are paid on the policy. Some endowment mortgages are 'with profits' and are designed to give the borrower a small additional lump sum at the end of the term over and above the money needed to pay off the loan and redeem the mortgage. A 'with profits' endowment mortgage will require higher monthly instalments.

A further form of mortgage is now being developed which is similar to the endowment mortgage. This is the pension mortgage, where the owner's private retirement pension is used as security for repayment of the capital borrowed. The capital is paid out of the lump sum which becomes payable to the borrower when the pension plan matures. No formal assignment of the pension can be made, and so lenders are really relying on their right to possession as security in the event of the capital not being repaid at the end of the agreed term. As with endowment mortgages, the borrower is required to pay interest on the outstanding capital throughout the term. Numerically this type of mortgage is as yet comparatively insignificant but is likely to become more numerous as the push to develop private pensions continues.

CHAPTER 32

Lender's right to possession

As the legal charge gives the lender a notional lease of the property, the lender will, subject to any agreement to the contrary contained in the deed, be entitled to take possession of the property as soon as the deed has been executed.[1] It is not necessary for the borrower to be in default. However, if someone other than the borrower has a right to possession in priority to that of the lender, the latter would be prevented from taking possession. (See below p322.) Obviously modern institutional lenders do not want possession of the property as they are anxious to ensure that they receive the regular repayments agreed with the borrower. The exercise of this right to possession will normally only be as a preliminary step to enforcing the security by way of sale with vacant possession in case of financial or other default under the mortgage. Unless the mortgage deed requires it, notice of proceedings for possession need not be given,[2] although a number of warning letters will usually be sent by a lender. It is unclear whether lenders must strictly obtain a court order to enforce their right to possession.[3] In practice, to ensure an ability to sell as mortgagees in possession, lenders do seek orders for possession. The extent to which Parliament has modified this common law right to possession is discussed in chapter 33.

Some charge deeds contain a clause effectively creating a notional tenancy between the lender and the borrower. This is called an 'attornment clause'. If the agreement contains such a clause then the lender must first terminate the tenancy before exercising its right to possession.[4] Such clauses are not common in modern institutional mortgage deeds.

---

1 Law of Property Act 1925 s95(4) and *Fourmaids Limited v Dudley Marshall (Properties) Limited* [1957] 2 All ER 35 and generally R J Smith 'The Mortgagee's Right to Possession – the Modern Law' (1979) *Conv* 266.
2 *Jolly v Arbuthnot* (1859) 4 De G & J 224.
3 See generally A Clarke 'Further Implications of s36 of the Administration of Justice Act' (1983) *Conv* 293.
4 *Hinckley and Country Building Society v Henny* [1953] 1 WLR 352.

CHAPTER 33

Courts' Powers to Deny Possession to Lender

As has been indicated above, the lender has an immediate right to possession of the mortgaged property. The court, when considering an application by the lender for an order for possession, has limited inherent and statutory powers to prevent the lender from obtaining possession.

Inherent power

The High Court has only an inherent discretion in possession proceedings to grant a short adjournment – for example 28 days – so as to allow any default to be remedied or for the loan to be paid off.[1] It has also been stated that the court's equitable powers extend to preventing a lender from taking possession 'except when it is sought bona fide and reasonably for the purpose of enforcing the security and then only subject to such conditions as the court thinks fit to impose'.[2]

This is a new proposition of equity from Lord Denning MR which was not supported by the other judges in the Court of Appeal, who reached a similar decision but without commenting on this dictum. The proposition has not, however, been overruled and gives scope for borrowers to argue, for instance, that if there is some other method of enforcing payment of arrears (such as a voluntary attachment of earnings order) then no order for possession should be granted. This would be particularly useful in cases where the lender's capital is not significantly at risk because there is plenty of equity in the property, ie the sale value of the property exceeds the outstanding debt.

---

1   *Birmingham Citizens' Permanent Building Society v Caunt* [1962] Ch 883.
2   *Quennel v Maltby* [1979] 1 All ER 568, CA at 571e.

Statutory Powers

There are two mutually exclusive statutory regimes which may be appropriate to assist a borrower in default under the mortgage. In the case of residential mortgages the court has powers to grant relief either by virtue of the Administration of Justice Acts 1970 and 1973 or alternatively under the Consumer Credit Act 1974. Where the mortgage is a 'regulated agreement' within the meaning of the 1974 Act (for which see p287 below), the provisions of that Act apply in place of those of the Administration of Justice Acts.[3] Where the mortgage relates to non-residential property then there will be statutory power to grant relief only if the agreement in question is 'a regulated agreement' within the 1974 Act.

In practice it is not uncommon for courts to treat consumer credit loans in the same way as loans to which the Administration of Justice Acts apply. It is important to remind district judges of the difference when dealing with consumer credit loans and to emphasise the fact that the court's powers under the Consumer Credit Act are wider than those under the Administration of Justice Acts.

Administration of Justice Acts 1970 and 1973

The Administration of Justice Act (AJA) 1970 Pt IV together with Administration of Justice Act (AJA) 1973 s8 (for which see appendix B) set out the court's principal powers to assist borrowers who are in default.[4]

The AJA 1970 s36(1) provides:

> Where the mortgagee under a *mortgage* of land which consists of or includes a *dwelling-house* brings an action in which he claims possession . . . (not being an action for *foreclosure* in which a claim for possession . . . is also made) the court may exercise any of [its] powers . . . if it appears to the court that in the event of its exercising the power the mortgagor *is likely* to be able within a *reasonable period* to pay *any sums due* under the mortgage or to remedy a default consisting of a breach of any other obligation arising under or by virtue of the mortgage. (Author's emphasis: these phrases are considered below.)

---

3   Administration of Justice Act 1970 s38A inserted by Consumer Credit Act 1974 Sch 4 para 30; Consumer Credit Act 1974 (Commencement No 8) Order 1983 SI No 1551 and County Courts Act (1984) s21(9).

4   See generally RJ Smith 'The Mortgagee's Right to Possession – The Modern Law' (1979) *Conv* 266 and A Clarke 'Further Implications of s36 of the Administration of Justice Act' (1983) *Conv* 293.

Section 36(2) provides that the court:

(a)   may adjourn the proceedings, or
(b)   on giving judgment, or making an order, for delivery of possession
      . . . or at any time before execution of such judgment or order
      may:
        (i)   stay or suspend execution of the judgment or order, or
        (ii) postpone the date for delivery of possession
for such period or periods as the court thinks reasonable.

By s36(3) any order made in exercise of any s36(2) powers may be made:

Subject to such conditions with regard to payment by the mortgagor of any
sum secured by the mortgage or the remedying of any default as the court
thinks fit.

The court is empowered by s36(4) to vary or revoke any condition
imposed. Section 36 is qualified by the AJA 1973 s8(2) which states,
in effect, that before exercising any of its powers it must appear to
the court not only that the borrower is likely to be able within the
reasonable period to pay off the missed monthly payments, but also
that it is likely that by the end of that reasonable period the borrower
will also have paid off the payments which have fallen due during that
period.

The court's powers apply equally to endowment mortgages, where
there is no obligation to repay the capital originally borrowed until the
end of the loan period, as they do to annuity (or repayment) mortgages,
where part of each monthly repayment is capital and part interest.[5] By
analogy, maturity loans (whereby only the interest on the capital
borrowed is payable) would also be included. Section 36 powers can also
be exercised whether or not there is default under the mortgage deed itself
– for example breach of some collateral agreement.[6]

The court has no power under the Administration of Justice Act 1973
s8 to assist a borrower unless the mortgage or an agreement under the
mortgage allows the borrower to defer payment of the principal sum after
it has become due. Where an agreement to secure a bank overdraft
provides that the sum owed shall only become payable on demand, then
there is no agreement to defer payment and so the agreement falls outside
the scope of section 8 of the 1973 Act.[7]

---

5   *Bank of Scotland v Grimes* [1985] 3 WLR 294, CA.
6   *Western Bank Ltd v Schindler* [1976] 2 All ER 393, CA and generally C Harpum 'A
    Mortgagee's Right to Possession and the Mischief Rule' (1977) 40 MLR 356.
7   See *Habib Bank Ltd v Taylor* [1982] 3 All ER 561, CA.

'Mortgage'

As indicated above there is no significant practical difference between a legal mortgage and a legal charge. Section 39(1) confirms that the expression 'mortgage' includes a 'charge' and that 'mortgagor' and 'mortgagee' should be similarly construed.

'Dwelling-house'

Section 39(1) defines dwelling-house as meaning any building or part of a building which is used as a dwelling. Section 39(2) amplifies this by expressly providing that the fact that part of the premises occupied as a dwelling is used as a shop, as an office or for business, trade or professional purposes does not prevent the premises from being a dwelling-house. It follows therefore that mixed business/residential user is covered by the Act.

'Foreclosure'

Although it is often said that a property is being foreclosed by a lender, in practice the common form of enforcement is that of taking possession and subsequent sale.

Foreclosure of residential mortgages is very rare as it is more complex and enforcement by possession and sale is sufficient as a method of enforcement. Foreclosure is technically quite different from the obtaining of possession and subsequent sale in that it involves the extinction of the borrower's equitable right to redeem the mortgage on the property and the vesting of the legal estate absolutely in the lender. An example will illustrate the difference.

> **Example:**   X borrows £15,000 by way of a mortgage from C Ltd. X repays £1,000 before C Ltd obtains possession of the property and sells it for £30,000. X would receive from C Ltd after the sale, £16,000 after redemption of the outstanding mortgage of £14,000. If C Ltd foreclosed on the property instead of taking possession and selling, X would lose the equity of £16,000, C Ltd would become the absolute owner of the property worth £30,000 and X would receive nothing.

In view of the draconian nature of foreclosure the courts are reluctant to grant foreclosure orders absolute and they put procedural obstacles in the way of a lender seeking such an order. Briefly, the procedure to obtain such an order is as follows. Once repayment of the mortgage money has fallen due – for example on breach of any term in the mortgage or after calling in by the lender – and it remains unpaid, the lender can apply for a foreclosure decree nisi. This order directs the taking of accounts between the lender and the borrower as to money paid during the term of the mortgage, and provides that if the borrower pays the remaining outstanding money by a particular date then the mortgage is redeemed and the debt discharged. If the mortgage is not redeemed by that date then the lender can apply to be granted the foreclosure order absolute. The lender then becomes the legal owner and the property is transferred to it. At the request of any person interested the court has the power[8] to order sale of the property instead of foreclosure. Normally such an order for 'judicial sale' would be granted so as to ensure that the borrower receives the balance of the sale price once the lender has been paid off. The court's dislike of foreclosure is such that, on occasion even after foreclosure order absolute, it will 'open' the foreclosure. As a result of this and the efficacy of other methods of enforcement, foreclosure is rarely used by lenders[9] although it may often be pleaded as part of the lender's claim for relief in addition to claims for sale and/or possession.

It seems likely that foreclosure is no longer possible in the case of 'regulated agreements' within the meaning of the Consumer Credit Act 1974 (see below p287) as s113(1) of the 1974 Act prevents a lender from obtaining any greater benefit by enforcing any security provided in relation to a regulated agreement than would be the case if no such security had been given. No authority on the point has been found but in view of the very restricted use of foreclosure the point may happily remain academic.

The Administration of Justice Acts add, to some limited degree, to the court's powers in cases where foreclosure is claimed. In effect, where foreclosure alone is claimed, the only statutory (as opposed to common law or inherent) power is adjournment. If the claim is for foreclosure and possession, there appears to be power to adjourn the foreclosure claim and to adjourn the possession claim or stay, suspend or postpone any order for possession.[10]

'Is likely'

The question of whether a borrower is likely to be able to pay any sums due within a reasonable time is one of fact for the judge on the evidence before him or her, whether on affidavit or oral evidence.[11] For this reason it is essential that the borrower(s) attend the possession hearing, otherwise

---

8   Law of Property Act 1925 s91(1), (2).
9   For a note on foreclosure in commercial mortgages, see E Bannister 'Foreclosure – A Remedy out of its Time?' (1992) EG 28 March.
10 Administration of Justice Act 1970 s36 and Administration of Justice Act 1973 s8(3). See generally S Tromans 'Mortgages: Possession by Default' (1984) *Conv* 91.
11 *Royal Trust Co of Canada v Markham* [1975] 3 All ER 433, CA and *Western Bank Ltd v Schindler* n6.

there will be no evidence before the district judge to allow him or her to exercise the court's statutory powers.

'Reasonable period'

The assessment of the 'reasonable period' is difficult but central to whether or not the court will grant the borrower relief. It has been stated, obiter, that in making the assessment the court must 'bear in mind the rights and obligations of both parties, including [the lender's] right to recover the money by selling the property, if necessary, and the whole past history of the security'.[12] More important is defining the length of the period during which arrears are to be cleared. Local practice varies considerably. Some district judges adopt a 12-month period and others have extended it to a two – or three – year period, or even longer. It is important to refer the district judge to the dictum of Scarman LJ, who commented: 'Since the object of the instalment mortgage was, with the consent of the mortgagee, to give the mortgagor the period of the mortgage to repay the capital sum and interest, one begins with a powerful presumption of fact in favour of the period of the mortgage being the "reasonable period".'[13] It has also been stated, obiter, that 'In a suitable case the specified period might even be the whole remaining prospective life of the mortgage'.[14]

> **Example:** In October 1980 A borrows £25,000 from a building society over a 15-year period, repayable at a rate of £200 per month. In October 1985 at the court hearing A is six months in arrears amounting to £1,200. If local practice dictates that arrears are cleared within 12 months of the court order A will need to show that s/he can pay £300 per month (being the normal monthly instalments of £200 and an additional £100 per month towards the arrears). If A cannot pay this then the lender will be granted an order for possession. If A can, then the Administration of Justice Act powers can be used. If Scarman LJ's dictum is adopted then A need only satisfy the registrar that s/he can pay £210 per month (being the normal monthly instalment of £200 and £10 towards the arrears, that is the £1,200 over the outstanding 120 months of the loan term).

Although it can be hard to persuade district judges to extend the length of the 'reasonable period', the benefits to the borrower are obvious. Provided that the equity in the property – that is the surplus value of the property arrived at after deducting the money outstanding under any

12   *Centrax Trustees v Ross* [1979] 2 All ER 952 per Goulding J at 957.
13   *First Middlesbrough Trading and Mortgage Company v Cunningham* (1974) 28 P & CR 69, CA at 75.
14   *Western Bank Ltd v Schindler* n6 at 400e, per Buckley LJ.

mortgages – is significant, it is hard to see what risk there is to the lender. It can be useful to clarify with the lender before the hearing whether it accepts that there is plenty of equity or to produce evidence to prove the amount of equity to show that the lender is not at risk. The green form scheme can be used to pay for the cost of an estate agent's valuation if one cannot be obtained free.

Where, however, there is no equity – that is, there would be a shortfall if the property were sold – it is possible to argue that the lender's interests are better served by a delay in possession being given up, particularly where there is some prospect of the market improving. The alternative view is that it in the lender's interest to allow sale to proceed at the earliest opportunity so that the loss to the lender is minimised.

'Sums due'

Most mortgage deeds enable the lender to 'call in' the loan at any time or else provide that the capital money in total becomes immediately payable in the event of any default. As originally drafted, the AJA 1970 s36 enabled the court to give relief to the borrower only if it were likely that s/he could pay any sums due under the mortgage. The court's power to give relief was therefore available only if the borrower could pay off any arrears and the outstanding capital which had invariably also become payable. To resolve this anomaly the AJA 1973 s8(1) redefined 'sums due' to make it clear that in the case of instalment mortgages or mortgages where payment was deferred in whole or part, the financial default to be considered at the hearing was limited to the normal instalments due but unpaid and that the provision for earlier repayment of capital contained in the mortgage deed was to be ignored.

> **Example:** B borrowed £25,000 from a building society repayable at the rate of £200 per month. The mortgage deed provided that as soon as B became in arrears with the repayments then the entire mortgage debt became repayable immediately. At the date of the court hearing B is six months in arrears. By virtue of Administration of Justice Act 1973 s8 the court can ignore the whole of the outstanding mortgage debt and treat as being immediately due only the arrears of £1,200.

It is not clear from the wording of AJA 1970 s36 and AJA 1973 s8, when read together, whether it is proper for the court in instalment mortgages to take into account interest which accrues on arrears and other payments which fall due as a result of being in arrears in determining a borrower's ability to pay off 'any sums due' over the reasonable period. It is submitted that given the wording of s8(1), the borrower should only be required to show that s/he is likely to be able to pay off the geniune arrears built up by the hearing and not that s/he can pay off those arrears plus any interest and other payments which may accrue over the reasonable period.[15]

Consumer Credit Act 1974

Where the mortgage is a 'regulated agreement' within the meaning of the 1974 Act, then the provisions of that Act apply in place of those in the Administration of Justice Acts.[16] Basically, an agreement under which an individual is supplied with credit not exceeding £15,000[17] will be a regulated agreement unless the agreement falls within the Act's 'exempt agreement' provisions.[18]

Loans which otherwise would be within scope of the Act are 'exempt agreements' in the following circumstances. All loans by local authorities secured on land are exempt. Alternatively, loans by building societies and the various banks, insurance companies, friendly societies and charities specified in the Consumer Credit (Exempt Agreements) Order 1989[19] are exempt provided the loans are secured on land and are for the purchase of land, or the provision of a dwelling or business premises. Additionally, loans by these lenders are exempt where they are for:

a) the alteration, enlargement, repair or improvement of a dwelling or business premises, provided the lender has already lent for the purchase of land or the provision of a dwelling or business premises; or alternatively
b) the alteration, enlargement, repair or improvement of a dwelling, such work to be undertaken by a housing association or other specified body.

In either case, to be exempt the loan must be secured on the property in question. Happily, in practice it is usually clear whether a loan falls within scope of the Consumer Credit Act.

The provisions of the Consumer Credit Act (CCA) 1974 are notoriously complicated, dealing as they do with a multitude of different types

15 For an interesting article on this and other points relating to the practice of mortgage possession proceedings, see District Judge Parmiter 'Wrongly Dispossessed?' (1992) LS Gaz 29 April.
16 See n3.
17 The limit of £15,000 was substituted for £5,000 from 20 May 1985 by the Consumer Credit (Increase of Monetary Limits) Order 1983 SI No 1878.
18 See Consumer Credit Act 1974 ss8 and 16.
19 Consumer Credit (Exempt Agreements) Order 1989 SI No 869; Consumer Credit (Exempt Agreements) (Amendment) Order 1989 SI No 1841; Consumer Credit (Exempt Agreements) (Amendment) (No 2) Order 1989 SI No 2337; Consumer Credit (Exempt Agreements) (Amendment) (No 3) Order 1991 SI 2844.

of credit transaction. The Act seeks to prescribe the way in which regulated agreements are entered into. Failure to observe any of these rules renders the agreement 'improperly executed' and so unenforceable without a court order.[20] Additionally the loan agreement must be in a prescribed form[21] and the Act lays down provisions for copies of the unexecuted agreement to be given to the borrower and a prescribed procedure for the execution of the agreement.[22] The provisions of the Act are not simple and reference should be made to the standard works on consumer credit law for details.[23]

In the context of possession proceedings, the CCA affords a borrower the protection of enforcement of the loan and mortgage by the lender only through a particular procedure in which the court has specific powers to give relief. The lender under a regulated agreement must serve a default notice before being entitled 'to recover possession of any . . . land' or 'to enforce any security'. The default notice must be in a prescribed form and specify the nature of the breach of the agreement being alleged.[24] If the borrower complies with the notice, the breach is treated as never having occurred.[25]

Receipt of a default notice by the borrower entitles her or him to apply to the court for a 'time order' by means of which the court can reschedule payment of money owed under the agreement. The time order provisions are dealt with below. Following a default notice, application[26] is by way of originating application on county court Practice Form N440. A court fee (currently £30) is payable, although the Lord Chancellor's Department may be amenable to waiving the fee on the ground of financial hardship. A simple covering letter asking for the fee to be waived setting out the applicant's financial circumstances should be sufficient. Alternatively the borrower can seek a time order in any possession action which the lender brings, following the expiry of the default notice. In most cases it will be advisable to seek a time order at the earliest possible date[27].

20   Consumer Credit Act 1974 s65.
21   Ibid s60; Consumer Credit (Agreements) Regulations 1983 SI No 1553.
22   Consumer Credit Act 1974 ss58, 61, 62, and 63.
23   See Guest and Lloyd *Encyclopædia of Consumer Credit Law* (Sweet & Maxwell), Goode and Yelland *Consumer Credit Legislation* (Butterworths), and Bennion *'Consumer Credit Control'* (Longman Professional).
24   Consumer Credit Act 1974 ss87 and 88 and Consumer Credit (Enforcement, Default and Termination Notices) Regulations 1983 SI No 1561.
25   Consumer Credit Act 1974 s89.
26   County Court Rules Ord 49 r4(5).
27   See generally D McConnell 'Time Orders on loans secured against property' January (1990) *Legal Action* 19, S Johnson and M Banks 'Time Orders' (1986) *Adviser*, No 1 p11; R Leszczyszyn 'Time Orders Revisited' (1990) *Adviser*, No 20 p22; E James 'Time orders and the Consumer Credit Act' March (1991) *SCOLAG* p40.

Assuming that the borrower does not pay off the arrears or remedy other default within the period specified in the default notice then the lender will be at liberty to issue a possession summons against the borrower. A mortgage securing a regulated agreement is specifically enforceable only on an order of the court.[28] The time order provisions,[29] together with the supplementary powers of CCA 1974 ss135 and 136, give the court powers to assist the borrower greatly in excess of those in the Administration of Justice Acts.

Consumer Credit Act 1974 s129(1) provides:

> If it appears to the court just to do so—
> . . .
>   (b)   on an application made by a debtor . . . under this paragraph after service on him of—
>   (i)   a default notice, or . . .
>   (c)   in an action brought by a creditor . . . to enforce a regulated agreement or security, or recover possession of any . . . land to which a regulated agreement relates,
> the court may make an order under this section (a 'time order').

It is clear from the wording of the section that, in the case of proceedings brought by the lender to recover possession, the court has the discretion to make a time order even if the borrower has not sought one or even if the borrower is not present in court. The only requirement is that it should appear to the court 'just to do so'. No specific form is prescribed in the Green Book for use in possession proceedings but it is advisable to amend Practice Form N440 so as to constitute a counterclaim for a time order. See precedent at p358.

In making an assessment whether it is 'just' to grant a time order, the court should have regard not only to the borrower's position but also to the creditor's interests. Where there has been a long history of default with only sporadic payments from the borrower, it would not be just to grant a time order where the only payments which the borrower can realistically afford are insufficient to cover the accruing interest.[30] In such circumstances it is therefore all the more important to ask the court to vary the interest rate under the agreement so that the revised payments are within the borrower's means (see below).

Section 129(2) provides:

> A time order shall provide for one or both of the following, as the court considers just—

---

28   Consumer Credit Act 1974 s126.
29   Ibid ss129 and 130.
30   *First National Bank plc v Syed & Syed* [1991] 2 All ER 250.

(a)   the payment by the debtor . . . of any sum owed under a regulated agreement or a security by such instalments, payable at such times, as the court, having regard to the means of the debtor . . . and any surety, considers reasonable;

(b)   the remedying by the debtor . . . of any breach of a regulated agreement (other than non-payment of money) within such period as the court may specify.

The court is required by the section to order payment of any money owed by instalments or the remedying of other default if it wishes to make a time order. However, expressly, having determined to exercise its discretion to grant a time order, the court must have regard only to the means of the debtor (and any surety) when considering the size and rate of instalments. It is not legitimate to look to possible hardship caused to the lender or its investors. Equally, there is no requirement that the arrears or any other monies owed be paid off within a 'reasonable period' or even by the end of the original contractual loan period. The court is given absolute discretion.

The court's power under s129(2)(a) enables it to order instalment payment of 'any sum owed'. Only in the cases of hire-purchase and conditional sale agreements may the courts deal with sums which fall due for payment in the future.[31] In mortgage cases, this would seem to rule out the rescheduling of anything other than the total of instalments missed by the date of the hearing. However, many legal charges provide that as soon as default occurs then the whole loan becomes immediately payable. Alternatively, in cases where the whole loan does not automatically become due on default, lenders may have 'called in' the loan before issuing proceedings. In other words, demand by letter for immediate payment of the outstanding loan may have been made in pursuance of rights given to the lender in the legal charge. This calling in letter is distinct from the statutory default notice. In practice, default notices refer only to missed instalments. In either case the entire outstanding loan (including missed instalments) will be a 'sum owed' and hence capable of being the subject of a time order. Advisers should consider all documents carefully, asking if necessary for lenders to provide copies of calling in letters as well as default notices.

It is interesting to note that in the only reported case to reach the Court of Appeal in which time orders have been discussed, it was stated, *obiter*:

> Moreover the remedy of a time order under the section would seem to be directed at rescheduling the whole of the indebtedness under the regulated agreement, the principal which has become presently payable as a result of default as well as the arrears and current interest.[32]

Some lenders have drawn up loan agreements and mortgage deeds in such a way that the outstanding principal does not become automatically due on default. In such cases the lenders have taken possession proceedings with a view to selling with vacant possession, where only the missed monthly instalments have become payable and the outstanding capital has deliberately not been 'called in'. In such circumstances it may be possible to persuade the court that there has been an implied demand for payment of all monies secured by the mortgage, implicit in the lender's conduct in seeking possession with a view to sale with vacant possession.[33]

The court's powers under this part of the CCA have yet to be considered in detail by the superior courts. However, on appeal to a judge in the county court it has been held that the power under s129, taken together with the power to vary the terms of an agreement under s136 (see appendix B), is sufficient to enable the court to reduce both the monthly payments and the rate of interest payable under a consumer credit agreement.[34] In appropriate cases the time order provisions may allow the courts to rewrite agreements so as, for example, to freeze interest, or alternatively to create maturity loans. The full extent of the court's powers under these time order provisions are still to be clarified by higher court authority.

It is important to recognise that the time order provisions are distinct from the 'extortionate credit bargain' provisions contained in CCA 1974 ss137 to 140.[35]

Allied to the time order provisions, is the related but distinct power to impose conditions or to suspend operation of an order. Section 135 provides:

---

33   *The 'Halcyon Skies' (No 2)* [1977] 1 Lloyd's Rep 222.
34   *Cedar Holdings Ltd v Jenkins* (1987) 10 August (unreported), Sheffield County Court. Noted at October 1987 *Legal Action* 19. Leave to appeal to Court of Appeal was granted but appeal was discontinued by Cedar Holdings. Cf *Ashbroom Facilities Ltd v Bodley* (1988) 10 November, unreported, Birmingham County Court, noted in 1991 Green Book p1131. See also *National Guardian Mortgage Corporation v Wilkes* (1991) 22 July (unreported) Luton County Court noted at October 1991 *Legal Action*, where it was accepted that s136 enabled the court to vary the interest rate. See also *Cedar Holdings Ltd v Thompson*, Croydon County Court, DJ Brown 20.9.91 noted at Spring 1992 *Quarterly Account* 8, where s136 was similarly used, and *Cedar Holdings Ltd v Bowley* Croydon County Court, DJ Brown 8.4.92 (unreported).
35   For commentary on the extortionate credit bargain provisions of the 1974 Act, see L Bently and G Howells 'Judicial Treatment of Extortionate Credit Bargains' [1989] *Conv* 164, and a Consultation Letter from the Director General of Fair Trading dated 7 February 1991.

If it considers it just to do so, the court may in an order made by it in relation to a regulated agreement include provisions—
  (a)   making the operation of any term of the order conditional on the doing of specified acts by any party to the proceedings;
  (b)   suspending the operation of any term of the order either—
      (i)   until such time as the court subsequently directs, or
      (ii)   until the occurrence of a specified act or omission.

This subsection empowers the court to suspend any order for possession it may make, whether conditionally on payment of specified instalments by the borrower or until a particular event (eg, default in an instalment order, or the date the property is sold or the borrower rehoused by a local authority). Where a court feels it appropriate to make a time order, any order for possession granted could be suspended so long as payment of the instalments under the time order is made.

It is specifically stated that any person, 'affected by a time order'[36] or 'affected by a provision'[37] included in an order under s135, may apply to the court for a variation or revocation in the case of a time order or a variation in the case of a s135 order. These are particularly useful provisions as they allow a lender to make application to the court for a variation of the terms of a time order where, for example, a time order has been granted on favourable terms to allow the borrower to overcome temporary difficulties. In this way it can be argued that the lender would not be prejudiced by the granting of a time order on terms generous to the borrower, as the lender would be able to come back to court to have those terms varied.

To date, the provisions of the CCA to give assistance to borrowers in default have not received sufficient prominence – particularly the time order provisions. It is important to emphasise to district judges hearing possession actions relating to regulated agreements that they have powers which are distinct and much wider than under the Administration of Justice Acts with which they are more familiar. In particular, the absence of any requirement to clear off arrears within the 'reasonable period' should be stressed. It is important to reflect on the fact that loans taken out for the initial purchase of a property (which is the case with the majority of first mortgages) have been seen by Parliament to warrant different treatment from loans taken out for consumer purposes which happen to be secured on a borrower's home.

36   Consumer Credit Act 1974 s130(6).
37   Ibid s135(4).

CHAPTER 34

Preventing the Lender from Obtaining Possession

Raising the necessary money

In practice, mortgage possession actions can normally be defended only by raising enough money to satisfy the lender or, failing that, persuading the court that it is right to exercise one of the statutory powers just described. In common with most debt cases this will involve minimising the borrower's expenditure and maximising the borrower's income.

Where the borrower is working, the question of income maximisation is largely one of ensuring that s/he is in receipt of any possible relevant additions to wages – income support, or family credit, housing benefit, maintenance payments, child benefit etc. A check on the borrower's tax coding should also be made. If the borrower is unemployed it is important to ensure that social security receipts are correct and complete. Any potential tax rebates should be claimed and any unfair dismissal or redundancy claims considered. It is also worth checking whether the borrower is protected by any mortgage protection plan by which an insurance company has agreed to make part or all of the mortgage repayments for a limited period of time following the borrower becoming sick or unemployed. Detailed consideration of these options is really outside the scope of this chapter and readers are encouraged to look at the booklet *Rights Guide for Home Owners*.[1] However, a brief synopsis of options relating to cutting mortgage costs may be useful here.

Reducing mortgage costs and assistance from local authorities

Although in law most lenders have quite wide-ranging powers to lend money as they wish, it is often the case that lenders may say that any proposed options for rescheduling the loan are not possible or practical. It

---

1 *Rights Guide for Home Owners* (CPAG/SHAC 9th edn October 1992). Available from SHAC, 189a Old Brompton Road, London SW5. See also P Harris 'Mortgage Arrears' (1992) *Adviser* No 10.

will be necessary to persevere and show that by reducing the mortgage costs it will be possible to meet future commitments. It is encouraging to note that more recently many local authorities are becoming responsive to the needs of owner-occupiers in difficulty.[2] The Council of Mortgage Lenders has also issued a practice statement on 'Handling of Mortgage Arrears' which sets out what the lenders can do to help.[3]

Reduction of repayments

Lenders (especially 'responsible lenders' such as local authorities and building societies) should be prepared to accept interest-only payments and defer capital repayments of annuity mortgages at least in the short term. This should prevent further arrears accruing providing payments are made, although the lender may require that the unpaid capital elements be paid off when normal repayments are resumed. If refused, it is worth contacting the chair of the relevant local authority committee or, in the case of building societies, the chief executive at the society's head office or possibly lodging a complaint with the building societies ombudsman.[4]

The Benefit Agency (BA) is required in most cases to pay interest on loans for the purchase or repair or improvement (as defined) of the home, where the borrower is in receipt of income support.[5] There is no BA obligation to pay the capital element in the monthly loan repayment or the monthly premium on the insurance policy in endowment mortgages, or to assist in maintaining the private pension contribution in cases of pension mortgages. Where neither claimant nor her or his partner is over sixty years old, the BA is obliged to pay only fifty per cent of the mortgage interest during the first 16 weeks of payment of income support. There are complicated provisions relating to entitlement to income support on interest on accrued arrears of interest, 'rolled up' and added to the capital, and to interest on loans other than for purchase, repair or improvement of the home where the loan was taken out by a separated partner and

---

2   See *Mortgage arrears: owner-occupiers at risk* (Association of Metropolitan Authorities 1986).

3   Council of Mortgage Lenders, 3 Savile Row, London W1X 1AR, Tel: 071–437 0655.

4   *The Finer Committee on One Parent Families* (Cmnd 5629, HMSO, 1974) at 6.117 stated 'we can see no reason why building societies or local authorities when they are mortgagees should not accept interest only, for many years if necessary, without hardship to their borrowers or investors', and see DoE Circ 78/77 Appendix A para 30 onwards. The Building Societies Ombudsman can be contacted at Grosvenor Gardens House, 35/37 Grosvenor Gardens, London SW1X 7AW. 071–931 0044.

5   Income Support (General) Regulations 1987 SI No 1967 regs 17(e) and 18(f) and Sch 3 paras 7 and 8.

payment is necessary to allow the claimant to continue to live in the home.[6] From May 1992, payments of income support in relation to a claimant's mortgage interest can be made direct to qualifying lenders when the full mortgage allowance is being paid.[7] It is important to note that the spouse of a sole legal owner has the statutory right to make the repayments to the lender.[8] This does not extend to cohabitees. Any spouse making payments in such circumstances may be able to claim that s/he has acquired an interest in the property by virtue of these payments. Borrowers should obtain proof from the BA that the interest payments will be paid and make this available to the lender.

Where the borrower took out a mortgage protection policy to pay the mortgage instalments in the event of unemployment or sickness, it is important to lodge the necessary claim form with insurers as soon as possible. Many of these policies set down a very short time scale within which a claim should be made. Do not, however, be put off lodging the claim after the time specified, as the insurers can extend the time at their discretion. Mortgage protection policies are commonly taken out with second mortgages or 'secured loans'.

Extension of term

In any annuity mortgage case it may be possible to extend the term of the loan so as to reduce the capital element and thus the amount of the monthly repayment. This is inapplicable if the lender is prepared to accept interest only. Extending the term of the loan involves entering into a new mortgage arrangement and it may be possible as part of that arrangement to have the existing arrears 'capitalised'. This involves the lender wiping out the arrears and increasing the outstanding capital by an equivalent amount. In this way the borrower can be given a fresh start.

Changing type of mortgage

In the case of an endowment mortgage, it is worth considering whether there would be a reduction in monthly payments by switching to an annuity mortgage. The amount of interest paid each month would remain the same but the monthly repayments of the capital over the remainder of the term or over an extended term may be less than the payments of the life insurance premium. The amount of capital originally borrowed from the

6 Ibid.
7 Social Security (Mortgage Interest Payments) Act 1992 and Social Security (Claims and Payments) Amendment Regulations 1992 SI 1026.
8 Matrimonial Homes Act 1983 s1(5).

lender would be reduced by the surrender value of the life insurance policy. However, a mortgage protection policy would have to be taken out to cover the possibility of the borrower's death before the end of the loan term. If the life insurance policy has been going for some years, more will be raised by selling the policy to an endowment policy investor. The borrower should contact a reputable insurance broker for details of how the policy could be sold on. It can be difficult to sell policies which have been in existence for only a few years.

Remortgaging

Where there are two or more mortgages (which is likely to mean fringe mortgage companies which charge high rates of interest), or even where there is one high interest rate loan, it is worth trying to persuade one of the 'social lenders' – local authority or building society – to 'remortgage' the lender.[9] This involves redemption of the existing loan(s) and replacement with a new mortgage agreement. It will be easier to persuade a building society to remortgage the defaulting borrower if at the time of the new mortgage the local authority agrees to enter into a form of mortgage guarantee to indemnify the building society in the event of the society suffering a loss because of the default.[10] It is worth arguing that the building society has in the future nothing to lose, as the money will be recovered either following repossession and sale or, if there is any shortfall, by the local authority meeting the shortfall under the terms of the guarantee. Local authorities should also be reminded of their housing obligations under the Housing Act 1985 Pt III where a possible permanent housing duty would be relevant in the event of dispossession. Extreme caution should be exercised when considering whether to remortgage with institutions other than building societies or other social lenders, as the terms offered may well be disadvantageous in the long term. The costs of remortgaging will also be considerable, as this will involve not only surveyors' and solicitors' costs but also the commission charged by the mortgage broker who arranges the remortgage. Where a borrower is 'threatened with homelessness' – ie, it is 'likely that he will be homeless within 28 days'[11] – it is useful to remind the housing authority of its duty[12] to 'take reasonable steps to secure that accommodation does not cease to be available for [the borrower's] occupation'. It is arguable that this duty may extend to requiring the authority to use one or more of its

9   Building Societies Act 1986 s10 and HA 1985 ss435(1), (3) and 439(3).
10   See HA 1985 s442 and DoE Circ 5/81.
11   HA 1985 s58(4).
12   Ibid s66(2).

powers outlined above to prevent dispossession. This duty, however, arises only where the authority is satisfied that the borrower is in priority need and not intentionally threatened with homelessness. See chapter 39 on Homelessness below.

Mortgage rescue schemes, sale and lease back

Lastly, it is worth considering, if all else fails, trying to persuade the local authority or, more likely, a housing association to purchase the property by agreement and to allow the borrower to remain in occupation as a tenant. A variant of this arises where the housing association buys a share of the property and the borrower remains in possession as joint owner. The local housing authority should be aware of any mortgage rescue schemes operating in its area.[13]

In practice it is quite common for a defaulting borrower who has purchased his or her previously council-owned property to request the local authority to buy the property back. Normally a local authority requires the Secretary of State's consent to 'municipalise' a property. However, there is a number of exceptions to this where local authorities are at liberty, without the Secretary of State's permission, to purchase a property from a private owner – these include purchase from defaulting local authority borrowers, people who are unable to remain as owner-occupiers because they are elderly, disabled or chronically sick and, arguably, owners who, following purchase by the local authority, will remain in occupation under a shared ownership scheme.[14]

13   On mortgage rescue schemes generally, see the CML's 'Mortgage Arrears and Possessions – Trends, Issues and Policy Initiatives' (23 December 1991); S Foster *Mortgage Rescue – What does it add up to?* (Shelter 1992); 'Mortgage Rescue – What Role for Housing Associations?' *Housing Associations Weekly* 10 January 1992; T Dwelly 'Abandoned' (1992) *Roof*, March/April p26.
14   DoE Circ 9/85, Annex A and B and also Housing Revenue Account Subsidy Determination 1990 Sch 3.

CHAPTER 35

Procedure and Tactics

Venue for proceedings

Proceedings for possession of a dwelling-house must be brought in the county court, unless the property is in Greater London in which case proceedings may be brought in the High Court.[1] In 1990, 2, 818 mortgage actions were commenced in the High Court in London.[2] Where, however, the loan is one regulated by the Consumer Credit Act 1974, proceedings must be brought in the county court. Proceedings must be issued in the county court district where the house is situated. In practice it is much more common for proceedings to be brought in the county court, and the procedure and tactics discussed in this chapter apply to proceedings in that court unless otherwise indicated.

Summons

Proceedings are brought by fixed date summons which will be endorsed with the hearing date as with other possession cases. The proceedings are for recovery of the property and are not an action to enforce the mortgage.[3] The time at which lenders issue proceedings will vary but can be when as little as two months' arrears have accrued. In practice, proceedings are brought to enforce payment with the deterrent that failure will result in possession being lost. The proceedings are the same whether the plaintiff is a first or subsequent mortgagee.

Depending on the terms of the mortgage deed, before issuing the summons the lender may send a 'calling in' letter. This specifies the amount required to be paid by the borrower to redeem the loan. The

---

1 County Courts Act 1984 s21 as amended by the High Court and County Court Jurisdiction Order 1991 SI No 724.
2 *Hansard* Vol 186 No 64 391–392 Written Answer 25 February 1991.
3 *R v Judge Dutton Briant ex parte Abbey National Building Society* [1957] 2 All ER 625.

mortgage deed may require the lender to make such a formal demand for the outstanding loan before it becomes payable in whole. Alternatively, the mortgage deed may provide that the whole outstanding loan becomes due immediately on default in which case the calling in letter is not necessary.

The particulars of claim attached to the summons are required[4] to specify certain details relating to the loan including, amongst others, the amount of the loan, the amount of any interest or instalment in arrears and the amount remaining due under the mortgage. In the normal way, the defendant(s) has 14 days within which to file any defence. Generally the only defence available will be to seek the benefit of the court's powers under the Administration of Justice Acts or Consumer Credit Act (see chapter 33 above). Although it is important to file a formal defence if any unusual point is to be argued, the courts will allow a defendant to seek such relief without any formal pleadings being served.[5] Usually all that will be applicable is a short defence claiming the protection of the Administration of Justice Acts or the Consumer Credit Act.

Parties to proceedings

It is, it seems, necessary to join as defendants in addition to the borrower(s) only those persons in occupation who are known to claim a right to remain.[6] Where a spouse is not a legal owner (the property being in the sole name of the borrower) s/he does not have the absolute right to be joined as defendant. Where such a spouse has registered a class F land charge, or a notice or caution pursuant to the Matrimonial Homes Act 1967 s2(7) or the Matrimonial Homes Act 1983 s2(8), s/he has the right to be notified of the action being brought by the lender against his or her spouse, and will be sent a copy of the particulars of claim. S/he does not have to be joined as defendant by the lender from the outset.[7] Whether or not any such charge, notice or caution has been registered, a spouse who is not a defendant may apply to be joined as a defendant 'at any time before the action is finally disposed of in that court' and shall be made a defendant with a view to meeting the borrower's liabilities provided that the court 'does not see any special reason against it' and the court is satisfied that s/he may be able to persuade the court to exercise any of its powers under the Administration of Justice Act 1970 or Consumer Credit

4   CCR Ord 6 r5.
5   See *Redditch Benefit Building Society v Roberts* [1940] 1 All ER 342, CA; CCR Ord 9 r9(2).
6   *Brighton and Shoreham Building Society v Hollingdale* [1965] 1 All ER 540.
7   Matrimonial Homes Act 1983 s8.

Act 1974.[8] It is important to appreciate that the spouse of a borrower defendant has no absolute right to be joined as defendant.

Obviously it is quite possible that a deserted spouse may not hear about the proceedings until the bailiffs come to execute a warrant for possession, but it would be possible for him or her to apply at that stage for relief. Occupiers (such as tenants) who wish to be joined as defendants to argue any point should apply ex parte by letter to the court and attend the hearing.[9] Alternatively, they could simply attend the hearing and ask to be joined as defendants then. An occupying tenant (who may well have no right to remain as against the lender) may need to apply to be joined as defendant so as to obtain a possession order for the purpose of application to the local housing authority for assistance under the homelessness provisions of the Housing Act 1985 Pt III. Advisers should consider the practice of the local housing authority before making any application because a tenant renders him or herself at risk as to costs. It is likely, however, that a lender would not usually take steps to recover costs against the tenant but would rely on recovery of costs against the security of the property (see below).

Evidence

As the matter will be heard in chambers unless the court directs to the contrary,[10] evidence may be given by affidavit without specific court order.[11] However, it is possible on the application of any party to obtain an order requiring the deponent to attend court for cross-examination. Usually, institutional lenders will make use of this facility as it is easier and more cost effective to give evidence by affidavit rather than incur the expense of attendance at court of management personnel. Pro forma affidavits are generally produced, which do little more than confirm the contents of the particulars of claim. The mortgage deed is usually exhibited to the affidavit as is any calling in letter. Where relevant, an up-to-date search certificate of HM Land Registry or Land Charges Department will also be exhibited to ascertain if any notice, caution or class F land charge has been registered to protect a spouse's rights of occupation under matrimonial legislation.

The borrower may wish to require attendance of the deponent to the affidavit where, for example, the lender is claiming arrears of payments

---

8   Ibid s8(2).
9   CCR Ord 15 r3.
10   Ibid Ord 49 r1.
11   Ibid Ord 20 r5.

which include separate interest charges on missed monthly payments so as to have this clarified for the court. Advisers can then argue that only bona fide missed payments should be taken into account in considering whether to suspend an order or not. Borrowers should consider the attendance of deponents only if there is some good reason, in view of the formidable position which lenders have in connection with costs and expenses (see below). The affidavit will usually be sent recorded delivery to the borrower before the hearing. However, the County Court Rules do not indicate any specific time limit by which the affidavit has to be served. Where insufficient time has been given, it would be open to the court to refuse to allow such evidence 'if in the interest of justice the court thinks fit'.[12]

Hearing and orders for possession

As stated above, the hearing of the action is normally in chambers and before the district judge.[13] Given the numbers of possession summonses being listed for hearing, in practice the court may well only expect to be able to spend as little as three minutes on each case. If any substantive argument is raised, then it is likely that the case will be adjourned to another date. In such cases the borrower should offer to make some payment towards the mortgage in the interim. As with many hearings in chambers, practice and procedure vary. Normally the lender's solicitor will outline the history of the case and advise on any change in circumstances since the date of the affidavit. If foreclosure has been claimed in the pleadings it is likely that the claim will be withdrawn provided that it is clear that some order for possession is to be granted. The original legal charge and a search for the purpose of identifying any rights registered under the Matrimonial Homes Act should be produced for examination by the district judge. Failure to produce either of these can be grounds for an adjournment. The borrower will then be asked to comment on the lender's case and to justify the court's exercise of any statutory power to postpone the lender taking possession. It is obviously essential that the borrower attends the hearing so as to give evidence to support the claim for statutory relief. Evidence which can be of use includes a letter of confirmation from the BA concerning payment of mortgage interest, evidence of future regular employment from a new employer, or a loan from friends or relatives, proof of remortgage

---

12   Ibid Ord 20 r9.
13   Originally Administration of Justice Act 1970 s38(3) (repealed by County Courts Act 1984 s148(3)).

facilities and an estate agent's valuation of the property. Where relief by way of a time order is being sought, realistic statements of income and expenditure should be available.

If when arranging the mortgage the borrower was required to pay for a mortgage indemnity policy, taken out by the lender to protect it in the event of a shortfall on sale following the borrower's eviction, this should be made clear to the district judge if there is any doubt about extent of the security. Since such a policy will indemnify the lender (either entirely or to a pre-set figure), it will not normally be prejudiced by giving any benefit of the doubt to the borrower. It is, however, important that the borrower is aware that the insurance company with whom the policy was taken out is in law entitled to seek to recover any payment made by it from the borrower. This is not, however, common in practice.[14]

As stated above, local practice varies but the court, when considering possible orders for suspended possession, may well be using a rule of thumb that arrears should be cleared within 12 to 24 months. District judges are generally now more willing to adopt a longer period than in the past. Advisers should seek to extend this period so that the amount of money required to be paid monthly towards the arrears is minimised. In cases falling within the Consumer Credit Act 1974, it is important to ensure that the district judge is aware that, when considering an application for a possession order, there is no statutory restriction requiring the arrears to be paid off within a 'reasonable period'. In addition, it is important also to ask her or him to consider making a time order (see p289) as well as suspending any order for possession granted in favour of the lender.

Any order giving statutory relief is likely to be in the following terms: 'an order for possession in 28 days, suspended so long as current instalments are maintained and £X is paid monthly off the arrears which have accumulated to the date of the hearing.' (See county court prescribed Form N31.) Effectively, the number of months it will take to clear off the arrears at £X per month is the 'reasonable period' referred to in the Administration of Justice Act 1970 s36(1) (see chapter 33 above).

Example: Ms X is required under the terms of her mortgage to pay £200 per month. She falls into arrears and at the date of the hearing she owes £1,000. If the court accepts 12 months as the 'reasonable period' then Ms X will need to satisfy the court that she can raise £283.33 per month towards the mortgage (that is current monthly instalments of £200 plus £1,000 divided by 12

14   See P Madge 'A False Security' (1991) *Adviser* May 1991 p28.

towards the arrears). If she cannot pay this amount over the next 12 months then the lender will be granted an absolute order for possession.

Usually the court will, unless the security is insufficient or threatened, be anxious not to grant an absolute order in favour of the lender. Where the court does not feel able to exercise its discretion either after hearing evidence from the borrower or where the borrower does not attend the hearing, then an order for possession in 28, or possibly 56, days will be given in favour of the lender.

Where the borrower's financial position is uncertain – for example, where s/he has recently applied for a job or where a fresh claim has been made for income support and the amount of help to come from the BA by way of income support is not clear – it is possible to ask for an adjournment for a short period to allow the issues to be clarified. Borrowers should if at all possible offer to make some payments in the interim.

If the borrower is not able to persuade the district judge to grant a suspended order for possession because the borrower is not able to meet the current payments and clear off the arrears over a reasonable period, some district judges have adopted a practice of granting an absolute order for possession effective some time in the future. This might be, for instance, an order for possession in six months' time. The rationale for this would seem to be that this will give a borrower who is not able to meet the statutory criteria for relief a period of time in order to improve his/her situation. If this proves to be the case, the borrower can apply to the court at that stage for a variation of the order for possession such that it is then suspended on terms. It can forcefully be argued that if a lender feels that at some stage during this period it is being prejudiced, it is always open to the lender as a party to the proceedings to make application for a variation of the order to reduce the period before which the order becomes effective.

Where it is clear that some form of statutory relief is to be given to the borrower, advisers should argue, where the Administration of Justice Acts apply, for adjournment on specified monthly payments by the borrower as opposed to a suspended order for possession. The advantage is that in default a further hearing would be required if adjournment was originally ordered; whereas a lender would be able to apply immediately for a warrant for possession without further hearing if the terms of a suspended order were breached.

By contrast, in the High Court, execution of an order for possession because of a breach of a suspensory term cannot take place without the defendant being given an opportunity to be heard.[15]

The court should not attach to a suspended order for possession a requirement that the warrant for possession should not be executed without leave of the court,[16] although in practice it is not unknown for such a requirement to be added.

The existence of a counterclaim for damages against a lender does not prevent the latter from exercising its common-law right to possession. Even where a meritorious counterclaim exists, eg, for negligence or breach of warranty arising out of a survey report on the condition of the mortgaged property, this does not allow the court to exercise its Administration of Justice Act discretion, as damages received by virtue of the counterclaim would not necessarily extinguish arrears by the end of a 'reasonable period'.[17] The position may be different, however, where the claim against the lender is by way of a set-off[18] or where the counterclaim is for rescission of the mortgage.[19] It is submitted that the situation of mortgages governed by the Consumer Credit Act 1974 may be different, in that the court's power to assist the borrower is not qualified by having to be satisfied that the arrears and accruing payments will be paid up to date by the end of a 'reasonable period'.

Where the borrower clears off all the arrears after the issue of the proceedings but before the hearing, the proper order is to adjourn the proceedings generally so that the action can be reinstated if further arrears accrue, rather than require the lender to issue fresh proceedings the cost of which will be borne by the borrower.[20]

Where a borrower is not able to satisfy the court that it should grant him or her any statutory relief, then the lender will be entitled to possession of the property. This may put the borrower in practical difficulty if some weeks are required to obtain alternative accommodation (either privately or from the local housing authority) where the lender is not willing to defer by consent the obtaining of physical possession. It is felt that the county court has sufficient inherent

---

15 *Fleet Mortgage and Investment Co v Lower Maisonette 46 Eaton Place Ltd* [1972] 2 All ER 737 and *Practice Direction* [1972] 1 All ER 576.

16 *Royal Trust Co of Canada v Markham* [1975] 3 All ER 433, CA.

17 See *Citibank Trust v Ayivor* [1987] 1 WLR 1157; *Barclays Bank plc v Tennet* (1984) 6 June CAT 242, noted at [1985] CLY 5, and A Pugh-Thomas 'Mortgagees and Counterclaims' (1988) LS Gaz 27 April p28.

18 See *Ashley Guarantee plc v Zacaria* (1991) *Independent* 7 October.

19 See *Barclays Bank plc v Waterson* (1988) Manchester County Court, noted at (1989) 10 CL 259.

20 *Greyhound Guaranty v Caulfield* (1981) 9 April Leeds County Court, noted at [1981] CLY 1808 and 1992 *County Court Practice* (Green Book) p25.

jurisdiction to postpone execution of the warrant for possession for a reasonable period.[21] However, it is clear that this power must be used judicially and the limits of this jurisdiction are unclear.

Appeals

Where a party is dissatisfied with a proposed order, that party has the right to require the summons to be adjourned to the circuit judge.[22] Where the objection is to the proposed exercise of discretion the adjournment should be to the circuit judge in chambers, but on a point of law to the circuit judge in open court. Appeal against a decision of the district judge to the circuit judge should be made on notice and served within 14 days.[23] However, it is important to recognise that as an order for possession granted by a district judge is a final order, the circuit judge's powers on appeal are limited and are akin to those of the Court of Appeal on an appeal from a county court judge. If the appeal relates to the exercise of discretion – eg, as to the terms of a suspended possession order – then the circuit judge can interfere only if s/he thinks that no reasonable district judge could have exercised her or his discretion in that way.[24] It is, for this reason, preferable to adjourn the summons to the circuit judge *before* a possession order is granted rather than rely on the circuit judge's limited powers on appeal. It would be necessary to apply for a stay of execution pending determination of the appeal,[25] although where the hearing by the circuit judge is likely to be heard reasonably quickly the bailiff's office may well unilaterally decide to take no action until that hearing is disposed of.

Warrants for possession

Pre-execution

Where an absolute order for possession has been granted at the hearing and any period of postponement has expired or where the terms of any suspended order have been broken, the lender is free to apply ex parte for the issue and execution of a warrant for possession. No further hearing is required. It is often only when the occupiers receive notification of the

21 See *Kelly v White, Penn Gaskell v Roberts* [1920] WN 220.
22 *London Permanent Benefit Building Society v De Baer* [1968] 1 All ER 372 and *Practice Direction* [1965] 3 All ER 306.
23 CCR Ord 37 r6.
24 See notes to CCR Ord 37 r6 in *County Court Practice 1992*.
25 CCR Ord 37 r8.

issue of the warrant that advice is sought. At this stage advisers should consider applying to set aside judgment, if there are grounds for doing so, before execution of the warrant, for example where the borrower did not attend the hearing because of non-receipt of the summons or illness. Application should be made on notice with a supporting affidavit, confirming the grounds set out in the notice of application (see precedent at p347). Where occupiers are not parties to the proceedings they may wish to make an application to be joined as defendants[26] as well as applying to have the order for possession set aside. Where a tenant occupies part of the property s/he may only be able to have judgment set aside in respect of the part s/he occupies.

A borrower in breach of a suspended order for posession can apply to have the order itself further suspended, or alternatively to have the warrant for possession suspended on terms. The Administration of Justice Act 1970 s36 may be used to stay or suspend execution of an order for possession 'at any time before execution of such . . . order'.[27] Similar scope is given to the court in respect of regulated agreements within the meaning of the Consumer Credit Act 1974.[28] Any application for such a further stay or suspension should usually be made on notice on Form N244 to the lender. It is advisable to make such an application (see precedent at p345) pending negotiations if there is any doubt as to whether a lender will agree to a stay.

Independently of the Administration of Justice Acts 1970 and 1973 and the Consumer Credit Act 1974, the court also has power in the CCR to extend the period of time for giving up possession and to reduce the rate of payments under any order.[29]

Post-execution

Once the bailiff has executed the warrant and the borrower is displaced, the court's statutory powers are exhausted. However, the court's inherent power to set aside judgment and to suspend the warrant for possession may still be of assistance.[30] Where the borrower can raise the money to redeem the mortgage prior to exchange of contracts on the lender's sale the court may restrain the lender from selling although separate proceedings

26 Ibid Ord 15 r3.
27 See also *R v Bloomsbury and Marylebone County Court ex parte Villerwest Ltd* [1976] 1 All ER 897, CA; *R v Ilkeston County Court ex p Kruza* (1985) 17 HLR 539 and *Hawtin v Heathcote* (1976) CLY 371.
28 Consumer Credit Act 1974 s135.
29 CCR Ord 22 r10 and Ord 13 r4.
30 CCR Ord 37. See also *Governors of Peabody Donation Fund v Hay* (1987) 19 HLR 145 and *LB Tower Hamlets v McCarron*, noted at September 1988 *Legal Action* 13.

would need to be brought. Where, however, an occupier is evicted by the bailiff and claims to have an independent right to remain as against the lender, for example as an occupier with a tenancy binding on the lender or as an occupier with a superior equitable interest (for which see pp313 and 322 below), s/he may apply to have judgment set aside or stayed so far as s/he is concerned and be allowed to defend the proceedings.[31]

Mortgagee in possession and sale

In the context of residential mortgages, the lender will be seeking possession of the borrower's home with a view to evicting the borrower and selling with vacant possession. As a disincentive to the taking of possession, the common law imposes some fairly ill-defined obligations on the lender after possession has been taken. In practice, particularly in a depressed property market, disputes between the lender and the borrower tend to arise over first the timing of the sale and, secondly, the sale price.

As mortgagee in possession, the common law imposes an obligation on the lender to 'take reasonable precautions to obtain the true market value of the mortgaged property at the date on which he decides to sell'.[32] Building society lenders are also under a statutory duty to 'take reasonable care to ensure that the price at which the land is sold is the best price that can reasonably be obtained'.[33] There appears in effect to be no difference between the two duties. However, it is clear that while there is an obligation to obtain the best price at the date of sale, the timing of that sale is left to the judgment of the lender. In *Bank of Cyprus Ltd v Gill* Lloyd J said 'the law as I understand it, is that a mortgagee in possession is entitled to sell at any time. He is not obliged to wait on a rising market or for a market to recover'.[34] In *Tse Kwong Lam v Wong Chit Sen* Lord Templeman put it this way: 'The mortgagee is not, however, bound to postpone the sale in the hope of obtaining a better price . . .'[35] However, in *Standard Chartered Bank Ltd v Walker* Lord Denning commented, *obiter*, 'There are several dicta to the effect that the mortgagee can choose his own time for sale, but I do not think that this means that he can sell at the worst possible time. It is at least arguable that, in choosing the time, he must exercise a reasonable degree of care'.[36]

This obligation on the lender in possession appears to protect the

31   *Minet v Johnson* (1890) 63 LT 507 and *Hawtin v Heathcote* n27.
32   *Cuckmere Brick Co Ltd v Mutual Finance Ltd* [1971] Ch 949 at p968H.
33   Building Societies Act 1986 Sch 4 para 1(1)(a).
34   [1979] 2 Lloyd's Rep 508 at p511.
35   [1983] 1 WLR 1349 at p1355.
36   [1982] 1 WLR 1410 at p1415.

borrower against an unreasonable sale in the sense of the sale not resulting in the bona fide proper price. In *Predeth v Castle Phillips Finance Co Ltd* Ralph Gibson said that 'the law allowed [the lender] to sell at the time which suited its convenience, provided, of course, the property was fairly and properly exposed to the market or sold at a price which was based upon such exposure'.[37] This duty is owed both to the borrower and also any guarantor[38] although it does not extend to persons claiming as beneficiaries under constructive, resulting or other trusts.[39] The borrower may bring an action for breach of duty against the lender, but a separate action in negligence may lie may lie also against the lender's selling agents.[40] Provisions in a legal charge purporting to exclude the lender's duty to take reasonable care do not exempt the lender if loss arises from the lender's failure to take such reasonable care.[41]

However, in a depressed market a borrower is more likely to be concerned about a delay in the sale being concluded and the fact that interest continues to accrue until the final redemption of the mortgage folllowing sale. The common-law 'duty to account' imposed on a mortgagee in possession may be of some assistance to borrowers in these circumstances. The extent of this liability has not been considered recently by the courts, and many of the old cases do not readily lend themselves to giving guidance to the position where modern institutional lenders take possession for the sole purpose of disposing of the premises with vacant possession. The liability to account operates in the borrower's favour by allowing the borrower on redeeming the mortgage to set off against monies due to the lender under the mortgage any rent or other profits received during the period of the lender's possession of the mortgaged property. If necessary the court can order the taking of accounts in redemption proceedings. This liability is a strict one, as it requires the lender to account not only for rents actually received from the date the mortgagee took possession, but also for rent which could have been received.

A mortgagee who goes into possession of the mortgaged property, and thereby excludes the mortgagor from control of it, is bound to account to the mortgagor, not only for the rents and profits which he actually receives, but

---

37   (1986) 279 EG 1355. See generally L Bentley 'Mortgagee's duties on sale – No place for tort?' [1990] Conv 431, J Marriott 'Sell and be sued? – the mortgagee's duty on sale' (1987) LS Gaz 30 September 2756 and H Wilkinson 'The mortgagee's duty to mortgagors and guarantors' (1982) NLJ 883.
38   n36.
39   *Parker-Tweedale v Dunbar Bank plc* (1990) *Independent* 9 January, CA.
40   See *Garland v Ralph Pay & Ransom* (1984) 271 EG 106.
41   See *Bishop v Bonham* [1988] 1 WLR 742, CA.

also for the rents and profits which, but for his wilful default or neglect, he might have received; that is, for everything which he has received, or might or ought to have received, while he continued in possession.[42]

A lender who refuses to rent out the property will also be liable to account for rent that could have been received. In the seventeenth-century case of *Anon*[43] it was held that the lender's liability to account on the basis of wilful default included the refusal to rent to a tenant who was capable of paying the going rent for the property. The short note of the case states:

> A Mortgagee shall not account according to the value of the land, viz. He shall not be bound by any proof that the land was worth so much, unless you can likewise prove that he did actually make so much of it or might have done so, had it not been for his wilful default: as if he turned out a sufficient tenant, that held it at so much rent, or refused to accept a sufficient tenant that would have given so much for it.

In *Brandon v Brandon*[44] it was held that the onus of proof is on the person alleging wilful default in not letting the property, and that the onus shifts to the lender where that person shows that the property can be let or has been let, and it is then up to the lender to show that s/he has been vigilant in attempts to rent the property.

While the two leading text books on the law of mortgages consider that this duty to account for notional rent does not arise where possession has been taken with a view to sale within a reasonable period,[45] the authority upon which the proposition is based does not in fact support that conclusion.[46]

The courts have been more restrictive in terms of imposing obligations on a mortgagee in possession in relation to repair of the property. It appears that there is some general obligation not to be negligent in relation to protection of the repossessed property, with the lender being under a duty to take reasonable steps to protect the property against vandalism.[47]

On completion of the sale the borrower will be entitled to be paid the balance of the purchase monies after the mortgage(s) has been redeemed. For that reason the borrower should notify the lender of his or her

---

42   *Halsbury's Laws* Vol 32 para 698.
43   (1682) 1 Vern 45.
44   (1862) 10 WR 287.
45   Fisher & Lightwood *Law of Mortgages* 10th edn 1988 Butterworths p368 and Cousins *Law of Mortgages* 1989 Sweet & Maxwell p215.
46   *Norwich General Trust v Grierson* (unreported) Stocker J, noted at [1984] CLY 2306.
47   See generally Fisher and Lightwood *op cit, Grierson* at n46 and H Markson 'Liability of lenders in possession' (1979) 129 NLJ 334.

whereabouts so that any balance can be forwarded to him or her where there are surplus proceeds of sale. However, where the sale proceeds are insufficient to pay off the mortgage in full, there is nothing at law to prevent the lender suing the borrower for the shortfall on the personal covenant in the mortgage deed.[48] Building societies, when selling as mortgagees, are obliged within 28 days of the completion of the sale to send to the borrower at his/her last known address by recorded delivery a notice containing certain prescribed particulars of the sale. This includes the date of completion, the sale price and the name of the purchaser. An offence is committed where, without reasonable excuse, this duty is not complied with.[49]

It is worth noting tht there is no need to obtain from the court an order authorising sale of the property after possession is obtained. The lender's right to sell the property will have arisen either under the terms of the mortgage deed or under the Law of Property Act 1925.

Costs

Advisers should, throughout, be conscious of the advantageous position which lenders are in concerning legal and other costs. In other types of litigation the normal rule is that costs follow the event – in mortgage cases prima facie the lender is entitled to all its 'costs, charges and expenses' reasonably and properly incurred in preserving the security or recovering the mortgage debt, including the costs of possession proceedings.[50] Costs of possession proceedings themselves will be allowed as being part of these 'just allowances',[51] even without mention in the court order. However, where the court orders taxation of the lender's costs in a possession action it will be on a standard basis and then it seems the lender is restricted, in the absence of terms to the contrary in the deed, to those standard basis costs.[52] Usually however the lender's position is so strengthened in the mortgage deed. The court has no authority to assess the lender's costs unless requested to do so by the lender.[53]

---

48   *Gordon Grant & Co Ltd v Boos* [1926] AC 781, PC.
49   Building Societies Act 1986 Sch 4 para 1 and Building Societies (Supplementary Provisions as to Mortgages) Rules 1986 SI No 2216.
50   *Drydon v Frost* (1838) My & C 670; *National Provincial Bank of England v Games* (1886) 31 Ch D 582, CA and *Sandon v Hooper* (1843) 6 Beav 246.
51   *Wilkes v Saunion* (1877) 7 Ch D 188.
52   *Re Adelphi Hotel (Brighton)* [1953] 2 All ER 498 and *Re Queen's Hotel Co Cardiff Ltd* [1900] 1 Ch 792.
53   *Principality Building Society v Llewellyn* (1987) 1 May (unreported), Pontypridd County Court, noted at [1987] CLY 2940.

In practice, lenders normally seek a specific order that there be 'no order as to costs' (or 'costs to security') or simply make no reference as to the costs at the hearing, relying on a mortgagee's apparent right to add costs to the security. It apears that a mortgagee is entitled to charge in addition to any standard basis costs, the sum required to make them up to the solicitor and own client costs which it will be charged by its solicitor if there is a right to do so in the mortgage deed.[54]

However, it is arguable that a lender is entitled to recover only what its own solicitor could properly charge following a taxation under the Solicitors Act 1974. Under that Act[55] the amount which may be allowed in the county court on taxation must not exceed the amount which would have been allowed in respect of that item on a standard basis. However, where the rights of the lender as to costs are extended by the terms of the mortgage deed, then that agreement is unaffected by the 1974 Act and taxation of the lender's costs will be on the basis specified in the mortgage deed.[56] In practice it is known for lenders to claim indemnification of all costs and expenses (including all solicitors' and estate agents' costs) when the mortgage is redeemed on sale.

While it is clear from the above that the lender is in a strong position as regards costs, the borrower can ask the court to restrict the lender's claim for costs in a number of ways. The lender's prima facie entitlement to the costs of the possession proceedings does not exclude the court's inherent jurisdiction to regulate the payment of litigation costs. Even where the mortgage deed provides for the lender's costs to be paid on an indemnity basis, the court has the discretion to override that contractual provision and to disentitle the lender from receiving those costs. Walton J put it this way: 'The court might very well take the view that, in the circumstances of any particular case, [the contractual right to costs on an indemnity basis] was a contractual provision which it ought to overlook and it ought not to give effect to.'[57] Where the lender has acted unreasonably in relation to the bringing of proceedings or in relation to some aspect of the proceedings, it is advisable to ask at the hearing for the court expressly to direct as part of the order that the lender 'be not at liberty to add any costs

---

54   *Gomba Holdings (UK) Ltd v Minories Finance Ltd (No 2)* [1992] 4 All ER 588, CA.
55   Solicitors Act 1974 s74(3).
56   *Tarrant v Speechly Bircham* (1986) 19 May (unreported), Slough County Court, noted at [1986] CLY 3193. See also 'Costs' (1992) EG 4 April for a short commentary on *Primeridge Ltd v Jean Muir Ltd* (unreported 1991) on the importance of the correct wording in mortgage deeds if the lender is to ensure that costs will be paid on an indemnity basis.
57   *Bank of Baroda v Panessar* [1987] 2 WLR 208 at 224D. See also *Gomba Holdings (UK) Ltd v Minories Finance Ltd (No 2) Supra.*

to the security' in relation to the proceedings or the particular hearing in question.

Additionally, the borrower, as the paying party to the proceedings, is entitled to ask the court to tax the lender's solicitors costs under Solicitors Act 1974 s70. The borrower has the absolute right to ask the court to tax the bill if objection is made within one month of delivery of the bill.[58] Outside this period the court may grant an order for taxation on such terms as it thinks fit.[59] However, no order for taxation will be granted after the expiry of 12 months from the bill's delivery in the absence of 'special circumstances',[60] and no order can be made at all more than 12 months after payment.[61] This would seem to be the case even if the borrower has not been told of the amount of the costs claimed by the lender's solicitors. Unfortunately, borrowers are very often not told of the fact that the bill has been delivered, or of the amount claimed and debited to the borrower's account.

Unfortunately, under this Act the party asking for the taxation of the costs will have to pay for the costs of the taxation proceedings unless s/he is able to persuade the court to reduce the amount of the costs to be paid by one-fifth of the sum claimed.[62] However, it is possible to identify a part only of the bill for scrutiny by the court and so restrict the risk of the consequences of the 'one-fifth rule'. It is advisable to ask the lender to provide details of its solicitors' bill of costs as soon as it is received, itemising the number of letters written and received, phone calls made and received, the time spent, the nature of the fee earned involved in the case and the hourly rate claimed and the work undertaken. Details of the amount of the disbursements involved should also be identified. From this it may be possible to assess whether a Solicitors Act taxation is advisable.

Subject to the mortgage deed a borrower is not personally liable for such costs[63] and does not have to pay them directly. They will be added to the security as part of the mortgage and paid out of the proceeds of the sale.[64] Lenders are entitled to add costs to the security even against a legally aided borrower and this will not be contrary to the Legal Aid Act 1988 s17 which restricts awards of costs against legally aided parties,[65] as technically the costs are recovered from the security and not the borrower.

---

58   Solicitors Act 1974 s70(1).
59   Ibid s70(2).
60   Ibid s70(3).
61   Ibid s70(4).
62   Ibid s70(9).
63   *Sinfield v Sweet* [1967] 3 All ER 479.
64   *National Provincial Bank of England v Games* n50.
65   *Saunders v Anglia Building Society (No 2)* [1971] 1 All ER 243, HL.

CHAPTER 36

Tenants of Borrowers

At common law a borrower had no power to grant a tenancy which was binding on the lender. Since 1925 borrowers have been given statutory power to grant certain types of lease.[1] However, this was subject to exclusion by the terms of the mortgage deed and in practice the power to grant tenancies is invariably excluded – either absolutely or without specific written approval.

Again, in practice, providing a borrower remains in control of the property and does not get into arrears the lender may not be interested in any third party occupation. It is clear that, irrespective of whether the tenancy is binding on the lender, as between the borrower/landlord and tenant, the tenancy will be binding on him or her if only by estoppel.[2] However, when a lender seeks to take possession, the position of tenants is normally dependent on whether the tenancy was granted before or after the mortgage deed was executed.[3]

Tenancies prior to date of mortgage

Registered land

In common with any purchaser of a legal interest a mortgagee takes the property subject to any interests which qualify as 'overriding interests' within the meaning of the Land Registration Act 1925 s70. Certain tenancies qualify as overriding interests.

A lease granted for a term not exceeding 3 years where the tenant is in

---

1 Law of Property Act (LPA) 1925 s99.
2 *Dudley and District Benefit Building Society v Emerson* [1949] 2 All ER 252, CA and *Chatsworth Properties v Effiom* [1971] 1 All ER 604, CA.
3 For an inventive article on the possibility of civil and criminal action against lenders for harassment of residential tenants, see D Barnsley 'Harassment of Tenants by Mortgagees' (1991) JSWL 220; see also S Robinson 'Helping Tenants of Defaulting Landlords' (1991) *Adviser* 23.

possession is effective to create a legal interest.[4] Such a tenancy need not be registered at HM Land Registry to bind the lender and will qualify as an overriding interest as being the rights of persons actually in occupation unless enquiries have been made and these rights are not disclosed.[5]

In addition, a lease for a term not exceeding 21 years also qualifies as an overriding interest[6] and, providing it is in writing, will be valid and binding on the lender whether or not the tenant is in occupation. In the case of registered land the mortgage is completed and becomes effective on the date it is executed.[7]

Unregistered land

The tenancy of a person who went into occupation prior to the mortgage will be binding on the lender if validly created, that is if the tenancy either was created formally by deed or was one capable of being created verbally, ie for a term not exceeding three years taking effect in possession at the best rent which can be reasonably obtained without taking a fine.[8] This will include weekly and monthly tenancies.

Pre-mortgage binding tenancies

Although it is conceivable that a borrower may have been able to allow tenants into a property in anticipation of the completion of the initial purchase, in practice, cases where a tenant has an interest binding on a lender are more likely to arise with second or subsequent mortgages. The effect of a binding tenancy will be that the lender cannot take possession as against the tenant unless, for example, the tenancy was granted following a notice under HA 88 ground 2. So long as the borrower is allowed to retain the property as against the lender s/he will be entitled to claim the rent and to sue for possession against the tenant.[9] If the lender claims possession in accordance with its common law right then the tenant is bound to pay the rent to the lender.[10] This includes any rent due but unpaid to the borrower at the time of the lender's demand.[11] Where

4   LPA 1925 s54(2).
5   Land Registration Act 1925 s70(1)(g); *Barclays Bank Ltd v Stasek* [1957] Ch 28 and *Bolton Building Society v Cobb* [1966] 1 WLR 1.
6   Land Registration Act 1925 s70(1)(k).
7   *Abbey National Building Society v Cann* [1990] 1 All ER 1085, HL.
8   LPA 1925 s54(2) and *Universal Permanent Building Society v Cooke* [1952] Ch 95, CA.
9   LPA 1925 ss99 and 141 and *Trent v Hunt* (1853) 9 Exch 14.
10   *Rogers v Humphreys* (1835) 4 Ad & E1 299.
11   *Moss v Gallimore* (1779) 1 Doug KB 279.

the lender takes possession and gives notice to the tenant, the tenant cannot set off against the rent a personal claim s/he has against the borrower.[12] A borrower executing a second mortgage deed after the granting of a tenancy to correct the terms of an earlier deed entered into before the granting of the tenancy does not replace the earlier deed so as to result in the tenancy being binding on the lender.[13]

Tenancies after date of mortgage

As indicated above, most mortgage deeds exclude the borrower's statutory power to grant leases, either absolutely or without the lender's specific permission. In such cases it has been held that a tenancy granted in breach of such a term in the mortgage deed is not binding as a protected tenancy within the RA on the lender although it remains binding as such on the borrower.[14] The principle will apply equally to tenancies under HA 88. The statutory tenant's 'status of irremovability' granted to a protected tenant on the ending of the contractual tenancy does not bind the lender if the original contractual tenancy was granted in breach of a term in the mortgage deed.[15] As a result, the occupying tenant will have no claim to remain once the lender exercises its right to possession. Until and unless something takes place to change the relationship, the tenant will as against the lender be a trespasser. The lender would not be entitled to demand payment of any arrears of rent due from the tenant to the borrower at the date the lender takes possession from the borrower.[16] Where a tenant is required by the lender to pay rent to it, the tenant can raise this as a defence to any claim by the borrower for the payment of rent.[17]

The occupier tenancy will, however, become binding on the lender if the lender does something expressly or by implication to recognise the tenant as its tenant.[18] As the original tenancy between the borrower and the tenant is a nullity so far as the lender is concerned, any tenancy created between the tenant and the lender must take effect as a new tenancy and will, other things being equal, be HA protected. An example of this was where a lender's solicitor wrote to the borrower's tenant informing him

---

12 *Reeves v Pope* [1914] 2 KB 284.
13 *Walthamstow Building Society v Davies* (1990) 22 HLR 60, CA.
14 *Dudley & District Benefit Building Society v Emerson* n2.
15 *Britannia Building Society v Earl* [1990] 2 All ER 469, CA; for a commentary see S Bridge 'The Residential Tenant and the Mortgaged Reversion' [1990] Conv 450.
16 *Kitchen's Trustee v Madders* [1949] 2 All ER 1079 CA.
17 *Underhay v Read* (1888) 20 QBD 209 CA.
18 See *Stroud Building Society v Delamont* [1960] 1 All ER 749.

that he should not pay any more rent to his 'former landlords' and making new arrangements for payment of rent.[19] The test is not one of intention but of objectivity – what would a reasonable person understand the relationship to be? In this case the court held that, by writing to the borrower's tenant in such terms, the lender was estopped from denying that it had accepted him as its tenant.

Mere knowledge of an unlawful tenancy coupled with a failure to take steps to evict the tenant does not have the effect of creating a tenancy.[20] Acceptance of rent by the lender from the borrower's tenant will create a yearly tenancy between the two parties, although the terms of the tenancy will not necessarily be the same as the tenancy from the borrower but will be such as are agreed or inferred from conduct.[21] However, a lender's requirement that payment of rent should in future be made to a receiver appointed under a legal charge as a formal agent for the borrower (as is normally the case with receivers) does not create a landlord/tenant relationship.[22]

It has been argued that the lender may act in such a way that, although falling short of creating a tenancy at common law, an equitable estoppel is raised precluding it from treating the tenant as a trespasser, relying on the normal equitable principles relating to estoppel.[23] It is thought that for this to happen, a lender who knew of the tenancy would have to act or refrain from acting at a time when the tenant was prejudicing him or herself (over and above paying rent) in reliance on that action or inaction. The essence of this would be that the lender was giving the tenant a false sense of security which resulted in the tenant acting reasonably in the circumstances but to his or her detriment. No direct authority is, however, known on the point.

The definition of 'mortgagor' in the Administration of Justice Acts as including 'any person deriving title under the original mortgagor'[24] does not include the borrower's tenant so as to enable that tenant to seek the protection of the Acts as if s/he were the borrower.[25] Where, however, a tenant does pay the rent to the lender to avoid eviction, s/he may deduct the amount actually paid to the lender from any future rental payments to the borrower.[26]

---

19   *Chatsworth Properties v Effiom* n2.
20   *Taylor v Ellis* [1960] Ch 368 and *Parker v Braithwaite* [1952] 2 All ER 837.
21   *Keith v R Gancia & Co Ltd* (1904) 1 Ch 774, CA.
22   *Lever Finance Ltd v Needleman* [1956] Ch 375 and LPA 1925 s109(2).
23   See A Walker 'Tenants of Mortgagors' (1978) 128 NLJ 773.
24   Administration of Justice Act 1970 s39(1).
25   See *Earl* at n15.
26   *Johnson v Jones* (1839) 9 Ad & E1 809; *Underhay v Read* (1887) 20 QBD 209, CA.

Under the Consumer Credit Act 1974 it would be open to a tenant who is joined as a defendant to seek to persuade the court to exercise its discretion to make a time order and to suspend any order for possession. The court is empowered[27] to make a time order and to suspend a possession order of its own volition where it is 'just to do so' in actions brought for possession of land to which a regulated agreement relates. It is clear that a time order must be directed at the borrower requiring payment by the borrower. However, in the face of potential proceedings by the tenant for breach of covenant for quiet enjoyment, the borrower may be persuaded to meet the payments required under the time order.

A tenant whose tenancy is invalid as against the lender is still a person interested in the equity of redemption and has the right to take a transfer of the mortgage on paying off the loan.[28] Similarly, as a person entitled to redeem the mortgage, the tenant can ask the court to order sale of the property with a view to buying it.[29]

Where occupiers are occupying the property under a tenancy which is not binding on the lender it has been held to be inappropriate for the lender to use the summary procedure under RSC Ord 113 or CCR Ord 24 to obtain an order for possession. The correct procedure is by way of fixed date action.[30]

A tenant evicted by a lender in these circumstances may be able to sue the landlord/borrower for breach of the limited covenant for quiet enjoyment. A similar right to claim damages for breach of an express covenant for quiet enjoyment may arise where there is a written lease.[31] However, there may well be practical difficulties in enforcing a monetary judgment against the borrower/landlord.

Tenants threatened with eviction in these circumstances should consider applying to be joined as defendants to the possession proceedings with a view to claiming damages against the landlord/borrower within those proceedings under CCR Ord 12 r5. Where an expedited hearing resulting in judgment can be arranged, or where it is possible to obtain judgment in default, it would be possible to register a charging order against the title. Assuming that there was sufficient equity the judgment would be satisfied on the lender selling the property.

---

27   Consumer Credit Act 1974 ss129(1) and (2) and 135.
28   *Tarn v Turner* (1888) 39 Ch D 456, CA.
29   LPA 1925 s91(2).
30   *London Goldhawk Building Society v Eminer* (1977) 242 EG 462.
31   *Carpenter v Parker* (1857) 3 CBNS 206.

Assured tenancies post-HA 1988

The HA 1988 introduced a new mandatory ground for possession against an assured tenant.[32] There was no corresponding ground under the RA 1977. The ground provides that the court must give an order for possession where (a) the mortgage was granted before the beginning of the tenancy, (b) the lender is entitled to exercise a power of sale conferred by the deed or under Law of Property Act 1925 s107, (c) the lender requires possession of the dwelling-house for the purpose of disposing of it with vacant possession *and* either (i) notice was given by the landlord not later than the beginning of the tenancy that possession might be required under this ground or (ii) the court considers it is just and equitable to dispense with the requirement of notice.

Assured tenancies created after the mortgage and in breach of a prohibition on the granting of tenancies will not be binding on the lender but will, however, be binding on the borrower as set out above. This ground for possession simply specifically empowers a lender to permit a borrower to create a tenancy without running the risk of the tenant's claiming security of tenure by virtue of the lender's permitting the tenancy to arise.

32   HA 1988 Sch 2 ground 2 see p187.

CHAPTER 37

Domestic Relationship Breakdown

It is common experience that the two most immediate causes of mortgage default are reduction of income following loss of employment and relationship breakdown. Where partners separate, it may be inevitable that the home will have to be sold as neither can afford to maintain the property on his or her sole income. However, where it is possible for one partner to maintain the property there are two additional problems for the remaining partner to consider over and above the continuing problem of paying for any existing mortgage. The first is preventing sale of the property and the second is preventing the property being used as security for further loan finance with the corresponding increased risk of eviction by a lender to obtain possession.

Sole ownership

Where the property is in the sole legal ownership of the departed partner the latter is free to sell or raise further mortgage finance. As a result, where the couple is married, it is important for the remaining spouse as soon as possible to register his or her statutory right to occupy the matrimonial home under the Matrimonial Homes Act 1983. In the case of registered land this should be done by way of a notice registered at HM Land Registry, or a class F land charge if the title is unregistered. If in doubt an Index Map search should be made to check if the property is registered or not. This is done by sending District Land Registry Form 96 to the Land Registry for the area in which the property is situated. Form 96 is contained in Explanatory Leaflet No 15 'The open register – a guide to information held by the Land Registry and how to obtain it', which is available free from the various land registries.

The effect of this will be, in practice, that the legal owner will not be able to sell or mortgage the property until the notice or charge is vacated. It is important to note that taking this step will have no effect on any prior mortgage and any arrears which may accrue under that loan. However, where such matrimonial occupation rights have been registered, prior to issue of proceedings a lender is required to give notice to the remaining spouse of any possession proceedings brought,[1] to name that person in the particulars of claim and to file at court a copy for service on that person. Such a spouse may then apply to be joined as defendant with a view to persuading the court to exercise its statutory powers.[2] The non-owning spouse has the right to make the mortgage repayments in respect of the matrimonial home and should do so if s/he can, in order to avoid loss of possession.[3] Where a spouse does not get to hear of the possession proceedings until after they have been instituted s/he has the right to seek to be joined as a party 'at any time before the action is finally disposed of in that court'[4] and will be made a party if the court does not see 'a special reason' against him or her being joined *and* if the court is satisfied that s/he may be able to meet the legal owner's mortgage liabilities either with or without the court exercising its Administration of Justice Act or Consumer Credit Act powers.

Where the remaining partner is not married to the legal owner the position is different. None of the provisions of the Matrimonial Homes Act 1983 will apply and s/he will normally have no right to contest the possession proceedings or to pay the mortgage instalments on behalf of the legal owner. Where, however, s/he has an equitable interest in the property which has priority over the interest of the lender, this will protect him or her against dispossession (see chapter 38 below).

Joint ownership

Where the property is in joint legal ownership, the departed partner obviously cannot sell or obtain further mortgage finance without the remaining partner's agreement as s/he would have to execute the necessary deed. It would, however, be open to the partner to seek a court order requiring sale of the property.[5] In the case of married couples the court has the normal wide-ranging power to transfer property as part of its matrimonial jurisdiction on divorce or judicial separation. As joint owners both partners will remain equally liable under the mortgage deed and will normally be joined as defendants in any proceedings brought by a lender.

1   Matrimonial Homes Act 1983 s8(3); CCR Ord 6 r5(1A) and County Court Practice Form N438.
2   Matrimonial Homes Act 1983 s8(2).
3   Ibid s1.
4   Ibid s8(2).
5   Law of Property Act 1925 s30.

Difficulties can arise where one joint legal owner forges the signature of the other on a deed creating a legal charge. In the case of unregistered land the beneficial interest of the owner who has created the forgery will pass to the lender, leaving the legal estate being held on trust for sale by the joint legal owners for the innocent legal owner and the lender. The lender would be able to seek a court order for sale under Law of Property Act 1925 s30. With registered land, the legal charge will be effective if registration at HM Land Registry is completed. The innocent joint legal owner's beneficial interest may, however, qualify as an overriding interest if s/he is in actual occupation.[6]

6   See generally P Thompson *Co-ownership* (Sweet & Maxwell 1988) pp98 and 134.

CHAPTER 38

Rights of Equitable Owners

This chapter considers cases where the legal title to a property is vested in the name of one or more people (the legal owners) but where another person has an interest in the property which is recognised in equity but falls short of being a legal interest. The most common example of this is where the matrimonial home is in the sole legal ownership of one spouse but where the other has an equitable interest. Such an occupier, who is not the legal owner, may defeat a possession claim by relying on equitable interests.

A legal charge is treated as a legal interest in land. Hence a lender who advances money secured by a legal charge is treated as a purchaser of a legal interest in the property which is being used as the security. In the case of unregistered land it is a basic principle of English land law that a bona fide purchaser for value of a legal estate (which will include a mortgagee) will take that estate subject to any equitable interests in the property of which the lender has notice, whether actual or constructive.[1] In the case of registered land, a purchaser takes the property subject to entries on the land register and any overriding interests, which can include the rights of persons in actual occupation except where enquiry is made of them and those rights are not disclosed.[2] The application of these general principles in the context of residential mortgages is considered in more detail below. In certain circumstances, therefore, occupiers who are not legal owners but who have some form of equitable interest in the property can effectively prevent the lender from obtaining possession. In this way the defaulting legal owner can seek to retain occupation under the protection of the equitable owner, without even making any further financial payments. The following is a brief outline only of what is a complicated and still developing area of residential land law.

---

1 Law of Property Act (LPA) 1925 ss199(1) and 205(1).
2 Land Registration Act 1925 s70(1)(g).

Creation of equitable interests

The courts have found it difficult to be consistent when deciding whether an occupying non-legal owner has acquired an equitable interest in a property. Many of the cases seem to depend on whether the judge feels that the justice of the situation demands intervention as against the legal owner and third parties. Sir Nicolas Browne-Wilkinson, who decided many of the leading cases, has even said:

> I do not think that the principles lying behind these decisions . . . have yet been fully explored and on occasion it seems that such rights are found to exist simply on the ground that to hold otherwise would be a hardship to the Plaintiff.[3]

No apology is made for not analysing the case law in detail; for a full explanation, reference must be made to the standard works on land law as well as family law, where many of the decisions have been reached in the context of relationship breakdown.[4] However, by way of example only, the courts have held that a non-legal owner has acquired an equitable interest by:

- paying directly for the purchase of a property which was conveyed into the legal owner's name[5]
- contributing towards the deposit paid on the purchase[6]
- helping with the construction of the house[7]
- regular and substantial direct financial contribution to the mortgage.[8]

Great weight is attached to financial contribution or direct contribution of money's worth.[9] Indirect financial contribution to the purchase of the property can result in the acquisition of an equitable interest, for example by pooling of resources or in some other way relieving the legal owner from

---

3   *In Re Sharpe* [1980] 1 WLR 219 at 223D.
4   See generally K Gray *Elements of Land Law* (Butterworths 1987) and S Cretney and J Masson *Principles of Family Law* (Sweet & Maxwell 5th edn 1990).
5   A resulting trust does not, however, arise from the fact that money was 'lent' to facilitate a purchase – see *Hussey v Palmer* [1972] 1 WLR 1286, CA; *Pettitt v Pettitt* [1969] 2 All ER 385, HL.
6   See *Burns v Burns* [1984] 1 All ER 244, CA at 264.
7   *Cooke v Head* [1972] 1 WLR 518, CA.
8   *Gissing v Gissing* [1971] AC 886, HL.
9   See *Lloyds Bank plc v Rosset* (1990) 22 HLR 349, HL; M P Thompson 'Establishing an Interest in the Home' (1990) *Conv* 314; s Gardner 'A Woman's Work . . .' (1991) 54 MLR 126; D Hayton 'Equitable Rights of Cohabitees' [1990] *Conv* 370 and P Sparkes 'The Quantification of Beneficial Interests: Problems arising from Contributions to Deposits, Mortgage Advances and Mortgage Instalments' (1991) *Oxford Journal of Legal Studies* Vol 11 p39.

expenditure on the property.[10] Alternatively, where the non-legal owner has acted to his or her detriment on the basis of assumed joint ownership, then the court may be prepared to recognise some equitable interest.[11]

Nature of equitable interests

The courts have also not been consistent in defining the nature of the interest accruing to the occupying non-legal owner who successfully argues that s/he has some form of equitable interest. The court may hold that the occupier is a tenant in common under a resulting or constructive trust. If this is the case the legal owner holds the property jointly on his or her behalf and on behalf of the non-legal owner.[12] An alternative basis for granting relief may be to find that the non-legal owner has rights under an irrevocable licence conferring some property interest binding on the legal owner and lender.[13]

Binding equitable interests

Legal ownership in one name

The legal considersations to be applied in deciding whether an equitable owner's interest in a property vested legally in another person binds third parties differ, depending on whether the land is registered or unregistered.

In the case of registered land, a lender taking a legal charge will take it subject to the interest specified in the land register and to any overriding interests:

> All registered land shall, unless under the provisions of this Act the contrary is expressed on the register, be deemed to be subject to such of the following overriding interests as may be for the time being subsisting in reference thereto . . .
>
> (g)   The rights of every person in actual occupation of the land . . . save where enquiry is made of such person and the rights are not disclosed.[14]

---

10   See generally S Cretney op cit n4; *Grant v Edwards* [1986] 2 All ER 426; J Warburton 'Interested or Not?' (1986) *Conv* 291.
11   *Midland Bank Ltd v Dobson* [1986] 1 FLR 171; *Coombes v Smith* [1986] 1 WLR 808; *In Re Basham (decd)* [1986] 1 WLR 1498; M P Thompson 'Estoppel and Clean Hands' (1986) *Conv* 406; J Montgomery 'A Question of Intention' (1987) *Conv* 16.
12   See *Kingsnorth Finance Co v Tizard* [1986] 2 All ER 54 and *Grant v Edwards* n9.
13   *In Re Sharpe* n3; and see *Bristol & West Building Society v Henning* [1985] 2 All ER 606, and noted at (1985) *Conv* 361. See generally references at n4 and n11.
14   Land Registration Act 1925 s70(1).

In *Williams & Glyn's Bank Ltd v Boland*,[15] the House of Lords held that the beneficial interest under a trust of an occupying spouse acquired by way of substantial contribution to the initial purchase price of the house is such an overriding interest capable of binding a lender. Whether someone is in 'actual occupation' is a question of fact. It does not necessarily involve the personal presence of the person claiming to occupy, although there must be some degree of permanence and continuity, which would rule out a fleeting presence. The relevant date for considering whether someone is in occupation is the date of execution of the mortgage not the date of registration at HM Land Registry.[16] Where the mortgage financed the initial purchase of the property and the purchase and the mortgage were simultaneous, the courts have been loath to allow an equitable owner's rights to take precedence over the lender's legal interest where the equitable owner knew, at the time, that the mortgage was being taken out, and have concluded that in these circumstances the equitable owner intended that her or his interest be postponed to that of the lender and so is estopped from claiming priority.[17] This postponement of the equitable owner's interest applies even to a subsequent remortgage taken out by the legal owner without the equitable owner's knowledge but limited to the extent of the original mortgage.[18] Where, however, the mortgage was genuinely granted after the property's acquisition by a borrower in whom the legal estate had already vested, where the beneficial owner was unaware of the creation of the legal charge, then that occupier's equitable interest will bind the lender.[19]

In the case of unregistered land, a mortgagee lending money on land by way of legal charge will take the security subject to any equitable interests in the property of which it has notice, whether actual, constructive or imputed. Actual notice is self-explanatory. Constructive notice is notice which the lender would have obtained 'if such enquiries and inspections had been made as ought reasonably to have been made' by the lender.[20] Imputed notice is the actual or constructive notice of the lender's agent, although only so far as notice was received by the agent in the case of the lender obtaining the mortgage.[21] It is not clear as to when a lender will be

---

15   [1980] 2 All ER 408.
16   See *Abbey National Building Society v Cann* (1990) 22 HLR 360, HL.
17   See *Paddington Building Society v Mendelsohn* (1985) 50 P & CR 244, CA and MP Thompson 'The retreat from 'Boland' ' (1986) *Conv* 57 and *Bristol & West Building Society v Henning* n13. See M Welstead 'The Mistress and The Mortgage' (1985) CLJ 354. See generally K Gray op cit n4.
18   *Equity & Home Loans Ltd v Prestidge* (1991) 24 HLR 76, CA.
19   *Williams & Glyns Bank v Boland* n15
20   LPA 1925 s199(1)(ii)(a).
21   Ibid s199(1)(ii)(b).

fixed with constructive notice or the lengths to which a lender has to go to discharge its duty to make reasonable enquiry. However, it seems that the courts will require not inconsiderable enquiries to be made – in one case it was held that a lender's agent visiting the property at a pre-arranged time was insufficient enquiry to discharge an obligation to find out whether a matrimonial home was occupied by a spouse who might have an equitable interest.[22] As with registered land, the courts have proved unwilling to allow a beneficial owner to bind a lender where s/he knowingly was to benefit from the legal owner's borrowing money by way of mortgage, although the court's reasoning is open to question.[23]

In practice, however, the question of whether an equitable owner's interest or right binds a lender is most likely to arise in cases of mortgages entered into after the initial purchase of the property.

Where a lender has taken a mortgage on a property which is subject to equitable rights in priority to its rights under the mortgage, it would remain open to the lender to sue the legal owner for repayment of the loan by virtue of any covenant to repay contained in the mortgage deed. If made bankrupt, the legal owner's trustee in bankruptcy could seek a court order for sale of the property under Law of Property Act 1925 s30. See p337 below.

Legal ownership in several names

Although there was initially some doubt, following the decision in *Boland*, the House of Lords, in *City of London Building Society v Flegg*,[24] confirmed that a lender who advances money on the security of a property where the legal title is vested in two or more persons as trustees for sale, is free from the concern of whether or not other persons may have equitable interests under such a trust[25] as in *Boland*. By virtue of the 'overreaching' provisions of the Law of Property Act 1925,[26] such a lender will take its interest by virtue of the mortgage free from all beneficial claims. The equitable owner's interests theoretically will attach to the capital money

---

22   *Kingsnorth Finance Co v Tizard* n12 and noted at (1986) 278 EG 981. See also P Luxton 'Clandestine co-owners: an occupational hazard for mortgagees?' (1986) NLJ 771 and M P Thompson 'The purchaser as private detective' (1986) *Conv* 283.

23   See *Bristol & West Building Society v Henning* n13 and MP Thompson 'Relief for first mortgagees?' (1986) 49 MLR 245.

24   (1987) 19 HLR 484, HL; see also W Swadling 'The Conveyancer's Revenge' (1987) *Conv* 451 and S Gardner '"Bleak House" Latest – Law Lords Dispel Fog?' (1988) 51 MLR 365.

25   LPA 1925 ss2 and 27 see also K Gray op cit n4.

26   LPA 1925 s36(1).

realised when the property is sold. Notice of beneficial interests in unregistered land and actual occupation in registered land is irrelevant.

It has been argued that a distinction needs to be drawn between persons who have a beneficial interest behind a trust for sale (where 'overreaching' will apply) and people who have a right to occupy the property under a form of estoppel licence (where overreaching would not apply).[27]

Mortgage consent forms

In an effort to avoid the risk of being landed with a binding equitable owner, some lenders now require adult intending occupiers who are not to be joined as parties to the mortgage deed to execute forms of consent or undertaking prior to completion of the mortgage. This is intended to postpone any equitable rights they may have, to after those of the lender. It is, however, by no means certain that these forms achieve the results that lenders are seeking. Executing such a form may act as an estoppel preventing the equitable owner from seeking to rely on his or her interest but some commentators doubt this.[28]

Undue influence and special relationships

Where a mortgage, guarantee or consent form was obtained through the exercise of undue influence, then the transaction is voidable at the instance of the person who entered into it.[29] To seek to avoid the risk of this being raised as a defence, many lenders advise borrowers and other persons who are involved in the proposed transaction, for example other persons with an interest in the security or guarantors, to seek independent legal advice before entering into the transaction. It is not clear whether there is a legal obligation on lenders to ensure that this advice is obtained.[30] Lenders

27   See M P Thompson 'Dispositions by Trustees for Sale' (1988) *Conv* 108; M P Thompson *Co-ownership* (Sweet & Maxwell 1988) p136 and *In Re Sharpe* n3 and K Gray op cit n4.
28   D Barnsley *Barnsley's Conveyancing Law and Practice* (Butterworths 3rd edn 1988) p62; Farrand *Emmet on Title* (Longman Professional 19th edn 1986) para 5.201.
29   *Lloyds Bank Ltd v Bundy* [1974] 3 All ER 757, CA; *National Westminster Bank plc v Morgan* [1985] 1 All ER 821, HL. See also *Petrou v Woodstead Finance* [1986] FLR 158, CA.
30   *Bank of Baroda v Shah* [1988] 3 All ER 25, CA; *Coldunell Ltd v Gallon* [1986] 1 All ER 429, CA. However, para 12.0 of the Code of Practice 'Good Banking' adopted by many of the major lenders (effective 16 March 1992) imposes an obligation on lenders to advise personal customers to take legal advice. See note in *Credit & Finance Law* Vol 4 No 7 February 1992 p49.

may be held responsible for any undue influence exerted on the borrower or an equitable owner which resulted in that person consenting to the mortgage.[31]

Before a transaction will be set aside for undue influence there must have been 'manifest disadvantage' to the person who was influenced.[32] Undue influence on that person can be either actual or presumed. The relationship of husband and wife does not of itself give rise to a presumption of undue influence, although in the case of married women giving security for their husbands' debts a creditor should take reasonable steps to ensure that the wife understands the nature of the obligation she is entering into.[33] However, a lender who simply leaves it to the borrower to obtain the signature of the third party will be bound by the borrower's conduct if the signature is obtained by undue influence or deceit.[34]

A bank may be liable to its customer in damages if it negligently advises as to the nature and effect of the mortgage to be entered into in its favour by that person, although a negligent misstatement falling short of undue influence will not result in the mortgage being set aside.[35]

31   See generally *Midland Bank plc v Perry* (1988) 56 P&CR 202, CA; *Midland Bank plc v Shephard* [1988] 3 All ER 17, CA, and *Barclays Bank plc v Kennedy* (1989) 58 P&CR 221, CA; M Dixon 'The Limits of Undue Influence Explained' [1989] CLJ 359; E Dunbill 'Mortgage and Other Securities: Fraud and Undue Influence: Husband and Wife' [1990] *Conv* 226, E Macdonald 'Undue Influence and Third Parties' (1990) *Journal of Business Law* 469 and P Chandler 'Tainted by Undue Influence – Role of the Intermediary' (1991) *Journal of Business Law* 333.

32   See Morgan n29 and *Bank of Credit & Commerce v Aboody* [1989] 2 WLR 759, CA.

33   See *Shephard* n31 and *Barclays Bank plc v O'Brien* (1992) *Times* 3 June.

34   *Kennedy* n31 and *Lloyds Bank plc v Egremont* (1990) CCLR 756, CA.

35   *Cornish v Midland Bank plc* [1985] 3 All ER 513, CA; E Jacobs 'Undue Influence, Negligence and the Bank-Customer Relationship' (1986) 83 LS Gaz 1712. See *Barclays Bank plc v Khaira* (1992) 89/17 LS Gaz 50. See also n32.

CHAPTER 39

Homelessness

Where it is clear that there is no way of avoiding the loss of the home either by forced voluntary sale or dispossession through the court it will be necessary to consider the various rehousing options available to the borrower.

It is advisable as soon as it becomes clear that a borrower may not be successful in retaining possession of the property that s/he should register on the waiting lists of any available housing associations, housing co-operatives and with the local housing authority. Many housing associations now have closed waiting lists so this may not prove possible. Similarly many local authorities do not accept active applications to go on the waiting list from owner-occupiers (although this may amount to an unlawful fetter on local authority discretion[1]). It is important, therefore, to consider the local position in each case.

The Housing Act 1985 Part III

Obviously the main form of assistance available to borrowers who have lost or are shortly to lose their property through mortgage default is the Housing Act 1985 Pt III. Reference should be made to the standard works on housing law for the detail of the general law relating to homelessness.[2]

In outline, the 1985 Act Pt III requires that the local housing authority is obliged to 'secure that accommodation becomes available' to a homeless person who is in priority need unless the authority is satisfied, following the making of enquiries, that the person became homeless intentionally.[3] Additionally, where an applicant who is in priority need is likely to become homeless within 28 days, the authority is obliged to take

1 See HA 1985 s22 and *R v Canterbury City Council ex parte Gillespie* (1986) 19 HLR 7.
2 See, for example, C Hunter and S McGrath *Homeless Persons – The Housing Act 1985 Part III* (LAG 4th edn 1992).
3 HA 1985 s65(3).

reasonable steps 'to secure that accommodation does not cease to be available for his occupation',[4] unless it can satisfy itself, following enquiries, that the applicant became threatened with homelessness intentionally. An applicant is in priority need if, amongst other things, s/he or a member of his or her family has dependent children, is pregnant, or 'is vulnerable as a result of old age, mental illness or handicap or physical disability or other special reason'.[5]

Where a local authority is satisfied that an applicant for assistance is homeless and in priority need but is homeless intentionally, then the rehousing duty is limited to securing accommodation for the applicant's use for such period as the authority considers will give him or her 'a reasonable opportunity of securing accommodation for his occupation'.[6]

The authority is also under a preliminary duty to applicants whom it has reason to believe are homeless and in priority need, to provide immediate accommodation pending the outcome of the enquiries[7] and to take reasonable steps to prevent the loss of or damage to the applicant's personal property if s/he is unable to protect or deal with it.[8]

When is a person homeless?

Local authorities will come under a duty only where a person is homeless or threatened with homelessness within the definition set out in HA 1985 s58. In essence, a person is homeless if there is no accommodation which that person is entitled to occupy. Clearly, where a borrower is evicted by a lender following possession proceedings, then the borrower is homeless within the statutory definition. However, the Housing and Planning Act 1986 s14(2) added a new subsection (2A) to s58:

A person shall not be treated as having accommodation unless it is accommodation which it would be reasonable for him to continue to occupy.

This raises the prospect of arguing that a borrower is statutorily homeless in anticipation of possession proceedings. Where, following a careful assessment of the borrower's financial situation and debt counselling, it is evident that dispossession is inevitable, then it is strongly arguable that it is not reasonable for the borrower to continue to occupy the property and that s/he is at that stage, immediately, statutorily homeless. Subject to

4   Ibid s66(2).
5   Ibid s59(1).
6   Ibid s65(3)(a).
7   Ibid s63.
8   Ibid s70.

the questions of priority need and intentionality being resolved in the borrower's favour, a local authority would then find itself obliged to provide permanent alternative accommodation even before the execution of any possession warrant. In this context it is worth reminding local authorities of the following observation by Kennedy J in the case of *R v London Borough of Hillingdon ex parte Tinn*:[9]

> As a matter of commonsense, it seems to me that it cannot be reasonable for a person to continue to occupy accommodation when they can no longer discharge their financial obligation in relation to that accommodation that is to say, . . . make the mortgage repayments, without so straining their resources as to deprive themselves of the ordinary necessities of life, such as food, clothing, heat, transport and so forth.

This point should be raised at the earliest opportunity to try to resolve the question of what rehousing duty, if any, falls on the housing authority prior to the lender taking possession proceedings. In this way legal costs (which will initially be borne by the borrower) can be avoided, as can the trauma of the borrower being evicted and the question of rehousing obligations being resolved only following dispossession. It may also give time to negotiate with, and if necessary to take proceedings against, the housing authority where a decision adverse to the borrower is reached.

Intentional homelessness and mortgage arrears

It is clear that the question of intentionality is central to whether or not a local housing authority will be under any duty to provide long-term accommodation. The Act defines a person as being intentionally homeless:

> . . . if he deliberately does or fails to do anything in consequence of which he ceases to occupy accommodation which is available for his occupation and which it would have been reasonable for him to continue to occupy.[10]

This is, however, qualified so that:

> an act or omission in good faith on the part of a person who was unaware of any relevant fact shall not be treated as deliberate.[11]

A person can be deemed intentionally homeless only if s/he satisfies both limbs of the definition. S/he must have deliberately done or failed to do

---

9   (1988) 20 HLR 305 at 308.
10   HA 1985 s60(1).
11   Ibid s60(3).

something in consequence of which accommodation is lost *and* it must have been reasonable for her or him to have continued to occupy the property. Each limb must be considered separately.[12] If it would not have been reasonable to have continued to occupy the property, then the applicant cannot be taken to be intentionally homeless.

Local authorities should also be reminded of the observation of Kennedy J in *Tinn* quoted above on the question of whether it would have been reasonable to continue to occupy the property where an unforeseen change in circumstances resulted in the borrower not being able to meet the mortgage repayments resulting in possession proceedings.

Further amplification by way of advice is given to authorities in the Third Edition of the Code of Guidance to the Act which states in para 7.4:

> The following points are relevant in determining intentionality.
>
> The act of omission must have been deliberate. An applicant should always be given an opportunity to explain an act or omission. Generally the following should not be considered deliberate:
>
> (a) . . .
>
> (b) where an applicant has lost his/her home or was obliged to sell it because s/he got into rent or mortgage arrears because of real financial difficulties (for example because s/he became unemployed or ill or suffered greatly reduced earnings or family breakdown) and could genuinely not keep up the rent payments or loan repayments even after claiming benefits and for whom no further financial help is available. In the case of mortgagors, authorities should look at the applicant's ability to pay the mortgage commitment when it was taken on, given his/her financial circumstances at the time;
>
> (c) where an owner occupier, who is faced with foreclosure or possession proceedings to which there is no defence, sells before the mortgagee recovers possession through the courts or surrenders the property to the lender.

The Code does not have the same legal force as the Act but local authorities should be referred specifically to this paragraph and required to justify departure from this advice.

It can be particularly difficult to overturn an intentionality decision where at the time the loan was taken out the income of the borrower and his/her family was objectively insufficient to meet the required monthly repayments.[13] In such cases it is essential to consider whether there are any members of the family who were not party to the decision to take out the loan, and for those persons to apply as homeless.

---

12   *R v Eastleigh BC ex parte Beattie (No 1)* (1983) 10 HLR 134.
13   See *R v Barnet LBC ex parte O'Connor* (1990) 22 HLR 486.

Reasons for mortgage default

It is the duty of the housing authority to make enquiries as to the circumstances surrounding the mortgage default and especially the reasons behind it. The borrower should be given an opportunity to explain the arrears or the sale. Advisers must ensure that all the relevant facts are made known to the authority. Where the borrower was not aware of, for instance, financial assistance with mortgage interest available from the BA, this should be indicated to the authority. A decision that the borrower is intentionally homeless, reached in breach of the duty to make enquiries, may be quashed by way of judicial review proceedings.[14]

Where it is feared that the partner with financial control in a relationship may be deemed intentionally homeless, it is advisable for a clearly separate application to be made to the authority under the 1985 Act Pt III by the 'non-responsible' partner. This would then require the authority to enquire as to whether the partner had acquiesced in the deliberate failure to make the mortgage repayments or to sell the property before s/he can be branded as 'intentionally' homeless.[15]

Very real difficulties can arise where the borrower decides to sell the property in advance of the lender taking possession proceedings where the borrower knows or thinks that there is no prospect of defending the lender's claim at court.[16] Many authorities will classify applicants who sell the property in such circumstances as intentionally homeless. The authority should be advised that a borrower has no reasonable prospect of preventing dispossession and reference should be made to para 7.4 of the Code as well as to the second limb of HA 1985 s60(1) on whether it would have been reasonable to continue to occupy the property.[17] It is wise before sale of the property to approach the authority to seek assistance in remortgaging and to discuss the financial position to show that the borrower has not been reckless in deciding to sell. However, there can be difficulties where the local authority considers that the borrower has not yet reached the stage where sale of the property is inevitable.[18] Where the authority has indicated that it requires an order for possession before it will treat the borrower as not intentionally homeless, then the order should be obtained but not endorsed 'by consent'.

14 *R v Wyre BC ex parte Joyce* (1983) 11 HLR 73.
15 *R v North Devon DC ex parte Lewis* [1981] 1 WLR 328.
16 See R Matthews and M Tierney 'Don't rely on the Safety Net' May/June 1985 *Roof* 13.
17 See *R v Eastleigh BC ex parte Beattie (No 1)* n12 and *(No 2)* (1984) 17 HLR 168; *R v Hammersmith and Fulham LBC ex parte Duro-Rama* (1983) 9 HLR 71, 81 LGR 702 and *R v LB Hillingdon ex parte Tinn* n9.
18 See *R v Leeds City Council ex parte Adamiec* (1991) 24 HLR 138.

Where an absolute possession order has been granted to the lender, or where the terms of any suspended order have been breached and it is not proposed to apply for any further stay of the order or warrant, it is advisable for the borrower and the adviser to contact the authority as early as possible, to alert the authority as to the position and to indicate that application(s) under the 1985 Act Pt III are being made. In this way the local authority can make its enquiries at the earliest opportunity. The lender should be approached to be asked to defer any enforcement of the warrant until such time as the authority's decision is known. If the lender is obstructive it may be possible to apply on notice for an order postponing execution of the warrant for possession under the court's inherent jurisdiction[19] pending the local authority's decision.

Protection of property

Advisers should also note that where an authority is or has been under a duty to provide any form of accommodation, whether temporary or permanent, it is also under a duty to protect the applicant's personal property.[20] It may be that the lender on enforcing the warrant for possession will be prepared to allow the borrower to leave furniture etc in the property pending sale of the house. It is worth clarifying this with the lender before the warrant is executed. If not, the housing authority should be reminded of this duty and asked to take the furniture into store. It is important to remind the local authority which is to deal with the homeless application that, where the lender is taking possession by virtue of a court order, this means with vacant possession, ie, possession without any furniture left on the premises.[21] Additionally, the authority should be told that the lender who takes possession is under the common law generally not under any obligation to look after items left on the premises pending their removal.[22] Very often the lender's rights in relation to furniture and other items left in the property are reinforced by terms in the mortgage deed.

The borrower should notify the lender of any change of address so that the balance of the sale money can be forwarded to him or her once the mortgage or mortgages have been redeemed.

19   See *Kelly v White, Penn Gaskell v Roberts* [1920] WN 220.
20   HA 1985 s70.
21   See *Norwich Union Insurance Society v Preston* [1957] 2 All ER 428.
22   See *Jones v Foley* [1891] 1 QB 730.

CHAPTER 40
Possession claims by unsecured creditors

Owner-occupiers of property are in certain circumstances at risk of possession claims by creditors who were, at least initially, unsecured creditors. Advisers should be alert to these possible actions when advising owner-occupiers in relation to their debts. The two ways in which owners can be evicted are by way of an application for sale (a) following a creditor obtaining a charging order, and (b) on application by the owner's trustee in bankruptcy. The two possibilities need to be looked at separately.

Charging orders

Under the Charging Orders Act 1979 a creditor may, after obtaining judgment against a debtor, apply to the court for a charging order and then register a charge in relation to property owned beneficially by a judgment debtor, whether alone or jointly with others.

Following judgment, application is made ex parte to the court for a charging order *nisi*, and once granted a notice or caution can be registered at HM Land Registry in the case of registered land or as a pending land action in the case of unregistered land. The debtor is then served with notice of the hearing of the application for the charging order to be made absolute. The onus is on the debtor to show cause why the order should not be made absolute. The court has discretion whether to grant the charging order and is required to take into account 'all the circumstances of the case and, in particular, . . . (a) the personal circumstances of the debtor, and (b) whether any other creditor of the debtor would be likely to be unduly prejudiced by the making of the order'.[1] The court should not

---

1   Charging Orders Act 1979 s1(5) and *Roberts Petroleum Ltd v Bernard Kenny Ltd* [1983] AC 192. For the exercise of the court's powers in the context of simultaneous divorce proceedings see also *Harman v Glencross* [1986] 1 All ER 545, CA; *Austin-Fell v Austin-Fell and Midland Bank plc* [1990] 2 All ER 455, and J Warburton 'Victory for the Sprinter' [1986] *Conv* 218. See generally M P Thompson *Co-ownership* (Sweet & Maxwell 1988) p98, and P Madge and R Leszczyszyn 'Charging Orders' (1992) *Adviser* p31.

grant the charging order where the size of the debt is small compared to the value of the property,[2] or where a county court judgment has been ordered to be paid by instalments unless and until the debtor has defaulted in payments.[3] In practice, however, it is not difficult for a creditor to obtain the charging order absolute.

Proceedings to enforce a charging order by sale of the legal interest can only be taken under CCR Ord 31 r4 (for the sale of a property the subject of a charging order) when the judgment debtor(s) alone own the beneficial interest in the property charged. However, since a charging order can be granted against the beneficial interest of a judgment debtor owned subject to a trust for sale with others,[4] a judgment creditor with a charging order in relation to that debtor's beneficial interest under such a trust for sale, as a 'person interested', is entitled to apply under LPA 1925 s30 for an order for sale.[5] In determining whether to grant an order for sale in such a case, there is no difference between a chargee under a charging order and a trustee in bankruptcy.[6] The court is expected to balance the interests of the creditor against the interests of the debtor's family, and the principles to be applied in the case of trustees in bankruptcy seeking orders for sale apply in same way.

Under CCR Ord 31 r4 the creditor can apply for an order for sale and for an order for possession by originating application with supporting affidavit, setting out the charging order which it is sought to enforce, the amount still outstanding to the creditor, details of prior mortgagees and the sums outstanding and the estimated sale price. The application is heard by the district judge. Happily, in practice, district judges are often unwilling to grant the creditor's application for sale and possession.

When seeking to contest the application for sale, it is important to emphasise the fact that the creditor is already well protected and to point out the detriment which will result to innocent members of the family if the sale is allowed to proceed. If the debtor is able to offer alternative ways of discharging the judgment debt, these should be put forward.

---

2   *Robinson v Bailey* [1942] 1 All ER 498.
3   *Mercantile Credit Co Ltd v Ellis & Others* (1987) *Times* 2 April, CA.
4   Charging Orders Act 1979 s2.
5   *Midland Bank plc v Pike* [1988] 2 All ER 434. See also N Price 'Charging Orders and Trusts for Sale' [1989] *Conv* 133.
6   *Lloyds Bank plc v Byrne* (1991) 23 HLR 472, CA.

Trustees in bankruptcy

When a person becomes bankrupt his/her property vests in the trustee in bankruptcy as soon as that person is appointed. The property is vested in the trustee without the necessity of any deed of transfer.[7] The trustee's duty is then to realise the bankrupt's assets and to distribute the estate in accordance with the Insolvency Act 1986.

Where the legal and beneficial estate is in the sole name of the bankrupt, then the trustee is at liberty to dispose of that asset without the need to consider the position of others. However, where the legal estate is in the joint names of the bankrupt and a third party, or where the bankrupt and a third party have beneficial interests, then the trustee is a 'person interested' who can apply under LPA 1925 s30 for an order for sale. The bankruptcy of a beneficial joint tenant operates as an act of severance, resulting in the property being held as tenants in common.[8] Where there is a spouse in occupation (but not a cohabitee) who has no legal or beneficial interest, then s/he will have to rely on any rights of occupation under the Matrimonial Homes Act 1983. A cohabitee who has neither a legal nor beneficial interest in the property will not be able to resist an application for an order for possession in advance of sale.

The Insolvency Act 1986 s336 provides that when considering applications for sale and possession of property by the trustee under both Matrimonial Homes Act 1983 s1 and LPA 1925 s30, the court shall make such order as it thinks just and reasonable having regard to:

a) the interests of the bankrupt's creditors,
b) the conduct of the spouse or former spouse, so far as contributing to the bankruptcy,
c) the needs and financial resources of the spouse or former spouse,
d) the needs of any children, and
e) all the circumstances of the case other than the needs of the bankrupt.[9]

The Act provides for a statutory presumption in favour of the creditors after a 12-month period:

---

7   Insolvency Act 1986 s306(1), (2). See generally M P Thompson *Co-ownership* (Sweet & Maxwell 1988) p103, and E Bailey and C Berry 'The Matrimonial Home in Bankruptcy' (1987) 137 NLJ 310 and 'Applications by the Trustee for Possession and Sale' (1987) 137 NLJ 347.
8   *Re Gorman* [1990] 1 All ER 717.
9   Insolvency Act 1986 s336(4).

... after the end of the period of one year beginning with the first vesting of
... the bankrupt's estate in a trustee, the court shall assume, unless the
circumstances are exceptional, that the interests of the bankrupt's creditors
outweigh all other considerations.[10]

While this statutory assumption would seem to favour the creditors
during the 12 months after the bankruptcy, it does not prevent an
application for sale/possession by the trustee during that period.
However, faced with a defended application during the initial period,
many trustees will prefer to wait this statutory period before making the
application.

The 1986 Act therefore allows for the enforcement of the interests of
creditors to be delayed, but not indefinitely. The statutory period of 12
months will in most cases allow a breathing space for the third party to
seek alternative accommodation. However, the Act allows this period to
be disregarded where there are 'exceptional circumstances'. The fact that
innocent third parties will be made homeless is not such as to prevent a
sale being ordered.[11] In *Re Citro*[12] it was held, by majority, that the
interests of the creditors will usually prevail over the interests of a spouse
and children, and that more than the ordinary consequences of debt and
improvidence would be necessary before the court would be able to
postpone sale for a substantial period. However, where relevant, it is
important to emphasise the personal circumstances of the debtor's family,
including, for example, the effect on the children's education, particularly
if they are shortly to take examinations. If this is the case, it may be
possible to have the order for possession suspended until after the
examination date.[13]

It follows that advisers are often left with little scope for man-
oeuvre when advising the bankrupt or occupiers affected by the
bankruptcy. It is, however, worth arguing that it is open to the trustee
to apply under Insolvency Act 1986 s313 for a charging order over
property in favour of the bankrupt's estate. If made, then such a
charging order becomes subject to the Charging Orders Act 1979 s3, and
the court will therefore have the power to impose conditions as to
when the charge becomes enforceable. Additionally, the bankrupt
may be allowed to remain living in the property notwithstanding the
bankruptcy, conditionally on him/her making payments towards

10   Ibid s336(5).
11   *Re Lowrie* [1981] 3 All ER 353.
12   [1990] 3 WLR 880, CA. Cf *Re Holliday* [1981] Ch 405.
13   See generally D Brown 'Insolvency and the Matrimonial Home – The Sins of the
     Fathers: *In re Citro (A Bankrupt)*' (1992) 55 MLR 284.

the mortgage and the other outgoings. The bankrupt does not, however, by virtue of this acquire any interest in the property.[14]

14   Insolvency Act 1986 s338.

Part V

Precedents

Public Sector Tenants

1 Notice of seeking possession

Housing Act 1985, section 83

This Notice is the first step towards requiring you to give up possession of your dwelling. You should read it very carefully.

1. To _____ (name(s) of secure tenant(s))

- *If you need advice about this Notice, and what you should do about it, take it as quickly as possible to a Citizens' Advice Bureau, a Housing Aid Centre, or a Law Centre, or to a Solicitor. You may be able to receive Legal Aid but this will depend on your personal circumstances.*

2. The [name of landlord] intends to apply to the Court for an order requiring you to give up possession of:

_____ (address of property)

- *If you are a secure tenant under the Housing Act 1985, you can only be required to leave your dwelling if your landlord obtains an order for possession from the Court. The order must be based on one of the Grounds which are set out in the 1985 Act (see paragraphs 3 and 4 below).*

- *If you are willing to give up possession without a Court order, you should notify the person who signed this Notice as soon as possible and say when you would leave.*

3. Possession will be sought on Ground(s) _____ of Schedule 2 to the Housing Act 1985, which reads:—

[give the text in full of each Ground which is being relied on]

- *Whatever Grounds for possession are set out in paragraph 3 of this Notice, the Court may allow any of the other Grounds to be added at a later stage. If this is done, you will be told about it so you can argue at the hearing in Court about the new Ground, as well as the Grounds set out in paragraph 3, if you want to.*

4. Particulars of each Ground are as follows:—

[give a full explanation of why each Ground is being relied upon]

● *Before the Court will grant an order on any of the Grounds 1 to 8 or 12 to 16, it must be satisfied that it is reasonable to require you to leave. This means that, if one of these Grounds is set out in paragraph 3 of this Notice, you will be able to argue at the hearing in Court that it is not reasonable that you should have to leave, even if you accept that the Ground applies.*

● *Before the Court grants an order on any of the Grounds 9 to 16, it must be satisfied that there will be suitable alternative accommodation for you when you have to leave. This means that the Court will have to decide that, in its opinion, there will be other accommodation which is reasonably suitable for the needs of you and your family, taking into particular account various factors such as the nearness of your place of work, and the sort of housing that other people with similar needs are offered. Your new home will have to be let to you on another secure tenancy or a private tenancy under the Rent Act of a kind that will give you similar security. There is no requirement for suitable alternative accommodation where Grounds 1 to 8 apply.*

● *If your landlord is not a local authority, and the local authority gives a certificate that it will provide you with suitable accommodation, the Court has to accept the certificate.*

● *One of the requirements of Ground 10A is that the landlord must have approval for the redevelopment scheme from the Secretary of State (or, in the case of a housing association landlord, the Housing Corporation). The landlord must have consulted all secure tenants affected by the proposed redevelopment scheme.*

---

5. The Court proceedings will not be begun until after

_____

[give the date after which Court proceedings can be brought]

● *Court proceedings cannot be begun until after this date, which cannot be earlier than the date when your tenancy or licence could have been brought to an end. This means that if you have a weekly or fortnightly tenancy, there should be at least 4 weeks between the date this Notice is given and the date in this paragraph.*

● *After this date, court proceedings may be begun at once or at any time during the following twelve months. Once the twelve months are up this Notice will lapse and a new Notice must be served before possession can be sought.*

Signed _____

On behalf of _____

Address _____

_____

_____

Tel. No _____

Date _____

2   Application to suspend warrant for possession (*Form N.244*)

IN THE ANYTOWN COUNTY COURT   CASE No

BETWEEN .... RAINBOW DISTRICT COUNCIL .... PLAINTIFF

AND .... WAYNE ROSS .... DEFENDANT

I wish to apply for an order:

suspending the warrant for possession issued by the Plaintiff on terms.

TAKE NOTICE that the grounds for this application are set out in the supporting affidavit attached to this application.

DATED 18 September 1992

Signed .... Jenny Brown Solicitor for .... ~~Plaintiff~~/Defendant

Address for .... Rainbow Community Law Centre ....

Service .... 1 Lavender Close, Anytown ....

THIS SECTION TO BE COMPLETED BY THE COURT

To the Plaintiff/Defendant

TAKE NOTICE that this application will be heard by the Registrar [or Judge]
at

on   at   o'clock

IF YOU DO NOT ATTEND THE COURT WILL MAKE SUCH ORDER AS IT THINKS FIT.

Address all communications to the Chief Clerk AND QUOTE THE ABOVE CASE NUMBER

THE COURT OFFICE AT

is open from 10 a.m. to 4 p.m. Monday to Friday.

IN THE ANYTOWN COUNTY COURT   CASE No

BETWEEN:

RAINBOW DISTRICT COUNCIL   Plaintiff

– and –

WAYNE ROSS   Defendant

AFFIDAVIT OF WAYNE ROSS

I, WAYNE ROSS, of 32 Small Street, Anytown MAKE OATH AND SAY AS FOLLOWS:-

1   I am the Defendant in this action.

2   On 25 June 1992 the Plaintiff was granted an order for possession in respect of 32 Small Street, Anytown in which I live. The learned District Judge suspended the order on my paying the then current rent of £33 per week together with an additional £5 per week towards the arrears of £650.

3   Following the hearing I made the necessary payments of £38 regularly each week. However, on 21 July 1992 my employer told me that, because of a reduction in demand for the product which my employer makes, he was having to lay off half the number of employees with immediate effect. As a result, following 24 July 1992, I received no wages and although I was able to claim housing benefit and income support I could not afford to make any payments towards the arrears as required under the term of the possession order.

4   On 10 September 1992 I was taken back on at work and am now again employed on a full-time basis. As a result I am now able to resume making payments under the terms of the order and to pay off the missed payments towards the arrears.

5   In the circumstances I would respectfully ask this Honourable Court to suspend the warrant for possession issued by the Plaintiff on terms.

SWORN at Anytown in the County of Anytownshire this 18th day of September 1992

Before me

Solicitor/Officer of the Court appointed to take affidavits.

3   Application to set aside order for possession (*Form N.244*)

IN THE ANYTOWN COUNTY COURT   CASE No

BETWEEN .... RAINBOW DISTRICT COUNCIL .... PLAINTIFF

AND .... ALICE SMITH .... DEFENDANT

I wish to apply for an order:

(1)   setting aside the order for possession dated 16 March 1992 granted in favour of the Plaintiff;

(2)   giving appropriate directions for the effective disposal of the action.

TAKE NOTICE that the grounds for this application are set out in the supporting affidavit attached to this application.

DATED 17 April 1992

Signed .... Jenny Brown Solicitor for the .... P̶l̶a̶i̶n̶t̶i̶f̶f̶/Defendant

Address for ...... Rainbow Community Law Centre ....

Service .... 1 Lavender Close, Anytown ....

THIS SECTION TO BE COMPLETED BY THE COURT

To the Plaintiff/Defendant

TAKE NOTICE that this application will be heard by the Registrar [or Judge] at

on   at   o'clock

IF YOU DO NOT ATTEND THE COURT WILL MAKE SUCH ORDER AS IT THINKS FIT.

Address all communications to the Chief Clerk AND QUOTE THE ABOVE CASE NUMBER

THE COURT OFFICE AT

is open from 10 a.m. to 4 p.m. Monday to Friday.

IN THE ANYTOWN COUNTY COURT   CASE No

BETWEEN:

RAINBOW DISTRICT COUNCIL   Plaintiff

- and -

ALICE SMITH   Defendant

AFFIDAVIT OF ALICE SMITH

I, ALICE SMITH, of 10 Small Street, Anytown MAKE OATH AND SAY AS FOLLOWS:-

1   I am the Defendant in this action.

2   I am the tenant of 10 Small Street, Anytown which I rent from the Plaintiff.

3   On 16 April 1992 I received a copy of the order for possession which had been granted to the Plaintiff on 16 March 1992. This was the first I had heard about the proceedings which have been brought against me. At no stage have I received any court summons for possession of my house nor have I been told by anyone on the Plaintiff's behalf that proceedings had been started.

4   I can only assume that if the summons was served by the court by post the envelope has gone missing somewhere in the postal system.

5   I wish to defend the proceedings brought against me and to counterclaim against the Plaintiff for damages for breach of repairing obligation and for an injunction to require the Plaintiff to undertake repairs for which it is responsible. There is now produced and shown to me marked 'WR' a form of draft defence and counterclaim which I wish to serve in these proceedings. [*Alternatively, a brief synopsis of the grounds for defence and counterclaim should be set out*].

6   I would respectfully ask this Honourable Court to set aside the order for possession dated 16 March 1992 and to give directions for the service of the pleadings and consequential directions for disposal of this action.

SWORN at Anytown in the County of Anytownshire this 17th day of April 1992

Before me

Solicitor/Officer of the Court appointed to take affidavits.

4 Particulars of claim of public sector landlord

IN THE ANYTOWN COUNTY COURT   CASE No

BETWEEN:

RAINBOW DISTRICT COUNCIL   Plaintiff

– and –

WAYNE ROSS   Defendant

PARTICULARS OF CLAIM

1 The Plaintiff is the freehold owner of premises known as 32 Small Street Anytown (hereafter 'the premises').

2 Pursuant to a weekly tenancy granted by the Plaintiff in or about 1987 the Defendant is the secure tenant of the premises within the meaning of section 79 of the Housing Act 1985.

3 The rent payable under the said tenancy is £33.09 due weekly each Monday.

4 The Plaintiff's claim is for termination of the Defendant's tenancy and possession of the premises.

5 The tenant is indebted to the Plaintiff for rent due and owing.

6 On the 26th day of May 1991 the Plaintiff served a Notice Seeking Possession of the premises upon the Defendant pursuant to and in accordance with section 83 of the Housing Act 1985.

7 The Ground upon which the Plaintiff seeks possession is that the Defendant has failed to pay rent lawfully due.

PARTICULARS

i) As at 24th March 1991 arrears of rent were due in the sum of £99.27.

ii) As at 26th May 1991 arrears of rent were due in the sum of £126.45.

iii) As at 28th July 1991 arrears of rent were due in the sum of £153.96.

8 The Plaintiff asserts that in all the circumstances it would be reasonable for an order for possession to be granted.

AND the Plaintiff claims:

1   AN ORDER terminating the Defendant's tenancy and for possession of the premises on the ground stated in the notice;

2   £153.96 arrears of RENT calculated up to 28th July 1991;

3   FURTHER RENT at £33.09 per week from that date up to the date possession is ordered to be given;

4   MESNE PROFITS at £33.09 per week from the date the tenancy is terminated to the date possession is obtained;

5   COSTS.

DATED THIS 29th day of February 1992

JOHN SMITH, Solicitor, Rainbow Town Hall, Anytown.

Solicitor for the Plaintiff who will accept service of all proceedings in this action on behalf of the Plaintiff at the above address.

To the District Judge and to the Defendant.

5 Defence and counterclaim of public sector tenant

IN THE ANYTOWN COUNTY COURT   CASE No

BETWEEN:

RAINBOW DISTRICT COUNCIL   Plaintiff

– and –

WAYNE ROSS   Defendant

DEFENCE AND COUNTERCLAIM

1 Paragraphs 1 2 and 3 of the Particulars of Claim are admitted.

2 The Defendant denies that the Plaintiff is entitled to termination of his tenancy and possession of the premises as claimed in paragraph 4 or at all.

3 No admission is made as to the service, form or effect of any Notice Seeking Possession.

4 No admissions are made as to any arrears of rent or level of the same and the Plaintiff is put to strict proof of the existence or level of any such arrears.

5 Further and in the alternative the Defendant asserts that he is entitled to set off against any rent otherwise due the sums hereunder counterclaimed.

6 Further and in the alternative the Defendant claims the protection of section 84 of the Housing Act 1985 and denies that in all the circumstances it would be reasonable for an Order of Possession to be made.

COUNTERCLAIM

The Defendant repeats paragraphs 1 to 5 above.

7 The Defendant is entitled to the benefit of the repairing covenant implied by section 11 of the Landlord and Tenant Act 1985.

8 In breach of the aforementioned covenant the Plaintiff has since on or about October 1988 failed to keep the property in repair.

PARTICULARS

i)   extensive crumbling to stone works on second floor;
ii)   roof leak to main roof;
iii)   rot to kitchen window-sill;
iv)   loose railings outside first-floor windows;
v)   defects to pointing to front wall;
vi)   broken tiles to back additional roof and defects to sand/cement fillet;
vii)   rear wall out of plumb;
viii)   sashes to left-hand window in front living room on first floor ill-fitting to frame;
ix)   sash frame to kitchen window loose in opening;
x)   skirting board in kitchen loose to rear wall below window;
xi)   loose baluster and loose nosing to lower flight of stairs between first and second floor;
xii)   joins to asbestos cement gas boiler flue pipe in main roof space cracked and leaking;
xiii)   no support to timber wall plates in main roof space which supports rafters to rear chimney breast on right-hand party wall within right-hand roof space;
xiv)   accumulation of debris in valley gutter and top of access hatch upstand to main roof;
xv)   pointing to main roof loose and broken away and zinc flashing loose to left-hand parapet;
xvi)   inadequate protection to slates to rear verge to right-hand side adjoining party wall;
xvii)   collar to ventilation duct to left-hand slope broken off and lying in valley gutter;
xviii)   hole in staircase;
xix)   dampness in second-floor rear bedroom;
xx)   cracks and chipped paint to asbestos covering of sitting-room and kitchen doors.

9   The Plaintiff has notice of the aforementioned defects by reason of numerous oral complaints to its employees since 1988, a complaint made to the Local Government Ombudsman by the Defendant dated 17th May 1990, complaints to Councillor Diocles Jones by the Defendant since October 1989 and visits by various employees of the Plaintiff's on diverse dates.

10   By reason of the aforementioned breaches of covenant, the Defendant has suffered loss, damage, injury and inconvenience.

PARTICULARS

i) decorations have been ruined with the result that the Defendant has spent £233.65 on decorating materials and a considerable time in redecorating;
ii) curtains valued at £30.00 were torn by the Plaintiff's workmen;
iii) carpets valued at £350.00 were ruined;
iv) the Defendant had to take 10 days off work with resulting loss of wages of £25.00 per day;
v) by reason of the dampness, the Defendant spent additional sums on heating which he estimates at £60.00 for each winter quarter;
vi) as a result of dampness to the property, the Defendant's son has suffered more from bronchitis than is normal;
vii) the Defendant's wife has been depressed and a strain has been placed on their marriage;
viii) considerable inconvenience due to the disrepair and due to dust caused by the Plaintiff's workmen.

11   Further and in the alternative the Plaintiff is in breach of the express or alternatively implied term to keep in repair the common parts of the building in which the premises are situate, and/or in breach of the Plaintiff's duty not to derogate from its grant and more particularly to ensure that the parts retained in its possession and control remain reasonably safe and do not cause damage to the Defendant or to the premises, and/or is in breach of section 4 of the Defective Premises Act 1972.

PARTICULARS

The Defendant repeats the particulars set out under paragraph 8(i) to (xx).

12   By reason of the breaches set out in paragraph 11 the Defendant has suffered loss, damage and inconvenience.

PARTICULARS

The Defendant repeats the particulars set out under paragraph 10(i) to (viii).

13   The Defendant claims interest pursuant to the County Courts Act 1984 s69 at such rate and for such period as this Honourable Court will allow.

14   The Defendant asserts pursuant to CCR Order 6 rule 1A that the value of this counterclaim exceeds £5,000.

AND the Defendant counterclaims:

1   DAMAGES;

2   AN ORDER for specific performance to remedy such of the above-mentioned defects as are still outstanding at the date of judgment herein;

3   A MANDATORY INJUNCTION;

4   INTEREST pursuant to the County Courts Act 1984 s69;

5   COSTS.

Dated this 9th day of April 1992

JENNY BROWN, Solicitor, Rainbow Community Law Centre, 1 Lavender Close, Anytown.

Solicitors for the Defendant who will accept service at the above address.

To the District Judge and to the Plaintiff.

Private Sector Tenants

6 Particulars of claim of private landlord

IN THE CLERKENWELL COUNTY COURT   CASE No

BETWEEN:

EDWARD LANDLORD   Plaintiff

– and –

JOSEPHINE WRIGHTON   Defendant

PARTICULARS OF CLAIM

1   By an agreement made on or about 10th September 1988 the Plaintiff let to the Defendant all that suite of rooms situated and known as first floor, three rooms, kitchen, bathroom and wc, being part of the building known as 25 Magnolia Road, London NW9 (hereinafter referred to as 'the premises') for the term of one month from 8th September 1988 and thereafter on a monthly tenancy at a rent of £28.20 per month payable in advance on the 8th day of each and every month.

2   The rent currently payable by the Defendant to the Plaintiff pursuant to the terms of the said agreement is £17.30 per week. The rent was registered on the 14th July 1989.

3   By Notice to Quit dated 19th July 1991 the Plaintiff by his agents duly determined the said tenancy on the 20th August 1991 but the Defendant wrongfully holds possession of the premises.

4   Arrears of rent up to and including rent due on 1st April 1992 amounted to £423.54.

5   The claim relates to a dwelling-house.

AND the plaintiff claims:

1   POSSESSION of the premises;

2   ARREARS of rent amounting to £423.54;

3   RENT AND/OR MESNE PROFITS at the rate of £17.30 per week from the 1st April 1992 until possession is given up;

4   COSTS.

DATED this 10th day of APRIL 1992.

Jones & Smith, 3 High Street, London W1.

Solicitors to the Plaintiff.

To the Chief Clerk and to the Defendant.

7   Defence and counterclaim of private tenant

IN THE CLERKENWELL COUNTY COURT   CASE No

Between

EDWARD LANDLORD   Plaintiff

– and –

JOSEPHINE WRIGHTON   Defendant

DEFENCE AND COUNTERCLAIM

1   Paragraph 1 of the Particulars of Claim is admitted.

2   Paragraph 2 of the Particulars of Claim is denied. The defendant avers that no notice of increase was served or received following the registration of rent by the Rent Officer on 14th July 1989.

3   No admission is made as to the service or validity of any Notice to Quit.

4   The defendant denies Paragraph 4 of the Particulars of Claim and puts the plaintiff to strict proof as to the level of any rent arrears.

5   Further and in the alternative the defendant maintains that she is entitled to set off the matters hereunder counterclaimed.

6   Further and in the alternative the defendant claims the protection of the Rent Act 1977 and denies that in all the circumstances it is reasonable for an order for possession to be made.

7   The defendant admits paragraph 5 of the Particulars of Claim.

COUNTERCLAIM

8   The defendant repeats paragraphs 1 to 7 above.

9   The defendant's tenancy is subject to an implied covenant that the plaintiff will keep in repair the structure and exterior of the property and keep in repair and proper working order the installations for the supply of water, gas and electricity and for sanitation and for space heating or heating water.

10   Further and in the alternative the tenancy is subject to an implied term that the plaintiff keep in repair the common parts of the building as a whole and/or that he should not derogate from his grant and more particularly to ensure that the parts retained in his possession and control remain reasonably safe and do not cause damage to the plaintiff or to the premises.

11   Further and in the alternative by virtue of section 4 of the Defective Premises Act 1972 the plaintiff owes a duty to take such care as is reasonable in all the circumstances to see that the defendant and other persons are reasonably safe from personal injury or from damage to their property caused by a relevant defect to the premises.

12   The plaintiff has breached the aforementioned implied covenants and failed to comply with the aforementioned statutory duty.

PARTICULARS

i)   The asbestos sheeting which constitutes the exterior walls to the rear bedroom is draughty and ill fitting and lacks adequate insulation.
ii) There is penetrating dampness to the bathroom.
iii) There is a broken sash cord to the window in the toilet.
iv) There is crumbling plaster to the walls to the staircase.
v)   There is a cracked pane to the window to the lounge.
vi) The surrounds to the windows to the lounge are rotting and portions of wood are missing.

13   The Plaintiff has had notice of the aforementioned defects.

14   By reason of the aforementioned breaches of implied covenant and/ or statutory duty the defendant has suffered loss, damage and inconvenience.

PARTICULARS

i)   The rear bedroom is uninhabitable during the winter and clothes and bedding kept in the aforementioned rear bedroom have been ruined due to mildew.

ii)   There is mould growth to the walls in the bathroom and peeling wall-paper in the bathroom.

iii) The defendant has had to decorate rooms as a result of damage caused to decorations by disrepair.

iv)   The defendant has had to spend additional sums for heating the property.

15   The Defendant claims interest pursuant to the County Courts Act 1984 s69 at such rate and for such period as this Honourable Court will allow.

16   The Defendant asserts pursuant to Order 6 rule 1A that the value of her counterclaim exceeds £5,000.

AND the defendant counterclaims:

1   AN ORDER for specific performance to remedy the above-mentioned defects.

2   DAMAGES.

3   INTEREST pursuant to Section 69 of the County Courts Act 1984.

DATED this 17th day of May 1992.

Brown & Sons, Solicitors, of 56 Main Street, London NW5.

Solicitors for the defendant who will accept service of proceedings at the above address on behalf of the defendant.

To the Chief Clerk and to the Plaintiff's Solicitors.

Mortgagors

8 Particulars of claim of building society

IN THE ANYTOWN COUNTY COURT   CASE No

BETWEEN:

RAINBOW BUILDING SOCIETY   Plaintiff

– and –

STEPHEN and JOSIE NEILL   Defendants

PARTICULARS OF CLAIM

1   By a legal charge dated 1 August 1990 made between the Plaintiff and the Defendants, the Defendants charged by way of legal mortgage the freehold premises known as 1 Cedar Street, Anytown to secure the repayment of the principal sum of £60,000 advanced to the Defendants by the Plaintiff with interest thereon.

2   In the said legal charge the Defendants covenanted to repay to the Plaintiff the said principal and interest thereon by monthly instalments pursuant to the rules of the plaintiff Society. At the date hereof the said instalment is £475 per month.

3   The Defendants have defaulted in making payments to the Plaintiff and arrears amount to £1,200. The amount remaining due under the said legal charge at the date hereof is £58,000.

4   The Plaintiff has not before the commencement of this action taken any proceedings against the Defendants in respect of the said principal money or interest.

5   The said premises include a dwelling-house within the meaning of Pt IV Administration of Justice Act 1970.

6   No land charge, notice or caution pursuant to s2(7) Matrimonial Homes Act 1967 has been registered in respect of the said premises and there is no person on whom notice of this action is required to be served in accordance with s2(8) Matrimonial Homes Act 1983.

AND the plaintiff claims possession of 1 Cedar Street, Anytown aforesaid.

DATED this 20th day of April 1992.

PETER BLACK, Solicitor, Rainbow Building Society, 3 Silver Street, Anytown.

Solicitor for the Plaintiff who will accept service of all proceedings in this action on behalf of the Plaintiff at the above address.

To the Chief Clerk and to the Defendants.

9   Defence of mortgagor to claim by building society

IN THE ANYTOWN COUNTY COURT   CASE No

BETWEEN:

RAINBOW BUILDING SOCIETY   Plaintiff

– and –

STEPHEN and JOSIE NEILL   Defendants

DEFENCE

1   Save that the Defendants make no admissions as to paragraph 3 and deny that the Plaintiffs are entitled to possession of 1 Cedar Street, Anytown as claimed or otherwise, the Particulars of Claim are admitted.

2   To the extent that any arrears of payments are found to be owing to the Plaintiff by the Defendants, the Defendants seek the protection of Pt IV of the Administration of Justice Act 1970.

DATED this 1st day of May 1992

JENNY BROWN, Solicitor, Rainbow Community Law Centre, 1 Lavender Close, Anytown.

Solicitors for the Defendants who will accept service at the above address.

To the Chief Clerk and to the Plaintiff.

10   Particulars of claim of finance company

IN THE ANYTOWN COUNTY COURT   CASE No

BETWEEN:

EQUITABLE SECURED LOAN COMPANY   Plaintiff

– and –

STEPHEN and JOSIE NEILL   Defendants

PARTICULARS OF CLAIM

1   By a legal charge dated 2 August 1990 made between the Defendants and the Plaintiff and supplemental to a Credit Agreement, the Defendants

i)   covenanted inter alia with the Plaintiff that on demand in writing made to the Defendants, the Defendants would pay to the Plaintiff the balance which should for the time being be due and owing to the Plaintiff and

ii) charged by way of legal mortgage the freehold property known as 1 Cedar Street, Anytown with payment of the principal sum interest and all other monies thereby covenanted to be repaid.

2   On 8 July 1991 the Plaintiff served on the Defendants a default notice pursuant to Consumer Credit Act 1974 s87 and on 11 August 1991 the Plaintiff served a final demand for payment of the sum of £1,876.89 being the balance for the time being due and owing.

3   The particulars required under Order 6 rule 5(1) are as follows:

i)   The amount of the advance was £1,550.00 repayable over 48 months.

ii) The rate of interest is 35% per annum.

iii) The monthly sum of £53.86 is payable to the Plaintiff in connection with the Charge on the 8th day of each month.

iv) At the date hereof, the arrears of payments due to the Plaintiff amount to £556.12 including accrued interest.

v)   At the date hereof, the total balance of principal and interest remaining due under the Charge is £1,979.81 exclusive of costs.

vi) The property has registered title and a class F Land Charge or a Notice or Caution pursuant to Matrimonial Homes Act 1967 s2(7), or a notice pursuant to Matrimonial Homes Act 1983 s8 has not been registered and no person is required to be served with a Notice under the said Acts.

4   The Plaintiff has not taken any other proceedings against the Defendants in respect of principal money and interest secured by the Charge or in respect of the said property.

5   The said property includes a dwelling-house within the meaning of Pt IV of Administration of Justice Act 1970.

AND the plaintiff claims possession of 1 Cedar Street, Anytown.

DATED this 28th day of April 1992

MAMMON & CO, 1 Lucre Street, Anytown.

Solicitors to the Plaintiff who will at that address accept service of all proceedings.

To the Chief Clerk and to the Defendants.

11   Defence and counterclaim for relief under Consumer Credit Act 1974

IN THE ANYTOWN COUNTY COURT   CASE No

BETWEEN:

EQUITABLE SECURED LOAN COMPANY   Plaintiff

– and –

STEPHEN and JOSIE NEILL   Defendants

DEFENCE

1   Save that no admissions are made as to sums owed to the Plaintiff paragraphs 1 to 5 inclusive of the Particulars of Claim are admitted. The Defendants assert that the said credit agreement referred to in the Particulars of Claim is a regulated agreement within the Consumer Credit Act 1974 and deny that the Plaintiff is entitled to possession of 1 Cedar Street, Anytown as claimed or at all.

COUNTERCLAIM

2   The Defendants repeat their Defence herein.

3   By virtue of the matters set out in the Schedule hereto the Defendants counterclaim for a 'time order' and/or other relief under Part IX of the Consumer Credit Act 1974.

AND the defendants counterclaim for:

1   RELIEF pursuant to s129 Consumer Credit Act 1974.

2   FURTHER OR OTHER RELIEF.

DATED this 10th day of June 1992

JENNY BROWN, Solicitor, Rainbow Community Law Centre, 1 Lavender Close, Anytown.

Solicitors for the Defendants who will accept service at the above address.

To the Chief Clerk and to the Plaintiff.

Schedule to defence and counterclaim

Case number

In the   Anytown   **County Court**

Plaintiff: Equitable Secured Loan Co

Defendants: Stephen and Josie Neill

---

1. What is your occupation?
BUS DRIVER

2. Your employer's name
ANYTOWN TRANSPORT AUTHORITY

Address
TRANSPORT HOUSE
EXCHANGE STREET, ANYTOWN

3. Money you receive *(give average weekly figures)*
Pay before deductions £190 APPROX

overtime, bonuses, fees, allowances,
commissions
£   —

Usual take home pay £ 127. *Pension* £ —

State benefits £ 14.50. *Other income* £ —

Contributions from your household £ —

4. If anyone depends on you financially, give their names and ages including any children.
KENNY (6)

IAN (2)

5. How much rent or mortgage should you pay?
£538.86 Anytown B. Soc (£475)
         Plaintiff (£53.86)

Is this weekly ☐ *or monthly* ☒
6. How much do you actually pay? £450
                                    approx.

7. What rates should you pay? £15.00
Is this weekly ☒ *or monthly* ☐

8. How much do you actually pay? £15.00

9. Do you have to pay under any Court Order?
Please give details including name of court, case number, amount still owing and instalment you pay.

---

10. What other regular payments do you have to make *(for credit, hire purchase etc?)*

Clothing club   £10 p.w.
HP furniture   £25 p.w.

---

11. Give details of any other regular expenses you wish the court to take into account.

Food, household materials
    and fuel bills   £50

---

12. Are the goods in your possession?
Yes ☐   *No* ☐   N/A

My proposals for payment are £36 per month to clear any arrears and thereafter the outstanding balance.

12   Notice of an assured shorthold tenancy

Housing Act 1988 section 20

- Please write clearly in black ink.

- If there is any thing you do not understand you should get advice from a solicitor or a Citizens' Advice Bureau, before you agree to the tenancy.

- The landlord must give the notice of the tenant before an assured shorthold tenancy is granted. It does not commit the tenant to take the tenancy.

- This document is important, keep it in a safe place.

To:

Name of proposed tenant. It a joint tenancy is being offered enter the names of the joint tenants.

1.   You are proposing to take a tenancy of the dwelling known as:

from [/ /19] to [/ /19]

day   month   year   day   month   year

The tenancy must be for a term certain of at least six months.

2.   This notice is to tell you that your tenancy is to be an assured shorthold tenancy. Provided you keep to the terms of the tenancy, you are entitled to remain in the dwelling for at least the first six months of the fixed period agreed at the start of the tenancy. At the end of this period, depending on the terms of the tenancy, the landlord may have the right to repossession if he wants.

3.   The rent for this tenancy is the rent we have agreed. However, you have the right to apply to a rent assessment committee for a determination of the rent which the committee considers might reasonably be obtained under the tenancy. If the committee considers (i) that there is a sufficient number of similar properties in the locality let on assured tenancies and that (ii) the rent we have agreed is significantly higher than the rent which might reasonably be obtained having regard to the level of rents for other assured tenancies in the locality, it will determine a rent for the tenancy. That rent will be the legal maximum you can be required to pay from the date the committee directs.

4.   [. . .]

To be signed by the landord or his agent (someone acting for him). If there are joint landlords each must sign, unless one signs on behalf of the rest with their agreement.

Signed

Name(s) of tenant(s)

Address of landlord(s)

Tel:

If signed by agent, name and address of agent

Tel: [   ]   *Date:* [19   ]

Special note for existing tenants

● Generally if you already have a protected or statutory tenancy and you give it up to take a new tenancy in the same or other accommodation owned by the same landlord, that tenancy cannot be an assured tenancy. It can still be a protected tenancy.

● But if you currently occupy a dwelling which was let to you as a protected shorthold tenant, special rules apply.

● If you have an assured tenancy which is not a shorthold under the Housing Act 1988, you cannot be offered an assured shorthold tenancy of the same or other accommodation by the same landlord.

13   Notice seeking possession of a property let on an assured tenancy

Housing Act 1988 section 8

- Please write clearly in black ink.
- Do not use this form if possession is sought from an assured shorthold tenant under section 21 of the Housing Act 1988 or if the property is occupied under an assured agricultural occupancy.
- This notice is the first step towards requiring you to give up possession of your home. You should read it very carefully.

- If you need advice about this notice, and what you should do about it, take it as quickly as possible to any of the following—
  - a Citizens' Advice Bureau,
  - a housing aid centre,
  - a law centre,
  - or a solicitor.

You may be able to get Legal Aid but this will depend on your personal circumstances.

1.   To: [   ]   *Name(s) of tenant(s)*

2.   Your landlord intends to apply to the court for an order requiring you to give up possession of—

[   ]   *Address of premises*

- If you have an assured tenancy under the Housing Act 1988, which is not an assured shorthold tenancy, you can only be required to leave your home if your landlord gets an order for possession from the court on one of the grounds which are set out in Schedule 2 to the Act.

- If you are willing to give up possession of your home without a court order, you should tell the person who signed this notice as soon as possible and say when you can leave.

3.   The landlord intends to seek possession on ground(s) [   ] in Schedule 2 to the Housing Act 1988, which reads
Give a full text of each ground which is being relied on. (Continue on a separate sheet if necessary.)

[   ]

- Whichever grounds are set out in paragraph 3 the court may allow any of the other grounds to be added at a later date. If this is done, you will be told about it so you can discuss the additional grounds at the court hearing as well as the grounds set out in paragraph 3.

4.   Particulars of each ground are as follows—

Give a full explanation of why each ground is being relied on. (Continue on a separate sheet if necessary.)

[   ]

- If the court is satisfied that any of grounds 1 to 8 is established it must make an order (but see below in respect of fixed term tenancies).

- Before the court will grant an order on any of grounds 9 to 16, it must be satisfied that it is reasonable to require you to leave. This means that, if one of these grounds is set out in paragraph 3, you will be able to suggest to the court that it is not reasonable that you should have to leave, even if you accept that the ground applies.

- The court will not make an order under grounds 1, 3 to 7, 9 or 16, to take effect during the fixed term of the tenancy; and it will only make an order during the fixed term on grounds 2, 8 or 10 to 15 if the terms of the tenancy make provision for it to be brought to an end on any of these grounds.

- Where the court makes an order for possession solely on ground 6 or 9, your landlord must pay your reasonable removal expenses.

5. **The court proceedings will not begin until after**

> | | |
> | --- | --- |
> | | 19 |

Give the date after which court proceedings can be brought.

- Where the landlord is seeking possession under grounds 1, 2, 5 to 7, 9 or 16 in Schedule 2, court proceedings cannot begin earlier than 2 months from the date this notice is served on you and not before the date on which the tenancy (had it not been assured) could have been brought to an end by a notice to quit served at the same time as this notice.

- Where the landlord is seeking possession on grounds 3, 4, 8 or 10 to 15, court proceedings cannot begin until 2 weeks after the date this notice is served.

- After the date shown in paragraph 5, court proceedings may be begun at once but not later than 12 months from the date this notice is served. After this time the notice will lapse and a new notice must be served before possession can be sought.

To be signed by the landlord or his agent (someone acting for him).

Signed

Name(s) of tenant(s)

Address of landlord(s)

Tel:

If signed by agent, name and address of agent

Tel: *Date:*   19

14   Judgment for plaintiff in action for recovery of land (*Prescribed form N.26*)

Order 22, Rule 1(1)

[*Title of proceedings, form N.200*]

It is adjudged that the plaintiff do recover against the defendant possession of the land mentioned in the particulars of claim enclosed with the summons in this action, namely: [*here describe the land as set out in the particulars*]

And that the plaintiff do recover against the defendant the sum of £   for rent and mesne profits and £   for costs (or his costs of this action to be taxed on scale   ), amounting together to the sum of £

It is ordered that the defendant do give the plaintiff possession of the said land on the

And that the defendant do pay the plaintiff the (total) sum mentioned above by (and do pay the amount of costs when taxed by that day or, if the costs have not been taxed, within 14 days of taxation)
Or (together with the amount of costs when taxed) by instalments of £   for every calendar month, the first instalment to reach the plaintiff by

Dated

Take Notice

To the defendant
If you do not comply with this order you may be evicted by the bailiff of the court and your goods removed and sold to pay the money judgment. If your circumstances change and you cannot pay, ask at the court about what you can do.

[*Add provisions on register of judgments, interest and payments from precedent 20 below*]

15 Judgment for plaintiff in action of forfeiture for non-payment of rent (*Prescribed form N.27*)

Order 22, Rule 1(1)

[*Title of proceedings, form N.200*]

It is adjudged that the plaintiff is entitled to recover against the defendant possession of the land mentioned in the particulars of claim enclosed with the summons in this action, namely: [*here describe the land as set out in the particulars*]

the rent of the land, amounting to £   , being in arrear and the plaintiff having a right of re-entry or forfeiture in respect thereof
And that the plaintiff do recover against the defendant the sum of £   for arrears of rent (and the sum of £   for costs (or his costs of this action to be taxed on scale   ), (amounting together to the sum of £   ))

It is ordered that the defendant do pay the (total) sum mentioned above into the court office <u>by</u> [*a date not less than 4 weeks from the date of the order*]
(and do pay the amount of the costs when taxed by that day or, if the costs have not been taxed, within 14 days of taxation)

And that unless payment of the said sum is made by the said date the defendant shall thereupon give possession of the said land to the plaintiff

And it is further adjudged that the plaintiff do recover against the defendant by way of mesne profits the sum of £
And it is ordered that the defendant do pay this further sum into the court office <u>by</u>

Dated

Take Notice
Failure to comply with this order may result in your eviction by the bailiff of the court and your goods being removed and sold or other enforcement proceedings being taken against you.
* This judgment has been registered in the Register of County Court Judgments. This may make it difficult for you to get credit.
[* Delete if debt is not to be registered]
• If you pay in full <u>within one month</u> of the date of judgment, you can ask the court to remove the entry and for a certificate proving payment.

• If you pay in full <u>after one month</u>, you can ask the court to mark the entry in the register as satisfied and for a certificate proving payment.

Payments into Court

You can pay the court by calling at the court office which is open from 10 am to 4 pm Monday to Friday. You may only pay by:

• cash
• banker's or giro draft
• cheque supported by a cheque card
• cheque (unsupported cheques may be accepted, subject to clearance, if the Chief Clerk agrees)

Cheques and drafts must be made payable to HM Paymaster General and crossed. *Please bring this form with you.*

By post
You may only pay by:

• postal order
• banker's or giro draft
• cheque (cheques may be accepted, subject to clearance, if the Chief Clerk agrees)

The payment must be made out to HM Paymaster General and crossed. This method of payment is at your own risk. And you must:

• pay the postage
• enclose this form
• enclose a self addressed envelope so that the court can return this form with a receipt

The court cannot accept stamps or payments by bank and giro credit transfers.

Note: You should carefully check any future forms from the court to see if payments should be made directly to the plaintiff.

---

16 Judgment for plaintiff in action of forfeiture for non-payment of rent where order refused under Rent Acts (*Prescribed form N.27(1)*)

Order 22, Rule 1(1)

[*Title of proceedings, form N.200*]

It is adjudged for the purposes of section 138 of the County Courts Act 1984 only, that the plaintiff is entitled to recover against the defendant possession of the land mentioned in the particulars of claim enclosed with the summons in this action, namely: [*here describe the land as set out in the particulars*]

the rent of the land, amounting to £   , being in arrear and the plaintiff having a right of re-entry or forfeiture in respect thereof

And that the plaintiff do recover against the defendant the sum of £   for arrears of rent (and the sum of £   for costs (or his costs of this action to be taxed on scale   ), (amounting together to the sum of £   ))

It is ordered that the defendant do pay the (total) sum mentioned above into the court office <u>by</u> [*a date not less than 4 weeks from the date of the order*]
(and do pay the amount of costs when taxed by that day or, if the costs have not been taxed, within 14 days of taxation)

For the aforesaid purposes only, that unless payment of the said sum is made by the said date the defendant shall thereupon give possession of the said land to the plaintiff

And it is further adjudged that the plaintiff do recover against the defendant by way of mesne profits the sum of £

And it is ordered that the defendant do pay this further sum into the court office <u>by</u>

And no order or judgment being made or given under the Rent Acts for the recovery of possession of the land.

It is ordered that no warrant shall issue to enforce the said order for possession.

Dated

Take Notice

If you pay the rent arrears and costs in full by the date specified at (2) above (or within such time as the court may allow) you will be entitled to keep possession of the property under the existing lease. However, if you fail to pay the rent arrears and costs, your landlord may take further proceedings to evict you.

* This judgment has been registered in the Register of County Court Judgments. **This may make it difficult for you to get credit.**

[* *Delete if debt is not to be registered*]

• If you pay in full within one month of the date of judgment, you can ask the court to remove the entry and for a certificate proving payment.

• If you pay in full after one month, you can ask the court to mark the entry in the register as satisfied and for a certificate proving payment.

[*Add provisions on payments into court from precedent 15*]

17 Judgment for plaintiff in action of forfeiture for non-payment of rent where order suspended under Rent Acts (*Prescribed form N.27(2)*)

Order 22, Rule 1(1)

[*Title of proceedings, form N.200*]

It is adjudged that the plaintiff is entitled to recover against the defendant possession of the land mentioned in the particulars of claim enclosed with the summons in this action, namely: [*here describe the land as set out in the particulars*]

the rent of the land, amounting to £   , being in arrear and the plaintiff having a right of re-entry or forfeiture in respect thereof

And that the plaintiff do recover against the defendant the sum of £   for arrears of rent (and the sum of £   for costs (or his costs of this action to be taxed on scale   ), (amounting together to the sum of £   ))

It is ordered that the defendant do pay the (total) sum mentioned above into the court office <u>by</u> [*a date not less than 4 weeks from the date of the order*]
(and do pay the amount of the costs when taxed by that day or, if the costs have not been taxed, within 14 days of taxation)

And that unless payment of the said sum is made by the said date the defendant shall thereupon give possession of the said land to the plaintiff

And it is further adjudged that the plaintiff do recover against the defendant by way of mesne profits the sum of £

And it is ordered that the defendant do pay this further sum into the court office <u>by</u>

And it is further ordered that execution on such order be suspended for so long as the defendant punctually pays to the plaintiff the said sum of £   and £   for mesne profits, making a total of £   , by instalments of £   per   , commencing on   the   in addition to the current rent of £   per   , and that no execution shall issue on such order when the said sum of £   has been paid.

Dated

Take Notice

If you pay the rent arrears and costs in full by the date specified at (2) above (or within such time as the court may allow), you will be entitled to keep possession of the property under the existing lease. In addition, if you keep to the terms mentioned in the final paragraph above, execution of this order for possession and payment will be suspended. If you become ill or out of work, ask you landlord to suspend the order until you are better or back at work. If he will not do so, you should ask the court officials to help you prepare an application to the judge.

* This judgment has been registered in the Register of County Court Judgments. **This may make it difficult for you to get credit.**

[* *Delete if debt is not to be registered*]

- If you pay in full <u>within one month</u> of the date of judgment, you can ask the court to remove the entry and for a certificate proving payment.
- If you pay in full <u>after one month</u>, you can ask the court to mark the entry in the register as satisfied and for a certificate proving payment.

[*Add provisions on payments into court from precedent 15*]

18 Suspended order for recovery of land (*Prescribed form N.28*)

Order 22, Rule 1(1)

[*Title of proceedings, form N.200*]

It is adjudged that the plaintiff do recover against the defendant possession of the land mentioned in the particulars of claim enclosed with the summons in this action, namely: [*here describe the land as set out in the particulars*]

And that the plaintiff do recover against the defendant the sum of (£ for arrears of rent and mesne profits and) £ for costs (or his costs of this action to be taxed on scale), (amounting together to the sum of £).

It is ordered that the judgment for possession shall not be enforced for days in any event, and for so long thereafter as the defendant punctually pays to the plaintiff the (arrears of rent, mesne profits and) costs by instalments of £ per in addition to the current rent.

And that the judgment for £ (and costs to be taxed) shall not be enforced for so long as the defendant pays the instalments of £ per .

And also that the judgment(s) shall cease to be enforceable when the (arrears of rent, mesne profits and) costs referred to above are satisfied.

CURRENT RENT £
(ARREARS TO DATE OF JUDGMENT £)
[*delete where judgment given for arrears of rent and mesne profits if any*]

The first payment must reach the plaintiff <u>by</u>

Dated

Take Notice

To the defendant
If you fail to comply with this order you may be evicted by the bailiff of the court and your goods removed and sold to pay the money judgment. If you become ill or out of work, ask your landlord to suspend the order until you are better or back at work. If he will not do so, you should ask the court office for help in preparing an application to the (district) judge.

[*Add provisions on register of judgments, interest and payments into court from precedent 20*]

19   Judgment for plaintiff in an action under a mortgage or charge (*Prescribed form N.29*)

Order 22, Rule 1(1)

[*Title of proceedings, form N.200*]

On hearing

and on reading

It is ordered that the defendant do deliver to the plaintiff by the
day of   19   , possession of the property comprised in a
mortgage (or legal charge) dated   and known as: [*here
describe the land as set out in the particulars*]

And that the plaintiff do recover against the defendant (the sum of
£   for principal money and or interest secured by the mortgage or
charge and) the sum of £   for costs, (amounting together to the
sum of £   ) (or his costs of this action to be taxed on scale   )

And that the defendant do pay the plaintiff the (total) sum mentioned
above <u>by</u>
(and do pay the amount of costs when taxed by that day or, if the costs
have not been taxed, within 14 days of taxation)
Or (together with the amount of the costs when taxed) by instalments of
£   for every calendar month, the first instalment to reach the
plaintiff <u>by</u>

Dated

[*Add 'Take Notice' from precedent 14 and provisions on register of
judgments, interest and payments from precedent 20*]

20 Suspended order for possession with no date fixed

IN THE ANYTOWN COUNTY COURT   CASE No

BETWEEN:

RAINBOW DISTRICT COUNCIL   Plaintiff

– and –

WAYNE ROSS   Defendant

Upon hearing the solicitor for the Plaintiff and the solicitor for the Defendant it is ordered that:

1   The Plaintiff is entitled to possession of the premises described in the Particulars of Claim and known as 32 Small Street, Anytown.

2   And it is ordered that the Defendant do deliver to the Plaintiff possession of the said premises on a date to be fixed on application by the Plaintiff.

3   And it is further ordered that the Plaintiff shall not be entitled to apply for an order fixing the date for possession and termination of the Defendant's tenancy for so long as the Defendant punctually pays to the Plaintiff the current rent together with £3.00 per week in respect of the arrears of rent which amount to £650.00.

4   Judgment be entered for the Plaintiff in the sum of £650.00 which sum to be paid by the Defendant at the rate of £3.00 per week in accordance with paragraph 3 of this order.

5   Any application to fix the date for the Defendant to give up possession shall be made to the District Judge in chambers.

6   This order shall be discharged when the Defendant has paid all the arrears of rent referred to above together with the current rent falling due after the date of this order. The first payment must reach the Plaintiff by the next date after the date of this order upon which rent is due under the terms of the tenancy.

7   There be no order as to costs save that there be legal aid taxation of the Defendant's costs.

DATED this 25th day of June 1992

―――――― Take Notice ――――――

To the defendant

If you do not pay in accordance with this order your goods may be removed and sold or other enforcement proceedings may be taken against you. If your circumstances change and you cannot pay, ask at the court office about what you can do.

(1)This judgment has been registered in the Register of County Court Judgments. This may make it difficult for you to get credit. When the money is paid in full (including any interest [delete if debt is not to be registered]) you can ask the court to mark the entry in the register as satisfied and for a certificate proving payment. You will have to provide proof and pay a fee. If you pay in full within one month the entry will be removed.

[delete if debt is not to be registered] If judgment is for more than £5000 the plaintiff may be entitled to interest.

―――――― Address for Payment ――――――

―――――― How to Pay ――――――

- PAYMENT(S) MUST BE MADE to the person named at the address for payment quoting their reference and the court case number.
- DO NOT bring or send payments to the court. THEY WILL NOT BE ACCEPTED.
- You should allow at least 4 days for your payment to reach the plaintiff or his representative.
- Make sure that you keep records and can account for all payments made. Proof may be required if there is any disagreement. It is not safe to send cash unless you use registered post.
- A leaflet giving further advice about payment can be obtained from the court.
- If you need more information you should contact the plaintiff or his representative.

The court office at

is open between 10 am and 4 pm Monday to Friday. When corresponding with the court, please address forms or letters to the Chief Clerk and quote the case number.

21   Adjournment on terms

IN THE ANYTOWN COUNTY COURT   CASE No

BETWEEN:

RAINBOW DISTRICT COUNCIL   Plaintiff

– and –

WAYNE ROSS   Defendant

Upon hearing the solicitor for the Plaintiff and the solicitor for the Defendant it is ordered that:

1   The Plaintiff's claim for possession of 32 Small Street, Anytown be adjourned generally on terms that the Defendant do pay the current rent plus £3.00 per week off the arrears which at the date of this order amount to £650.00.

2   In the event that the Defendant fails to make any payment as provided for in paragraph 1 above there be liberty to the Plaintiff to apply for a possession order on 7 days' notice with leave for such an application to be supported by affidavit evidence setting out details of the arrears then due and any other matters relevant to the matters of reasonableness.

3   Judgment be entered for the Plaintiff in the sum of £650.00 which sum to be paid by the Defendant at the rate of £3.00 per week.

4   There be no order as to costs save that there be legal aid taxation of the Defendants's costs.

DATED this 25th day of June 1992

——— **Take Notice** ———

To the defendant

If you do not pay in accordance with this order your goods may be removed and sold or other enforcement proceedings may be taken against you. If your circumstances change and you cannot pay, ask at the court office about what you can do.

(1)This judgment has been registered in the Register of County Court Judgments. This may make it difficult for you to get credit. When the money is paid in full (including any interest [*delete if debt is not to be registered*]) you can ask the court to mark the entry in the register as satisfied and for a certificate proving payment. You will have to provide proof and pay a fee. If you pay in full within one month the entry will be removed.

[*delete if debt is not to be registered*] If judgment is for more than £5000 the plaintiff may be entitled to interest.

——— Address for Payment ———

——— How to Pay ———

- PAYMENT(S) MUST BE MADE to the person named at the address for payment quoting their reference and the court case number.
- DO NOT bring or send payments to the court. THEY WILL NOT BE ACCEPTED.
- You should allow at least 4 days for your payment to reach the plaintiff or his representative.
- Make sure that you keep records and can account for all payments made. Proof may be required if there is any disagreement. It is not safe to send cash unless you use registered post.
- A leaflet giving further advice about payment can be obtained from the court.
- If you need more information you should contact the plaintiff or his representative.

The court office at

is open between 10 am and 4 pm Monday to Friday. When corresponding with the court, please address forms or letters to the Chief Clerk and quote the case number.

Part VI

Appendices

Appendices

Instructions checklist

Public and private sector occupiers

Occupiers
Full name, address, dates of birth, occupation, income and savings, relationships between.

Name of tenant(s)
Name and address and relationship to occupier.

Status
Protected/statutory/secure/assured tenant/restricted contract, successor tenant.

Details of accommodation
Room/flat/house, shared facilities, location in house.

Landlord/agent/solicitor
Name, address, telephone number, reference number.

Rent
Amount (inclusive/exclusive), arrears, rent registration, any irrecoverable rent.

Written agreement
Tenancy agreement, rent receipts, rent book.

Pre-tenancy notices
Type of notice, date and method of service.

Date of commencement of tenancy

Date of commencement of occupancy

Notice to quit / notice of intention to seek possession

Court proceedings
Previous proceedings, current proceedings, hearing date, date of receipt of summons.

Correspondence

Details of any previous arrangements to remedy default

Regular financial commitments
Maintenance, court orders, HP etc.

Rehousing obligations
Children, pregnancy, vulnerability.

Mortgagors

Occupiers
Full name, address, dates of birth, occupations, income and savings, relationships between.

Legal owner
Name and address, relationship to occupier.

Mortgagee / solicitors
Name, address, telephone and reference numbers, priority (first, second etc).

Type of mortgage
Repayment/endowment/pension.

Date of mortgage

Legal title
Freehold/leasehold, registered/unregistered land.

Payments
Monthly instalments, arrears.

Date of commencement of occupancy

Equitable owners
Previous properties occupied as such, details of contribution to purchase, financial/other detriment.

Correspondence

Court proceedings
Previous/current proceedings, hearing dates, date of receipt of summons.

Details of any previous arrangements to remedy default

Amount required to redeem mortgage

Value of property with vacant possession

Insurance cover
Mortgage indemnity policy, mortgage protection policy.

Regular financial commitments
Maintenance, court orders, HP etc.

Rehousing obligations
Children, pregnancy, vulnerability.

Statutory materials

Administration of Justice Act 1970 s36

ACTION BY MORTGAGEES FOR POSSESSION

Additional powers of court in action brought by mortgagee for possession of dwelling-house

36.—(1)   Where the mortgagee under a mortgage of land which consists of or includes a dwelling-house brings an action in which he claims possession of the mortgaged property, not being an action for foreclosure in which a claim for possession of the mortgaged property is also made, the court may exercise any of the powers conferred on it by subsection (2) below if it appears to the court that in the event of its exercising the power the mortgagor is likely to be able within a reasonable period to pay any sums due under the mortgage or to remedy a default consisting of a breach of any other obligation under or by virtue of the mortgage.

(2)   The court—
    (a)   may adjourn the proceedings, or
    (b)   on giving judgment, or making an order, for delivery of possession of the mortgaged property, or at any time before the execution of such judgment or order, may—
        (i)   stay or suspend execution of the judgment or order, or
        (ii)   postpone the date for delivery of possession,
for such period or periods as the court thinks reasonable.

(3)   Any such adjournment, stay, suspension or postponement as is referred to in subsection (2) above may be made subject to such conditions with regard to payment by the mortgagor of any sum secured by the mortgage or the remedying of any default as the court thinks fit.

(4)   The court may from time to time vary or revoke any condition imposed by virtue of this section.

Administration of Justice Act 1973 s8

Extension of powers of court in action by mortgagee of dwelling-house

8.—(1)   Where by a mortgage of land which consists of or includes a dwelling-house, or by any agreement between the mortgagee under such a mortgage and the mortgagor, the mortgagor is entitled or is to be permitted to pay the principal sum secured by instalments or otherwise to defer payment of it in whole or in part, but provision is also made for earlier payment in the event of any default by the mortgagor or of a demand by the mortgagee or otherwise, then for the purposes of section 36 of the Administration of Justice Act 1970 (under which a court has power to delay giving a mortgagee possession of the mortgaged property so as to allow the mortgagor a reasonable time to pay any sums due under the mortgage) a court may treat as due under the mortgage on account of the principal sum secured and of interest on it only such amounts as the mortgagor would have expected to be required to pay if there had been no such provision for earlier payment.

(2) A court shall not exercise by virtue of subsection (1) above the powers conferred by section 36 of the Administration of Justice Act 1970 unless it appears to the court not only that the mortgagor is likely to be able within a reasonable period to pay any amounts regarded (in accordance with subsection (1) above) as due on account of the principal sum secured, together with the interest on those amounts, but also that he is likely to be able by the end of that period to pay any further amounts that he would have expected to be required to pay by then on account of that sum and of interest on it if there had been no such provision as is referred to in subsection (1) above for earlier payment.

(3) Where subsection (1) above would apply to an action in which a mortgagee only claimed possession of the mortgaged property, and the mortgagee brings an action for foreclosure (with or without also claiming possession of the property), then section 36 of the Administration of Justice Act 1970 together with subsections (1) and (2) above shall apply as they would apply if it were an action in which the mortgagee only claimed possession of the mortgaged property, except that:—

(a) section 36(2)(b) shall apply only in relation to any claim for possession; and

(b) section 36(5) [*transitional provisions*] shall not apply.

Consumer Credit Act 1974 ss129, 130, 135 and 136

Time orders

129.—(1) If it appears to the court just to do so—

(a) on an application for an enforcement order; or

(b) on an application made by a debtor or hirer under this paragraph after service on him of—

   (i) a default notice, or

   (ii) a notice under section 76(1) or 98(1); or

(c) in an action brought by a creditor or owner to enforce a regulated agreement or any security, or recover possession of any goods or land to which a regulated agreement relates, the court may make an order under this section (a 'time order').

(2)   A time order shall provide for one or both of the following, as the court considers just—

(a)   the payment by the debtor or hirer or any surety of any sum owed under a regulated agreement or a security by such instalments, payable at such times, as the court, having regard to the means of the debtor or hirer and any surety, considers reasonable;

(b)   the remedying by the debtor or hirer of any breach of a regulated agreement (other than non-payment of money) within such period as the court may specify.

Supplemental provisions about time orders

130.—(1)   Where in accordance with rules of court an offer to pay any sum by instalments is made by the debtor or hirer and accepted by the creditor or owner, the court may in accordance with rules of court make a time order under section 129(2)(a) giving effect to the offer without hearing evidence of means.

(2)   In the case of a hire-purchase or conditional sale agreement only, a time order under section 129(2)(a) may deal with sums which, although not payable by the debtor at the time the order is made, would if the agreement continued in force become payable under it subsequently.

(3)   A time order under section 129(2)(a) shall not be made where the regulated agreement is secured by a pledge if, by virtue of regulations made under section 76(5), 87(4) or 98(5), service of a notice is not necessary for enforcement of the pledge.

(4)   Where, following the making of a time order in relation to a regulated hire-purchase or conditional sale agreement or a regulated consumer hire agreement, the debtor or hirer is in possession of the goods, he shall be treated (except in the case of a debtor to whom the creditor's title has passed) as a bailee or (in Scotland) a custodier of the goods under the terms of the agreement, notwithstanding that the agreement has been terminated.

(5)   Without prejudice to anything done by the creditor or owner before the commencement of the period specified in a time order made under section 129(2)(b) ('the relevant period')—

(a)   he shall not while the relevant period subsists take in relation to the agreement any action such as is mentioned in section 87(1);

(b)   where—

(i)   a provision of the agreement ('the secondary provision') becomes operative only on breach of another provision of the agreement ('the primary provision'), and

(ii)   the time order provides for the remedying of such a breach of the primary provision within the relevant period,

he shall not treat the secondary provision as operative before the end of that period;

(c) if while the relevant period subsists the breach to which the order relates is remedied it shall be treated as not having occurred.

(6) On the application of any person affected by a time order, the court may vary or revoke the order.

Power to impose conditions or suspend operation of order

135.—(1) If it considers it just to do so, the court may in an order made by it in relation to a regulated agreement include provisions—

(a) making the operation of any term of the order conditional on the doing of specified acts by any party to the proceedings;

(b) suspending the operation of any term of the order either—

(i) until such time as the court subsequently directs, or

(ii) until the occurrence of a specified act or omission.

(2) The court shall not suspend the operation of a term requiring the delivery up of goods by any person unless satisfied that the goods are in his possession or control.

(3) In the case of a consumer hire agreement, the court shall not so use its powers under subsection (1)(b) as to extend the period for which, under the terms of the agreement, the hirer is entitled to possession of the goods to which the agreement relates.

(4) On the application of any person affected by a provision included under subsection (1), the court may vary the provision.

Power to vary agreements and securities

136. The court may in an order made by it under this Act include such provision as it considers just for amending any agreement or security in consequence of a term of the order.

Index

Furniture
common parts, in, 32
deterioration of, as ground for
possession, 32 196
ill treatment of, ground for
possession against Rent Act
protected tenant, 132
suitable alternative
accommodation, availability
of, 125

Grounds for possession
Rent Act protected tenant,
against. *See* Rent Acts
secure occupier, against. *See*
Secure occupier

Gypsies
administrative law defences, 244

Harassment
counterclaim to proceedings, 227
Hardship
suspended possession order,
effect of, 53
Hearing
mortgagor, action by, 301–305
High court
forfeiture, relief from, 106
judicial review, application for,
51
jurisdiction, 50
possession order, discretion
relating to, 249
Holiday lets
out of season, possession against
Rent Act protected tenant,
149–150
Rent Act evasion, 82–83
tenancy preceded by, termination
of assured tenancy, 187
Home
only or principal home rule, 7–8
Homeless person
bed-and-breakfast
accommodation, 61

Homeless person *cont*
council-owned property,
placement in, 59–60
housed as homeless, 267
housing association, statutory
duties of, 66–67
non-council-owned
accommodation, placement in,
61
security of tenure, exclusion of
accommodation from, 9
short-term leasing, growth of, 61
squatter as, 265
Homelessness
intentional, 265–267 331–332
mortgagor, action by,
generally, 329
Housing Act 1985 Part III,
329–334
protection of property, 334
possession procedure,
deemed application, 267
generally, 263
housed as homeless, 267
intentional homelessness, 265–
267
possession order expired, 265
protection of property, 267
squatters, 265
threatened homelessness, 263–
264
unreasonable to remain, 265
threatened, 263–264
when occurring, 330–331
See also Homeless person
Hospital treatment
long-term, tenant receiving, 18
Hostel
security of tenure, exclusion of
resident from, 10
Housing action trust
existing tenants, effect of transfer
on,
access for renovation, 70–71
challenging rent, 70
generally, 69